B. Wells

The History of Taranaki

A Standard Work on the History of the Province

B. Wells

The History of Taranaki
A Standard Work on the History of the Province

ISBN/EAN: 9783337339166

Printed in Europe, USA, Canada, Australia, Japan

Cover: Foto ©ninafisch / pixelio.de

More available books at **www.hansebooks.com**

THE

HISTORY OF TARANAKI

BY

B. WELLS:

A STANDARD WORK ON THE HISTORY OF THE PROVINCE.

"It appears to me to be a noble employment to rescue from oblivion those who deserve to be eternally remembered, and by extending the reputation of others, to advance at the same time our own."—

PLINY THE YOUNGER.

NEW ZEALAND:
EDMONDSON & AVERY, "TARANAKI NEWS" OFFICE, NEW PLYMOUTH.

1878.

THE

HISTORY OF TARANAKI

BY

B. WELLS:

A STANDARD WORK ON THE HISTORY OF THE PROVINCE.

"It appears to me to be a noble employment to rescue from oblivion those who deserve to be eternally remembered, and by extending the reputation of others, to advance at the same time our own."—

PLINY THE YOUNGER.

NEW ZEALAND:
EDMONDSON & AVERY, "TARANAKI NEWS" OFFICE,
NEW PLYMOUTH.

1878.

PREFACE.

The Establishment of the European Settlements of Taranaki was attended with no ordinary difficulty. Not only had the heroic pioneers to contend with the primeval wilderness which received them when they landed on the Taranaki shores, and a barbarous and turbulent race of aborigines, but also with the inability of the Plymouth and New Zealand Companies to fulfil in a satisfactory manner the work of colonisation which they had undertaken. The records of these proceedings are few and very scarce, death has removed some of the chief actors in them and age has dimmed the memories of others; it seemed therefore right to me, having a love for the work and having more than ordinary opportunities for its accomplishment, to collect, arrange, and publish all the more important documents and traditions relating to these affairs. My labors having been brought to a close, I am able now to present to my fellow settlers a lasting memorial of those truly heroic deeds in which a majority of them have taken part, and which have happily resulted in the foundation of a beautiful home for us in a fertile land and under genial skies, and in adding another Province to that Empire on which the sun never sets. I am persuaded that this little work will be generally welcomed in the Province whose history it relates, and that it will have the use of all history by extending the lives of its readers into the past by leading them to the sources of existing things, and therefore to a deeper comprehension of them, and by examples of heroism and patient endurance incite a repetition of such virtues. I desire very cordially to express my thanks for aid rendered to me in the preparation of this work to F. A. Carrington, Esq., M.H.R., late Superintendent of Taranaki; Major Charles Brown, Civil Commissioner; R. Parris, Esq., late Civil Commissioner; Major Charles Stapp, Commanding Taranaki Militia and Volunteers; C. D. Whitcombe, Esq., Commissioner of Crown Lands; Mrs. S. Popham King; Miss Kate Flight; G. D. Hamerton, Esq., Coroner; J. B. Lawson, Esq., Clerk to the Provincial Council of Taranaki; Mr. F. U. Gledhill, and Mr. Max. D. King.

In passing the work through the press I have received every assistance from Messrs. Edmondson and Avery, the printers.

B. WELLS.

"News Office," New Plymouth,
    March 31st, 1878.

CONTENTS.

CHAPTER I.

MAORI traditions respecting the Morioris.—Resemblance of the Maoris to a tribe in India.—Affinity of the Maori and Indo-European tongues.—Resemblance of Maori customs with those of a tribe in China and with those of the ancient Africans.—Indian ship's bell found in New Zealand.—Remarkable resemblance of some Maori and Egyptian words ... 1

CHAPTER II.

The canoes of the Maori immigrants.—The naming of the Taranaki rivers and hills.—The Etymology of some Maori common names.—The arrival of the Ngatiawa at the Bay of Islands—They double the North Cape and enter the Waitara—They subdue the aborigines and establish themselves at Ngapuketurua—They roam about the island—They send a taua to assist Rauparaha—They flee to the Chatham Islands, and return to Taranaki—The location of the hapus.—Maori antiquities ... 4

CHAPTER III.

Description of Pukerangiora.—Description of Ngamotu.—Waikato spies arrive in a canoe.—War party of Waikatos arrive at Waitara—The assault on Pukerangiora—The Massacre of the Garrison—The cannibal feast—The attack and defence of Ngamotu—The defeat and retreat of the Waikatos.—Visit to Poarama ... 7

CHAPTER IV.

Discovery of New Zealand.—Juan Fernandez.—Tasman sights Taranaki.—Captain Cook names Mount Egmont.—M. Marion du Fresne ... 12

CHAPTER V.

Commerce with New Zealand.—Arrival of the Missionaries.—Kororareka The British Resident.—Native Confederation.—The New Zealand Company—Grant of Charter—Difficulties of the Company—Relinquishment of Charter—Debt Cancelled ... 15

CHAPTER VI.

Despatch of the Tory—Arrival of the Tory in Cook Strait.—Richard Barrett.—Guard the whaler.—Wreck of the Harriet.—Rev. H. Williams.—E. Puni and Warepori.—Sale of land by Ngatiawa.—Colonel Wakefield sails northward—Anchors off the Sugarloaves.—Dr. Dieffenbach and Barrett land at Ngamotu ... 19

CHAPTER VII.

Dr. Dieffenbach obtains a view of Egmont and Ruapahu—Description of the Ngamotu rocks—Description of the Huatoki, Henui, and Waiwakaiho rivers—Starts for the Mountain—Travels up the right bank of the Waiwakaiho—Returns unsuccessful to Ngamotu—Makes a second attempt to reach the Mountain—The ascent—Returns to Ngamotu—Starts to the Waitara—Visits Mokau—Buys the land of the natives.—The deed of sale 23

CHAPTER VIII.

New Zealand made a dependency of New South Wales.—Captain Hobson appointed Lieutenant-Governor.—Mr. Somes remonstrates with Lord Palmerston.—Arrival of Governor Hobson.—The Treaty of Waitangi. —A French expedition arrives at Akaroa 43

CHAPTER IX.

The establishment of the Plymouth Company.—Despatch of the Chief Surveyor.—Taranaki overland exploring expedition—The expedition reaches Ngamotu.—Colonel Wakefield's letter to the Plymouth Company.—The prospectus of the Company.—Arrival of Mr. Carrington in Wellington—He sails in the Brougham on an expedition in search of a site for a settlement—Selects Taranaki—Lands at Ngamotu with his staff 48

CHAPTER X.

Despatch of the William Bryan.—Failure of Wright's Bank.—Port to be called Port Eliot.—Mr. Cutfield's letter describing the landing of the pioneers.—Commencement of trouble with the natives.—Mr. Cutfield sows the first European seeds.—Despatch of the Amelia Thompson— Farewell dinner at Plymouth—God Speed the Ship.—Bahia.—Arrival at New Plymouth.—Arrival and wreck of the Regina.—Arrival of the Oriental.—Captain Liardet 59

CHAPTER XI.

Governor Hobson—His service in the Royal Navy—Attempts to establish a town at the Bay of Islands—Founds Auckland—Opposes the settlement of Wanganui and Taranaki—Constitutes a Legislative Council.—Te Kaka of Waikato visits Taranaki to claim the land by right of conquest.- Governor Hobson purchases the rights of Waikato —Proclaims a commission to inquire into land claims by Europeans.— Mr. Spain appointed commissioner.—New Zealand constituted a distinct Colony.—The Governor attempts to curtail the New Plymouth settlement.—Financial difficulties of the Government.—Governor Hobson's death 74

CHAPTER XII.

Arrival of the Timandra.—Moorings laid in the roadstead.—Colonel Wakefield visits the settlement—Appoints Mr. Wicksteed Resident Agent.—Mr. Wicksteed's report.—Death of Mr. C. Brown, senr.— The Nairn's employed to open a bridle path behind the Mountain.— Quarrels between settlers and natives.—Introduction of horses.—The Chief Surveyor's horse.—State of the settlement.—Return of the Ngatiawa slaves.—The first Waiwakaiho bridge.—Arrival of the Blenheim.—Another quarrel with the natives 81

CHAPTER XIII.

Arrival of the Essex.—Captain Cooke drives cattle and sheep from Wellington.—Mr. E. J. Wakefield visits the settlement.—Reduction of expenditure.—Notice to the Chief Surveyor that his services are no longer required.—Arrival of the Thomas Sparks.—Reduction of wages.—The Wairau massacre.—Governor Shortland's proclamation.—Mr. Wicksteed's report.—Erection of the first mill and brewery.—Appointment of Rev. W. Bolland.—Arrival of the William Stoveld.—Arrival of the Himalaya.—Governor Fitzroy 93

CHAPTER XIV.

Scarcity of food.—Natives cut the timber on Captain Cooke's section at Te Hua.—State of the settlement.—Arrival of the Theresa—Mutiny on board.—Arrival of the Bella Marina.—Arrival of Colonel Wakefield and Mr. Commissioner Spain.—Mr. Spain's award.—Threatenings of the natives.—Messengers despatched to Auckland.—Arrival of the Governor by H.M.S. Hazard, and of Bishop Selwyn, Rev. J. Whiteley and Mr. Maclean overland.—Temporary concilliation of the natives effected.—Governor again visits the settlement and reduces New Plymouth to a block of 3,500 acres.—Extracts from the reports of Messrs. Forsaith and Maclean.—Extract of a letter from the Rev. John Whiteley.—Wi Kingi's letter to the Governor.—Other reports and letters relating to the affairs of the settlement 102

CHAPTER XV.

Rev S. Marsden. Rev. J. F. Churton. The Church Society for New Zealand. Arrangement for the endowment of a Bishopric. Despatch of Mr. Wicksteed to the colony as agent. Nomination of Rev. G. A. Selwyn to the office of Bishop—Consecration—Presentation of Communion service at Windsor—Description of the service. The Bishop sails for Sydney. His arrival in Auckland—His tour of his diocese—Description of his journey to New Plymouth. Waimate College. Cathedral library. First confirmation. The Company's grant for churches. Appointment of Rev. W. Bolland to New Plymouth—His zeal. Church building committee—Collecting materials—Laying the first stone. Fever in the parsonage. Death of Rev. W. Bolland. Appointment of Rev. H. Govett, B.A. Brief notice of other clergymen. Roman Catholic Church. Appointment of Bishop Pompallier by Pope Gregory XVI—Lauds in the North—Takes up his abode at the Bay of Islands. Father Pezant visits Taranaki. Chapel built in Courtenay-street. Arrival of Father Tressallet. Church built in Devon-street. Rev. Father Pertius. Rev. Father Rolland—His bravery. Fathers Binfield and Lampillia. Wesleyan Methodist Church. Mission established at Wangaroa—Missionaries driven away. Re-establishment of the Mission at Hokianga. Mr. Creed sent to Ngamotu. Mr. Skevington sent to Taranaki proper. Wesleyan Chapel built in Brougham-street. Captain King and Mr. Wicksteed wish to hold a horticultural show in the chapel and are refused. Wesleyans orderal to remove their chapel. Mr. Gronbe commences the erection of a sandstone chapel in Courtenay-street—Sells it to the Wesleyans. Mr. Turton. The Grey Institution. Death of Mr. Skevington. Arrival of Mr. Whiteley. Mr. Ironside. Other Ministers. Primitive Methodist Church. Origin of Primitive Methodism. Bible Christians. Mr. Veale gives a site for a chapel. Mr. Ward preaches on the town bridge—Bible Christians accept him as their minister—Takes up his residence at Te Henui—Attempts to preach to the Maoris who threaten to tomahawk him—Succeeded by Mr. Long.

Chapels built at Bell Block and Hurdon. Return of Mr. Ward—His sufferings during the war. Erection of Queen-street chapel. Arrival of Mr. and Mrs. Waters. Arrival of Messrs. Dumbell, Standrin and Clover. Congregationalism in New Plymouth. Mr. Groube arrives in the Timandra—Conducts service in a raupo whare—Attempts to erect a sandstone chapel in Courtenay-street—Builds a timber chapel in Devon-street. His sufferings during the war. Leaves for Melbourne. Presbyterianism in Taranaki. Rev. J. Thom visits the settlement—Conducts the service in the Independent Chapel—Induces the Military Settlers to petition the Church of Scotland for a Minister. The ordination of the Rev. R. F. Macnicol—His arrival. The building of the kirk. Mr. Macnicol accepts a call from Auckland. Rev. T. Blain. Lay Ministry. Rev. M. S. Breach. Death of Rev. J. Thom. The Baptist cause. Laying foundation stone of chapel. The trustees. Building shut up 122

CHAPTER XVI.

Mr. Day goes to Sydney in the Slaines Castle to buy cattle and goods. The Paul Jones conveys eighteen despairing settlers to Adelaide. Maoris build a church at Mangoraka of materials stolen from the settlers. Dreadful storm and loss of the schooner Richmond on Kawhia bar. W. Bayly's barn and wheat stack burned at Mangoraka. Mr. Bolland returns from Auckland overland with the news of the appointment of a new Governor. Sir George Grey—His birth and education—Joins the 83rd Regiment—Commands an expedition sent to the interior of Australia—Assumes the Governorship of Australia— Arrives in Auckland—Brings the war in the North to a close—Is invested with the Star of the Order of the Bath—Chooses Tamati Waka Nene and Te Puni as his esquires—Settles the land claims in New Plymouth—Establishes Pensioner Settlements in Auckland— Delays the proclamation of the Constitution—Returns to England His literary works—He receives the degree of Doctor of Civil Laws at Oxford—Is appointed Governor of the Cape Colony—Is reappointed Governor of New Zealand—Tries diplomacy and fails— Breaks the power of Waikato—Treats his prisoners in a weak and ridiculous manner—Proceeds to England—Returns and retires to the Kawau—Accepts the office of Superintendent of Auckland— Enters Parliament and becomes Premier of the Colony. Origin of the Union Mill. Arrival of the Marianne. Letter from Mr. Gladstone to Governor Grey. Suicide of Mr. Williams. Arrival of the Madras and Ralph Bernal. Constabulary Barracks built. Site and plan for the hospital. Bells Falls discovered. Arrival of the Elora. Death of Richard Barrett. Arrival of the Inflexible with Governor Grey. The Governor's instructions to Mr. Maclean. Quarrel among the Puketapu. Purchase of Tataraimaka. Death of Rev. W. Bolland. Mr. F. D. Bell supersedes Mr. Wicksteed as Resident Agent. Bishop Selwyn lands from the Undine. Quarrel between the Puketapus and Taranakis of Omata. Arrival of Lieutenant Collinson, R.E. and Corporal Henderson, R.A. on secret service. The Grey and Omata Blocks purchased. Land allotted to the whalers. Dr. Wilson and Mr. Hulke leave Wanganui for Taranaki. Mr. Devenish brings a herd of cattle from Wellington. The Governor revisits New Plymouth. Mr. Bell purchases Bell Block of the Puketapu. The Waikanae migration. Kiugi settles on the south bank of the Waitara. Opening of the Omata block. Establishment of the Grey Institution. Death of Colonel Wakefield. Severe earthquake. Table of Waikanae migration 135

CHAPTER XVII.

Depression. State of New Plymouth in 1849. Compensation. Arrival of the Barque Cornwall. Dates of Conveyances of Blocks. Major Lloyd molested at Omata 147

CHAPTER XVIII.

Company resign their Charter to the Crown. Arrival of the Acheron. Consequences of gold discovery in Australia. The *Taranaki Herald* published. Constitution proclaimed. Reduction of price of Waste Lands of the Crown. Election of the first Superintendent. Election of the first members of the Provincial Council. Death of James Foreman. Departure of Sir George Grey. Severe earthquake. Difficulties of negotiation with the natives. Purchase of the Hua and Waiwakaiho Block. Te Puni seizes all the open land on the Block. Murder of a native at Kaipakopako. Death of Simon Crawley. Mary Rodgers murdered at Omata by Cassidy. A tract against land selling printed, and published among the natives. Deaths of Richard Eaton and William Holloway. Earthquake. Public Works Ordinance—First election under it. Arrival of Acting Governor Wynyard. Arrival of the Duke of Portland with troops. The Bishop publishes a pastoral letter. Arrival of Governor Brown. Natives cut a line across the ranges 150

CHAPTER XIX.

The Puketapu hapu—Their ancient home. The chief Rawiri. Land-leaguers and anti-land-leaguers. Rawiri and his men while cutting a line are fired on by Katatore and his men. Death of Rawiri. Great excitement. Appeal to the Government. Colonel Wynyard fears to interfere with the matter. Efforts made to settle the quarrel. Katatore offers land to the Government. Death of Rimene. Ngatiruanui besiege Ihaia—Ihaia retreats to Mahoetahi—Joins Arama Karaka. Settlers petition for military protection. Arrival of detachments of the 58th and 65th Regiments. Tragical death of Katatore. The burning of the Ikamoana pa. Ihaia retreats to Mimi. Ihaia Kirikumara 158

CHAPTER XX.

Governor Gore Browne. Origin of the Anti-land-selling League. Origin of the King movement. Mr. Cutfield elected Superintendent. First publication of the *Taranaki News*. The second session of the Maori Parliament. Public Debt Apportionment Act. Calling out of the Taranaki Militia. Death of Captain Dawson. Death of John Wright. Change of the name of the Province to Taranaki 166

CHAPTER XXI.

Puketapu natives receive payment for the Tarurutangi Block. Preparations for erecting a bridge over the Waiwakaiho. Volunteer regulations—Election of officers. Arrival of the Iris with the Governor. Conference with the natives. Te Teira of Waitara offers land to the Governor. Maori statistics. Opening of the Waiwakaiho bridge. The Council Chambers burnt. Contraction of the town of New Plymouth. Wiremu Kingi Whiti Rangitaki 174

CHAPTER XXII.

The Taranaki war. Minutes of the Executive Council. Instructions to Mr. Parris. Natives stop the survey at the Waitara. Proclamation of martial-law. Settlers remove into New Plymouth. Commencement of hostilities. Defection of Manahi. Engagement at Waireka. Reports of the engagement. Narrow escape of Mr. Parris. Requests for aid made to the Australian Colonies. Arrival of reinforcements. Captain Richard Brown. Battle of Puketakauere. Death of Hugh Corbyn Harris. Death of John Hurford. Wreck of the George Henderson. Death of Ephraim Coad and Henry Crann. Attack on Mahoetahi. Death of John Hawken. Death of Joseph Sarten. Taking of Matarikoriko. Expedition to the South. Attack on the Huirangi Redoubt. Death of Captain W. C. King. The sap. Death of Captain Strange. Death of E. Messenger. Death of Lieutenant McNaughten 186

CHAPTER XXIII.

Arrival of Tamihana. Hapurona hoists the white flag. Arrival of the Governor, Ministers, Mr. D. Maclean and Tamati Waka Nene. Arrival of General Cameron. Terms offered to the insurgents. Declaration of Hapurona. Sickness. Mr. C. Brown re-elected Superintendent. Arrival of reinforcements from India. Colors presented to the Taranaki Militia and Volunteers. Bank of New Zealand opened. Sir George Grey re-appointed Governor. Bishop Selwyn attempts to travel along the coast. Canon Stowell's opinion of the Taranaki settlers. Death of E. G. Wakefield. Wreck of the s.s. Lord Worsley. Wreck of the Orpheus. The Governor with his Ministers arrive by the Harrier for the purpose of reinstating the Province. Compensation. Troops take possession of Tataraimaka. Warning of ambuscades 226

CHAPTER XXIV.

Massacre at Oakura. Abandonment of the Waitara purchase. Attack on Katikara. The Maori toll-gate. Hapurona sends a challenge. Rebels take possession of a spur of the Kaitake Ranges. A fishing party of the rebels attacked by an ambuscade of the 58th Regiment near Kaitake. Death of Mr. Patterson. Rebels disturbed at Mangorei. Skirmish at Kaitake. Defeat at Ahuahu. Origin of Pai Marireism. Defeat of rebels at Sentry Hill. Capture of Manutahi, Mataitawa, and Te Arei. Colonel Maxwell Lepper. Disbanding of the old Militia. Native murders at Kaipikari. Death of Frank Roebuck. General Cameron arrives at Patea. Military settlers and Bushrangers embark for Patea. Accidents to the surf boats. Death of Joseph Hawke. Expedition embarks for the White Cliffs. Demand of the Imperial Government for payment for the troops employed in the Colony. Scheme for the settlement of Tikorangi. Skirmish at Whatino. Colonel Warre attacks the rebels inland of Warea. Revocation of the proclamation of martial-law. Engagement at Warea. General Cameron resigns the command of the army in New Zealand. Wreck of the steam transport Alexandra. Arrival of General Chute. Embarkation of the Imperial Forces 235

CHAPTER XXV.

Confiscation—Military settlements. Arrival of Military settlers. Lands proclaimed under the Military Settlements Act, 1863. Area of lands confiscated. Exodus of Military settlers. Occupation of other

confiscated lands. The Waste Lands Board. Establishment of
Inglewood 257

CHAPTER XXVI.

General Chute marches from Wanganui—Attacks Otapawa—Marches through the forest—Emerges at Mataitawa—His reception at New Plymouth—Proceeds to Patea. Waiwakaiho bridge swept away. Death of Roby, at Manutahi. First sale of land at Waitara. Disturbance at Patea. Attack at Turuturumokai. Capture of Te Ngutu o Te Manu. Repulse at Ruaruru. Major Von Tempsky. Repulse at Okutuku. The Brothers Hunter. The massacre at the White Cliffs. Rev. John Whiteley 265

CHAPTER XXVII.

Peace. The iron sand. Provincial Government. Land fund. Local Government. Immigration and public works. New Plymouth harbor. Electric telegraph. Judicature. Literary Institute. Education. Hospital. Botanic Garden. Acclimatisation. Victories of peace ... 288

CHAPTER XXVIII.

Taranaki pioneers. Mr. F. A. Carrington. Captain Henry King. Mr. Charles Brown, senr. Mr. Chilman 298

List of Ships 309
Bibliography 311

THE HISTORY OF TARANAKI.

CHAPTER I.

THE MAORIS.

THERE is a tradition among the Maoris that their forefathers came to New Zealand in certain canoes from a country called Hawaiiki, and that on their arrival they found the land thinly populated with a race short and plump, but physically inferior to themselves, called Moriori. The concluding part of this tradition is borne out by the fact of a people of that name and character having existed at the Chatham Islands within the memory of the present generation. It has also been confirmed by the discovery in the Waikato district of a number of skeletons arranged round a circular pit in an erect position, each with a block of wood upon its head, which was a mode of burial adopted in certain cases by the Morioris of the Chatham Islands. The Maoris are members of the brown portion of the Polynesian family, their language being a dialect of that spoken in the Sandwich Islands, and there are strong reasons for supposing that the family migrated from India at an early date. Mr. Thomson, of Otago, who has spent many years in India, says in a valuable paper in the "Transactions of the New Zealand Institute" that there is in that country a people who bear a very strong resemblance to the Maoris. The fierceness of the passions of the Maori, and the occasionally dusky hue of his skin, would lead us to suppose that he has African blood in his veins, and Mr. Thomson supposes that the original inhabitants of India were Ethiopians and that they were driven out by the influx of Aryans. The analogy between the Maori and Indo-European tongues is very striking. Mr. Fairburn, writing on this subject in the "Transactions," observes that "the definite and indefinite articles in Maori are *te* and *he*, the latter pronounced ha, which are nearly identical with the English *the* and *a*. The Maori *ko* is also interchangeable with our *to*, and like it is a sign of the dative case." Mr. Fairburn also observes that "it is a mistake to suppose Maori to be a section of the Turanian group of tongues. It is rather a mixture of the Indo-European and Semitic. Maori—Moriori—Malay—Maure—Moor—the evident relationship between these names indicate that the Maori is a fierce cross between the Arab and the Ethiopian. Again, the name Maori seems to indicate that this people came from the East; Maori—Malay—that is to say an inhabitant of Malacca or Malaka—bears evident affinity to the Maori words *marangai* the east, *arangi* rising, and *maranga* to arise. The Maori contains many old Arabic and Egyptian words." There is a singular circumstance in connection with this subject mentioned by Professor Max Muller in his "Chips from a German Workshop"—" In the Chinese province of Yunnan there are tribes of aborigines —not Chinese—called Mau-tze or soil-children, who salute as they did when first observed by Marco Polo in the thirteenth century by rubbing noses." The identity of this mode of salutation with that practised by the Maoris, the approximation of their names in sound and signification—for the word Maori signifies native—are at least very remarkable. Still more remarkable are the resemblances we can trace between existing Maori customs and some which have become obsolete among certain tribes of Africans. In Max Muller's review of the "Zulu Nursery Tales," by the Rev. H. Calloway of Natal, he says:—" There is one feature in these stories which to a great extent attests their antiquity. Several of the customs to which they allude are no longer in existence among the Zulus. It is not for instance any longer the custom among the natives of South Africa to bake meat by means of heated stones, the recognised mode of cooking among the Polynesians. Yet when Usikulumi orders a calf to be roasted he calls upon the boys of the kraal to collect large stones and to heat them. There are several other peculiarities which the Zulus seem to share in common with the Polynesians. The avoiding of certain words which form part of the names of deceased kings or chieftains is a distinguishing feature of the Zulu and Polynesian languages. If a person who has disappeared for some time and is supposed dead returns unexpectedly to his people, it is the custom both among the Zulus and Polynesians to salute him first by making a funeral lamentation. There are other coincidences in the stories of both races which make it more than probable that at some distant period they had lived either together or in close neighbourhood."

A circumstance strongly tending to show that oceanic communication existed between India and New Zealand in ancient times is the fact that in the interior of the Northern Island of New Zealand part of a ship's bell has been found, bearing an inscription in very ancient Tamil, which was thus translated in Ceylon :—" Mohoyden Buks Ship's Bell." Proof is also not wanting of an intimate connection between the Maori and the Egyptian at some very distant date. *Ra* is the term used by the Maori as expressive of day and the light of the sun, and it was used in precisely the same sense by the ancient Egyptians. A magnificent hymn to the sun, recently translated by

M. Marietta and attributed to the 12th Dynasty, begins thus:—
"Thou awakenest beneficially Ammon-Ra." In the Egyptian Ritual of the Dead the Divinity is made to say, "I am Ra, at his rising in the beginning, he who governs that he has made." In the Egyptian Trinity *Ra* is also the solar agent. The idea is also entertained that Pharaoh, the general title of the kings of Egypt, corresponds to the Egyptian phra or ra the "sun," which is written as an hieroglyphic symbol over the titles of kings. The similarity in sound and meaning of the Egyptian word *typhon* with that of the Maori *taipo*, both being the name of the Spirit of Evil, is also not a little remarkable.

CHAPTER II.

THE HISTORY OF THE NGATIAWA TRIBE.

ACCORDING to the tradition of the tribes the ancestors of the Maoris came to New Zealand in several successive migrations. The first canoe that reached this country was named Matahourua, and was commanded by a chief named Kupe, who took possession of the country by naming all the mountains and rivers from Wanganui to Patea. The next canoe that arrived was called Aotea, and was commanded by the chief Turi, who gave names to all the rivers and mountains from Patea to Aotea. Some of these names are poetical, most are expressive, some are gross, and of some the meaning is obscure. Taranaki, the name given to the great mountain, is derived from *tara*, a peak or prominence, and *naki* probably from *ngaki*, clear from vegetation, signifying the barren or treeless mountain. It was customary in old times for the distant tribes to call this mountain Pukehaupapa, which is a common appellation for a snow clad mountain like Mount Taranaki. Waitara, one of the most considerable rivers in the Taranaki district, signifies mountain stream. Te Henui, another river, signifies the great sin. Huatoki, fruitful in worms. Tapuae, the echo of footsteps. Oakura, the spot where the sun lingers. Among the rocks and capes— Paritutu, the great sugarloaf rock, signifies the rising precipice; Moturoa, the tall Island; Motumahanga, the twin island; Ngamotu, the islands, and Omata, near to the headland or cape.

According to Mr. John White the ancestors of the Ngatiawa came to New Zealand in a canoe named Tokomaru, commanded by the chief Manaia, who having murdered a number of men who were working for him felt himself under the necessity of seeking fresh fields. Manaia made the land in the vicinity of the Bay of Islands, and coasting along he doubled the North Cape, stretched along the bight of the West Coast and eventually entered the Waitara river where he took up his abode. From this latter circumstance the tribe took its name Ngatiawa, signifying the tribe of the river. Manaia found the district occupied by a tribe called Ngatimokotorea of whom he had not previously heard. They were not a warlike race and were easily overcome by the new arrivals. Manaia killed many of them, others escaped, and a portion of them intermingled with the conquerors. Tradition assigns Ngapuketurua as the most ancient settlement of the Ngatiawa. This place is situated on the west bank of the Waiongona river among a number of singular volcanic hills, and has been more recently called Mahoetahi, or the grove of mahoe trees. This spot seems to have been chosen for the large extent of good land in its vicinity, and from the facility it afforded for forming a number of fortified villages. The Ngatiawa are said to have been in old times a very restless race, and of all the tribes in New Zealand they were the most numerous and powerful. They are now located in the north end of the North Island, in the Bay of Plenty, at Taranaki, on both shores of Cook Strait, and at the Chatham Islands. They migrated first to the Bay of Plenty, and after a brief stay there went up the East Coast to the Thames, and ultimately to the North Cape. In the course of their wanderings they drove the tribes out of each district which they visited. They overran all the Ngapuhi district in the north, and were the cause of that portion of the Ngatiwhatua, who were located at the North Cape, coming south and joining the main body at Kaipara, and having by force of numbers taken all the land on the west coast to the north of Wangarei, they claimed it as their rightful property, not only by the law of might, but also because of having buried their dead in the sacred places of the tribes of the land. For they had, according to the native law, proved the power of their own heathen customs relative to the dead to be superior to that of the tribes into whose territory they had come. There is a small river to the north of Hokianga called Wangape, near to which H.M. sloop of war Osprey was wrecked. In the neighbourhood of this stream there is an old repository of bones which are, it is said, the remains of the people of the Ngatiawa tribe. The native laws relative to the burial of the dead are very strict. It is supposed that to bury the dead of an inferior tribe in the same place where the superior chiefs are interred without the consent of the relatives of these chiefs would cause the gods of the superior chiefs to destroy the tribe of the relatives of the inferior persons so buried. Hence, the circumstance of the Ngatiawa having buried their dead in utter disregard of such consent proved their undisputed right to the district,'not only by the law of force, but also by that of superior rank. The restless disposition of the Ngatiawa led them again to the south, and in this migration the tribe divided, part going by the West Coast, and part by the East Coast. The chief of the West Coast party took with him a tame lizard. The Maoris are not more in fear of any known thing than of a lizard, and this tame one became the passport of the Ngatiawa from Hokianga to Taranaki. Being in the midst of enemies, and reduced in numbers by the division of the tribe, they had to travel circumspectly. The East Coast party went by water and landed at the Bay of Plenty, taking possession of the district they still retain. The West Coast party settled at the home of their ancestors on the banks of the Waitara river and in the neighborhood thereof, where they remained till many of the tribe were induced to go to the south to assist the great chief of Kawhia, the renowned Rauparaha, in his exterminating wars. Quarrelling with that chief, the Ngatimutunga hapu fled from Wellington in the English brig Rodney in 1836 to the Chatham Islands, where they destroyed a great number of the Moriories and enslaved the rest. In 1870, having sold their possessions in the islands to Europeans, many of them returned to Taranaki and were located north of the Urenui, where they rapidly decreased in numbers and are now nearly extinct. Taranaki was originally the name of the district inhabited by the Taranaki tribe south of the Sugarloaves, and Tokomaru the name of that extending from the Sugarloaves to the White Cliffs; but the whole district lying round the mountain is called by the Europeans Taranaki. The hapus of the Ngatiawa in the district settled as follows :—Atiawa at the White Cliffs, Pukerangiora near the junction of the Waitara and Manganui rivers, Ngatimarua, Ngatimutunga, and Ngatirahiri north of the Waitara; Ngatimaru on the Waitara, considerably inland and to the east of the mountain; Puketapu south of the Waitara on the mount in Puketapu Bay, where in old times the crimson veronica flourished, and Ngamotu at the Sugarloaves, a spot attractive by reason of the excellent fishery afforded around the basis of the islands and the fastnesses of the rocky pinnacles.

Maori antiquities abound in the shape of old forts and pits, and stone axes. The Ngamotu pa was until very recently in existence. The ruins of a very strong pa were observable before the war on the top of Marsland Hill in New Plymouth. The name of this stronghold was Pukaka. The ruins of a very strong pa near the North Head of the Waiwakaiho River are still observable. The intrenchments around it are equal to European military works. This pa was called the Rewarewa. It is said to have been constructed to withstand an assault of the Taranaki tribe during some intertribal quarrel, and that it was garrisoned by 2000 men. A few Maoris resided at this pa when some of the early settlers arrived, but it has been deserted for many years. 'The mount opposite to the landing place at New Plymouth was called Pukeariki, or the hill of chiefs, on account of its being the burial place of some of the principal chiefs of the district. It was held sacred by the natives for many years after the arrival of the Europeans, but is now doomed by the Harbor Board to be levelled in order that it may form part of the town.

CHAPTER III.

THE FALL OF PUKERANGIORA AND THE DEFENCE OF NGAMOTU.

PUKERANGIORA is the abrupt termination of a high ridge on the banks of the Waitara River, situate about seven miles from the river's mouth. In the course of ages the waters of the stream have eroded the foot of the hill and caused at this spot a high and steep escarpment, the verge of which forms a strong military position. On this account the spot was selected by a hapu of the Ngatiawa as a fit site for their pa. The spot received its name from the fact of the hill being in old time clad with rangiora, a well known shrub remarkable for its large leaves, green on the upper surface, and covered with a white and papery epidermis beneath. The prospect from this hill is very fine, and in addition to the Waitara valley, embraces much of the Tokomaru district between the river and the Sugarloaves. Owing perhaps to the abundance of food yielded by the neighbourhood the population was numerous. The river beneath furnished them with mullet, eels, lampreys, and other fish. On the good land of the district they raised in their gardens large crops of maize, potatoes, kumera, taro, calabashes, melons and pumpkins. The extensive forest in the immediate vicinity furnished them with fat arboreal pigeons and luscious tuis, besides abundance of rats. Through the forest a long narrow path, some three days' journey in length, led to the shores of Cook Strait, and was probably intended to aid in a retreat in case of a successful assault from the enemy. At the time of which we write the garrison of the pa had been considerably reduced by many of the warriors having gone to the South with Rauparaha to assist him in his wars.

Everyone who has caught a glimpse of the settlement of Taranaki has seen those peaked rocks which are known to the settlers as the Sugarloaves, and to the Maoris as Ngamotu—the islands. Geologists tell us they are composed of trachytic breccia, cemented with volcanic mud. They are, probably, the fragments of the lips of a great crater which existed in by-gone ages. The adventurous youth who climbs their lofty summits, finds their peaks perforated with pits, which were excavated by the natives to serve as hiding places for their persons and food, in time of war. He may also, perchance, light upon a weapon of green nephrite, for the neolithic age of Maoridom has given way to that of iron within the memory of the present generation.

In the neighborhood of these rocky islets a pa had stood from time immemorial, which next after Pukerangiora, was the strongest fortress of the Ngatiawa tribe in the district. Not that the site was particularly commanding, but it embraced a good view of the sea-beach—the highway in ancient times, and was in close proximity to the pitted pinnacles. The spot was also sheltered from the prevailing winds, so that extensive gardens could all be cultivated to perfection, and in the partially sheltered bay in front of the Pa there was excellent fishing ground, and abundance of fish.

It was early summer in the year 1831, when a Waikato canoe came to Ngamotu for a cargo of that Maori delicacy, dried shark. The strangers excused themselves by saying that the fish in question were scarce in their district, while here they are abundant. Friendly greetings were exchanged, the fish prepared, the canoe, which was damaged, repaired, and the Waikatos sent back in peace. Little did the Ngatiawas think these men were spies; such, however, was their character, and in a month afterwards—December, 1831—a taua consisting of nearly 4,000 Waikatos was at the Waitara. The enemy at first scattered himself about in disorderly parties at Tikorangi and its neighborhood. A few Ngatiawas soon fell into his hands; these were sacrificed to Tu, the god of war, and Wiro the evil spirit. Soon an unsuspecting party of twenty-five persons, returning from a distant village, was taken, slain and devoured. A panic seized the Ngatiawas, who flew to their stronghold with such precipitation that they had not time to procure any quantity of provisions. Next the enemy destroyed all their sacred places, crossed the river and attacked the Pa. He was, however, repulsed, and fell back with the loss of four chiefs and several men of inferior grade. For twelve successive days the enemy made repeated assaults, but was constantly repulsed, and lost in these attacks thirty-six men. Famine and watchfulness now reduced the garrison to a state of despondency. Instead of stealing away under the cover of the night, they made the mistake of attempting an evacuation in the day time. The enemy perceiving this, pursued and captured numbers of the half famished wretches. Then mothers threw their children over the precipice, and leaped themselves into the river below to avoid a more dreadful fate at the hands of their sanguinary foes. The captives were driven into whares and guarded by sentinels armed with sharp tomahawks. On that day the Waikatos glutted themselves with the flesh of the slain. On the morrow morning, nearly two hundred prisoners were brought out; those who were well tatooed were beheaded on a block for the sake of their heads. Some of the remainder were slain by a blow or cut on the skull; on others every refinement of cruelty was practised, particularly the thrusting of a red hot ramrod up the bowels. Children and youths were cut open, eviscerated, spitted, and roasted over fires made from the defences of the dismantled Pa. In the afternoon, a similar massacre took place, and so greedily did some of these vampires feast that they died from the effects of their gluttony. The feast was *graced* with the tatooed heads of the slain, which were stuck on short poles, and placed *vis-a-vis* with the captors, who would at times pause in their feasting to address them with the most insulting expressions. Having finished the work to their satisfaction, the Waikatos proceeded to the Sugarloaves to attack Ngamotu Pa, the garrison of which consisted of eleven Europeans and three hundred and fifty Maoris. The presence of the Europeans, who were possessed of four carronades, somewhat intimidated the enemy; but he remembered that he was strong in numbers; moreover, he determined, if possible, to effect his object by treachery.

At daybreak on a morning of February, 1832, the watchers discovered the enemy advancing in his usually disorderly manner along the beach. Every preparation was immediately made for his reception. All the provisions at hand were taken within the pa, the walls of the whares were defended with earth or sods, and the guns were got into position. The garrison possessed no round or grape shot, accordingly scraps of iron and stone were improvised for the occasion. Fearful of the kind of reception he should meet with, the enemy halted, deliberated, and then signalled for a parley. Then a Waikato chief advanced along the beach to the front of the pa, and the Ngamotu chief came out alone to meet him. The two sat down on the sand, rubbed noses, and commenced the tangi. The Ngamotu chief enquired what his people had done to provoke the anger of Waikato, and wished to know whether it were wise for Maoris to destroy each other for the benefit of strangers. The Waikato chief could not reply to this question, and promised to return peacefully; "but first," said he "let us into your pa to embrace our friends." This could not be acceded to. In less than an hour after this parley the Waikatos danced the war dance in front of the pa, fired a volley, and charged, but were repulsed with loss. The next day, while shots were exchanging, a Ngatiawa chief in a fit of valour rushed from the pa in the direction of the enemy, discharged his piece and retired. Before he could reach the pa he fell shot through the back, and a party from the enemy rushed to take him, while another party of his friends flew to protect him. Then followed a skirmish in which several fell or were taken prisoners. Several Waikato chiefs now advanced to the pa with expressions of the purest affection, and advised the besieged to surrender; some of the Maoris felt inclined to comply, but the English would not hear of it. On the fourth day of the siege, a slave came to the pa with a message requesting another parley. The two chiefs met again on the beach in front of the pa. The Waikato chief professed to be ashamed of his former perfidy, and promised to withdraw his people immediately. When this news reached the pa the foolish people wished to invite the Waikatos to a friendly dance, but the English and many of the natives feared treachery. Then followed quarrelling. One man, the son of a chief, threw himself on a fire in a fit of vexation, and burned himself so severely that he died a few days afterwards. Two sisters quarrelled; one who had confidence in the promise of the enemy ran out of the pa to prove his good faith, but she was taken and cut to pieces within sight of her friends, and her flesh washed in the streamlet from which the garrison procured their water, to tapu it, so that they should not be able to drink it. An assault was next made and bravely resisted, after which a sap was commenced under the pa, but this work was frustrated. Firebrands were also thrown into the pa, but by the vigilance of the people no damage was sustained by them. In the midst of the siege the schooner Currency Lass, of Sydney, came in with supplies for the Europeans. The enemy tried to take her, but was prevented by the vigilance of the master, Mr. Love. One of the besieged managed to board her under the enemy's fire, and to return to the pa unhurt. A message was now sent to the pa, desiring that Mr. Love, who had landed, would return to the schooner and there confer with the Waikato chief. The meeting took place, and ended precisely as the other parleys had done, the wily chief's treacherous intentions being apparent. Strange as it may appear, business was carried on at times between the contending parties. For blankets and tobacco the Englishmen bought muskets and ammunition of the enemy while skirmishes were going on around them.

The enemy now built mounds, from which, under cover, he could fire down into the pa. During a brisk trade a quarrel arose about a musket, during which three Waikatos were killed, and were afterwards roasted, and eaten. The next day one of the carronades burst without seriously hurting any of the besieged. The enemy cheered by this accident, sent a message stating that he should storm the pa at day break on the following morning. The siege had now lasted for three weeks, and the enemy's food was getting short, for he had not a single slave or prisoner left to cut up into rations. That night many of the besieged slept as soundly as though perfect peace reigned around, but others, with the Englishmen, kept an anxious watch. At the first dawn of the day the assault was made by the whole force of the enemy. Amid terrific yells, the fences were cut, and a party was within the pa before some of the besieged were well awake. A brave and faithful little band of the besieged fought with the energy of despair, cutting off the retreat of those who had entered the pa. British courage now rose to heroism. The three remaining carronades were served with celerity and precision, the missiles which they belched out inflicting horrible wounds in the bodies of the assailants. The enemy charged again and again, until at last a panic seized him, and he retreated, dragging his dead chiefs but leaving his wounded. Three hundred and fifty mutilated bodies lay around the pa, some dead and some living. Then the Ngamotus rushed out to wreak vengeance on the wounded. Some were burned alive. One prisoner had a tomahawk thrust into his mouth, while an incision was made in his throat, and a wretch drank his warm flowing blood. He was then quartered, and his heart sent as a present to an old chief. A traitor coming to the pa in the hour of victory was seized, tortured, and slain. The dead which the enemy had buried were exhumed and devoured. The beach in the vicinity of the pa presented a horrible spectacle, portions of human bodies lay scattered about, and the dogs fed on human entrails. Ngatiawa lost thirteen chiefs in this fight; these were buried with barbaric honours. Each chief had eight muskets and a quantity of ammunition buried with him, and for each ten slaves were killed, to become servitors in the *reinga*, or spirit land.

The Waikato never repeated their attack, though they threatened to do so; and the remnant of the Ngatiawa finding themselves too weak to oppose effectually any renewed attack from Waikato migrated with their women and children, and rejoined their relatives at Otaki, Wellington, Queen Charlotte's Sound, and other places. A few forlorn wretches clung to the land of their fathers, stealthily cultivating small gardens in the depth of the forest. A party of fugitives from Pukerangiora sought refuge in the Kaiauai gorge, situated between the Pouakai ranges and Mount Egmont, where they were discovered and slain by the relentless Waikato. A man named Mangu fell shot through the neck at Pukerangiora and was left for dead. Seeing a favourable opportunity he snatched up a young child which had been spared, and placing it astride on his shoulders he started off with it along the forest path which led to Cook Strait. Fear of pursuit impelled him onward, and he fed the child with the forest berries which overhung the path and threw water up to its mouth with his hand, not daring to put it down. Ihaia and Tiraurau, chiefs of Ngatiawa have borne testimony to the desolation of the land after the Waikato raid : "All was quite deserted, the land, the sea, the streams and lakes, the forest, the rocks were deserted ; the food, the property, the works were deserted ; the dead, the sick were deserted ; and the land marks were deserted."

In the summer of 1873-4 we paid a visit to Ngamotu Pa and found its aged chief and three or four of his people working in an adjoining garden. We addressed him as Poaruma, but he told us that that was no longer his name for he had joined Israel ; alluding to a superstition then prevalent among the Maoris. We asked him the name of the chief who defended the pa against the Waikato, and the names of the Europeans who assisted in its defence. The old man's memory seemed at fault, but after a time we gleaned from him that the name of the chief was Warepori, and the names of the Europeans were Barrett, Love, Akerau, probably Akers, Tamiriri, probably Wright, Kopiri probably Phillips, and Oliver. On the neighbouring island, known as Mikotahi, there is an inscription which probably records the arrival of one of these men ; it is as follows :—JOHN WRIGHT, October, 1829.

CHAPTER IV.

THE EUROPEAN DISCOVERY OF TARANAKI.

THE DISCOVERY of New Zealand is popularly attributed to Abel Jansen Tasman, a Dutch navigator, who, under a commission from Anthony Van Diemen, the Governor-General of the Dutch East India Company, sailed on a voyage of discovery from Batavia on the 14th August 1642, and made the shores of New Zealand on the 13th December of that year. The journal of this navigator contains a clear admission that he was not the discoverer of the country, for in it he says, "the land which I found in my chart marked New Zealand, I have called Staaten Land." Bleau, a Dutchman, who died four years before Tasman commenced his voyage, published a large folio atlas in which, indistinctly, a line of coast is shown with the name against it—" Zelandia Nova." There is strong probability that Juan Fernandez, the Spanish navigator, was the actual European discoverer of these islands. In the year 1574, sailing from the coast of Chili, in about the latitude of forty degrees, in a small vessel with some of his companions, he reached in about a month a Terra Firma which was fertile and pleasant, and inhabited by a race of white people, well made and dressed in a species of woven cloth, and who were of an amiable disposition. The country contained several rivers which fell into the sea, and it appeared better and richer than Peru. Native tradition concerning the arrival of a ship, and the introduction of the dog and pig, together with the names given to these animals by the Maoris, tend to corroborate the idea of Spanish intercourse with this country at an early date. On the Admiralty Chart of the Indian Ocean of 1827, against the draft of the group appears this note :—" New Zealand discovered and named by Tasman, 1642, but whose Eastern Coast was known to the Portuguese about 1550," and also against Cook's Strait, east side—" Gulf of the Portuguese, 1550." On old charts also, the East Cape is marked as Cabo Formosa. Tasman, who had under his command the yacht "Heemskirk," and the fly-boat "Sea Hen," appears from his chart to have made the coast at Cape Foulwind on the west coast of Nelson. Coasting to the North he entered Massacre Bay and came to anchor there; apparently without the slightest provocation he was attacked by war canoes full of armed Maoris and lost several of his men. This induced him to weigh anchor and sail to the eastward. He then anchored off the mouth of the Pelorus River, and again weighing he made still farther to the eastward, but not perceiving the strait, and having, as he says, the land all about him, he 'bouted ship and made for the westward and northward. On the 26th December, after the subsiding of a north-easterly gale, Tasman sighted Mount Egmont and the coast of Taranaki. To Cape Egmont he gave the name of Cabo Pieter

Boreels. Bearing off the land he failed to discover the Sugarloaves, but he approached the coast near to Kawhia, and then sailing northward discovered the cape which he named after his patron's daughter, afterwards his wife, " Cape Maria Van Diemen."

Captain James Cook was sent by the British Government, in 1768, to Tahiti to observe a transit of Venus over the sun's disc. After reaching that island and making a successful observation of the transit, which occurred on June 3rd, 1769, he sailed southward and made the coast of New Zealand on the 6th October of that year. Sailing northwards from Poverty Bay, and doubling the North Cape, he came in sight of Mount Egmont at 7 o'clock on the evening of Wednesday, January 10th, 1770. "At this time," says Cook, "Albatross Point bore N.E., distant nearly two leagues, and the southernmost land in sight bore S.S.W. ½ W., being a very high mountain and in appearance resembling the Peak of Teneriffe. In this situation we had thirty fathoms of water, and having little wind all night we tacked about four in the morning, Thursday, 11th, and stood in for the shore. Soon after it fell calm, and being in forty-two fathoms water, the people caught a few sea-bream. At eleven a light breeze sprang from the west, and we made sail to the southward. We continued to steer S. by W., and S.S.W. along the shore, at the distance of about four leagues, with gentle breezes from between N.W. and N.N.E. At seven in the evening we saw the top of the peak to the southward above the clouds, which concealed it below. At noon, on the 12th, we were distant about three leagues from the shore which lies under the peak, but the peak itself was wholly concealed by clouds; we judged it to bear about S.S.E., and some remarkable peaked islands which lay under the shore, bore E.S.E., distant three or four leagues. At seven in the evening we sounded and had forty-two fathoms, being distant from the shore between two and three leagues. We judged the peak to bear east, and after it was dark we saw fires upon the shore. At five o'clock on the morning of Saturday the 13th we saw for a few minutes the summit of the peak, towering above the clouds and covered with snow. It now bore N.E.—it lies in latitude 39° 16′ S., longitude 185° 15′ W., and I named it MOUNT EGMONT, in honor of the Earl. It seems to have a large base, and to rise with a gradual ascent; it lies near the sea and is surrounded by a flat country of pleasant appearance, being clothed with verdure and wood, which renders it the more conspicuous, and the shore under it forms a large cape, which I have named Cape Egmont. It lies S.S.W. ½ W., twenty-seven leagues distant from Albatross Point, and on the north side of it are two small islands, which lie near to a remarkable point on the main, that rises to a considerable height in the form of a sugar loaf."

The next navigator who approached the shores of Taranaki was M. Marion du Fresne, a Frenchman, who made the land here on the 10th February, 1772. He named the mountain Le pic de Mascarin, after the name of his ship. This unfortunate commander was shortly afterwards killed and eaten by the Maoris at the Bay of

Islands. Crozet, one of his officers, in his narrative of this sad affair, says :—"The natives treated us with every show of friendship for thirty-three days, with the intention of killing and eating us on the thirty-fourth." It is supposed that the French unwittingly broke the tapu, by taking some drift-wood from the shore for the ship's use, on which the tapu had been laid. Colonel Wakefield, in his despatches mentions the presence of a Russian man-of-war on this coast, and of a trigonometrical measurement of the mountain by a German mathematician on board, but of this event we possess no farther account.

CHAPTER V.

THE NEW ZEALAND COMPANY.

THE discoveries of Captain Cook, in the South Seas, led to the formation of a British penal settlement at Botany Bay, or more strictly speaking at Sydney, in New South Wales. The British commercial spirit was quickly manifested in the young colony, and was fostered to a considerable extent by the need of home freight for the ships visiting the colony. Whales, especially those yielding sperm, were known to abound in the surrounding seas, and vessels were fitted out and despatched for their capture. Flax (phormium) and spars for masts and yards of ships were known to be in abundance in New Zealand, and small trading vessels were sent thither to barter with the natives for these commodities.

In 1814 the Rev. S. Marsden, senior chaplain of New South Wales, started on a missionary tour to New Zealand, preaching his first sermon in the country at the Bay of Islands on Christmas Day of that year. Shortly after this visit, Church of England and Wesleyan Mission stations were established in the neighborhood of the Bay. It having been discovered that whales abounded on the New Zealand Coasts, whaling vessels were sent thither from Sydney, and shore parties were also established in spots favourable for the business of catching whales and preparing the oil. Traders from Sydney visited the rivers and maritime villages of the Islands, giving manufactured goods for scraped flax and for spars. These people after establishing a trade left agents, whose business it was to collect cargo during the absence of vessels. The Maoris very quickly appreciated the benefits of trade, bringing as it did to them many comforts and conveniences to which they had heretofore been strangers. Iron pots for cooking, blankets, clothing, and tobacco were in special request. Each tribe, nay, each hapu sought to have a resident pakeha trader, and to these traders chiefs' daughters were freely given to wife. The Bay of Islands soon became a port of refreshment for whaling ships of various nations; here they could refit, procure spars, firewood, potatoes and pigs. On the Kororareka beach a small town sprang up, peopled with whalers, traders, absconding seamen, and escaped convicts, and in this Alsatia, where no law but that of might prevailed, scenes were enacted which tended to undo much that the missionaries had attempted for the improvement of the Maoris. In consequence of the representations of the local authorities of New South Wales, and of a letter to King William the Fourth from thirteen New Zealand chiefs, praying for the protection of the British Crown, Lord Ripon, on the 14th June, 1832, despatched Mr. Busby to the Bay of Islands, as British resident, accrediting him to certain officers of the Church Missionary Society, and thereby treating the country as a foreign state. Mr. Busby, on his arrival, was hailed by the roughs as a man-of-war without guns, because he came among them in a state of legal and administrative helplessness. In 1834, in consequence of the assumptions of the Baron de Thierry, the Resident, assisted by Missionaries, attempted to establish a Native Government, a number of chiefs being procured to form a confederation, and to declare the independence of the country. On 29th April, 1834, General Bourke, Governor of New South Wales, transmitted to Lord Stanley a proposal from Mr. Busby for establishing a national flag for the tribes of New Zealand in their collective capacity, and advised that ships built in the islands, and registered by the chiefs, should have their registers respected in their intercourse with the British possessions. Sir R. Bourke reported that he had sent three patterns of flags, one of which had been selected by the chiefs, and that the chiefs had assembled with the commanders of the British and three American ships to witness the inauguration of the flag, at which inauguration the officers of H.M.S. Alligator were also present. The flag had been declared to be the "National flag of New Zealand," and being hoisted, was saluted with twenty-one guns by the Alligator, British ship of war. On 21st December, 1834, a dispatch was addressed to Sir R. Bourke by Lord Aberdeen, approving of all these proceedings in the name of the king of Great Britain. A copy of a letter sent to the Admiralty was also sent stating that they had instructed their officers to give effect to the New Zealand registers and to acknowledge and respect the National flag of New Zealand.

Attempts were made by public companies to colonise New Zealand in the years 1825 and 1837, which were resisted by the Government. In 1833, Mr. Edward Gibbon Wakefield published his "View of the Art of Colonisation," the principle of his system being that the new lands of the colonies should be sold in small allotments at low prices to settlers, and the funds thus obtained be expended in carrying out fresh emigrants. This system was adopted by the founders of South Australia, and it was with a view of colonising New Zealand on this plan that on the 22nd of May, 1839, the New Zealand Company was formed with the following directory :—

Governor : The Earl of Durham.
Deputy-Governor : Joseph Somes, Esq.
Directors : The Right Hon. Lord Petre.
John William Buckle, Esq.
Russell Ellice, Esq.
Ralph Fenwick, Esq.
James Brodie Gordon, Esq.
William Hutt, Esq., M.P.
George Lyall, Esq.
Stewart Majoribanks, Esq.
George Palmer, Esq., M.P.
John Pirie, Alderman.
Sir John Sinclair, Bart., M.P.

John Abel Smith, Esq., M.P.
William Thompson, Esq., Alderman, M.P.
Colonel Torrens.
Sir Henry Webb, Bart.
Arthur Willis, Esq.
George Frederick Young, Esq.

To these the following names were afterwards added :—
T. A. Hankey, Esq. ; T. Weeding, Esq. ; J. Ellerker Boulcott, Esq. ; A. Nairne, Esq. ; Hon. F. Baring, M.P. ; Sir W. Molesworth, Bart. ; Viscount Ingestre, M.P. ; J. R. Gowen, M.P. ; E. G. Wakefield, Esq. ; John Hine, Esq. ; Hon. F. Tollemache, M.P. ; H. A. Aglionby, Esq., M.P. ; Alderman Copeland, M.P. ; R. D. Mangles, Esq. ; C. Buller, Esq. ; W. King, Esq. ; Sir Ralph Howard, Bart., M.P. ; Viscount Courtenay, M.P. ; Sir J. L. Goldsmid ; A. Hastie, Esq. ; J. Pilcher, Esq. ; G. Lyall, Esq. ; Alexander Currie.

The names of these gentlemen are a sufficient proof of the respectability of the Company. Thirteen of them were members of Parliament, three were aldermen of the city of London, and the majority of the remainder were either princely merchants, or extensive ship owners. The Company did not so much seek for direct personal gain as for a fresh outlet for British commerce, and a field of emigration for the over-populated districts of Britain in a time of great commercial depression. . That object was ultimately attained, but it was in the face of a fierce and powerful opposition. Opposed by the Colonial Office, and denied a Charter, the Company engaged in the forlorn hope of colonising a land ostensibly governed by a flimsy confederacy of native chiefs, who might possibly one day attempt to devour each other ; but in reality, ruled so far as there was any government, by a missionary hierarchy. After the Company had despatched their pioneers, circumstances arose which rendered it impossible for the Government to withhold a Charter. One was accordingly granted on 12th February, 1841. Owing to the opposition of many of the Church of England missionaries in New Zealand to the unjust and arbitrary measures of Governors Hobson and Fitzroy, and owing also to the Wairau massacre, the Company were compelled to suspend operations in 1844. In consequence of this the Imperial Parliament passed two Acts, one in 1846 granting to the Company a loan of £100,000, and another in 1847 giving them an additional loan of £136,000, with this proviso, that if they could not repay the money in 1850 they were to discharge the debt by surrendering their charter and property to the Crown. In 1850 the charter was relinquished, and a New Zealand Settlement Bill passed the Imperial Parliament, by which Act the debt of £236,000 was cancelled, and the directors were to have five shillings an acre for their property in the island ; in other words £268,370. In 1852, when a constitution was granted to New Zealand, one fourth of the price of all lands sold was appropriated for the payment of the capital and interest of this debt, and the directors offered to cancel it on the immediate payment of £200,000. In 1856 a Bill passed the General Assembly of New Zealand authorising the borrowing of this sum which was to be paid off by the middle Island Provinces on condition that their revenue was not taken to purchase native lands in the North Island. With the aid of the Home Government the money was borrowed in 1857, and at a meeting of the directors of the Company in 1858 the debt was paid.

CHAPTER VI.

THE OPERATIONS OF THE NEW ZEALAND COMPANY.

ON May 13th, 1839, the New Zealand Company despatched from the Port of London their first ship, the Tory, 400 tons, Captain Chaffers, laden with British manufactured goods for the purpose of barter. Captain Chaffers was singularly fitted for the command of this vessel, being one of the best navigators in the royal navy, and having been master of the Beagle surveying ship when Captain Fitzroy was making for the Admiralty a survey of the New Zealand coasts. On board were Colonel Wakefield, the brother of Edward Gibbon Wakefield, the Company's principal agent, a gentleman who had distinguished himself in Spain and Portugal as an intrepid commander of a regiment of Lancers ; Mr. Edward Jerningham Wakefield, his nephew and secretary; Doctor Ernst Dieffenbach, of Berlin, and Fellow of the Royal Society of England, the Company's naturalist; Mr. Heaphy, draughtsman; Mr. John Dorset, Company's agent; and Nati, a Maori interpreter.

After a good passage of ninety-six days they sighted New Zealand, and on the following day came to anchor in Queen Charlotte's Sound. The Maoris paid friendly visits to the ship and the Europeans paid frequent visits to the shore. After staying at the anchorage till the 31st, they weighed and took the ship up to Terawiti. Here Richard Barrett came on board from a whale-boat, and Colonel Wakefield engaged him as his factotum—as pilot, interpreter, and Maori agent. Barrett was born at Rotherhithe, near London, and came out to Sydney, from whence he removed to New Zealand, living and marrying with Ngatiawa, with whom he traded and fought. He had with him a powerful negro who had escaped from an American ship, and went by the name of Sippy or Scipio. At Terawiti Colonel Wakefield came in contact with Guard, an old whaler, who conducted him in a boat to the Pelorus river; he being a man well acquainted with that part of the coast. In 1827, being then master of a trading vessel, Guard had taken shelter from a gale in the Pelorus. On 29th April, 1834, while being conveyed with his wife and family from Sydney to Port Underwood, in the whaling ship Harriet, Capt. Hall, he was wrecked on the coast of Taranaki proper, not far from Cape Egmont. For six days friendly relations were maintained between the shipwrecked people and the Maoris; the plunder of the wreck probably diverting the attention of the latter. The vessel had a quantity of soap on board, a substance with which the Taranaki were totally unacquainted. Supposing it to be food, they cooked it in their ovens, and ate a quantity of it. After this a quarrel arose in which twelve sailors and twenty-five natives were killed, and Mrs. Guard, two children, and ten seamen made prisoners. Guard and several sailors were allowed to depart on promising to return with powder as a ransom for the others. Guard proceeded to Sydney and represented the matter to the Government, which sent H. M. S. Alligator, Capt. Lambert, to rescue the prisoners. This was effected, but according to Thompson, in a treacherous manner; many Maoris were killed, and two villages destroyed.

Hearing that the Rev. Henry Williams had sent a message to the Maoris at Wellington, advising them not to sell their land, and promising to visit them shortly in his schooner, Colonel Wakefield determined to reach that spot as quickly as possible. This Mr. Williams was, in his younger days, an officer in the Royal Navy, and he is said to have been on board the Shannon at the time she engaged the Chesapeake in the American War of 1813. After that he took holy orders, and came to New Zealand as a missionary in 1823, taking up his abode at the Bay of Islands, where he built a schooner, and navigated it himself to Sydney and to various parts of the New Zealand coast. He was a most uncompromising opponent to colonization, but he laid claim to twenty-two thousand acres of land, out of which he was awarded nine thousand acres. He died in 1872, at an advanced age.

On the 20th September, the Tory entered Port Nicholson, being piloted thither by Richard Barrett. E. Puni and Warepori, two principal chiefs of the Ngatiawa, came on board, and entertained with satisfaction Colonel Wakefield's proposal to buy the land. On the 2nd November, the Tory was again in Queen Charlotte's Sound. Under this date Colonel Wakefield writes :—" The Natives here, some of the ancient possessers of Taranaki, are very desirous that I should become the purchaser of that district, in order that they may return to their native places without fear of the Waikato tribes. They will yield all their claims on the district to the Company, but stipulate for the same reservation of land for Mr. Barrett and the children of the late Mr. Love as for the Native chiefs; these two Englishmen having lived for so many years among the Ngatiawa during their wars, and having had children born of Maori wives on the spot, have long been considered as belonging to the tribe." On 8th November, 1839, a deed was executed in Queen Charlotte's Sound, by which the Ngatiawa conveyed to the Company all the land from the Mokau river past Taranaki, Wanganui, and Wellington, to Cape Tikukahore, in latitude 41° on the East Coast. This deed was personally signed by thirty Maoris, and by two by proxy. The chiefs E Hawe and E White signed it, and the hapus signed as follows :—Puketapu ten, and one by proxy; Ngamotu sixteen; Taniwa one; Ngatimaru one; the chief E Riri signed by proxy. The witnesses were :—Richard Barrett, Richard Lowry, George Doddney, and Himiona.

Having completed this business in Cook Strait, Colonel Wakefield resolved to proceed to the North to view some land at Kaipara, which the Company had bought of the New Zealand Association. On his way he determined to leave Dr. Dieffenbach and Barrett at Ngamotu, and to take them up on his return. The following is his account of the voyage :—

"SUGARLOAF ISLANDS,
"Wednesday, November 27th, 1839.

"At length, after a tedious voyage of nine days from Kapiti, being only 130 miles off, having experienced much bad weather and three gales of wind, we anchored this morning in nine fathoms water, at two miles from the land to the north of these islands. The gale had left a heavy swell which caused a great surf on the beach, so as to prevent a boat landing. Mr. Barrett, with Te Aurau and E Whare, whom you will recollect I brought from Port Nicholson, went near the land in a boat, and succeeded, after some time, in making themselves recognised by the inhabitants. Two chiefs swam off to the boat through the surf and came on board the ship. This specimen of communication with the shore will give a bad opinion of the place as regards its roadstead, and I can say nothing to palliate it. It is completely open to the north-west, and never accessible but after a long calm or south-east wind, both of which are rare events. Ships, moreover, would have a difficulty in going to sea, if a gale came on suddenly. No talking on the part of the natives took place in the boat; surprise at seeing their old friends, and the national custom preventing any demonstration of feeling; but after coming on board an affecting scene took place, in which one of the new comers described the wretched existence that he and his companions had led since the mass of the tribe had migrated to Cook Strait, six years ago. Continual war had been carried on against them by the Waikato people; and nothing but the refuge afforded by the Sugarloaf peaks had preserved the small remnant, not amounting to more than fifty, who still held their ground, with occasional assistance from their southern neighbors. They expressed great anxiety respecting their future fate; hoped their enemies now being missionaries would no longer persecute them; but declared their intention not to remove from, but to die on the land of their grandsires. Mr. Williams had been here a fortnight ago, and had left at Otamatua, where the original Taranaki people live, many missionary books and some instructors. The country to the south of Mount Egmont, after doubling the Cape, appears extremely valuable; an immense table land extends as far as the eye can reach, no part of which is free from vegetation. The finest flax grows nearly to the sea side. Immediately at the base of the mountain, towards the sea, many volcanic appearances present themselves in the confused assemblage of hillocks, the nature of the rocks, and the black sand surrounding them. The mountain commences at about twenty miles from the coast, and slopes down gradually to the north for at least forty miles. Within this slope and the sea is a fertile undulating plain, covered with small timber and abundant vegetation. It is belted by a narrow ridge of sand hummocks, and in its fertility and general appearance strongly reminds one of French Flanders, to which its dangerous and inconvenient coast further assimilates it.

"Thursday, November 28.

"It being impossible to collect the chiefs whose consent is requisite for the transfer of the land from Manawatu to Mokau, under at least a week, and having been detained so much by baffling winds, I determined not to remain longer here, but to leave Mr. Barrett, who would be an efficient agent in the transaction, from his intimate knowledge of the territory I am desirous to acquire, from his personal influence with the chiefs, and from the acknowledged claims he has by marriage and the birth of his children on the land. He accordingly landed this morning with his wife and children, with instructions to assemble the numerous chiefs on a coast line of 150 miles in a month's time, when I am to return to make the payment for the different districts, and to receive the written assent of the chiefs to the sale.

"Notwithstanding the qualities of the soil of the Taranaki district, which are allowed to be superior to those of any land in these islands, such is the difficulty of communicating with it by water, that I do not see any probability of settlers being placed there for some years. Looking, however, to the future, and to the interests of the Company's future representatives, and hoping that by the unconquerable energies of the British inhabitants, this country will shortly assume a different aspect as regards its interior communications,—sanguinely hoping even to see commenced such an undertaking as the construction of a road from this district, and that of all the valuable land to the northward of Port Nicholson, a distance of not more than 156 miles, in which, however, many obstacles in the mountain ranges occur, I cannot but be anxious to obtain this fine territory. The many conflicting interests and divisions of the occupants, whose numbers and places of residence you will find in the table, would render it almost impossible for any individual without shipping and large means at his disposal to acquire this portion of country; and the agent I have employed is from his connection with the natives, perhaps the only man who could negotiate the bargain, I have every hope that on my return here the completion of it will be effected.

"Dr. Dieffenbach, the naturalist, also remains on shore here with the view of ascending Mount Egmont, and of examining the country in the neighborhood. As it could seldom happen that a man of science should have the opportunity of being put down here, with a family who could protect him in what has hitherto been considered, with reason, the wildest part of New Zealand, with time to examine the most important district as regards mineralogy in these islands, and to be taken off again when he had achieved his object, I strongly recommended him to stay here in preference to proceeding to Kaipara, which has been visited by many naturalists, and presents nothing so worthy of the examination of the learned. We got under weigh so soon as the party had landed, and with a fair wind stood to the northward."

CHAPTER VII.

THE ADVENTURES OF DOCTOR DIEFFENBACH IN TARANAKI.

DR. ERNST DIEFFENBACH, the New Zealand Company's naturalist, in his work entitled "Travels in New Zealand" thus describes his adventures and explorations in the Taranaki district :—

" On the 22nd of November we obtained the long-wished-for view of Mount Egmont, and also of the Ruapahu, both of which were to a great extent covered with snow. But they were soon again hid from our view; and it was only on the 27th of November, after having experienced much bad weather and several severe gales, that we anchored to the northward of the Sugarloaf Islands, about two miles from the shore. Soon after we had cast anchor a waterspout rose not far from us. The weather had now begun to clear up; and I scrutinised the sides and lofty summit of Mount Egmont, which, once thrown up by the mysterious fires of the deep, was now apparently in a state of repose, to discover whether there was any possibility of ascending it, an undertaking which had never yet been achieved.

" We had brought from Port Nicholson one of the principal chiefs, Tuarau, who was delighted to see the land of his birth and to assist the Company's agent in the purchase of it. Our boat, which was sent ashore, was unable to land on account of the surf, but brought back two natives who had plunged into the foaming sea and swum to it. The meeting on our deck between them and Tuarau was almost solemn; they did not utter a word, and struggled to conceal the deep feelings which evidently agitated them.

" Our anchorage was not regarded as safe ; and as the continual gales of the last few days had left a heavy swell, which made communication with the shore difficult and hazardous, it was determined that the Tory should proceed on her voyage to the northward, and that Mr. Barrett should remain in Taranaki to keep possession of the land for the New Zealand Company. I immediately resolved to stay with him, and we landed on the morning of the 28th. I could not have found a better opportunity for examining a district so little known, and determined to occupy the time until the return of the Tory in ascending Mount Egmont, which I expected would prove in more than one respect an interesting and profitable achievment. I must mention that Mr. Barrett had lived for several years near the Sugarloaf Islands, prior to the period when almost all the original natives yielded, after a long-continued contest, to the tribe of the Waikato, who live about sixty miles to the northward. The natives of Taranaki migrated to the eastward, and settled on both sides of Cook's Straits, and especially at Kapiti, Port Nicholson, and Queen

Charlotte's Sound. Only a few remained, who could not be persuaded to leave the land of their forefathers, for which, indeed, all migrated tribes evince the greatest predilection, and cherish the hope that, by the help of the European colonists, they will one day be able to return and recover their lost territory. Since the removal of the majority, the small remnant of the original natives of Taranaki had lived a very agitated life, often harassed by the Waikato, and seeking refuge on one of the Rocky Sugarloaf Islands, at times dispersed into the impenetrable forest at the base of Mount Egmont, sometimes making a temporary truce with their oppressors, but always regarded as an enslaved and powerless tribe. They could not, however, be induced to join their relations, and the reader can well imagine with what joy they hailed the arrival of their old friend Barrett, and how they cherished the hope of rising from the degradation in which they had lived for so long a time, and again becoming an independent tribe.

"We landed to the northward of Paritutu, or Sugarloaf Point, a dome-like cone of trachytic porphyry, which rises to about 500 feet, and stands quite by itself. We turned our whale-boat over, and made preparations for passing the first night under it.

"As soon as we had landed the Tory weighed her anchors, and with a favourable breeze, was soon out of sight.

"On the beach, from which large sand-hills here rise, I picked up many specimens of the neat and delicate shells Spirula australis.

"The land near the beach is, in some parts, covered with shrubs; in others the loose sand here and there acquired some solidity from the roots and fibres of a running carex, which is the first preparatory step to its becoming fit for other plants. In several places behind these sand-hills lagoons of fresh water are found, which abound with ducks, but contain no other fish than some large eels, in order to catch which the natives formerly cut through the sand-hills and emptied the lagoon. Round these lagoons the vegetation was very rich, and amongst the shrubs was the handsome Apeiba autralis, which I observed here for the first time.

"Towards Sugarloaf Point, large boulders, all consisting of volcanic rocks of apparently an old date, as basalts, greenstones, trachyte, augitic rock, &c., were cemented together into an extremely solid conglomerate, which appeared to extend like a stream of lava from Mount Egmont into the sea, but cannot be traced far. Where the water washes these rocks, the conglomerate is peculiarly hard, and this is caused by a chemical action of the salt water, either on the particles of the iron pyrites, with which several of the rocks abound, and which often cover the pebbles with a metallic crust, or else on the black titanic-iron-sand which is found on the beach. In some places this chemical action is accompanied by the development of a good deal of heat, which is perceived where, at the retiring tide, the sea leaves ponds of water between the rocks. A strong smell of sulphuretted hydrogen gas may also be observed about a mile from high-water mark. The natives have a whimsical story of an *Atua* (spirit), who they say was drowned here, and is still undergoing decomposition.

"In some places the sandy downs at a little distance from the shore are covered with a hard crust of oxydated iron-clay, which forms the most fantastic shapes of tubes, saucers, &c., evidently owing to the oxydation of the particles of iron in the sand by water and air, and subsequent adhesion to each other. All this interested me much, proving a former extensive activity of volcanic powers, the centre of which was Mount Egmont, situated at a distance of twenty-five miles; its summit afforded me a never-failing object of attraction when it was free from clouds, or when the morning or evening sun gilded its snowy summit with a rosy hue.

"Aqueous formations were visible on both sides of Sugarloaf Point; they consisted of cliffs of yellow clay, and in some places contain formations not of coal or lignite, but of wood embedded in discoloured blackish earth. Towards Mokau these formations are especially visible, and form everywhere one of the most remarkable features in the geology of New Zealand. Elevated about ten feet above the level of the sea, they consist, according to all that I could ascertain, of the remains of trees belonging to species still existing in the island, and are an indubitable proof that an elevation of the land above the level of the sea has taken place at a period when the same vegetation existed as at present. I never found any remains of animals in these formations, which are however irregular and interrupted.

"It is a question of great interest to geologists, to what cause is to be ascribed the formation of those extensive coal-fields which form the principal source of our industry,—whether they have taken their rise from the submersion of a whole forest, or the floating of uprooted timber in estuaries of the sea or lakes, or whether they are due to the submersion of peat-beds. Guided by the principle that the former epochs in the earth's history can be best deciphered by studying her present aspect and the alterations which are going on before our eyes, I have arrived at the opinion that our coal formations were formerly peat; that the timber which is deposited in estuaries or inland lakes will ultimately become lignite or brown coal, which has lost scarcely any of the qualities of wood. A river which brings vast masses of wood to the sea must of necessity deposit them in a very unequal manner, mixed with alluvium of various descriptions, and must imbed in this formation such testaceous animals as are living near the spot. Such is the case at present with the New Zealand rivers; such are the lignitic formations which we observe at present above the level of the sea in this country; and of the same nature are the mines of lignite which are worked in many parts of Germany. Will anybody contend that it is possible by any agency —whether by the pressure of a superincumbent formation, or by igneous causes from below, or by both agencies combined—to convert that mixture of trees and earthy or mineral substance into the homogeneous substance which is spread out in such regular stratifications, and which we call coal? I, for my part, cannot credit the possibility of such a change. It is different with peat, which occupies large tracts in the countries out of the tropics, very often in horizontal and equal layers, and which we see imbedding trees in an upright position. If artificially compressed it resembles coal far more than does any lignitic substance that I have ever seen. I have brought specimens of peat from the Chatham Islands, taken from a layer not in actual formation, but covered by a loamy earth several feet in thickness. In these specimens, which it was evident were formerly pure peat, I can observe a conchoidal fracture and lustrous appearance greatly resembling coal, whilst in other parts of the same specimen the gradual transition from true peat is evident. I am well aware that eminent geologists have contended for the double origin of coal, and others will only admit the simple one from wood; but they will, probably, come to a different conclusion if they turn their attention more to present processes, and divest their minds of preconceived ideas regarding a difference of phenomena in former days.

"One of the Sugarloaf Islands also consists of aqueous deposits, namely, yellow and soft sandstone. But the rest of these islands are steep and conical masses of a greyish trachyte, containing much feldspar, with scarcely any vegetation on them beyond the Phormium tenax, Mesembryanthemum australe, Pteris esculenta, Peperomia d'Urvillei, Microcalia australis, epacris, linum, &c. Numerous seaweeds float at their base, amongst which were the Laminaria flabelliformis, Sargassum carpillifolium, Marginaria urvilliana, &c.

"I found about twenty natives near Sugarloaf Point; the place seemed only a fishing station; the remainder of the Taranaki tribes lived either on concealed potatoe-plantations, or farther south near Cape Egmont. On our arrival being known, they assembled around Mr. Barrett, and with tears welcomed their old friend. In a singing strain of lamentation they related their misfortunes and the continual inroads of the Waikato. The scene was truly affecting, and the more so when we recollect that this small remnant had sacrificed everything to the love of their native place. I perceived in the evening how much they stood in dread of the Waikato. A fire had been observed in the direction of Kawhia, and the fear that the Waikato were again on their way to Taranaki kept them awake during the greater part of the night.

"The principal village of the Taranaki natives formerly stood a little to the eastward of Sugarloaf Point. Besieged by the Waikato, who had come in great numbers from Kawhia, they effectually kept them at bay, with the help of Mr. Barrett and eight other traders, who at that time lived with them in the village. Three pieces of cannon in their possession made great havoc amongst the Waikato. The exasperation on both sides was great, and the prisoners captured at occasional sorties were devoured. The Waikato at last raised the siege, and returned to Kawhia; nevertheless the Ngatiawa resolved to quit the district, and, 2,000 in number, they started together with the Europeans. This took place in November, 1832. At a second attack the Waikato destroyed the pa, of which now scarcely any vestige remains, with the exception of the fosses; the cannons had been spiked by the Ngatiawa on their departure, and were still lying on the beach.

"South of Sugarloaf Point to Cape Egmont and Waimate, the country, as I ascertained from many subsequent excursions, slopes very slowly from Mount Egmont to the sea-coast. In fact the country is so level round the base of Mount Egmont that the latter seems almost to rise immediately from the plain. The coast forms a cliff of moderate height, and consists of a yellowish sandy loam—an excellent substratum for a rich mould which covers the top, and which increases in depth towards the foot of the mountain. Near the sea-shore the soil is light, intermixed with sand. In general the land for three or four miles from the coast is open, and covered with a uniform vegetation, especially of flax or fern; in the little dales, however, are groves of trees, or swamps covered with bulrushes and reeds.

"A countless number of small streams here discharge themselves into the sea: scarcely a mile was passed without our crossing a streamlet, which was sometimes knee-deep. They came from Mount Egmont, or from several small lagoons situated between it and the coast.

"The Sugarloaf Islands are five in number: the three nearest the shore are Pararaki, Paparoa, and Mikotahi; then Moturoa; and afterwards Motumahanga, which is the outermost. Besides, there are some rocks and reefs. The native name for them, as well as for the whole district near Sugarloaf Point, and for the tribe formerly living near them, is Ngamotu—the Islands.

"To the northward of Sugarloaf Point are three small creeks—the Huatoki, the Henui, and the Waiwakaiho. Everywhere on their banks are traces of former cultivation and of native villages, but now no one lives here: thus the finest district in New Zealand is almost uninhabited—a sad instance of the mutual hatred existing among savage clans.

"The natives could not understand what induced me to ascend Mount Egmont; they tried much to dissuade me from the attempt, by saying that the mountain was *tapu*, that there were *ngarara* (crocodiles) on it, which would undoubtedly eat me; the mysterious bird 'moa,' of which I shall say more hereafter, was also said to exist there. But I answered that I was not afraid of these creations of their lively imagination, and if they wanted large payment for their land I must first go and look at it; that it was possible—though not very probable—that the monikoura (money-gold) was found on the mountain, and that if, through their refusing to provide me a guide, I was the first to reach the summit, I should make the mountain *tapu* for myself, according to their own law. An old Tohunga, or priest, was therefore persuaded to show the way as far as he knew it, and with him, and an American man of colour, I started on the 3rd of December. Tangutu-na-Waikato, as the worthy chief was called, was particularly qualified for the office of guide on this expedition.

In the wars between the Ngatiawa and Waikato, the latter had carried away his two wives into slavery; he himself escaped to the mountain, where they were unable to find him. There he lives by himself, as all his kindred are gone, and cultivates small patches in the impenetrable forest, which supply him with food. The Waikato often chased him, but he was always fortunate enough to escape. The old man was renowned for his skill in the arts and the·mystic lore of a priest of his nation, and had lately become a zealous missionary; and although he almost invariably kept his *puka puka* (hymn and prayer books) upside down when he pretended to sing his psalms or read the service, yet what he sung or said pretty nearly corresponded with the text, as he knew the books by heart. A mat of his own manufacture, as he had no female to work it for him, was his only dress; a· hatchet his only weapon. We did not take much provision with us, as the party in Ngamotu had little to spare, and as we had no means of carrying it. I trusted to my gun and to the stores of Tangutu in the bush.

"Our road led us along the beach to the northward. We crossed the Huatoki and Henui creeks, and then turned into the interior over the downs and hillocks of the coast which were covered with fern and flax, overshadowed here and there by a picturesque ti (Dracæna australis). About two miles from the coast we came into a low shrubby forest where the soil consisted mostly of a very dark vegetable mould. Tangutu had here cleared a place in the middle of the bush, where he had formed a clean and well-weeded garden, planted with potatoes, taro, onions, water-melons and pumpkins. Not far from this point we crossed the river Waiwakaiho, a rapid but not very deep stream, with a broad and pebbly bed, all the pebbles consisting of hard and blue trap-rock. About a mile farther we passed another deep creek—Mangoraka a tributary of the Waiongona, where my guide had another potatoe-field. The forest consisted generally of tawa; here and there might be seen a majestic rimu pine, or rata, bearing crimson flowers. There were many aborescent ferns, and in the deepest shade grew the Nikau palm (Areca sapida). Sometimes we came to an open spot, several square miles in extent, probably cleared by natives, but now grown over with the highest Phormium tenax I ever saw. The leaves in many instances were twelve, and the flower-stalks twenty feet long; the flowers contain a kind of sweet liquid in considerable quantities, the extraction of which forms a favourite occupation among the New Zealand children. The cryptogamous plants, ferns, jungermannias, and mosses, bear in New Zealand rather an undue proportion to the phanerogamous—a circumstance which is unfavourable to the rearing of bees. I am not aware that there is any native bee in New Zealand, but in certain seasons the European bee would find a great quantity of honey and wax in the Phormium tenax. Bees have been introduced into New Zealand from New South Wales. My excellent friend, the Rev. Richard Taylor, at Waimate, had a hive, and they were thriving remarkably well; but in that neighbourhood many European plants had been introduced,

"The country began now to rise a little, but the elevation was so slight as to be scarcely perceptible. Everywhere vegetation appeared most vigorous, and the primeval forest was often almost impenetrable, on account of thick creepers, and the briers, tataramoa (*rubus*), of which several species are found, and which tore our hands and faces severely. We scarcely ever obtained a view of the sun, and the shade of the trees produced a delightful coolness, although the thermometer in open places rose to 90°, and at six in the evening on a hill it stood at 80°. We did not see many birds, and I need scarcely repeat that the most perfect silence reigned through the forest. Although we walked on a track, it was one visible only to the eyes of Tangutu; and it was not until after much practice that I could distinguish, in the turning or the pressure of a leaf, indications that the path had ever been trod by mortal feet. My guide went patiently forward, carrying a heavy load for me, without a murmur, although a priest and a person of consequence among his own people. We soon came to another potatoe-field of Tangutu, where he had a house; he here entered the forest, and quickly returned with some fern-root and some dried shark which he had concealed, and which greatly increased our scanty stock or provisions. In consequence of the insecurity of their persons and property, it is very usual with the Taranaki natives to have plantations of this sort in the forest, which are often known to the proprietor alone, and to which he can fall back in times of need. Frequently Tangutu would on a sudden make me stop on the way, and, entering the forest, would return either with a dried fish, or with some oil contained in a dilated joint of kelp, with which he would grease his dark and glossy hair; sometimes he brought a handful of leeks, which were always welcome.

"At sunset we arrived at the clear summit of the hill, where we found several houses for provisions, which are always built on posts, to guard against the rats, and also two other houses. A thick forest surrounded this place on all sides. The plantations of potatoes, all belonging to Tangutu, and planted with his own hands, were in tolerably good order. There was no want of provisions; and pigeons, potatoes, leeks, taro, cabbage, turnips, and the young shoots of Sonchus oleraceus were all at our command.

"Before it was quite dark, flights of the Austral Nestor passed over our encampment, shrieking in a dismal manner, and alighted for a moment on one of the dead trees at the skirt of the forest, to watch with a stupid curiosity what was going on below; but they soon became quiet, with the rest of the inhabitants of the forest. In the twilight there was also a small bat flying about, but I did not succeed in shooting one. During the day a sandfly (*ngamu*), a tipula, is very troublesome in New Zealand, especially near the sea-shore; and, diminutive as they are, they are perhaps the most bloodthirsty animals that exist, attacking all the most exposed parts of the body. With the last ray of the sun they all disappear, but are immediately replaced by the mosquitos, which, however, are numerous only in particular spots, such as the cleared places of the forest. We had taken our abode in an old house, where the rats ran over us all night, and two species of smaller animals, not to be named to ears polite, were by no means scarce. An old native house is a hotbed for all vermin, and after this night's experience I always preferred sleeping in the open air, or under my own tent, which I found by far the most comfortable.

"Before sunrise on the 4th of December the thermometer stood at 44°. We took an east-south-east direction, and after descending the hill we had to pass a large creek flowing to the eastward. Our road lay over gently undulating hills, which were covered with a dense forest. The cabbage-palms were the highest I ever saw. We passed several other streams, and at noon halted at another plantation belonging to our guide. He rested here during the day to arrange our provisions for the continuance of the journey. This field was situated at the side of a river, which rolled over a pebbly and rocky bed, and was canopied by the trees on its banks. From the high towai trees a graceful moss hung down in long festoons. This creek was the Mangoraka, which we passed the day before.

"The temperature here at noon was 91° in the sun and 72° in the shade, and I found the heat very oppressive.

"I could not prevail upon Tangutu to start the next morning, as this was his last plantation. The sky was overcast, and he said that the weather would be bad for several days. We had some dried shark and potatoes, with maize, but not sufficient to last us many days. Birds are everywhere scarce, and too small to be worth powder and shot. One bird that I found here is of a new species; it is called E Ihi, and belongs to the class of the honey-eaters. Another bird, the tierawaki (Icterus rafisater Less.,), is very common. It is as large as a blackbird, of a jet-black plumage, with red-brown coverlets on the wings and tail. It has two small orange-coloured appendages at the base of the beak. This bird is seen on the lower branches of trees, is very lively, and has a loud penetrating note. It always screams when anything attracts its attention—huei, huei, tierawak, tierawak. It feeds principally on fleshy berries, but also on coleopterous insects.

"Pouring rain lasted during this and the following day. On the afternoon of the 7th, the weather having somewhat cleared up, we started, but had not proceeded far before the rain again compelled us to halt. It must be observed that travelling through the bush in New Zealand is rather a scrambling affair, and with a load is very fatiguing, and cannot be kept up for a long time. Fifteen miles I considered a very good day's work, even in the open parts of the island. We took up our quarters under the shelter of a rata-tree. Several species of the kind to which this enormous tree belongs were common; but the pukatea was the most frequent. I was roused in the night by the psalm-singing of old Tangutu, who could not sleep, and was probably afraid that *Atua* was determined to oppose our ascending the sacred mountain by means of the bad weather which had now set in.

"On the 8th we several times crossed the Mangoraka. Its banks are steep, and from one of them Tangutu dug out a titi; this bird, a Procellaria, or mutton-bird as it is commonly called, has many peculiarities. In the month of December it comes from the sea to the mountains inland, especially to the fore-hills of Mount Egmont. Here the female, which is at that time very fat, but afterwards becomes thin and emaciated, lays one egg, which is remarkably large for the size of the bird. Instead of building a nest, she deposits and covers over her egg in a deep channel under the roots of trees, or at the sides of a cliff, and never leaves the place until the egg is hatched. The natives believe that during this period the female takes no food, and have accordingly named it " the bird of one feeding " (*He manu wangainga tahi.*)

"On the 9th we travelled for some time on the right bank of the Waiwakaiho river, which is the largest of those that take their rise on the northern side of Mount Egmont. Although of very unequal depth, it is a true mountain stream; it rolls over a broad bed of boulders and pebbles, and often rises suddenly when the snow melts, or when the rain has been heavy. Its banks were moderately elevated; on their top the land was flat, and the whole was covered with forest of the wildest and most primeval aspect. We passed numerous tributaries of this river, some of which were of considerable depth, owing to the late rains, which had also formed stagnant pools between the roots of old trees. At one place Tangutu conducted us into the bed of the river, whence we had the satisfaction, for the first time since we had entered the forest, of seeing Mount Egmont, which rose to the south-by-west, covered with snow, but with its summit hid in the clouds. The dense forest on both sides of the river formed, as it were, a framework to the picture. My guide suddenly stopped at the bank near this point, and, clearing away with his hatchet a few of the young towai-trees, chanted some hymns, and begged me to read a chapter from St. Paul's Epistle to the Romans. On my asking the reason of this sudden procedure, he told me that many years ago, going with a party to fetch kokowai (red ochre), from the foot of the mountain, they had been surprised at this spot by a party of Waikato, and that in the struggle which ensued his mother had been killed. He had never, he said, visited that spot without paying a tribute to her memory.

"We stopped for the night on a low island in the Waiwakaiho, called Waiwiti, grown over with kahikatoa (Leptospermum), intermixed with a junceous plant the Hamelinia veratroides of Achille Richard (Astelia Banksii), the seeds of which form the food of the kiwi and weka (Apterix australis and Rallus australis). The island bore evident marks of being frequently overflowed, as large stems of drifted trees were collected on it. The river Waiwakaiho is extremely well adapted for the application of water-power to manufactories and mills; and the whole district of Taranaki, as far as I have yet seen, rivals any in the world in fertility, beauty, and fitness for becoming the dwelling-place of civilised European communities.

"Our provisions grew very scanty; and when on the following day the sky was again overcast, and the rain poured down in torrents, I almost gave up the hope of ever reaching the summit of Mount Egmont, especially as Tangutu now frequently lost all trace of the right direction. We proceeded, however, along the left bank of the river, wet to the skin. The trees over which we had to clamber were extremely slippery, and, although they preserved their outward shape, we often sunk knee-deep into their soft and decayed substance. To appease our hunger we had nothing but the young shoots of a fern, or the mucous undeveloped leaves of the Cyathea medullaris; these, with the heart of the cabbage-palm, and, in open spots, the roots of the Pteris esculenta, are, generally speaking, the only eatables that can be obtained in a New Zealand forest. The rain had made my gun useless—a matter, indeed, of less consequence, as there was no game, and very few of the smaller birds. The confidence shown by these birds proved that they are not often disturbed by the approach of man. The boldest was a fly-catcher of an ashy colour, which hopped continually over the rotten trees, searching for insects. It builds its nest on the lowest branches of small trees, where they join the stem, and constructs it neatly of moss, lining it inside with the soft and villous cover of the young undeveloped leaves of the Cyathea medullaris.

"The rain continued during the 10th and 11th, and all our provisions were gone. We could procure no dry wood to make a fire; we had no tent with us, and got but little shelter from the trees. During these nights the forest assumed a beautiful appearance: the fallen trees, and almost the whole surface of the ground sparkled in a thousand places with the phosphorescence of the decayed matter;—we seemed to have entered the illuminated domain of fairy-land.

"When the weather cleared up we determined to return, abandoning, for the present, the attempt to reach the summit of the mountain. Taking a different track from that by which we had come, we again stood on the sea-shore on the evening of the 15th of December.

"During our absence plenty had reigned at Ngamotu: the natives had daily gone out fishing, and the quantity of fish they took was so great that they were enabled to dry large numbers in the sun for store. Pigs and potatoes had also been brought from the southward. A Waikato chief, with his followers, had come on a friendly visit from Kawhia, and there was apparently a good understanding between them and the natives at this place. The abundance of food enabled me to start again on the 19th, determined, at all hazards, to accomplish the ascent of the mountain. I persuaded E Kake, one of the chiefs, to accompany me, who took a slave with him, and sent on before a female slave to one of his plantations which lay in our route, with an order to prepare maize-cakes for us to carry as provisions. The companions of my last trip again accompanied me, and our party was joined by Mr. Heberley, a European, who had come with us from Teawaiti, where he had lived for several years as a whaler, and who was most expert in finding his way through all the difficulties attending such an expedition as this. This time I was more fortunate. Although we took a different route, in order to obtain provisions at the settlements of E Kake, in four days we reached our last halting-place at the foot of the mountain. We had to walk for some distance along the rocky bed and through the icy water of the Waiwakaiho; but notwithstanding the force of its rapid current, which often threatened to throw us down, we heeded not the difficulty, as we had the gratification of seeing the summit of the mountain directly before us. We climbed at last up a ridge rising on the left bank of the river, and running in a north-east direction from Mount Egmont. This ridge is very narrow, and forms, towards the river, a sharp escarpment; nor was it without much difficulty that we reached its crest. Higher up is a frightful precipice, close to the edge of which we had to walk. Lying down, we looked over into the deep gorge, which appeared to have been split asunder by volcanic agency, and to have been hollowed out more and more by the action of the river. This ridge was still covered with wood; but, as we ascended, the trees gradually became less lofty, and soon gave way to stunted shrubs. Low and crooked pines, especially totara and miro, and the manuka, gave a character to the vegetation as affiliated kinds of trees do to the mountain-crests of Europe. I found one plant of a new pine two feet high, and very much resembling the Taxus baccata of Europe. The thermometer rose during this day to 76°, and when we halted in the evening, shortly before sunset, it stood at 61°, but fell back immediately afterwards to 51°, and the cold became very severe; our altitude was about 5,500 feet. We prepared to rest amidst the stunted and dwarfish shrubs amongst which I observed the Dracophyllum rosmarinifolium, Solidago arborescens, and several other compositous plants. We were able to obtain sufficient firewood a little way down the sides of the ridge, where we found many bleak and dry stems of large dimensions.

"The escarpment which I have mentioned consisted of a blue basaltic lava, overlaid to the depth of from ten to fifteen feet by a formation of fragmentary rocks, boulders, and pebbles, which however, I could not accurately examine.

"Scarcely any birds were to be seen at this height; the cry, however, of the parrots re-echoed from the woody gorges; and a little bird, which is peculiar to these heights, busied itself in our neighborhood; it is related in shape and habits to our Sitta, but is much smaller, and of a dark-green plumage. It is the Acanthisitta tenuirostris of our Index, and called piwauwau by the natives.

"Not far from this point the ridge forms a platform from which rises the pyramidical summit. We reached the platform by descending into a deep gorge which an arm of the Waiwakaiho river has scooped out of the blue lava. We walked with ease in the rocky channel thus formed, and soon came to the source of this arm, which took its rise from under a frozen mass of snow which filled up the ravine and remained unmelted, although it was now in the middle of summer. This place, however, is not to be regarded as lying within the limits of perpetual snow, as the duration of this frozen mass resulted from the fact that the influence of the sun was obstructed by high walls rising on both sides. There was very little vegetation here; I collected, however, a Viola, a primulaceous and ranunculaceous plant, a Myosotis, and the Microcalia australis, the southern representative of our daisy, which it much resembles. We now began to ascend the cone, which consisted of cinders, or slags of scoriaceous lava, of various colours—white, red, or brown,—and had been reduced almost to a gravel, so as to offer no resistance to our feet. These volcanic products can be distinguished in their lithological characters from scoriæ of the Auvergne. We soon came to the snow, at a point of about 1,500 feet below the summit. The limits of perpetual congelation in New Zealand correspond nearly with the result obtained by calculation according to Kirwan's formula, which, taking 59° as the mean annual temperature of New Zealand, would give the limit of perpetual snow 7,204 feet; deducting this number from 8,839 feet, which is about the height of Mount Egmont, we have 1,635 feet below its summit as the lowest point at which snow is perpetual. Vegetation had long ceased, not from the great elevation, but from the entire absence of even a patch of soil where plants might take root. In the ravines, as I have already observed, the snow was found much lower down.

"As soon as we reached the limits of perpetual snow, my two native attendants (the third had been left behind at the last night's halting-place) squatted down, took out their books, and began to pray. No native had ever before been so high, and, in addition to that awe which the grand scenes of nature and the solemn silence reigning on such heights produce in every mind, the savage views such scenes with superstitious dread. To them the mountains are peopled with mysterious and misshapen animals; the black points, which he sees from afar in the dazzling snow, are fierce and monstrous birds; a supernatural spirit breathes on him in the evening breeze, or is heard in the rolling of a loose stone. It is this imaginative superstition which gives birth to the poetry of infant nations, as we see in the old tales of the Germans, which evidently have their origin in the earliest ages of the race, and bear the impress of the ethics and religion of a people not yet emerged from barbarism; but with the Polynesians these fears lead to gross superstition, witchcraft, and the worship of demons. My native attendants would not go any farther, not only on account of their superstitious fears, but because, from the intensity of the cold, their uncovered feet had already suffered severely. I started, therefore, for the summit, accompanied by Heberley alone. The slope of the snow was very steep, and we had to cut steps in it, as it was frozen on the surface. Higher up we found some support in large pieces of rugged scoriæ, which, however, increased the danger of the ascent, as they obstructed our path, which lay along a narrow ridge, while on both sides yawned an abyss filled with snow. However, we at length reached the summit, and found that it consisted of a field of snow about a square mile in extent.

[It is really but an acre in extent.] Some protruding blocks of scoriæ, of a reddish-brown colour, and here and there slightly vitrified on the surface, indicated the former existence of an active volcano. A most extensive view opened before us, and our eye followed the line of coast towards Kawhia and Waikato. The country over which we looked was but slightly elevated; here and there broken, or with irregular ramifications of low hills, towards the snowy group of the Ruapahu in the interior, which bore N. 60° W. [It really bears east.] I had just time to look towards Cook's Straits and distinguish Entry Island, when a dense fog enveloped us, and prevented all further view. Whilst waiting in the hope that the fog would disperse, I tried the temperature of boiling-water with one of Newman's thermometers, and found it to be 197°, the temperature of the air being 49°, which, taking 55° as the mean of the temperatures at the summit and the base, would give 8,839 feet as the height of Mount Egmont; the whole calculated according to the tables given in an article in the London 'Geographical Journal,' vol. iii., and communicated by Lieutenant-Colonel W. H. Sykes, F.R.S.

"I have above mentioned that the cone, forming the summit of Mount Egmont, rises from a platform. The cone of cinders and scoriaceous lava is separated from this platform by a deep saddle, which descends laterally towards the side of the mountain. The high rocky walls, near the source of the Waiwakaiho, show the composition of the exterior cone to be a hard lava of bluish-grey colour, which sounds to the hammer like phonolite or clink-stone, and breaks into large tabular fragments. The wall where this rock is seen is fissured in a perpendicular direction. There seems to be a great scarcity of simple minerals in the principal rock of which this mountain consists.

"The natives have no historical account of any eruption of Mount Egmont, and maintain that the country at its base is less subject to movements of the earth than any other parts of the islands, especially those which are the most mountainous. They have, indeed, tales which, if divested of their figurative dress, might be referred to the recollection of former volcanic activity; such is their account that the Tongariro and Mount Taranaki are brother and sister, and formerly lived together, but quarrelled and separated.

"The branches or buttresses which Mount Egmont throws out towards the sea-coast and to the interior being of inferior height, the cone itself appears to be very isolated. A ridge of hills runs towards Cape Egmont; another, that on which we made the ascent, goes to the north-east-by-east, and a third towards the interior, in the direction of the Ruapahu and the still active volcano of Tongariro.

"On the summit of the mountain I found the entire skeleton of a rat, carried there, no doubt, by a hawk.

"After staying for some time on the summit, in the vain hope that the clouds which enveloped us would disperse, we retraced our steps, and accomplished the descent with comparative ease. The natives expressed their joy at seeing us again, as they had already given us up as lost. We encamped on the bank of the left branch of the Waiwakaiho amidst trees of the Leptospermum species. Our resting-place—which, from finding the boiling-point to be 207° Fahrenheit, while the mean temperature of the air was 57°, I calculated to be 2,699 feet above the level of the sea—was the utmost limit of the excursions of the natives; at this spot they obtain the best sort of kokowai in the bed of the river, which was for some distance quite yellow from a solution in its waters of this ochreous substance, which glazed the rocks with a metallic coating. Immediately on our arrival our native companions set to work to make baskets of rushes and flax-leaves, for the carriage of this muddy ochre, which they dug out from swamps formed by the Waiwakahio at its banks. This substance was afterwards slowly dried at the fire, and, by further burning and preparing, a fine vermillion was obtained, which they carried home as an acceptable present to their families. This ochre is formed in great quantities in many places of New Zealand, where water has become stagnant, and is constantly deposited either from the iron contained in vegetables or from the ferruginous soil. I have often seen the natives forming weirs at stagnant creeks in order to obtain it. They use it for many purposes; when mixed with shark's oil, it forms a durable paint for their houses, canoes, and burying-places; it is also universally in request to rub into their faces and bodies. The custom of besmearing the body in this manner is common to almost all barbarous nations, and is adopted for objects widely differing. When going to battle, the savage bedaubs himself in order to strike terror and fear into the heart of his enemy; when joining in the funeral ceremonies or the festivities of his tribe, he employs the same means to increase the beauty of his appearance; the custom of covering themselves with a thick coating of this substance at the death of a relation or friend may have a symbolical meaning, reminding them of the earth from which they have sprung, and is similar to the practice prevailing among Oriental nations of mourners heaping ashes on their heads. The New Zealander also regards this pigment as a good defence against the troublesome sand-flies and musquitos. Whether it is the cause of the sleekness of the skin for which the natives are so remarkable, I will not pretend to say; as this may be owing to their frequent bathing and continual exposure to the air, or, which it is still more probable, may be a characteristic feature of the Polynesian and other coloured races, in consequence of a greater development of the vascular pupillæ between the epidermis and cutis than is the case with the white or Caucasian races.

"But to return from this long digression. The Waiwakaiho was at this point confined between high walls overshadowed by trees; here and there large masses of the cliffs had fallen into the bed of the river. In future times this picturesque valley, as well as Mount Egmont and the smiling open land at its base, will become as celebrated for their beauty as the Bay of Naples, and will attract travellers from all parts of the globe.

"On the 28th of December we again reached the beach without accident, and with somewhat better reason to be satisfied with our success than on our last return. I found a large number of natives at Ngamotu from the Otumatua and Waimate assembled for the purpose of selling the whole Taranaki district. As the return of the Tory was daily expected, the beach looked as if a fair was being held on it. A European also had arrived from Kawhia, accompanied by many natives, for the purpose of dissuading those at Taranaki from ceding to the Company their territorial rights; not, however, from any disinterested intention, or for the sake of the Taranaki natives, but because some parties were anxious to buy the land for themselves, either from the small remaining body of the original native proprietors, or, if they would not agree to the terms proposed, from their conquerors, the Waikato tribes. It was said that the missionaries were much concerned in these transactions.

"On the 31st I started in the boat for the Waitara, which is twelve miles to the northward of the Sugarloaf Islands. This river has a bar at the entrance, over which there is only five feet of water at low the tide, but inside the bar it deepens considerably, and two miles from its mouth I found the depth to be two fathoms and a half. The Waitara does not take its rise in Mount Egmont, but comes from a hilly range which runs from Tongariro in a south-westerly direction, and is called Rangitoto. [The Manganui and other tributaries of the Waitara flow from Mount Egmont.] It flows through a fertile and open country. About twelve miles from its mouth, and situated on the left bank, was formerly a large and prosperous village, called Pukerangiora, peopled with 1,500 of the Ngatiawa tribes. About ten years ago it was taken, after a very long siege, by the Waikato, and nearly 500 of the inhabitants were slaughtered, fifty of them by the hand of Te Wherowhero, who is at present a great 'Mihanere' (as the natives call those who have adopted Christianity, from the word missionary), and lives at Waitemata or Manukau; the rest of the population was carried away into slavery. There are no natives here at present, nor is there any trace of the path which formerly led from Pukerangiora round the base of Mount Egmont to the districts of Cook's Straits.

"I returned in the evening delighted with the general aspect of the country.

"We were now in the middle of summer; the weather was very agreeable; the thermometer in the afternoon stood in the shade at 86°, rising to 100° in the sun, and generally falling in the evening to 62°. But I must observe that we were living amidst the sand-hills of the coast, which were often so much heated that I could not bear to walk upon them. But we were never a week without rain, and sometimes had a thunder storm, after which a delightful coolness pervaded the atmosphere. The rivulets always retained their quantity of water; the humidity in the forest rarely ceased; and the mosses and ferns continued as fresh as ever. Fishing was attended with great success, and I often had occasion to admire the expertness of the women in diving for crawfish in the surf near the Sugarloaf

Islands. The New Zealanders, men women and children, swim well, and can continue the exertion for a long time; in common with the North American Indians, they swim like dogs, not dividing the water, as we do, with the palm of the hands, but paddling along with each arm alternately. Bathing was one of our favourite amusements, as there was a beautiful pond of fresh water immediately behind our hut, and great was the mirth and good fellowship at our daily bathing-parties.

"In the beginning of January two messengers of the Ngatiawa tribe, who had been enslaved by the Waikato, arrived from Kawhai; they brought intelligence that the Ngateraukawa had sent to the Waikato to request their aid in exterminating warfare against the Ngatiawa tribe in Waikanae, in revenge for their losses there. They also told us that the Waikato were prepared to make an immediate descent on us, in order to prevent the natives of Taranaki from selling any of the land, which they regarded as their property. In consequence of this information we prepared for defence, in case a tribe of the Waikato should attack us during the night, although I did not think that our party had anything to fear. It was impossible to sleep, as the natives talked all night as to the possible result of a conflict with the Waikato. On the following morning they advised us to shift our habitation to Moturoa, the largest of the Sugarloaf Islands, and to take all the women and children with us. The men resolved to remain on the mainland opposite the island, and to provide us with necessaries; if the Waikato should make a descent, they might thus more easily resist, or fly towards the mountain. We followed their advice, and lived on Moturoa during the rest of our stay, as we daily expected the arrival of the Tory. This island is a conical rock, extremely steep, about one mile in circumference and 300 feet high; the formation is trachyte. The rock contains much augite and feldspar, and includes here and there fragments of a different formation. The augite appears often in nests; and the micaceous iron-ore occurs in thin veins. The summit was scarcely accessible, but the native women, with their children on their backs walked up and down the hill, and along steep precipices, with the utmost unconcern. From time immemorial Moturoa has been a place of refuge and security for the Ngatiawa tribes, but more so of late, since the departure of the greater portion of them. Wherever there was a platform, or level space on the rock, they had built dwelling-houses and stores, in which they kept wood and provisions. In case of an attack, they could, if watchful easily keep off an enemy. We took possession of a good house on the north-west side of the island, about 190 feet above the water, and placed in a dry niche, with the rock overhanging it. The vegetation of the island is confined to flax, cabbage, and parsley, which grow in the interstices of the rock.

"On the 10th I started on an excursion to Mokau, situated three day's journey from the Sugarloaves, in order to visit a large tribe of the Waikato living there. The son of the chief of that tribe, who had come to Taranaki a few days before, accompanied me as a guide. On the hard sandy beach which lies to the northward of the Sugarloaves, we passed the Huatoki, the Henui, and the Waiwakaiho rivers. The escarpment of the coast shows here volcanic boulders, kept together by yellow loam. This formation is covered with sand. From the Waiwakaiho to the river Mimi the shore consists of sandy downs. We passed the latter river at low water. At its right bank is an escarpment, which consists entirely of sharp-edged volcanic fragments. A whale was lying on the beach, which seemed to have been stranded a few days before. An enormous quantity of driftwood was imbedded in the sand, intermixed with human bones, probably the remains of the cannibal feasts held during the seige of Pukerangiora. We slept on the banks of the Waitara river, after having passed several smaller streams. From this point the seashore becomes elevated; the cliffs consisting of a stiff blue clay, with a formation of yellow loam above it. We travelled for the greater part of our route over fertile fern-hills, with beautiful groves of trees. The vegetation continued down to the water's edge.

"We passed the rivers Onaero and Urenui; the latter flowed with a sluggish stream through a deep bed of white mud. After we had crossed this river we heard voices at a distance, and soon came up with a European, who had been sent by the Wesleyan missionary in Kawhia, and was travelling for missionary objects to the southward. With him was a large party of Waikato natives, and also men, women, and children belonging to the tribe of the Ngatiawa at the Sugarloaves. They had been taken into slavery during the last war, and had been obliged to live at Kawhia; but now their masters had allowed them to go to Taranaki for the purpose of paying a visit. They saluted us very heartily, rubbing noses and shaking hands, and an old woman began a lamentation over me. I found that she was the mother of Barrett's wife. The undisguised joy and sorrow she expressed when I told her of the fortunes or trials of her daughter and grandchildren, showed me once more how equally Nature has distributed amongst the whole of the human family the kindly affections of the heart, which are not the privilege of any one race or color, nor increased by civilization, which indeed too often blunts and destroys them.

"The country near the sea-coast bears, in many places, the traces of former extensive native cultivation, and the ruins of several pas. Here formerly lived the Ngatitoma and Ngatimotunga tribes, the present inhabitants of the Chatham Islands, who migrated there many years ago. The whole district between Taranaki and Mokau has not at present a single inhabitant, although one of the most favored districts of New Zealand.

"Near the Urenui river we again reached the sea-shore; the cliffs were here about a hundred feet high; the lowest formation was a marly clay. About twenty feet above the level of the sea was a formation of wood, very little altered or carbonized, and ten feet in thickness, but irregular; above that was a loamy soil. From the lowest formation I dug out a quantity of protophosphate of iron; it is found in small pieces or balls, is of an earthy consistence, and of a pale blue colour; the natives call it *pukepoto*, and when freed from the earthy particles and washed it is esteemed highly as paint. A little farther on the shore becomes very picturesque; it consists of a micaceous, soft yellowish, sandstone, which the waves of the sea have worn into the most fantastic shapes; sometimes it resembles the wall of a fort with round towers, and surrounded by balconies, crowned with beautiful shrubs. In some parts, and at one particular level, large boulders of trap-rock protruded out of the wall, the soft mixture in which they had been deposited having been washed away; in fact, the whole shore had the appearance of having been artificially cut out. This formation extended as far as Mokau, which place we reached the following day. My arrival was espied from the first pa, which is built on a hill near the outlet of the river. I was welcomed with a salute of musketry, and conducted in the midst of the assembled chiefs, who were dressed in their best attire. The sale of the lands and the colonization of the country by Europeans, engrossed their whole attention, and formed the subject of our interview. On the following day we went several miles up the river, and visited some other pas, which were numerously inhabited; we were everywhere received with the most studied attention. Disunion had, however, been spread amongst them by the arrival of some native missionaries, sent from the Wesleyan establishment at Kawhia. The larger and more respectable part of the little community were not well inclined to them, as an idea prevailed that the missionaries sought to convert them only with a view to their own aggrandizement.

"These natives, which are a subdivision of the tribe of the Waikato, and are called Ngatimaniapoto, seem to be in very prosperous circumstances. The river Mokau, which takes its rise in the mountains of Rangitoto, a hilly range running near the western coast, flows through a very fertile and moderately hilly district. On its banks are well-cultivated spots, bearing potatoes, maize, melons, and taro; the natives were also growing a great proportion of the tobacco they consumed in the year. Flax covers extensive districts; and the industry formerly displayed in manufacturing mats has not yet entirely disappeared. The settlement never having been reached by European visitors or ships, these natives had retained their unsophisticated virtues. They sometimes, indeed, have come in contact with Europeans at Kawhia, where they exchange their pigs for foreign commodities. A brig once entered the river, and from the general aspect it appeared to me as if there was sufficient depth over the bar for vessels of moderate burden, at all events for steamers. Inside the bar I sounded, and found three fathoms; according to the natives, there is one fathom and a half over the bar at low water. Inside the headlands the river takes a sharp turn, and forms a deep and completely sheltered basin.

"I returned to Taranaki accompanied by the principal chiefs of

HISTORY OF TARANAKI. 41

Mokau, and greatly satisfied with the reception they had given me, and reached the Sugarloaf Islands after an absence of eight days.

"After we had waited a great length of time for the return of the Tory, a brig, the Guide, arrived on the 31st January, having on board some gentlemen belonging to the Tory, and bringing the intelligence that she was refitting at the Kaipara, having grounded on the bar at the entrance to that harbour. This news relieved us from the anxiety which we had felt as to the possibility of securing the Taranaki district for the New Zealand Company; as since my arrival churchmen and laymen had vied with each other to obtain possession of that district.

"On the arrival of the Guide a liberal price was given to the natives for their land, and the good will of the Waikato purchased by presents. Thus the New Zealand Company became proprietors of the finest district in New Zealand, which offers to the colonist, besides its natural resources, the advantage of there being no natives on the land, with the exception of the small remnant of the Ngatiawa tribe at Ngamotu.

"Since the above was written the settlement of New Plymouth has been established at Ngamotu, or Sugarloaf Point, which must be prosperous even without a harbour, which is wanting there, as it possesses cultivable land, extensive facilities of land communication both with Cook's Straits and along the coast to Mokau and Kawhia, and, as I can state from my own experience, a very delightful climate."

On the 15th February, 1840, the Maoris of the district signed a deed of sale to the Company, of which the following is an extract:
"Know all men by these presents, that we the undersigned, chiefs of Ngamotu, near Mount Egmont, in New Zealand, have this day sold and parted with all our rights, titles, claims, and interests, in all the lands, islands, tenements, woods, bays, harbors, rivers, streams, and creeks, within certain boundaries, as shall be truly described in the deed, unto John Dorset, Esquire, his executors and administrators, in trust for the Governor, directors, and shareholders of the New Zealand Land Company, in London, their heirs, administrators, and assigns forever. * * * * And in order to prevent any dispute or misunderstanding, and to guarantee more fully unto the said Governors, directors, and shareholders, of the New Zealand Land Company of London, their heirs, administrators, and assigns forever, true, undisputed possession of the said lands, islands, tenements, woods, bays, harbors, rivers, streams and creeks, we, the said chiefs, for ourselves, families, tribes and successors forever, do hereby agree and bind ourselves to the description following, which constitutes the boundaries of the aforesaid lands, islands, tenements, woods, bays, harbors, rivers, streams and creeks, now sold by us, the undersigned chiefs, to the said John Dorset, this 15th day of February, in the year of our Lord, 1840, that is to say, from the mouth of the Wakatino river, along the seashore by Te Kawau, Oman, Tongaporutu, Te Oro, Parininihi, Puka, Arawa, Perairou, Otumatua, Wakariwa,

Orapapa, the Mimi river, Arapawa, the Urenui river, Te Pianga, Onaero, Waiaua, Te Tanewha, Turangi, the Waitara river, Waiorua, Waiongona, Rewatapu, Te Puketapu, the Pohui river, Waita, Mangate, Matakitaki, the Puka lagoon, the Waiwakaiho river, Pukaweka, the Henui river, the Huatoki river, Kawaroa, Te Arawata, Pukatuti, Waitapu, Otaki, Mataipu, Arakari, the Ongeonge lagoon, Te Tutu, the islands of Ki Mikotahi, Moturoa, and Motumahanga, commonly called the Sugarloaf Islands; Te Kutu, Paparoa, Paritutu, commonly called Sugarloaf Point; Wahine, Taranaki, Mataora, Motuotomatea, Arakawi, Ahanui, Porapora, Waioratoki, Waireka, Omata, Te Wairiri, Opo, Otiti, Tapuwairuru, Kakiorangi, Omura, Oakura, Wakau, Wairau, Waimoku, Otupota-te-Wairiri, Ahuahu, Oraukiwa, to Hauranga; the said seashore at low water mark forms the north-western boundary of the said lands, islands, tenements, woods, bays, harbors, rivers, streams and creeks. From the Hauranga on the seashore, a line striking inland by Patua, Heringa, Pawaka, Te Kiri, Pouakai, and from the said Pouakai to the summit of Taranaki, commonly called Mount Egmont, forms the southern boundary of the said lands. * * * * * . * From the summit of Taranaki, a line striking by Taumataitawa, Purakahua, Wakahinangi, Ratapiho, Pukarimu, Mangotoku, Wakaikatoa, Makahu, Wangaihu, Moangiha, Te Kopua, Te Waitetanga, Wangamomona, Makuri, Te Po, to the river Wanganui, and from the said river by Te Tangitangi, Mangohewa, Paringa, Pukekura, across the Onaero river, to Te Tuahu, by Kaipikiri, Wakamahuki, Tupari, Pukewakamaru, across the Urenui river by Puketarata, across the Mimi river by Rangiurapaki, Waitaoura, Te Pokuru, across the Papatiki by Turangarua, Romanu, Pukakao, Te Awera, across the Wakarumu and Waipikaho rivers, by Paraninihi, Timinuka, and Wangatorowai, on the said Wakatino river, and down the said river and its mouth, forms the eastern and northern boundary of the said lands, islands, tenements, woods, bays, harbors, rivers, streams and creeks. And we, the aforesaid chiefs, do hereby acknowledge for ourselves, families, tribes, and successors forever, to have this day received a full and sufficient payment for the aforesaid lands, islands, tenements, woods, bays, harbors, streams and creeks.

"In witness whereof, the said Chiefs of the first part, and the said John Dorset of the second part, have hereunto put their hands and seals this 15th day of February, in the year of our Lord 1840."

Here follow 72 signatures of Maoris; also that of John Dorset, Acting Agent for the New Zealand Land Company.

The deed was witnessed by Richard Barrett, George Doddney, and Ernst Dieffenbach, M. D.

On the 10th February the Doctor left the roadstead of Taranaki, and arrived at Wellington on the 21st of the same month.

CHAPTER VIII.

THE BRITISH ASSUMPTION OF SOVEREIGNTY.

AFTER the British Government had fully and unmistakeably recognised the independence of New Zealand, it discovered that in so doing it had made a serious mistake. A despatch from the Governor of New South Wales, bearing date 9th September, 1837, and covering two reports illustrative of the then state of New Zealand ; one from Captain Hobson, commanding H.M.S. Rattlesnake, and the other from the British Resident, brought about a Treasury Minute sanctioning the despatch to New Zealand of a British Consul and eventual Lieutenant Governor, also an advance from the revenues of New South Wales on account of his expenses. By letters patent under the great seal of the United Kingdom, bearing date 15th June, 1839, the former territories of New South Wales were extended so as to comprehend any part of New Zealand that might be acquired in sovereignty by Her Majesty ; and by a commission under the royal signet and sign manual, bearing date 30th July, 1839, William Hobson, Esq., captain in Her Majesty's navy, was appointed to be Lieutenant-Governor " over any territory which may be acquired in sovereignty by Her Majesty in the islands of New Zealand." Captain Hobson was instructed by the Marquis of Normanby to seek the aid of the missionaries in coaxing the Maoris into the cession of the sovereignty of the country to the British Government, and to win over their consent thereto by presents or other pecuniary arrangements. On 7th November, 1839, Mr. Somes, Deputy Governor of the New Zealand Company, addressed a letter to Lord Palmerston, Secretary of State for Foreign Affairs, complaining that the Colonial Office refused in any way to acknowledge the New Zealand Company, and urging the immediate assumption of sovereignty over New Zealand by Great Britain on the following grounds :—" We are assured that this question engages the attention of various commercial bodies, and of a large portion of the public press in France ; that the sovereignty of England in New Zealand is denied ; that the French Government is urged either to join in that denial by protesting against the colonisation of the islands by England, or to claim an equal right with England to plant settlements there. We are not without fear that some such protest or claim should be admitted by your lordship's department, as it appears to have been admitted by the Colonial department ; and we are therefore desirous of laying the following statement before your lordship :—

" It appears that the agitation of this question in France has been produced by the publication of a Minute of the British Treasury, made at the instance of the Colonial department, and bearing date 19th July, 1839, and also an extract from certain instructions recently given by that department to Captain Hobson—two documents by which the Crown of England seems to repudiate the sovereignty of New Zealand. The apparent repudiation consists of an acknowledgment of the sovereignty of the native chiefs, from whom Captain Hobson is to procure, if possible, a cession thereof to Her Majesty. It is this acknowledgment, according to all our information, which has given occasion to the pretensions now urged in France. That which England, it is contended, instructs her officer to procure, if possible, she admits that she does not possess, and she thereby admits the right of France either to obtain sovereign jurisdiction in New Zealand by the means which Captain Hobson is directed to employ, or, if France should prefer that course, to sustain the independent sovereignty of the natives. The argument appears conclusive. It becomes very important, therefore, if it is of great importance to England to prevent the establishment of French power in the midst of the English colonies of Australasia, that your lordship should be made aware of the acts of the British Crown which lead to a conclusion directly at variance with that which may be drawn from the said minute and instructions."

Capt. Hobson sailed to Sydney in H.M.S. Druid. Arriving in safety, he took the oaths of office, and then sailed with a small party of subordinate officers to New Zealand in H.M.S. Herald, arriving at the Bay of Islands on 29th January, 1840. On the following day he issued two proclamations, one announcing his commission, and the other the refusal of the Queen to recognise any titles to land not derived from or confirmed by herself. The Governor by the aid of the British Resident and Missionaries, and by presents of a few casks of tobacco and bales of blankets, obtained the cession, or rather recession, of the sovereignty of the country, and in eight days after his arrival the Treaty of Waitangi, of which the following is the text, had been drawn up by the Missionaries, and signed by many of the natives of the Bay of Islands.

THE TREATY OF WAITANGI.

"Her Majesty, Victoria, Queen of the United Kingdom of Great Britain and Ireland, regarding with her royal favor the native chiefs and tribes of New Zealand, and anxious to protect their just rights and property, and to secure to them the enjoyment of peace and good order, has deemed it necessary, in consequence of the great number of Her Majesty's subjects who have already settled in New Zealand, and the rapid extension of emigration both from Europe and Australia which is still in progress, to constitute and appoint a functionary properly authorised to treat with the aborigines of New Zealand for the recognition of Her Majesty's sovereign authority over the whole, or any part of those islands. Her Majesty, therefore, being desirous to establish a settled form of civil government, with a view to avert the evil consequences which must result from the absence of the necessary laws and institutions, alike to the native population and to her subjects, has been graciously pleased to empower and to authorise me, William Hobson, a captain in Her Majesty's royal navy, Consul and Lieutenant-Governor over such parts of New Zealand as may be, or hereafter shall be, ceded to Her Majesty, to invite the confederated and independent chiefs of New Zealand to concur in the following articles and conditions :—

"Article the First.—The chiefs of the confederation of the united tribes of New Zealand, and the separate and independent chiefs who have become members of the confederation, cede to Her Majesty, the Queen of England, absolutely and without reservation, all the rights and powers of sovereignty which the said confederation or individual chiefs respectively exercise or possess, over their respective territories, as the sole sovereign thereof.

"Article the Second.—Her Majesty, the Queen of England, confirms and guarantees to the chiefs and tribes of New Zealand, and to the respective families and individuals thereof, the full, exclusive, and undisturbed possession of their lands and estates, forests, fisheries, and other properties which they may collectively or individually possess, so long as it is their wish and desire to retain the same in their possession. But the chiefs of the united tribes, and the individual chiefs, yield to Her Majesty the exclusive right of pre-emption over such lands as the proprietors thereof may be disposed to alienate, at such prices as may be agreed upon between the respective proprietors and persons appointed by Her Majesty to treat with them on that behalf.

"Article the Third.—In consideration thereof, Her Majesty, the Queen of England, extends to the natives of New Zealand her royal protection, and imparts to them all the rights and privileges of British subjects.

[Signed.]   "W. HOBSON.

"Now, therefore, we the chiefs of the confederation of the united tribes of New Zealand, being assembled in congress at Victoria, in Waitangi, and we the separate and independent chiefs of New Zealand, claiming authority over the tribes and territories which are specified after our respective names, having been made fully to understand the provisions of the foregoing treaty, accept and enter into the same in the full spirit and meaning thereof.

"In witness whereof, we have attached our signatures or marks, at the places and dates respectively specified.

"Done at Waitangi, this 6th day of February, in the year of our Lord, 1840."

Here follow 512 signatures.

On 21st May, 1840, Governor Hobson issued two proclamations at Russell, Bay of Islands, one declaring the Queen of Great Britain's sovereignty over the Northern Island of New Zealand, and the other asserting her sovereignty over the whole of the New Zealand Islands.

On the 20th February, 1840, the Secretary of the New Zealand Company, at the desire of the directors, wrote to Lord John Russell, enclosing extracts from the *Journal de Havre*, a French newspaper, from which it appeared that a French expedition had been despatched for the purpose of founding a colony at Bank's Peninsula, in the Middle Island of New Zealand, and that the French entertained the idea of forming a penal settlement in that locality. The Company at the earliest opportunity forwarded to their principal agent a despatch containing all the intelligence they could glean with respect to the doings of the French, and instructed him to aid Governor Hobson in frustrating their designs to the utmost of his power. Governor Hobson, on receiving intelligence of the expected arrival of the French, immediately despatched Capt. Stanley in H.M.S. Britomart to Akaroa. The following is that officer's report of his expedition.

"Capt. Stanley, R.N., to Lieut. Governor Hobson :

"Her Majesty's Ship Britomart, at sea, 17th Sept. 1840.

"Sir :—I have the honor to inform your Excellency that I proceeded in Her Majesty's sloop under my command to the port of Akaroa, in Banks' Peninsula, where I arrived on the 10th of August, after a very stormy passage, during which the stern boat was washed away, and one of the quarter boats stove.

"The French frigate L'Aube had not arrived when I anchored, nor had any French emigrants been landed.

"11th August—I landed, accompanied by Messrs. Murphy and Robinson, police magistrates, and visited the only two parts of the bay where there were houses; at both places a flag was hoisted, and a court, of which notice had been given the day before, was held by the magistrates.

"Having received information that there were three whaling stations on the southern side of the Peninsula, the exposed position of which afforded no anchorage for the Britomart, I sent Messrs. Murphy and Robinson to visit them in a whale boat. At each station the flag was hoisted and a court held.

"On the 15th August the French frigate L'Aube, Capt. Lavaud, arrived, having been four days off the point : On the 16th August the French whaler, Comte de Paris, Captain Langlois, having on board 57 French emigrants, arrived.

"With the exception of M. Billingi, from the Jardin des Plantes, who is sent to look after the emigrants, and who is a good botanist and mineralogist, the emigrants are all of the lower order, and include carpenters, gardeners, stonemasons, laborers, a baker and a miner, in all 30 men, 11 women, and the rest children.

"Capt. Lavaud, on the arrival of the emigrants, assured me on his word of honor, that he would maintain the most strict neutrality between the British residents and the emigrants, and that should any differences arise betweeen them he would settle matters impartially.

"Capt. Lavaud also informed me, that as the Comte de Paris had to proceed to sea whaling, that he would cause the emigrants to be landed in some unoccupied part of the bay, where he pledged himself they should do nothing which could be considered hostile to our Government, and that until fresh instructions should be received from our respective Governments, the emigrants should merely build themselves houses for shelter, and clear away what little land they might require for gardens.

" Upon visiting the Comte de Paris, I found that she had on board, besides agricultural tools for the settlers, six long 24-pounder guns mounted on field carriages.

" I immediately called upon Captain Lavaud to protest against the guns being landed. Captain Lavaud assured me that he had been much surprised at finding that guns had been sent out in the Comte de Paris, but that he had already given the most positive orders that they should not be landed.

" On the 19th August, the French emigrants having landed in a well sheltered part of the bay, where they could not interfere with any one, I handed over to Messrs. Murphy and Robinson the instruction intrusted to me by your Excellency to meet such a contingency.

" Mr. Robinson finding that he could engage three or four Englishmen as constables, and having been enabled, through the kindness of Capt. Lavaud, to purchase a boat from a French whaler, decided upon remaining.

" Capt. Lavaud expressed much satisfaction when I informed him that Mr. Robinson was to remain, and immediately offered him the use of his cabin and table as long as L'Aube remained at Akaroa.

" Mr. Robinson accepted Capt. Lavaud's offer till he could establish himself on shore.

" On 27th August I sailed from Akaroa for Pigeon Bay. * * *
" I have the honor to be, etc.,
" W. M. STANLEY, R.N."
" To his Excellency, Lieut. Governor Hobson,
New Zealand."

By letters patent, bearing date 16th November, 1840, the Islands of New Zealand were erected into a separate territory, and on the same date Lieut. Governor Hobson was commissioned Governor and Commander-in-Chief over the said territory.

CHAPTER IX.

THE FOUNDATION OF THE SETTLEMENT.

AT A PUBLIC meeting held in the town of Plymouth, England, on the 25th of January, 1840, was formed the Plymouth Company for colonising New Zealand from the West of England, with a capital of £150,000, and with the following gentlemen as its directors and officers :—Governor :—The Earl of Devon. Deputy-Governor :—Thomas Gill, Esq. Directors :—Sir Anthony Buller, Capt. Bulkley, Charles Briggs Calmady, Esq., J. Collier Cookworthy, M.D., Nathaniel Downe, Esq., Lord Eliot, M.P., Richard Willis, Esq., Thomas Gardner, Esq., William John Gilbert, Esq., John Hine, Esq., George Leach, Esq., Sir Charles Lemon, Bart., M.P., E. W. W. Pendarves, Esq., M.P., Edward St. Aubyn, Esq., R. Hippesley Tuckfield, Esq., Right Hon. Sir Hussey Vivian, Bart., M.P. Trustees :— Lord Courtenay, John Buller, Esq., Thomas Gill, Esq. Managing Director :—Thomas Woollcombe, Esq. Superintendent of Emigration :—J. C. Matthews, Esq. The Company purchased from the New Zealand Company 10,000 acres of their newly-acquired land, and on the 13th of August despatched their chief surveyor with a staff of officers and men, by the barque London, to select a site for their settlement and to commence the surveys. On the 26th of August the Company made a further purchase of 50,000 acres from the New Zealand Company, which sent out instructions to Colonel Wakefield to give Mr. Carrington (the Company's Surveyor), every assistance in his power in making the selection. On the 27th August, 1840, in obedience to instructions received from the Surveyor-General, an overland exploring expedition left Wellington for Taranaki. It consisted of Messrs. Stokes and Park, surveyors; Mr. Heaphy, draughtsman to the Company; Mr. Dean, a volunteer, and six men, bearers of blankets and provisions. After a very fatiguing journey of a month's duration, the party reached the Sugarloaves, and after a very brief stay, retraced their steps to Wellington.

"Our resting place," Mr. Stokes reports, "was within sight of the Sugarloaf Islands, which we reached the following afternoon, after a fatiguing walk over the rocky beach, crossing in succession the Waimariri, the Timaru, the Oakura, the Tapuae, and the Ongeouge, we passed over a high sand hill, running down to Sugarloaf Point, and descended to the pa on the other side, which is a small collection of huts, without even a fence, and containing very few natives. The house in which we slept during our stay at Ngamotu had been built by the Maoris in expectation of the arrival of immigrants among them, and was intended for their reception. It was the longest house we had met with, being 140 feet long, and 18 feet wide, having seven doors or openings, and a rude verandah in front, about three feet wide. There are two others in progress, one on either side of that just described; they are to be the same width with the first and 90ft. long. The houses are near the anchorage, on the edge of a terrace which skirts the beach from Sugarloaf Point to the eastward, following the curved line of the bay. The anchorage is formed by three islands and the reefs connected with them, called, from their conical shape, the Sugarloaves; the fourth of these conical hills terminates Sugarloaf Point. The district is called from them Ngamotu, 'the islands;' and Moturoa, 'the tall island.' The highest of these rocks has an elevation of from four to five hundred feet (503 ft). On the farthest island the natives keep their property and provisions, to secure them from a sudden incursion of the Waikato tribes. The soil from the beach to the hills, which are a quarter of a mile distant, is rich and black, and has evidently, in more prosperous days, been under cultivation. There is not much wood in the immediate neighborhood; and the natives bring the wood, used in the construction of their houses, a distance of some miles. All their time of late has been occupied with the erection of houses, even to the neglect of their potatoe grounds. They speak of nothing else but Port Nicholson and the settlers there, and all their questions are directed to that point. The day after our arrival it rained heavily, but the next day we were able to go into the country as far as the wood. The ground in the immediate neighborhood of the beach has been already described; beyond this it is rather broken. After crossing a small stream, we ascended a hill of very moderate elevation, on the top of which there is a level space of several hundred acres, the low hills on each side sloping towards it; this is covered with fern of luxuriant growth, indeed, from the hills near the beach to the wood is mostly overgrown with fern. Beyond this, the ground again becomes more broken, until passing a small stream we entered the wood. We were now obliged to think of returning. From Patea to Ngamotu, from various causes we had found it extremely difficult to procure provisions, and at Ngamotu the difficulty was still greater. There is no settlement between Ngamotu and Mokau, so that it was impossible to proceed any farther. I have been since informed that there really is a scarcity along the coast. We regretted this the more, as the district of Waitara, the country immediately beyond Ngamotu, and the land on the other side of Mount Egmont, is said to be more valuable than any portion of Taranaki we had seen. The Waitara is said to have its rise in the Wanganui District. It flows through a level country of the richest description, and after a long and winding course, in which it is navigable for boats the whole way, falls into the sea beyond Ngamotu. We could hardly refrain from wishing that a small vessel had taken us direct to Taranaki with provisions and supplies, to have rendered us independent of every contingency, and enabled us to devote that time which must now be consumed in retracing our steps homeward over the same ground we had already traversed, to exploring and gaining a more perfect knowledge of this district. We left Ngamotu on 27th September on our way back to Port Nicholson, and arrived at Patea in six days."

About four months after this expedition had been sent from Wellington by the Surveyor-General to explore the Taranaki country, Colonel Wakefield wrote the following despatch to the Secretary of the Plymouth Company of New Zealand :—

"Wellington, New Zealand,
"22nd December, 1840.

"Sir,—I take the advantage of a ship going direct to Bombay to write to you shortly for the overland mail, and have the honor to acknowledge the receipt of your letter of the 13th August last. Having received by the Martha Ridgway instructions from the Court of Directors in London regarding the New Plymouth Settlement, I was prepared to recommend a place of location to Mr. Carrington. Since that gentleman arrived here, I have seen the instructions given to him by the Board of Directors; and feeling that great responsibility attaches to him, I have refrained from pressing any particular place upon him, until he has seen all that is eligible in the Company's possessions. I have placed the barque Brougham at the disposal of Mr. Carrington, with a recommendation to proceed in her immediately to Queen Charlotte's Sound, Blind Bay, and Taranaki, with full instructions as to the advantages and capabilities of each place. I have also induced Mr. Barrett, who is better acquainted than anybody I know with these coasts, to accompany the expedition. Mr. Carrington will proceed, I believe, on his tour of inspection in a few days. As regards the relative merits of the three places I have named, you will be partially informed by my correspondence with Mr. Ward, already published. Queen Charlotte's Sound presents an unexceptionable harbor, and it will be for Mr. Carrington to say whether he considers the available level land in it sufficient for the purposes, present and prospective, of the settlement. It strikes me that the hilly nature of the country throughout it would hold out few inducements to British cultivators, until they become better acquainted with the nature of this country, the cleared fern lands of which have been much over-estimated. Blind Bay has a safe anchorage, under Adele Island, and a large flat clear district, with sufficient timber for all purposes, at a distance of fifteen miles from it, but the removal of immigrants with their goods to which would be a serious drawback to the place. Its position in the Strait is good, the prevalent winds allowing ships to enter and leave the bay at nearly all times. The vicinity of the high mountains at the back renders the climate less agreeable than that of the Northern Island. Taranaki, the district abreast of the Sugarloaf Islands, has but one disadvantage. It has no harbor. The roadstead is not unsafe for ships well found in ground tackle, and formerly numerous traders used to lie there whilst unloading. Considering the genial climate and fertile soil, the vast space of easily available territory, the land communication with numerous settlements, and the facility of transporting produce to Port Nicholson, or Australia by means of small craft which can anchor under shelter of the islands with safety; seeing in fact, that the only obstacle to the rapid rise of a settlement there is the inconvenience to large ships from Europe, which might be remedied by a breakwater or mole connecting the largest island with the main—a work infinitely less formidable than that which in modern times has made the name of our English Plymouth familiar to the world—I cannot but recommend Taranaki as the most eligible place for the settlement of her offspring. Permit me to assure the directors of the Plymouth Company, through you, that duly sensible of the flattering recommendation to their surveyor to learn my opinion on this subject, I shall spare no pains to insure to the immigrants, under their auspices, the most favorable location, and to assist the officers of the Company by my advice and exertions upon all occasions.—I have &c.,

"WILLIAM WAKEFIELD."

The following prospectus had meanwhile been issued by the directorate of the Company, and preparations were being made to despatch immigrants immediately on the receipt of intelligence that a site for the New Plymouth settlement had been selected:—

"THE PROSPECTUS OF THE NEW PLYMOUTH COMPANY.

"The New Plymouth Settlement is intended to consist of three classes of land: (1.) The town land, comprising 2,200 sections of a quarter of an acre each: (2.) The suburban lands, comprising at least 1,150 sections of 50 acres each. All sales in England will be confined, until further notice, to actual colonists, on the following terms:—(1.) With a view to distribute as generally as may be practicable the advantages to be derived from the possession of preliminary lands, no application from an individual colonist will be entertained for more than eight allotments of lands, each allotment containing one section of town land, and one section of rural land. (2.) Two hundred and fifty allotments are set apart as above mentioned at the price of £75 for each allotment, and applications for the same are to be made in writing to the undersigned, which, if accompanied by a deposit of £10 in respect of each allotment, will entitle the applicant to receive separate land orders for each town and rural section, with such priorities and rights of selection as are hereinafter mentioned, in exchange for the residue of the purchase money. (3.) The numbers signifying the priority of choice for the town sections have been selected on a fair average from the 1,000 numbers of choice which have fallen to the Company in the general ballot above referred to. These selected numbers are deposited in a wheel, from which the purchaser's number will be drawn in the presence of three Directors and the applicant, if he chooses to attend, either in person, or by his agent. The purchasers will be entitled to such town sections as may have been chosen by the Company's Agents in virtue of the priority of choice signified by the numbers so respectively drawn. The purchasers will also be entitled to select the rural sections from any land in the Plymouth Settlement surveyed and declared open for choice as rural sections, at the time and according to the order of presenting the land order in the Colony, subject only to the regulations of the land office for preserving fairness and regularity of choice. (4.) The sum of £50, in respect to every £75 received for each allotment as above, will be transferred to the Emigration Fund, and a purchaser to the extent of £300 will be entitled to an allowance from the said Fund towards the passage of himself and family to the Colony, at the rate of £25 per cent. on the amount of his purchase money—provided that no person will be entitled to a larger allowance on the above mentioned account than will pay his own passage and that of his family, according to the rates which will be issued from time to time by the Court of Directors. The residue of the Fund will be expended in the conveyance of laboring emigrants to the Colony. Any person proceeding to New Zealand with a view to purchase land in this settlement from the Company, will receive liberal allowances in passage money, etc., particulars of which may be obtained at the office.

"WILLIAM BRIDGES,
"Secretary."

By the date of the following letter from the Company's Surveyor, Mr. F. A. Carrington, to his brother, it will be seen that the party sent by the Surveyor-General to explore Taranaki had returned and reported the result of their expedition long before the arrival of that gentleman in New Zealand.

"Ship London, Port Nicholson Harbor,
"December 14th, 1840.

"I have just now heard that there is a vessel to sail to-morrow morning for Valparaiso, and although it is past eleven o'clock at night, and I am much tired with running about I cannot do less than send you a few lines. Capain Blisset sails, perhaps, in two or three days. By him I send letters which I expect you will get long before this reaches you, I shall therefore say but a few words.

"We had a fine passage, touched nowhere, tried to make Tristan d'Achuna, but could not on account of contrary winds. We were 185 days from land to land, and anchored in this place on the morning of the 12th. The scenery is beautiful, and the climate lovely, the only thing in the least against it being the frequency of very stormy winds. Wellington on account of its harbor will no doubt become a great place and the grand depot of the Islands. The land is neither what I could wish, nor what I expected, there being no level ground, but immensely steep hills, covered with evergreen woods to the waters' edge. The surveying goes on but slowly on account of the heaviness of the country. Things are very far from being right with regard to the confidence in the Government. I shall strain every nerve to be off from here as soon as possible and fix upon a locality for New Plymouth. My next letter shall tell you much. I cannot say what I wish now as there is to be a meeting on Tuesday to settle, if possible, the present hitch; I have not time to write more.

"Your affectionate Brother,
"F. A. CARRINGTON."

EXPEDITION IN SEARCH OF A SITE FOR THE NEW PLYMOUTH SETTLEMENT.

Colonel Wakefield, in accordance with the instructions he had received from London to afford Mr. Carrington all the aid in his power in the selection of a suitable site for the New Plymouth Settlement, placed the barque Brougham at his disposal for that purpose. This vessel was singularly fitted for the service, being small and easily handled, and possessing a hull of singular strength. Fortunately, the particulars of this exploration have been preserved, and are as follows:

Journal of Mr. R. H. Aubrey, attached to the Surveying Staff at New Plymouth:—

"Port Nicholson, February 2nd, 1841.

"We left Port Nicholson on an exploratory expedition with a fine S.E. breeze on 8th January, and steered our course in the first instance for Taranaki. Mr. Barrett, who was the chief agent employed in effecting the purchases of land for Colonel Wakefield, accompanied us in the double capacity of pilot and interpreter, and it is impossible we could have met with a person better qualified for the task. He has resided for fifteen years in New Zealand, and, from his constant intercourse with the natives has become well acquainted with their language, manners and habits. To this he unites a thorough knowledge of the coasts, especially of Cook's Strait, in which there is not a cove, however unimportant, that has not, at some time or the other been visited by him. He has seen many reverses of fortune, and had some remarkable escapes. More than once, he tells us, he has been tied to the stake preparatory to becoming a meal for one of the chiefs. Two years ago he married a chief's daughter, and from that moment obtained great influence over the whole of the tribe. He has derived considerable benefit in a pecuniary point of view, from the manner in which he exerted himself for the Company. A large wooden house, originally the property of Dr. Evans, now belongs to him, and is the best hotel in Wellington. His wife and several of her relations accompanied him to Taranaki, part of which formerly belonged to them; and even now they are in possession of a considerable tract of land where they intend settling. The scene that ensued on their landing baffles description; such lamenting, crying, and rubbing noses I never before witnessed—a most extraordinary manner of testifying their joy, and one that was exceedingly amusing to us. We reached our destination the following evening, and anchored in a very unsheltered situation close to the Sugarloaf Islands. Luckily the breeze subsided or we might have had to slip and run with the loss of a cable. The lateness of the hour compelled us to defer landing till next day. In the meantime our fishing tackle was brought into requisition and a couple of hours enabled us to catch seventy-five large snappers, the smallest of which weighs four pounds. They are similar in appearance to the English mullet, and are capital eating. At daybreak on the

10th Mr. Barrett landed his family, and shortly afterwards Mr. Carrington, Messrs Baines, Nesbit, Rogan, and myself went on shore with our guns. The natives to the number of at least one hundred were assembled on the beach, busily employed in landing Mr. Barrett's goods and chattels, which was not done without difficulty, for although it was a dead calm the surf ran high. They gave us a hearty welcome, and having gone through the ceremony of shaking hands, which lasted some time, we were invited into their whares or huts to partake of a collation of fern root and cold water. We next proceeded to take a view of the country, which was not done without difficulty, for almost at every step we were stopped by impenetrable barriers of evergreens and ferns, the latter in many cases considerably above our heads. There are three houses close to the beach built of reeds by the natives for Mr. Barrett; one of which is 96 feet long. I was astonished at the ingenuity displayed in the erection of these buildings. With no other materials than reed, native grass, that grows in abundance, and flax which serves for ligatures, are they able to construct houses, comfortable, and of considerable durability. Near to a small lagoon I picked up the skull of a New Zealander, and having mentioned the circumstance to Mr. Barrett, he informed me that seven years ago a great battle was fought on that spot, at which he played a distinguished part, his party being besieged. Their pa, or native fort, was surrounded by deep trenches, which are still visible, and defended by several guns, which are at present lying on the beach spiked and dismounted. Although not more than 300 men they succeeded, he says, in keeping at bay upwards of 3,000 of the enemy. He relates many horrible and disgusting atrocities that were committed on this occasion. The country about Taranaki is unquestionably better adapted for agricultural purposes than that in the environs of Port Nicholson. For twenty or thirty miles along the whole coast before we reached the Sugarloaves it presented a continuation of flat land. Mount Egmont rises in the back ground, towering far above the surrounding hills, and when the clouds are for a moment withdrawn from the snow clad summit the sight is exceedingly beautiful. The want of a harbor, however, is an insuperable objection to our fixing the site of the settlement here, not one point along the coast having even a cove which could afford shelter to the smallest coaster. There is a very fine beach at Ngamotu, to the north of which is a reef on which the surf during a north-wester is said to break with great fury. Taranaki would undoubtedly become of great importance if a road could only be made from Port Nicholson; her superfluous produce could then be safely and expeditiously transported to a market.

"On the 11th it was our intention to have visited the Waitara, of which Mr. Barrettt speaks in high terms. Rainy weather, however, compelled us to defer this until the 12th. We started accordingly at day-break, and after rowing for five hours under what might be termed a tropical sun, reached the entrance. Its appearance was, however, inferior to the description he had given. It is unquestionably a fine river, considerably wider than the Hutt, but it is not, and I fear never can be made capable of admitting any but vessels of the smallest tonnage. A bar extends across the entrance. Soundings were taken at high water, and the depth found to average from eight to twelve feet upon it, but there was a considerably greater depth both inside and outside of it. We rowed up the river for nearly three miles, and found its banks covered with a luxuriant vegetation which quite surpassed my expectations. The wretched beings farming it appeared much surprised to see us pounce upon them in so unexpected a manner; but the sight of Mr. Barrett soon dispelled any fears they may have entertained respecting their personal safety. I was too tired to think of returning to the ship that night. In anticipation of this we had brought a tent which we lost no time in pitching, after which we made a hearty meal upon pork and potatoes steamed in a native oven. Having a few hours of daylight left, we determined on making the most of it, and accordingly took a walk into the brushwood, which presented obstructions at every step, and at last we were compelled to give it up without accomplishing our object so satisfactorily as we could have wished. What we did see quite satisfied us that if brought into cultivation the banks of the Waitara might become the garden of the Pacific. There are no hills to contend with as at Port Nicholson, and the size of the timber, with few exceptions, presents but few obstacles to the clearance of the land. Nothing can surpass the quality of the soil if we are to judge from the luxuriant vegetation springing up everywhere. Some potatoe stalks growing at the native settlement exceeded four feet in length. Wild cabbage is also to be found here in the greatest profusion, affording a delicious vegetable. But what chiefly attracted my attention was the Indian corn. This is a plant which I have seen cultivated in France, Spain, and Italy, but never did I see it come to greater perfection than here. These are, I think, sufficient proofs of the fertility of the soil. We had reason to repent the situation we had chosen for pitching our tent. The middle of the bush certainly sheltered us from the rays of the sun during the day, but when night came, notwithstanding a roaring fire to keep them off, we were devoured by sandflies and mosquitos. These pests, as you may imagine, entirely banished sleep, and so covered our hands and faces with venomous bites, that anyone not knowing the circumstances would have thought we were just recovering from an attack of the measles. Our appearance, in short, was most wretched, and great was our delight at finding ourselves on our way back. But our troubles were not yet at an end; for in going down the river at low water we ran aground on the bar, and it was only by leaping out and lightening the boat that we could get her off. A cold bath was rather unpleasant just then, especially as we had no time to doff our clothes, but we endured this additional trouble with the most patient and heroic resignation. At length we reached the Brougham in a most woeful plight, and a few hours after weighed anchor, and set sail for Blind Bay. Contrary winds and calms kept us knocking about the Straits for two days.

"On the evening of the 15th we anchored in Port Hardy. The weather from the time we left Taranaki was lovely in the extreme, and re-called to my mind the sunny clime of Italy. Port Hardy is by far too mountainous ever to be made available as a settlement, the hills rising almost perpendicularly from the waters edge, covered with verdure to their summits. The harbour, were it anywhere else, would leave nothing to be desired, but owing to the land being totally unavailable, it can never become a station of any importance. A few natives came off in a canoe, looking almost as miserable as their brethren at the Waitara. We bartered tobacco with them for potatoes and turnips.

"On the 16th we left Port Hardy for Astrolabe Roads. We had a fine run through the bay, and anchored on the 17th within gunshot of Fisherman's and Adele Islands. The country immediately in front of our anchorage presented equally as mountainous an appearance as any that I had previously seen. At the distance of ten or twelve miles to the left, flat land was plainly discernible. Having fired a gun to apprise the natives of our arrival, three of them shortly afterwards came on board, and appeared delighted to see Mr. Barrett, whom they greeted with the friendly appellation of 'E Diki!' by which name he is known to all the New Zealanders. They expressed a wish that he should visit their settlement, which they described as being about eight miles distant on the banks of the Motueka river. It was, however, too late to think of going there, and we agreed to postpone our excursion until the following day. In the mean time we went on shore near the ship, and soon obtained a plentiful supply of birds, among which I may enumerate the shag, red-bill, several of the gull species, sand-pipers, and terns. While enjoying this sport I made a few observations which may prove interesting. This part of the coast abounds in granite precisely similar to the Cornish; a fine white sandstone, admirably calculated for building is equally plentiful, and from a few specimens I obtained, there can be but little doubt but that marble will be found amongst it. I also collected some curious mussels.

"On the 18th we visited the Motueka settlement, situated on a sandy flat, which is nearly covered at high water, although nearly three miles from the sea. We had some difficulty in reaching it, the tide at the time being on the ebb. On our return the river presented a fine appearance, being in some places nearly as wide as the Thames at Westminster, but very shallow everywhere. The natives had prepared a homely meal of fish and potatoes, to which we did ample justice; in fact it was impossible for any human beings to be kinder or more attentive than they were to us. This was the largest settlement we had visited, forming quite a little village, and surrounded as usual by the native stockade. The men for the most part are fine athletic fellows, but I regret to say I cannot bestow any praise on the appearance of the women, who were without exception the most degraded, hideous, dirty set of human beings I ever set my eyes upon. The appearance of the land did not answer Mr. Carrington's expectations, being chiefly low, swampy, and liable to inundations. Level land apparently extended to a very considerable distance; it was therefore necessary to employ another day in the examination. Accordingly, early on the 19th we again sallied forth, fully prepared for a long walk, and accompanied by several of the natives, who acted as guides. The country throughout was as level as a bowling green, but the soil had not the richness of that of Taranaki, as it was chiefly of a sandy description, and covered with dwarf flax and stunted fern. After walking for a considerable distance and fording several rivers we reached a magnificent forest, many of the trees of which might serve for the mast of a large ship. The country here bore the same swampy appearance as that nearer to the settlement. Ducks, pigeons, and terns were plentiful, and afforded capital sport. To my great surprise I saw several quails, and succeeded in killing one. I found it similar in every respect to those I have seen in Italy. By the account of the natives they are plentiful, not only here, but also on the level land that surrounds Mount Egmont. I left Blind Bay with regret; it was the only part of New Zealand I had seen which came up to my ideas of the romantic and beautiful. I allude of course to the scenery about Adele and Fisherman's Islands, and not to that at Motueka, which has no advantages of this description to boast of. It began to blow immediately we left Blind Bay, and the wind increased to a gale as we neared Queen Charlotte's Sound, which we entered on the 21st, the day after leaving the bay. Thanks to our pilot we soon came to an anchor in East Bay. The weather here bore a strong contrast to that we had lately experienced. As soon as it moderated a man named Nott came off with goats milk, vegetables, and poultry, which we purchased of him at high prices. He was one of the most disgusting blackguards I ever met with, but I believe a very good specimen of a whaler.

"On the 22nd we left East Bay and ran up to Tory Channel, where we anchored close to the whaling station of Mr. Thoms. We found him to be a much more respectable man than the other individual. He has a very snug house and a capital garden, containing all sorts of vegetables, which appeared to be thriving exceedingly well. Queen Charlotte's Sound would be appropriately termed the Bay of Harbours, the whole of it consisting of a succession of channels and coves, every one of which contains water sufficiently deep to float a ship of war close into the shore. The character of the land is however mountainous, which is much to be regretted, for did it contain any flat land there would not be a place in the world better adapted for a settlement. We left Tory Channel on the 24th, ran across the Strait in six hours with a fine south-easter, and anchored at Port Nicholson the sixteenth day after our departure."

Mr. Carrington having determined to fix the site of the Plymouth Settlement at Taranaki, sailed thither with his staff and party of intending settlers in the barque Brougham, which anchored at Ngamotu on 12th February, 1841. Here, in the graphic language of one of his chain-men, 'he turned his party loose into the fern like wild pigs.'

Writing to Mr. Woollcombe, under date May 4th, Mr. Carrington says:—"All the harbors of New Zealand are surrounded with mountains and hills too steep for cultivation, even to the water's edge. I have therefore been obliged to take a roadstead, but at the same time that I lament the want of a harbor, I have much pleasure in informing you that I have selected a place where small ones can be easily made, and with trifling expense, close to the town, abundance of material being on the spot. We now have the best anchorage—hard sand and clay, and vessels have only one wind to be uneasy about, that is the N.W. This wind has been blowing but twice since I have been here, and then a ship might have remained. The prevailing wind is S.W. From my own observation, and from what Mr. Barrett has told me, I believe that this wind blows for nine months in the year. The Sugarloaf rocks shelter from this wind. The fact is the wind is either as I have named or else off the land. I have fixed the town between the rivers Huatoki and Henui. The former two miles from this (Moturoa), and the latter three. Two or three brooks also run through the town, and water is to be had in any part of it. The soil, I think, cannot be better. There is much open, or fern country, and abundance of fine timber. We have also fine rivers between this and the Waitara, a distance of about twelve miles. I have twice been up this river, once at low water for three miles. The banks are parallel, and the country and river beautiful. I once had made up my mind to have the town there, but the almost constant surf upon the bar has caused me to prefer this place. A good roadstead is certainly before a bad harbour. There is thirteen-and-a-half feet of water at high tides at Waitara, and inside the bar plenty for a large ship. However, it would never do for the town, owing to the surf. As you will see by my journal, I have minutely examined about seven or eight hundred miles of coast. The Plymouth Company has the garden of this country. All we want is labour, and particularly working oxen. I trust this scrawly letter will be excused as I am writing in a wretched hovel with many annoyances at my elbow."

The following letter from Captain Cooke, of Te Hua, to Mr. Woollcombe, explains Mr. Carrington's oversight of the snug little harbor of Wakatu, or as it is now called Nelson Haven, when exploring in Blind Bay:—"The next day we arrived at Nelson Haven. It occasioned great surprise to many of the colonists at Taranaki when informed of a settlement at Blind Bay, that Mr. Carrington should have overlooked it in his exploratory voyage in the Brougham. This mystery to my eyes was now cleared up, for the harbor which is formed by a narrow bank of boulders running out in a semi-circular direction from the main land, is nearly invisible until you are within it when off Pepin Island. From this cause I believe not a soul on board the Brougham knew anything about Wakatu or Nelson Haven."

CHAPTER X.

THE DESPATCH OF THE PIONEER SHIPS.

IN NOVEMBER, 1840, preparations were made in Plymouth, England, for the despatch of a pioneer vessel to the Plymouth Company's settlement at Taranaki. For this service the barque William Brian, 312 tons, commanded by Captain Maclean, was selected. Previous to the departure of the expedition a dinner was given to the pioneer emigrants, at which Mr. E. G. Wakefield was present. The emigrants were chiefly from Cornwall, Sir William Molesworth having made great efforts to induce a number of agricultural and mining laborers who resided on his estates or in their neighborhood, to enter into the scheme. Much enthusiasm prevailed at the meeting, and each emigrant was promised a town section in the town of New Plymouth, on his arrival. The dejeuner took place on the 30th October, the Earl of Devon being in the chair, and on the previous day the proclamation of the British Sovereignty of the Islands of New Zealand was published in London in the Government Gazette. Mr. Gibbon Wakefield was in London at the time, and on hearing the important news he immediately started for Plymouth by the mail coach, and arrived there in the midst of the feast, where he was called upon by Lord Devon to communicate to the assembly the intelligence he had brought from London. The vessel sailed from Plymouth Sound on the 19th November, 1840, Mr. George Cutfield, a naval architect, and late of H.M. Dockyard, at Devonport, being in charge of the expedition. On board were Mr. Richard Chilman, of London, who, on the voyage, was appointed clerk to Mr. Cutfield; Mr. Thomas King, of London; and Mr. A. Aubrey, son of Colonel Aubrey, of the Horse Guards. Mr. Weeks was the ship's surgeon. In the steerage there were 42 married, and 22 single, adults, and 70 children. After a favorable voyage the vessel entered Cloudy Bay for orders, on the 19th March, 1841. Finding no one in the Bay able to give him any information respecting the site of the new settlement, Mr. Cutfield hired a cutter and proceeded to Wellington, for the purpose of seeing Col. Wakefield on the subject. After a brief stay he returned with a pilot, and with orders to proceed to Taranaki. The William Brian again set sail on the 28th March, and came to anchor off the Sugarloaves at six o'clock on the evening of March 30th, 1841.

Scarcely had the Plymouth Company commenced operations, when they were involved in pecuniary difficulties by the failure of their bankers, Messrs. Wright and Co., of London. This misfortune resulted in a deed of agreement, dated 10th May, 1841, by which the Plymouth Company was merged in the New Zealand Company, the Directors of the Plymouth Company continuing to act in connection with the New Zealand Company, under the title of the West of England Board.

It was determined by the New Zealand Company, while the negotiations for the merging were pending, to name the new port after that of a residence of Lord St. Germains, in Cornwall, and the following instructions to that effect were sent out to the Colony:—

"F. D. Bell, to Colonel Wakefield:
"New Zealand House,
"April 22nd, 1841.
" It is the particular desire of the Court of Directors that the shore on which New Plymouth may be built should be called Port Eliot, which is the name of a residence of Lord St. Germains, in Cornwall. The Directors wish that the compliment to Lord Eliot were as adequate to the debt of gratitude which all the settlers in British New Zealand, no less than this Company, owe to his Lordship, as the name is suitable to that harbor which is destined to be the chief port of arrival for the emigrants from the west of England."

The following letter from Mr. Cutfield to the Directors of the Plymouth Company gives a detailed account of the landing and initial works of the pioneers:—

"Mr. Cutfield, to the Directors of the Plymouth Company:
"New Plymouth, Taranaki,
"May 2nd, 1841.
" Gentlemen:—Being fully immersed in business, and living in a very rough way, almost in the open air, I am not in the condition to correct my rough journal, and send you a copy. I cannot, however, allow the ship to depart without writing some short account of the 'pioneer expedition,' since it debarked on the shores of New Zealand.
"We left Cloudy Bay on Sunday, 28th March, and on the following Tuesday evening came to anchor to the eastward of the Sugarloaf Islands, at about a mile and a half from the shore. On the following morning we landed the whole of the passengers, and all the live stock we intended for New Zealand when we left England. I erected tents, and procured different places of shelter for the people from Mr. Barrett—rough certainly, but better than being out of doors. From the time of our landing until the 6th of April, we were constantly employed unloading the vessel and landing the goods on a bank, just above high water mark, having fortunately during the whole of the time most beautiful weather. You have already, I believe, been apprised of the site for the town being fixed two miles east of the Sugarloaves, between two small rivers, called respectively the Huatoki and Henui. I have, in consequence, to remove the stores and baggage along the land and over the Huatoki, which is about 50 feet across, to the storehouse in the town. In order to do this I have had to construct a bridge over the river. You will be fully aware of the great difficulty we have had in the transit of these goods with the small means at our disposal, which consists of but one timber dray, two hand carts, and six wheelbarrows,

the narrow wheels of all cutting deeply into the sand. The traction had to be entirely manual. A pair of bullocks or a horse would be of invaluable service to us, and a great saving of expense to the Company.

"On the 6th the ship left for Port Hardy, to take in ballast. On her leaving, I commenced with the storehouse and bridge. The former took all the carpenters three weeks, and so much of the timber was lost by hoisting it in and out of the ship, and by rafting, that I feared I should not be able to get the building up in a respectable way. The bridge was built by laborers who had to carry all the timber used in its construction, and some of it a distance of two miles. I think it is strong enough for a horse and a well loaded cart. The storehouse being up, and the bridge finished, I commenced on the 29th removing stores, and continued doing so till the return of the ship, when we in part broke off from this duty, to unload. Captain Maclean has shown great energy in landing the stores, and has done everything in his power for our welfare.

"This is a fine country with a large quantity of flat land, but every part is covered with vegetation—fern, scrub and forest. The fern, on good land, is generally from four to six feet high. There are thousands of acres of this land which will require but a trifling outlay to bring into cultivation.

"Rats are numerous, and we require arsenic and a good breed of terriers, or I fear that our stores and produce will suffer. Few natives have been living here since the war with the Waikato tribe, about seven years since, consequently, pigs and potatoes are scarce, and, as the native population is likely to increase, I fear provisions will be still more scarce before the spring. I have, therefore, purchased all the stores Capt. Maclean can spare. We are on very good terms with the natives. Mr. Barrett has done everything in his power to assist us in landing the cargo with one of his whaleboats, for which I shall have to pay him.

"Strong, warm clothing, and large blankets will, for a long time, be the best articles to barter with the natives. There is, at this time, no demand for guns or powder; blankets! blankets! is all the cry. Nails and tools they already appreciate, and they will, I trust, soon take to agricultural implements. They are quick in understanding, but are very dirty and idle. Finer men I never saw, but the women are by no means prepossessing. Since we have been here there has been much talk of the Waikato tribe coming. Should they come with a bad feeling, I shall be prepared for them; however, I hope they know better than to molest the whites.

"Not having the means myself, I am endeavoring to make arrangements with Mr. Barrett for building a large boat of from five to eight tons, of a suitable construction for landing on these sands. I hope to accomplish this by the arrival of the next ship, otherwise, it will be difficult to unload her. Our small boats are ill fitted for this service.

"Moorings for a 600 tons ship would here be of essential service; vessels then might go to sea at a few minutes' warning, and in threatening weather, might go to sea at night, and return in the morning. Hoping that what I have done since I landed on these shores may meet with your approval, I am, etc.,

"GEORGE CUTFIELD."

Mr. Carrington commenced operations by cutting a base line for his survey from the great Sugarloaf toward the Mountain. Owing to the dense vegetation which clothed the face of the country, it was found impossible to survey any large portion of the land without first cutting lines through the high fern and the scrub and forest. Accordingly, most of the working people in the little community, together with some natives, were employed in this labor. While so engaged, Mr. Carrington's first dispute with the natives arose, the particulars of which we shall give in his own words: "I employed nine natives when first I commenced the works in New Plymouth, with the few white men I had, namely, six laborers, who came out in the Slaines Castle, and who joined me after my return from exploring the coast. Some time prior to the 8th of March, 1841, while engaged in cutting lines on the banks of the Huatoki, I went to a bend of the river with a man named Enoka, and a man of the name of Whiti, a petty chief. These two men were the farthest in the bush with me, and I made signs, not being able at that time to speak a word of the language, for them to go to work. They looked at me very curiously, and I recollect they uttered the words *E koe tito*, which mean "you are a liar." I did not know what this meant at all. After looking at me for a moment, they threw off their mats and stood stark naked, and began clapping their hams; I thought my doom was fixed. In less than a minute, however, they were at work most vigorously. All that ended very well, and it all went off for two or three days. Then they were joined by some natives from the interior, who said that we should not cut any more. They flourished their tomahawks, and danced, and yelled, and I thought we should all be massacred; however, it all became quiet. We went to Barrett, and got him to send for a man of the name of Joseph Davis, as an interpreter; and the next day, after some little explanation, and my drawing on the ground some squares, and showing them that this was the land of the natives, and this the land of the Europeans, and that the land had all been bought, they admitted that the land had been sold, and everything went on again peaceably, and, as I thought, all right; but it appeared afterwards, when the next misunderstanding arose, that they supposed I meant only that piece of land which I had marked was sold; it was a very small patch, and belonged to a native named Poarama, a chief of Ngatiawa, who had been captured by Waikato, and afterwards liberated." Mr. Carrington discovered that the discontent of the natives arose from the fact of their not having received all the goods which had been promised them for the land. He accordingly wrote to Colonel Wakefield on the subject, who sent the articles by the schooner Jewess, which was unfortunately wrecked near to Kapiti while on her voyage, and her gear and cargo plundered by the natives on that part of the coast. A few weeks after the arrival of the William Bryan, a party of Waikatos came and asked for *utu*, for some whares they had built near to the settlement on speculation, expecting that the white people would be very glad of them on their arrival, but, as the price they asked was considerably too high, the purchase was refused, and a present being made to the chief, the party returned satisfied.

Huts built in the native manner, of rushes and sedges, served as temporary dwellings for the pioneers. Rations were served out to all hands from the Company's store on Devon street, which was in after years the Court House, and is, at the time we write, the Police Station. Near to this building Mr. Cutfield sowed the first English garden seeds. At a meeting of settlers with the Company's Agent, wages were fixed at 7s. per day for mechanics, and 5s. per day for laborers. A smithy and carpenter's shop were erected, and sawyers and boat-builders set to work. The boys were employed cutting fern preparatory to the sowing of wheat. On the 27th June, the Speculator came into the roadstead with the news that a charter had been granted to the Company, and that Britain had not quite ignored her adventurous sons in New Zealand; also, that the Company had despatched the Amelia Thompson from Plymouth. In the middle of July a fresh supply of provisions was obtained from the schooner Lapwing, and all the spare hands were employed cutting lines for the town.

On the 25th March, 1841, the barque Amelia Thompson, 480 tons, Capt. Dawson, was despatched from Plymouth for New Plymouth, with the following persons—Capt. Henry King, R.N., Chief Commissioner of the New Plymouth Colony, his lady and son; Mr. Edwin Brown, lady and two children; Capt. Davy and son; Capt. Cooke; Mr. Webster, lady and three children; Miss Baker; Mr. Wallace and son; Mr. Merchant and lady; Messrs. C. Brown, junior; W. and H. Halse, Ibbotson, Goodall, Lewthwaite, St. George, Marshall, Mr. Evans, ship's surgeon; eight in the intermediate, and 156 in the steerage; total, 187 passengers.

FAREWELL DINNER AND DEPARTURE OF THE FIRST COLONISTS TO NEW PLYMOUTH.

The Plymouth Company of New Zealand having resolved on giving a farewell dinner to the cabin passengers of the Amelia Thompson, previous to her departure for her destination, the entertainment took place on Friday, 19th March, at Whiddow's Royal Hotel. The following Directors of the Plymouth Company were present:—Capt. Charles Bulkeley, of Stonehouse; Richard Fillis, Esq., of Plymouth; George Leach, of Stoke; and Dr. Thorburn, Princess-square, Plymouth. The cabin passengers present were:—Captain Henry King, R.N.; Captain L. H. Davy, late of the Bengal Army; James Webster, Esq.; William and Henry Halse, Esqrs., of St. James' Palace, London; George John Cooke, Esq., late of the 11th Regiment; Charles Brown, Esq., of Plymouth; Mr. John Wallace, of Birmingham; Messrs.

Edwin Brown, Isaac Goodall, and John Lewthwaite, of Halifax, Yorkshire; Mr. Edmund Marshall, of London; Mr. Thomas Ibbotson, Mr. Charles Merchant, and Mr. St. George, of Staffordshire. A few friends of the gentlemen from the neighborhood, who were passengers, were also invited. The officers from the Company's establishment, including W. Bridges, Esq., Secretary; and Mr. J. Matthews, Accountant, and Superintendent of Emigration, were also present. Messrs. Saunders and Haswell, the Company's Shipping Surveyors; Mr. John Borwarva, and a few other gentlemen were among the guests.

The Chair was taken at six o'clock by Thomas Gill, Esq., Sub-Governor of the Plymouth Company of New Zealand, who was supported on his right by Captain King, Chief Commissioner of the Company's Settlement; and on his left, by J. Watson, Esq., the representative of a numerous body of purchasers of land in the settlement. Thomas Woollcombe, Esq., Managing Director, officiated as Vice-President. About forty gentlemen sat down to dinner, which was served up in Mrs. Whiddow's usual style, and consisted of every luxury that could be desired. The healths of the "Queen," the "Queen Dowager," "Prince Albert," and the "Royal Family," were drunk with the usual honors, followed by the "Army and Navy," acknowledged by Captain Bulkeley and Captain King, on behalf of their respective services.

T. Woollcombe, Esq., then rose, and after addressing some observations on the particular event which had called them together, in which everyone present must take an especial interest, and none more so than himself; he begged to propose a toast, which, apart from all political feelings, would, he was certain, call for the approbation of all present. Whatever might be the opinions of gentlemen with respect to the political career of the Noble Lord, the Secretary for the Colonies, he was sure all would join him in applauding the statesmanlike and generous manner in which he had now taken up this great and interesting Colony. It was owing to the manliness and courage with which Lord John Russell had practically acknowledged, and fearlessly corrected the error which had been originally committed with regard to New Zealand, that the Colony now stood in its present proud position in this great commercial country. He therefore begged to propose the health of the "Noble Secretary for the Colonies." The toast was warmly received, and drunk with great applause.

The Chairman then proposed the health of "Captain King," the Chief Commissioner of the Colony. He was a gentleman of high moral feeling, of great worth, and whose energies had prompted him to accede to the wishes of the Directors in undertaking the arduous task of superintending the social condition, and the formation of a compact, which shall descend to future generations. In this gentleman, he observed one on whom they could all rely; and in whom they could place the most undivided confidence. The health of Captain King was received and drunk with the greatest enthusiasm.

Captain King, in rising to return thanks for the honor conferred upon him, wished also to allude to the manner in which the Directors had brought them together upon the present occasion, and which he deemed most honorable to them. It was always more or less painful to take a final farewell of friends, but much depended upon the way in which it was done. On the present occasion, most of the intending colonists had youth on their side, and those who had not, had perseverance; and the pleasure derived from the confidence of success inspired by these was sufficient to counterbalance every feeling of fear or regret. Nothing beyond this was necessary but unanimity among themselves. He begged to thank the Chairman for the honor conferred upon him, and the company present, especially for the manner in which they had responded to the call of the Chairman in drinking his health. Captain King concluded by proposing the health of the "Chairman, Thomas Gill, Esq." which was enthusiastically responded to by the assembly.

The Chairman could not suffer the observations of Captain King to pass without attention, and, at the same time that he assured them of his own endeavors to do his duty, he was fully convinced that every one who had acted with him had strained every nerve to do theirs. One thing he might safely say, that there never was a set of men more enthusiastic with regard to their object, and that the welfare of the settlement, and the well-being of the colonists were equally desired by them all. As regarded the Colony, their efforts would still be unceasing, for it was their intention to send out another ship immediately, in succession to that noble vessel, the Amelia Thompson, which would take the present intending colonists out. In doing this, the same attention would be paid to the health, convenience, and comfort of every individual, as had been shown in the present instance. When he looked back at colonisation as it was carried out formerly, and made a comparison between that and the mode which was now adopted, he must say that the misery and suffering endured in the one case, and the convenience of arrangement, and comfort and pleasure, arising out of it in the present instance, afforded a marked and pleasing contrast. The class of persons now assembled round the table was, in fact, such as would reflect credit on any place, so that, in addition to the marked improvement in the mode of going from one climate to another, an equal change had taken place in the class of individuals who left their native land for the country of their adoption. The facilities of emigration, he would add, were in a progression so rapid that we should shortly be enabled to go from one country to another with as little difficulty as we formerly stepped from our own door to that of our neighbor; and the establishment of a regular line of steam packets in the Pacific would, he doubted not, be carried out eventually, to the great benefit of our colonies in the southern hemisphere, and to none more so than to the Colony of New Zealand.

T. Woollcombe, Esq., said he hoped he might be permitted to explain to those assembled the objects which the Company had in view in sending out the Chief Commissioner. He had much pleasure in assuring them that these objects were no farther of a commercial nature than to realise a reasonable profit upon the goods which they shipped to supply the colonists themselves. Competition with the settlers formed no part of their enterprise, and their instructions to their officers were that they were on no account to enter the market in this character, either as regard the necessaries of life or the disposal of land. (Cheers). With their permission he would read to them the Company's intention respecting land. [Mr. Woollcombe then read to the company the Chief Commissioner's instructions, which were received with the warmest approbation.] He believed that all who were concerned in the enterprise were animated strongly by these feelings, which he might say were cradled in these counties. From the west of England had proceeded the early founders of that great and glorious colony of England, the United States of America, towards which, notwithstanding any transient cloud which might lower for a time on the political horizon, every true Briton would look with pride and reverence. Those bold and energetic men whom he now addressed were departing from their native land on a mission which he firmly believed would end in bringing great glories to this country, and would add another brilliant page to the records of our commercial greatness. To ensure this they need only recall the deeds of their forefathers in a like cause, and they would render New Plymouth as celebrated as any part of the United States. They would carry with them the blessings of civilization, and they would attain the dearest reward of all exertion—the consciousness of having achieved their own fortunes and independence.

C. V. Bridgman, Esq., of Tavistock, rose and begged that he might be allowed to propose the health of the Vice-President. In making this request, he hoped he should not be considered an intruder. This, he was sure, would not be the case, for, besides the interest which he felt in the colony itself, he was connected by ties of relationship with one who held an important office on board the Amelia Thompson—he meant the surgeon, James Evans, Esq.—whom he hoped to have met at this interesting party, but whose paramount duty to the emigrants had detained him on board. He begged to propose the health of Thomas Woollcombe, Esq.

The Vice-President, in returning thanks, wished to observe that the pride and satisfaction which he felt in having done his own duty to the best of his ability, was not greater than the pleasure which he experienced from seeing his humble efforts crowned with success, through the aid and cordial co-operation of his brother directors. He could not do anything by halves, and he knew of no cause in which he had been engaged which had afforded him so much gratification as this one of aiding in the establishment of a colony of Britons in the southern hemisphere.

The Chairman proposed the toast of "Ships, Colonies, and Commerce," which was duly honored.

The Chairman begged to remark that although the ladies formed no part of the present company, they would not be absent on board, and would be found a most essential ingredient in the Colony at New Plymouth. It had hitherto been an error in emigration to leave this very important part of a social community out of the question, and great inconvenience had been the result. He must say, however, that all would feel deeply indebted to those ladies who, on the present occasion, had had the resolution to embark themselves on so long a voyage, and whose patient endurance of trial—so proverbial of the softer sex—had given them the courage to adventure on administering to the wants and comforts of their fellow passengers. He would conclude by drinking the health of the ladies on board the Amelia Thompson.

Mr. Webster returned thanks on the part of the ladies.

The Chairman felt convinced that the preceding toast would give satisfaction to all interested persons, both present and absent, but he was sure that there was one among them who would take an especial interest in seeing that the comforts of the ladies themselves were not overlooked—he meant the commander of the Amelia Thompson, Captain Dawson, whose health he now begged to propose.

Captain Dawson's health was drunk with much enthusiasm.

Captain Dawson said he felt highly honored by the marked manner in which the President had alluded to his humble services. When he first heard of the Plymouth Company of New Zealand, he happened to be in Scotland, and ever since the expedition had been made known to him, he had felt an especial interest in it, and that interest had increased up to the present moment. He was sure that this feeling could never subside, for the more he saw of the Company the more convinced he was that the liberality and kind support which had been accorded to him would be continued until his mission was crowned with success; and they might rely upon it that the comforts of the ladies would meet with his especial attention.

Mr. Charles Brown, sen., of Laira Green, begged to make a few remarks before the company separated. He was not going out himself in the Amelia Thompson, but he was nevertheless equally interested, on account of one in whose welfare he was immediately concerned, and whom he intended speedily to follow. He could see clearly that in matters of this kind no good could be accomplished unless every man acted *truly* for himself, which was the reverse of selfishness, for if every man acted well for himself he would also act well for the community.

Mr. Watson rose to propose a bumper toast. He stood there as one of the early purchasers of land, and the representative of a large portion of proprietors. In the first instance they found opposed to them not only the Government but the press, and against these the directors had to contend in all their early proceedings. How had they acted in this emergency, however? Had they flinched from their duty? No. If any gentlemen were present who had witnessed the assembling of the merchants of London on this interesting subject, he was sure they would coincide with him in his opinion. The Government at length had met all their wishes, and they had now the satisfaction, not only of being severed from a convict Colony, but of enjoying all the blessings of the British Constitution. The emigrants now leaving Plymouth he was sure would have all the comforts of a house on board the vessel in which they were about to embark, and a wide field was opened for their labor on their arrival out. Here, in England, they were pressing too closely upon each other, and all their united exertions were insufficient to keep the body and soul together; there, he doubted not, but that they would be enabled not only to live comfortably, but also to lay by sufficient in store of the good things of this world to ensure an old age of ease and happiness. Nor had they forgotten the Aborigines. They were going to join them in the wilderness and to aid in rendering it the abode of civilized men, and when their country would be converted from a waste into a paradise what remained to them would be infinitely more valuable than the whole had been in a state of desolation. The directors were entitled to the thanks and good wishes of all for having laid the foundation of accomplishing so much, both for them and the natives, and he begged now to conclude by drinking their health in a bumper.

T. Woollcombe, Esq., returned thanks on behalf of the Directors.

Mr. Charles Brown, jun., having obtained the consent of the Chairman to propose the health of the Officers of the Company, it was drunk with enthusiasm.

Mr. Bridges returned thanks on behalf of himself and brother officers.

Mr. Lewthwaite proposed the health of Captain Haswell.

Captain Haswell returned thanks.

The company separated at an early hour of the evening.

The Amelia Thompson got under weigh on Thursday morning, and on passing the Impregnable, lying in the Sound, was greeted by every soul on board, the ship's band playing the National Anthem.

The beautiful schooner Regina, which had just been launched, and belonged to Messrs. Row and Billing, of Plymouth, had been chartered by the Directors for the purpose of conveying the baggage and stores of the emigrants who were shut out from the Amelia Thompson. She was to sail on the Saturday following the farewell banquet. The cargoes of the two vessels were estimated to considerably exceed £20,000.

GOD SPEED THE SHIP.

[Written by Mr. S. H. Stokes, of Truro, on the departure of the Amelia Thompson, for Taranaki, New Zealand.]

God speed the ship! her anchor's up,
  Her sails are spreading in the breeze,
With filling eyes and foaming cup,
  We now commit her to the seas;

And as she leaves old England's shore
   Hark! from yon stately vessel's side
What well-known strains are wafted o'er,
   The waves that swell with conscious pride;
See, see the "meteor flag" unfurled,
   At once the lofty yards are mann'd,
And with such cheers as daunt the world
   The bold adventurers leave their native land.

God speed the ship to that far isle
   Where in the vast Pacific Main
Another Albion seems to smile,
   And Britons find their home again;
Green hills appear with streamlets clear
   And waving woods and showery skies,
And Ocean loves to murmur there
   While many an echoing cave replies;
There birds chime in the matin hour,
   And when the trembling stars grow bright
Sweet voices from the woodland bower
   Remind the swain of England's summer night.

God speed the ship! her company
   Have hearts as tender as they're true;
Good bark! Oh bear them gallantly
   The deep's tempestuous perils through;
A dear, a sacred charge is thine,
   Good ship be staunch, be strong, be swift,
Soon may the glorious Southern Sign
   Its cross above the waters lift,
To prompt perchance some grateful hymn
   "A holy and a cheerful note,"
Such as did once on Ocean's brim
   By the remote Bermudas sweetly float.

God speed the ship! For conscience sake
   No more the Briton leaves his home,
In transatlantic wilds to make
   With forest boughs his temple dome;
Not thus with cheers and blessings went
   The Pilgrim Father's from the coast;
Some silent prayers to heaven were sent
   For good men to their country lost;
Few, few, to bid farewell stood by,
   And hastening from the lonely shore
The exiles 'neath a lowering sky
   Heard but the sea birds scream and billow's roar.

God speed the ship! God speed the ship!
  To all on board a long adieu!
In the blue waves the white sails dip,
  And soon elude my anxious view;
    Yet like the faithful Albatross
In thought I'll track the rapid bark,
  With her the burning line I'll cross
And seek the Bay with pine woods dark,
  Where safe from storms on some blythe morrow
The eager crew will leap to land,
  And on the soil their ploughs shall furrow
The flag of England plant, 'mid cheers that shake the strand.

When the Amelia Thompson reached the South American coast, Captain King determined to put into Bahia, one of the most important ports of Brazil, for water and refreshment, and from thence he sent the following letter, descriptive of the early part of the voyage, to Mr. Woollcombe :—

"On board the Amelia Thompson,
"Bahia, May 7th, 1841.

"Sir,—I wrote you, per Lord Auckland, on 22nd April, in latitude 4° 27′ N., longitude 23° 17′ W., and now beg to communicate, for the information of the Directors, that we crossed the Equator on the 23rd April, in longitude 25° 38′ W., since which the prevailing south winds having carried us so far to the west on the Brazilian coast as Bahia, and the ship making little progress in consequence of light variable winds, I considered it a favourable time to run in and break the monotony of the voyage which was visibly depressing both cabin and steerage passengers, as well as to give the people a supply of water for washing their clothes and refreshing them by a change of provisions, fruits and vegetables, which I hope will contribute to their health for the remainder of the voyage. Since my last, one female infant has been added to the number of steerage passengers, and I am very sorry to say we had a death yesterday, Mr. Merchant losing his youngest son in convulsions from teething. We anchored in this fine harbor on Wednesday afternoon, shall complete watering the ship this afternoon, and intend sailing to-morrow morning, when we hope to meet with favorable winds to convey us to our destination before we anchor again.—I am, &c.,

"HENRY KING."

The Amelia Thompson after a long, but pleasant voyage, and after anchoring in Cloudy Bay, anchored in Port Nicholson on the 2nd of August. Sailing from thence on the 13th she again anchored in Cloudy Bay for the purpose of taking in ballast. She again set sail and anchored in New Plymouth roadstead on the 3rd of September. This being the period of the vernal equinox the weather was stormy; Captain Dawson also was in much dread of the coast, and put to sea every time the sky threatened, going out so far that he could scarcely get back again till the fine weather was over; the consequence of which was that the unloading of the ship occupied a considerable time.

The schooner Regina, 174 tons, Captain Browse, after a stormy passage arrived at Port Nicholson on the 31st August. On the 27th of September she sailed for New Plymouth, conveying as passengers from Wellington, Captain Liardet, R.N., the Company's Agent, and Messrs. Dorset and Smith. The Regina experienced a succession of gales from the time of leaving Plymouth till she arrived at Wellington. In Cook Strait she only escaped a lee shore and certain destruction by a press of sail which her tough masts enabled her to carry. She arrived at New Plymouth on the 3rd of October, and landed part of her cargo, but owing to the stormy weather had several times to put to sea; on one of these occasions she ran to Port Hardy for ballast. About half-past two o'clock on the morning of the 5th of November, she from some unexplained cause drifted from the anchorage opposite to the town on to the long reef, and became a total wreck. There was a swell rolling in from the N.E. at the time of the accident, and the sky was hazy with light rain, but there was little or no wind. The crew were rescued without any difficulty, for the sea was sufficiently calm to permit a small boat to reach the wreck from the shore. This disaster was severely felt in New Plymouth; it gave the settlement an ill name as a place of danger to shipping, it deprived the Colony of a much needed coasting vessel, and was the cause of the loss of a quantity of valuable goods and machinery.

The ship Oriental, 506 tons, Captain Wilson, which left Plymouth on June 22nd, arrived at New Plymouth on November 19th. She brought seventeen cabin passengers and seventy-four in the steerage. Great despatch was made in landing the passengers and cargo, notwithstanding which the Captain had to slip his cable and thereby lost an anchor and chain.

The pioneers who came out in the London with Mr. Carrington, in the Slaines Castle, and in the William Bryan, located themselves in whares in that part of the town at the junction of Queen Street, and St. Aubyn Street, which in the early days was called Devonport. The immigrants by the Amelia Thompson and Oriental encamped near to the beach till they could get "cob" and timber houses constructed. By the 4th of November the survey of the town had been completed, and the sections were ready to be given out to the purchasers. The promise made of the gift of a town section to each of the heads of the families of the pioneers who came in the William Bryan was never fulfilled. After pressing their claims for a considerable period they were allowed the privilege of selecting sections in St Michael's Square at £5 each. This concession was accepted by many of the poorer settlers and thus the quarter lost its original name for that of Poverty Square, its popular designation to this day.

CAPTAIN LIARDET, R.N.

Owing to the merger of the Plymouth and New Zealand Companies, the appointment of Captain King as Chief Commissioner of the

Colony of New Plymouth was but of a temporary character. Shortly after the departure of the Amelia Thompson the Company chose Captain Liardet, formerly of H.M.S. Powerful, and a friend of Colonel Wakefield, to be their permanent Resident Agent at New Plymouth. This officer had served on the coast of Syria and was present at the bombardment of St. Jean d'Acre as a flag Captain of Admiral Napier's. He was a bold sailor-like fellow, and a perfect gentleman. He sailed for New Zealand in the barque Whitby, 347 tons, Captain Lacy, which left Gravesend on the 27th of April, 1841, and arrived at Wellington on the 18th of September of the same year. The Whitby with the Will Watch conveyed the first expedition to Nelson, Captain Liardet having as a fellow passenger the late lamented Captain Wakefield, who was afterwards killed at the Wairau by the red-handed Rauparaha. On Tuesday evening, 20th of September, Captains Wakefield and Liardet were entertained at a public dinner at Barrett's Hotel, Wellington, at which seventy gentlemen sat down. After the customary loyal toasts had been given, and the health of Captain Wakefield had been drunk, Dr. Evans gave "Captain Liardet and prosperity to New Plymouth." In doing so he paid a high compliment to the gallant Captain for his Naval reputation, and referred to his recent exploits at the siege of St. Jean d'Acre. They now found him, he said, abandoning the prospects of his profession, and engaged in the satisfactory work of transplanting Englishmen to a land enriched with the bounties of nature, and that was far more satisfactory than the work of destroying, however just and honorable the cause of the warfare might be. In the gallant Captain, the New Zealand Company had an enthusiastic admirer of their plans, and he (Dr. Evans), was sure nothing would be wanting on Captain Liardet's part to give proper effect to them. The toast was responded to with three times three and one cheer more. Captain Liardet briefly returned thanks, and said, "Since I have seen New Zealand I like it, and intend to make it my home." Captain Liardet sailed from Wellington for Taranaki in the schooner Regina, which arrived at New Plymouth on the 3rd of October. After a brief stay at Taranaki he returned to Wellington in the schooner Ariel, arriving there on the 25th of October. On his arrival in Wellington he found the Oriental, from Plymouth, about to sail to New Plymouth. He took passage in her and again arrived at New Plymouth on the 19th of November. By this ship came Mr. Charles Brown, senior; and Mr. Watson, late master of the Amelia Thompson, returned in her from Wellington with the intention of settling at New Plymouth. Captain Liardet's period of effective service in the settlement was exceedingly brief, for ten days after his return he met with a very serious accident which nearly cost him his life, and which is thus described in a letter by one of the pioneer settlers :—

"On 29th November, 1841, Captain Liardet and Mr. Watson met with a dreadful accident at a quarter to ten in the morning, near to our tent. It was found necessary to clear the vent of a small four-pounder gun lying on the beach, which had been recovered from the wreck of the Regina. To effect this, Captain Liardet, assisted by Mr. Watson and a seaman, elevated the muzzle of the gun by resting it upon another gun lying at right angles to it. He then threw into the chamber a few ounces of loose powder, and cautiously dropped a fire-stick down the muzzle. The brand failed to reach the powder, and no explosion took place. Some five minutes after this, thinking the brand was extinguished, the Captain and Mr. Watson attempted to lower the muzzle, and while so engaged the loose powder reached the still burning brand, exploded and dreadfully scorched both their faces. The faces of both were blackened and covered with blood, and it was feared they would both lose their sight. As Captain Liardet came out as the representative of the Company, and we placed the utmost confidence in him, the accident is most deeply to be regretted."

Mr. E. J. Wakefield thus bears testimony to the worth of this officer :—

" Captain Liardet has given unbounded satisfaction during his short administration of office. High-minded and generous and possessed of great moral and physical courage, this well-known type of the British naval officer had soon acquired the devoted love and respect of the colonists, whose energies he had undertaken to direct. They felt that he was to be depended on in any emergency which might befall them ; and while his powers of mind thus secured general confidence, his very commanding personal appearance, combined with the affability of a gentleman, and the frank-heartedness of a sailor, to make him the universal favorite of his little society."

Captain Liardet having partially recovered, left New Plymouth for Sydney in February, 1842. From thence he proceeded to England, in the ship Caroline. Both he and Mr. Watson recovered their sight, but the gallant Captain never returned to New Zealand. Shortly after his departure, some young men, his nephews, came out, and were bitterly disappointed to find that their uncle had been compelled to return to England. Liardet Street, New Plymouth, is the only token that remains to perpetuate the memory of this once promising Resident Agent.

CHAPTER XI.

GOVERNOR HOBSON.

CAPTAIN WILLIAM HOBSON, the first Governor of New Zealand, served as lieutenant at Jamaica, in 1823, when it was found necessary by Sir Charles Rowley, the commander-in-chief of that station, from the swarms of pirates annoying British commerce in those seas, to fit out two schooners to go in search of them. Lieutenant Hobson volunteered, and was put in command of the Lion, on which service he distinguished himself by taking several piratical vessels, with their crews and most notorious chiefs, whom he brought to punishment. Subsequently he himself fell into their hands, and his reputation for generosity and courage alone saved him and his comrades from a violent death. It is said that some of the incidents of this transaction furnished Michael Scott materials for one of the most interesting passages in "Tom Cringle's Log." A short time after this, for his remarkable bravery Lieutenant Hobson was made a Commander and was appointed to the Ferrett, and again was sent among the pirates. At the paying off of the Scylla, to which vessel he had been removed, in 1828, he was promoted by the Lords of the Admiralty to the rank of Post-Captain. He afterwards commanded the Rattlesnake, detached from the East India station to New Zealand, and it was his connection in this manner with the islands that led to his appointment as the first Governor.

The hopes which had been raised by the Governor's proclamation of the Sovereignty of Her Britannic Majesty over New Zealand were doomed to disappointment. To the intense disgust of the settlers who came out under the auspices of the New Zealand Company, the Governor, instead of fixing the seat of Government at Wellington, made an abortive attempt to establish himself at the Bay of Islands, by purchasing one of the islands in the Bay of a whaling Captain, named Clendon, for the enormous sum of £13,000. Being thwarted in this foolish business, he proceeded to the Waitemata, or river of sparkling waters, and on its banks founded the City of Auckland. Governor Hobson's hostility to the colonists of the Company is probably attributable to his having unreservedly thrown himself into the hands of the Rev. Henry Williams and other missionaries of the Bay of Islands.

Owing to the facilities which its magnificent inland waters offer to navigation and trade, and also to its rich gold fields, Auckland has risen to be one of the chief cities of the Colony; but in the early days of Colonial history it was a wretched vampire, preying upon the vitals of the Company's settlements. Possessing but little good land in its immediate vicinity, and scarcely any agricultural population, its community was composed of the Governor and his officials, a few scamps from Sydney and Parkhurst Prison, a clergyman, and a few immigrants crimped from the Company's settlements. Here sat the Legislative Council, composed chiefly of Government officials, and here alone were the High Courts of Justice established. One of the Governor's early acts was the appointment of Maori Protectors, who were chosen from among the missionaries and partook of all their anti-colonial prejudices.

During the period in which New Zealand remained an appendage of New South Wales, the settlers of Wellington sent a deputation to the Governor-in-Chief complaining of the grievances which they suffered at the hands of Lieut.-Governor Hobson, which resulted in the following correspondence :—

"Lieutenant-Governor Hobson to Governor Sir George Gipps.
"Government House, Russell,
"December 29, 1840.

" Sir :—Referring to your Excellency's letter, dated and numbered as in the margin, covering copies of communications made to the deputation from Port Nicholson by your Excellency, and informing me of the conditions on which the settlers are to remain undisturbed on the lands they have taken possession of, I do myself the honor to inform you that notice has been published in the Port Nicholson papers by Captain Smith, R.A., who signs himself Surveyor-General of the New Zealand Company, that plans of the district of Wanganui and Taranaki were ready for inspection, and that the selection therein would take place on Monday, February 4th, 1841.

"I have to request that your Excellency will furnish me with instructions as to the course I should pursue to prevent the serious consequences that must inevitably result from the Company apportioning lands so distant from their settlement, in contravention of your Excellency's conditions, reservations, and limitations as expressed in Enclosure D, the lands of Taranaki being distant one hundred miles from Port Nicholson, and those of Wanganui being far beyond the limits of any block including Port Nicholson that can be comprised within 110,000 acres.

"I have the honor to be
"W. Hobson."

" Governor Sir George Gipps to Lieutenant-Governor Hobson.
" Government House, Sydney,
" January 12th, 1841.

" Sir :—I had the honor to receive your despatch of 29th December, informing me that a notice has been published in a newspaper at Port Nicholson that plans of the districts of Wanganui and Taranaki are ready for inspection, and that selections therein would take place on Monday, 4th February, the notice being signed by a person who calls himself Surveyor-General to the New Zealand Company ; and I have, in consequence, to desire that you will, without loss of time, direct the Police Magistrate at Port Nicholson to notify in the most public mannner possible that no such selections will be acknowledged by Her Majesty's Government, nor any titles whatsoever derived from the New Zealand Company, beyond the lands of 110,000 acres taken in one continuous block round Port Nicholson.

"I have the honor to be, etc.,
"GEORGE GIPPS."

On the 3rd May, 1841, the Governor, by proclamation, constituted a Legislative Council in the following terms: "And I do hereby proclaim and declare that Her Majesty has been pleased to appoint a Legislative Council for the Colony of New Zealand and its dependencies, and to appoint and direct that such legislative council shall consist of the following members:—His Excellency, the Governor for the time being; the Colonial Secretary for the time being; the Attorney General for the time being; the Colonial Treasurer for the time being; and the three senior Justices of the Peace, nominated as such in any commission of the peace to be issued by me, the said Governor and Commander-in-Chief, or by the Governor, or acting Governor for the time being."

In a despatch to the Secretary of State, dated 13th November, 1841, the Governor thus writes concerning the claims of the Waikato tribe to the land at Taranaki:—"At Taranaki the powerful tribe of Waikato threatens to dislodge the settlers, because they did not buy the land from them, they claiming it by right of conquest." Again, on the 13th December, the Governor thus addresses the same Minister:—"Now Te Wherowhero claims Taranaki by right of conquest, and insists that the remnant of the Ngatiawa are slaves; that they live at Taranaki by sufferance, and that they have no right whatever to sell the land without his consent."

In December, 1841, a party of Waikatos under the chief Te Kaka, paid a visit to New Plymouth respecting their claim, causing considerable alarm to the unsophisticated settlers by their warlike bearing. Their war dance is thus described by Mr. T. W. Shute, a well known pioneer, in a letter to a friend at Plymouth:—

"New Plymouth,
"December, 1841.

"This day we have had a much finer sight than ever you saw on the Hoe with soldiers. A part of a strange tribe of natives have arrived here, and something appears to have occurred which does not please them. They were all armed with double-barrelled guns, and met the natives residing here in a place appointed for the purpose. When they came in sight of the place they began to run, and a Ngatiawa chief ran to meet them, casting a stick, *taiaha*, towards them. When they came up as far as the boundary, they sat down for a little time, and then got up at the command of their leader and commenced the war dance. The chiefs then commenced speaking to each other, one at a time, at the end of which they engaged in a feast. The food consisted of a large quantity of potatoes, cooked for the occasion, with meat, fish, rice, pease and Indian corn, dished up in three-legged iron pots. The *piece de resistance* consisted of a pig, split down like a fish, and cooked whole. You may be sure it was a fine sight. The Waikato is one of the largest tribes of the island. We have but 150 of the original tribe of this district here, the others having been killed in war or taken captive, and it is only since we have been here that these have returned from captivity."

By means of trifling presents this party was induced to return in peace to Waikato, where shortly after the Governor prevailed on Te Wherowhero to part with his claim to the land, on the terms shown in the following translation of the deed of sale :—

"Know all men by this paper, that we, chiefs of Waikato, do let go and sell these lands of ours to George Clarke, the protector of natives, for Her Majesty, the Queen of England, her heirs and successors, whether male or female; the land, and all things that are on or under this land, we sell to George Clarke, the protector of natives, for an estate for the Queen, her heirs and successors, whether male or female, forever.

"The beginning of the northern boundary is at Tongaporutu, the western boundary is along the seashore between Tongaporutu and Waitotara, the southern boundary is from Waitotara inland by Piraunui.

"We receive these payments on behalf of the tribes of Waikato for their interest in the said lands, namely, one hundred and fifty pounds in money, two horses, two saddles, two bridles, and one hundred red blankets.

"Witness our names and signs :—

"Written in Auckland, on this thirty-first day of January, in the year of our Lord, one thousand eight hundred and forty-two.

"Te Kati,
"Te Wherowhero.

"Witness:
"J. Coates,
"George Clarke,
"Sub-Protector."

The Treaty of Waitangi gave to the British Crown a pre-emptive right to all the lands in New Zealand. Before the Treaty the New Zealand Company and others had made extensive purchases of lands from the natives, and to meet these cases it was recommended by the Colonial Office and notified by the Governor's Proclamation "That in order to dispel any apprehension that it is intended to dispossess the owners of any land acquired on equitable conditions, and not in extent or otherwise prejudicial to the present or prospective interests of the community, I do hereby further proclaim and declare that Her Majesty has been pleased to direct that a Commission shall be appointed, with certain powers to be derived from the Governor and Legislative Council of New South Wales, to inquire into and report on all such claims on lands." To investigate these claims and to adjudicate upon them the Colonial Office commissioned Mr. Spain, an English barrister, who left London on this mission in the ship Prince Rupert, on the 21st April, 1841. The vessel was unfortunately wrecked at the Cape of Good Hope, but Mr. Spain managed to reach Wellington in the brig Antilla, on December 8th, and Auckland on December 24th.

The next important event which took place was the political detachment of New Zealand from the Colony of New South Wales, and the erection of the islands into a separate Colony. This was effected by letters-patent from the Queen, and by the Governor's proclamation thereof, as follows :—

" Proclamation by his Excellency Captain William Hobson, Governor and Commander-in-Chief in and over the Colony of New Zealand and its dependencies.

" Whereas Her Majesty has been pleased by letters-patent, under the seal of the United Kingdom of Great Britain and Ireland, bearing date the 16th day of November, in the year of our Lord 1840, to erect the islands of New Zealand into a separate territory, by the name of Her Majesty's Colony of New Zealand. Now, therefore, I, the Governor and Commander-in-Chief, by commission under the great seal appointed, do hereby notify and proclaim that under Her Majesty's said letters-patent the islands of New Zealand are henceforth to be designated and known as Her Majesty's Colony of New Zealand and its dependencies. And I do further notify and proclaim that Her Majesty has been pleased to direct that the three principal islands of New Zealand heretofore known, or commonly called the North Island, the Middle Island and Stewart's Island, shall henceforth be designated and known respectively as New Munster, and New Leinster, of which all Her Majesty's subjects are hereby required to take notice.

" Given under my hand and seal at Government House, Auckland, this 3rd day of May, in the fourth year of Her Majesty's reign, and in the year of our Lord, 1841.

" (Signed)   WILLIAM HOBSON, Governor.
" By his Excellency's Command,
" (Signed)   WILLOUGHBY SHORTLAND."

New Zealand having been constituted a distinct Colony, Mr. Spain's Court of Land Claims had to be legalised by an Act of the New Zealand Legislative Council, and accordingly an Ordinance was passed to that effect on 9th June, 1841. There was other legislation upon the subject, but the above Ordinance was ultimately acted upon, subsequent Acts being disallowed by the Imperial Government.

Mr. Carrington's surveys extended from Paritutu to the Taniwha, situated about three miles on the east side of the Waitara river. The Governor, however, for some reason attempted to curtail the New Plymouth Block, the particulars of which appear in the following correspondence :—

HISTORY OF TARANAKI. 79

"Governor Hobson to Colonel Wakefield.
"Barrett's Hotel, Wellington, September 6th, 1841.

"Sir:—Understanding that some doubt is entertained as to the intentions of the Government with respect to the lands claimed by the New Zealand Company, in reference both to the right of pre-emption vested in the Crown, and to conflicting claims between the Company and other purchasers, it may be satisfactory to you to know that the Crown will forego its right of pre-emption to the lands comprised within the limits laid down in the accompanying Schedule, and that the Company will receive a grant of land, as may by any one have been validly purchased from the natives; the Company compensating all previous purchasers according to the scale fixed by local Ordinance. You are at liberty to give the utmost publicity to this communication.—I have the honor to be,
"WILLIAM HOBSON.

"Schedule of Lands referred to in the above letter:—Fifty thousand acres, more or less, to be surveyed and allotted by the said Company in the neighborhood of New Plymouth, the boundaries whereof are as follows, viz.:—The coast line from Sugarloaf Point extending in a northerly direction ten miles in direct distance; from thence a line at right angles with the coast line eight miles; from thence by a line parallel with the coast line ten miles; and thence by a line parallel with the Northern boundary to the sea coast at Sugarloaf Head."

These ten miles entirely excluded the Waitara district. On 15th October, 1841, Mr. Carrington pointed out the injury this would be to the settlement, as follows:—

"Mr. Carrington to Captain Liardet.
"New Plymouth, 15th October, 1841.

"Sir:—I have this morning read in the *New Zealand Gazette* of the 11th of September, a copy of a letter and Government notice forwarded by his Excellency Governor Hobson to William Wakefield, Esq., bearing date 5th September, 1841. I am not a little grieved to find that one of these notices will militate most seriously against this settlement, and will, if enforced, blast all hope for the colonists. I therefore lose not a moment in informing you of the position in which we are now placed, and hope you will, with the least possible delay, communicate with his Excellency, praying that the said notice may be cancelled."

On 15th November, 1841, Colonel Wakefield wrote to the Company: "I am about to apply to the Governor for an extension of the block at Taranaki, to the amount of 30,720 acres." On the 25th April, 1842, Governor Hobson wrote to the Resident Magistrate at Taranaki, Captain King: "I have purchased Te Wherowhero's claims, as well to your block of land as that which extends thirty miles to the north of what Colonel Wakefield pointed out to me as your northern boundary. * * * * I have permitted the Waikatos to settle near you, but by no means to infringe on you. They will locate on your northern frontier. * * * Have the goodness to point out to Mr. Whiteley your boundary line, and to inform him on behalf of the natives where they may go without interfering with the settlers."

During his visit to Wellington Governor Hobson placed Capt. King, Capt. Liardet, Capt. Cooke, Mr. Cutfield, and Mr. W. Halse, in the commission of the peace.

Governor Hobson's troubles increased daily. Some of the officers he had brought from Sydney had turned out badly. He found it very difficult to raise a revenue, and his government became involved in a debt of £100,000. Everybody but the missionaries was dissatisfied with him. Memorials asking for his recall were sent home both from Auckland and the Company's settlements. The newspapers lashed him unmercifully. Weakened in body and mind by paralysis, he sank under his political and physical afflictions, and died on the 10th of September, 1842, in the 49th year of his age, and the thirty-first month of his government of New Zealand. In the words of Dr. Thompson, "Auckland is his monument."

CHAPTER XII.

THE EVENTS OF 1842.

THE first event of importance which happened in 1842 was the arrival of the barque Timandra, 382 tons, Captain Skinner, which left Plymouth on the 2nd of November, 1841. She brought 212 passengers, and moorings for the roadstead, consisting of two sets of anchors, chains and buoys. The Timandra laid one set of these moorings at about two miles from the shore. Of the other set the chains and buoys were landed on the beach, one anchor was lost in an attempt to convey it to the shore on a raft, and the other was taken by the vessel to Sydney, where it remained at Mr. David Moore's Wharf till the wharf dues on it equalled its value, when it was sold or appropriated to pay expenses.

The following letters convey a good idea of the events of this period, and the condition of the settlement at this time :—

"Captain Cooke to Mr. Woollcombe.
"New Plymouth, April 16th, 1842.
"In consequence of poor Liardet's accident, and the consequent derangement of affairs, Colonel Wakefield determined upon visiting this place, taking Nelson *en route*. The Brougham, a very fine barque, chartered by the Company, being at his disposal, he sailed from Wellington on 2nd March, accompanied by Mr. Murphy, the Chief Police Magistrate at Wellington, and myself. After calling at Nelson we arrived here on Sunday, the 20th. We found to our great delight that the Timandra had arrived, remaining almost a fortnight, enjoying the most lovely weather during the whole of her stay, and landed her cargo and passengers with perfect safety. We made fast to the buoy she had laid down, and went on shore. It came on to blow in the night from the N.W., when the old Brougham slipped and stood out to sea, where she lay to until the end of the gale. Captain Robertson said that there was now no more danger in coming to Taranaki than to any other port in New Zealand. Colonel Wakefield remained here three days, and expressed himself delighted with the country and its fertility. Mr. Murphy also was loud in its praises. I mention this latter fact as I hear there is a probability of his being our future agent. He is an active, intelligent, gentlemanly person. Soon after my arrival here a small vessel came in from Port Nicholson with eight working bullocks and a horse, which I had purchased at that place. Four of these bullocks were for King and Cutfield; they were landed in admirable order, and I have had the satisfaction of seeing them plough every day. Colonel Wakefield's visit has been productive of some good results. A road to the Waitara has been commenced, and a bridle path to Wanganui

is talked of. When the latter is effected I shall be able to ride to Port Nicholson in five or six days. You will receive by Captain Liardet a specimen of the coal (shale), that our miners have discovered on the Waitara.—I am, &c.,

"J. G. COOKE."

[EXTRACT.]

" Letter from an Early Colonist to a friend in London.

"Taranaki, April 18th, 1842.

" With regard to the progress of the settlement, we are laboring under the serious disadvantage of having no capitalists here. The capabilities of the place are very great, for although I admit the great drawback of having no harbor, yet, from all we can learn of the neighboring settlements, we decidedly have the advantage as far as land is concerned. But we want money to develop the resources of the place. I am convinced that for persons intending to farm this is the most eligible location, as I doubt not by the time we have produce to export we shall have convenience for so doing in the shape of a jetty or small harbor, as projected and forwarded to the New Zealand Company. As a consequence of the small amount of capital here, we are without those two aids to the advancement of a settlement, a bank and a newspaper, both of which with a population of 1,000 we should be able to support if we had a due proportion of monied men. I wish the Company would hold out some tempting inducement to capitalists, for the district is extensive and easily available for cultivation."

Colonel Wakefield fortunately did not select Mr. Murphy for the post of Resident Agent in the room of Capt. Liardet, who by his accident had been compelled to resign his appointment, for that " perfect gentleman" speedily fell into irretrievable disgrace. On the 5th of May Mr. John Tylson Wicksteed was despatched from Wellington to Taranaki by the Brougham, to undertake the duties of the resident agency. Mr. Wicksteed was in some respects a remarkable man. He was one of the most fluent speakers we have ever heard, and a scarcely less ready writer. In his early days he was sub-editor of the London Spectator under Mr. Rintoul, the friend of Mr. Edward Gibbon Wakefield, and of Sir William Molesworth. Under these circumstances his connection with Colonial affairs can be easily accounted for. In order to propitiate the Church party, the New Zealand Company not only devoted a portion of its funds to the building of churches in the Colony, but it offered to give 2,000 acres of land on condition that the Church Society would purchase an equal quantity, towards the endowment of a bishopric in New Zealand. As the Agent of the Church Society for the purpose of administering this land, Mr. Wicksteed came to the Colony, in the London, in December, 1840. Mr. Rintoul is said to have declared that in Mr. Wicksteed he lost a valuable assistant. The services of an energetic man of business were much needed in the settlement, for the changes which had taken place in the office of Agent, and the accident which had prevented Capt. Liardet from attending to his duty, had left the Company's affairs in New Plymouth in a very complicated state. To Mr. Wicksteed we are chiefly indebted for the history of what may not be inappropriately termed the dark ages of Taranaki history, that is, of the period between 1842 and 1848, a period as cheerless as ever fell to the lot of a colony, when retrogression took the place of advancement, and nothing but the dogged courage of Britons could have stood against the flood of adversity which came over the infant settlement. It was Mr. Wicksteed's custom to write a monthly report to the principal Agent; and the following is an extract from his first report:—

"New Plymouth, June 1st, 1842.
"I found the surveys in a sufficient state of forwardness to justify the publication of a notice that a selection of rural lands would take place on the 20th June, 1842. I have reason to believe that very nearly if not all the land sold—being 8,200 acres—will be selected on the day named; in which case there will be a surplus of surveyed land to meet future sales of not less than 4,000 acres, the quantity to be offered for choice being upwards of 12,000 acres.

"The conclusion of the contracts for cutting lines has thrown many unemployed laborers on the Company's hands; but there is reason to believe that when the rural lands are given out on the 20th instant, a considerable portion of this labor will be absorbed by the proprietors, several of whom are ready to commence farming operations upon a small scale. At present all applicants for employment are put on the Waitara Road on the reduced wages of 16s. per week and rations.

"The principal difficulty in opening up communication with the Waitara district is in making a safe passage across the river Waiwakaiho, which is wide, with a stony bottom, a very rapid current, and subject occasionally to floods. The cost of a substantial bridge would be so great, that for the present I think of providing a good raft with ropes fastened to trees or stakes on each bank, such as are used in America for crossing much larger and more rapid rivers. I have no doubt that a small toll to pay for the repairs of the raft and ropes, and the wages of a ferryman, would be cheerfully paid.

"A surveyor's party of twenty-four men and boys depart this day for the Waitara district to stake out the sections, so that any proprietor or agent may at once be put on his sections after the day of selection.

"In concluding this report I ought to add that the general appearance of things is improving, and that a spirit of cheerfulness begins to prevail among the settlers."

In June Mr. Charles Brown, senr., died of apoplexy, after but seven months' residence in the Colony.

Mr. Wicksteed being anxious to open up communication with Wellington by means of a road through the forest, sent two of Mr. Nairn's sons in June to Patea, to engage a gang of twelve Maoris to cut a bridle road from the coast to a point east of Mount Egmont.

After these were set to work one of the brothers returned to New Plymouth, and with another gang proceeded to cut another line from Mataitawa to meet the line from Patea. Mr. E. J. Wakefield in his journal thus writes concerning this line :—

"The Agent of the New Plymouth Settlement had determined to cut a bridle-road inland of Mount Egmont, to connect New Plymouth with the coast of Cook Strait somewhere between Waimate and Patea, by an easier and shorter route than that round the coast. This object had at length been effected, notwithstanding the opposition of the great body of the natives on the Cook Strait side, entirely by native labor.

"A Wesleyan missionary residing at Waimate, named Skevington, had made the most strenuous efforts to overthrow the scheme, telling the natives that the road was made with a view to seize their lands, and that it was nothing but a design upon them which ought to be viewed with the utmost suspicion. Accordingly, the natives had refused to allow egress to the road at Waimate, Manawapou, or Patea.

"But a Maori, named Pakeke, who at New Plymouth had become acquainted with the Nairn family, at once gave the plan his cordial support, and engaged that his own especial followers should do the work. He appointed Waingongoro, or the snoring river, as the place of egress on the coast, as his out-cultivations were on the edge of the wood near the valley of that river.

"Upon this the missionary raised such a hornet's nest about his ears, that though he had formerly lived in Waimate Pa, and had been one of the most zealous attendants on Mr. Skevington's religious instruction, he removed his own family and retinue to a new village which he built at the mouth of the river where the road was to emerge, and suddenly but resolutely abjured his profession of Methodism and called himself a Churchman. His following all did the same, and the most revolting religious feud ensued. The road, however, was finished, and we met a party of workmen at Manawapou who were on their way to show the guns, in which they had insisted on receiving the principal part of the payment, to their friends at an inland settlement, between the rivers Manawapou and Patea."

The despatches of the Resident Agent bear unmistakable evidence that increasing pressure was brought to bear upon him to induce retrenchment in the Company's establishment. The reason for this may be found in the fact that very few men of capital came out to New Plymouth, the labor market was overstocked, and the Home and Colonial Governments hampered the Company as much as possible. In June, 1842, Mr. Weekes, the Colonial Surgeon, resigned his appointment, and the Agent reported that the two remaining surgeons, Messrs. Evans and St. George, were sufficient for the wants of the settlement. In this month some dispute arose about the native reserves. The settlers who possessed land orders were permitted to draw lots for priority of choice of sections, and it was originally intended that the Maoris who were to have every tenth section returned to them were to draw lots with the settlers, or some qualified person was to draw for them. A quantity of rural land had been surveyed, and a day was fixed for the drawing of the lots. Those holders of land orders who wished to obtain land in this block drew, but, by some unexplained circumstance, Capt. King, who had been appointed, *pro tem.*, Protector of Aborigines, failed to draw for the Maoris. But when the 20th of June arrived, the day for selecting the land, Capt. King protested against the selection, because no numbers had been drawn for the Maoris, and claimed the right of selecting for them by virtue of authority received from the Government. Mr. Wicksteed refused to receive Capt. King's protest or to entertain his proposal, because the Directors had instructed their Agents to select for the Maoris, for fear that others in selecting for them should interfere with a privilege they had given to Europeans, of selecting sections in contiguity with those of relatives and friends. The Agent was anxious that the Maoris should have their land in a block by themselves. The idea of mixing up the Maoris and Europeans arose from a desire to benefit the natives as much as possible, but in practice it did not answer, for the British husbandman found the Maori a bad neighbor, permitting his pigs to trespass, his curs to worry the sheep, and his neglected fields to produce rich crops of groundsel, docks, and other kinds of noxious weeds.

Now commenced those troubles with the natives, which resulted in driving off the settlers from their newly-acquired farms, and ultimately in the Taranaki war. The following letters of the Resident Agent describe the particulars of the first of these difficulties :—

" Mr. Wicksteed to Colonel Wakefield.
"New Plymouth, July 25th, 1842.

" Sir :—The settlers in this part of the Company's territory have recently had some difficulty with the natives, the particulars of which I think it right to state, as they are liable to misconstruction.

" You are aware that a considerable number of natives have lately been liberated by the Waikatos, who, some years ago, overran the Taranaki district, and carried off a large portion of its inhabitants as their slaves. The manumitted natives are now returning to this district, and not having been parties to the sale of the land to the Company, now complain that they have neither potatoe grounds nor *utu* in money or recompense. In point of fact, however, the native reserves are sufficient for a population twenty-fold larger than that likely under any circumstances to belong to Taranaki ; and I cannot discover among the malcontents a single person who, according to the custom of the natives, has or had a right to sell the land. On the contrary, many of those who did sell the land have distinctly warned me not to enter into any bargain or treaty with these returned slaves.

"Not being encouraged by me to expect any *utu*, some of these natives had resource to violence, and entered a section on the Mangoraka, belonging to a very peaceable settler named Pearce, burnt down his cottage and destroyed some raupo for thatching. They then proceeded to the next section where the Messrs. Bayly had put up their tent and were commencing their farming operations. They were very furious, brandishing their tomahawks, and attempted to tear down the tent; but the Baylys, very resolute and strong men, resisted, and a sort of scuffle or wrestling match ensued between one of the brothers and a native who acted as champion of the assailants. Twice Bayly threw the Maori but was thrown himself the third time; whereupon the natives crowded round him and one apparently was going to cleave his skull with a tomahawk, when a bystander levelled his fowling piece at the native who then gave way. There were about thirty natives and six white men. A parley ensued, and they agreed to refer the case to me.

"Accordingly the 'mob' of natives came to my house two days after, and there I told them of my determination to put the white settlers on their land, and to call upon the police magistrate to send any native who broke the peace into prison; at the same time assuring them that any chief who had any real title to the land should receive such compensation as Mr. Spain on his arrival might award. They very well knew they had no such chief among them, and being also certain that I should protect the settlers, they promised to give the Baylys no farther annoyance; and they are now very good friends with the settlers, working for them, sleeping in the same tent, and apparently quite satisfied with the excellent land reserved for them in or near that part of the country.

"Another affair of the same kind happened soon after at the Waitara. A body of armed natives drove Messrs. Goodall and Brown, agents of large absentee proprietors, off their section lying on the north side of the Waitara, cut down trees and brushwood, and declared their resolution to keep the settlers to the south of the Waitara. I perceived the necessity of stopping this at once, especially as the real chiefs assured me that the rioters had no claim whatever to the land, and only intended to terrify me into paying *utu*. The day after the riot I called upon Captain Cooke, a magistrate, to swear in a body of special constables, and that gentleman administered the oaths in the presence, and with the sanction of Captain King, the chief police magistrate. I put twelve muskets and fifty ball cartridges into the boat, and accompanied by Mr. Cooke, who nominally commanded the party, proceeded to the Waitara, and there we swore in the surveying men, making our force twenty-eight men.

"As I fully expected, this demonstration had the desired effect. A long talk with the natives ended in their entire submission, and promise of better behavior in future. Mr. Cooke told the ringleader that on the next occasion of his breaking the peace he would himself go to the pa and arrest him and send him for trial to Port Nicholson. We crossed over the river, formally took possession of the land, fired a volley by way of and *tapu*, then, but not before, I gave away a few blankets and some tobacco. The principal natives at the Waitara, as well as here, expressed their satisfaction at the proceeding. Among the settlers there is but one opinion in its favor, and I have received thanks on every side. At present all is quiet, and I think will continue so. I wish it to be particularly observed that I had the express authority and countenance of the magistrates throughout; and that I took, what the event proved to be, the best means of preventing an otherwise inevitable collision with the natives. * * * *

"I have the honor to be, etc.,
"J. T. WICKSTEED."

THE INTRODUCTION OF HORSES TO TARANAKI.

Mr. E. J. Wakefield thus describes the panic of the Maoris on the coast between Wanganui and Patea when they first saw a horse :—" I was not seen by the inhabitants of the pa until close to the river Whenuakura. They then ran down to the beach. By this time I had plunged into the river, which here flows over soft and shining sands. The horse's body was nearly hidden; and though many of my old friends here had recognised me and shouted '*Tiraweka! Haeremai!*' they evidently thought that a native was carrying me on his shoulders. There were now nearly a hundred natives collected, many of whom had never seen a horse before, crowding over each other to give me the first greeting. With two or three vigorous plunges the horse suddenly emerged from the water and bore me into the middle of them. Such a complete panic as ensued can hardly be imagined. They fled, yelling, in all directions, without looking behind them; and as fast as I galloped past those who were running across the sandy flat and up the steep path leading to the Tihoe pa, they fairly lay down on their faces and gave themselves up for lost. Half-way up the hill I dismounted, and they plucked up courage to come and look at the *kuri nui* or 'large dog.' The most amusing questions were put to me as to its habits and disposition. 'Can he talk?' said one; 'Does he like boiled potatoes?' said another; and a third, 'Mustn't he have a blanket to lie down upon at night!' This unbounded respect and admiration lasted all the time that I remained. The horse was taken into the central courtyard of the pa; a dozen hands were always offering him Indian corn, grass, and sow-thistles, when they had learned what he really did eat, and a wooden bowl full of water was kept constantly replenished close to him; and little knots of curious observers sat round the circle of his tether-rope, remarking and conjecturing and disputing about the meaning and intention of every whisk of his tail or shake of his ears."

In October and November, 1839, the Rev. W. Williams was at Waikanae with some horses, for the purpose of establishing a mission there. He also came up the coast as far as the Sugarloaves, leaving books and native catechists at Otumatua, near to Opunake, but it is doubtful whether he brought a horse with him beyond Waikanae. When the William Bryan arrived the only horses in the district were a mare and foal belonging to Richard Barrett, and shortly afterwards the mare was killed by falling into a Maori pit. The first horse landed on the beach was brought from Kawhia, in a sailing vessel, for the use of Mr. Creed, the Wesleyan Missionary. As soon as it reached the shore, William Marshall leaped upon its back, and rode up and down the beach. On the 24th October, 1841, the animal being ill, Mr. Creed brought it to the tent of a gentleman who possessed some knowledge of the veterinary art, for the purpose of getting it bled. William Marshall, who was near at the time, took hold of the animal's foreleg, which caused it to paw at him and strike him in the abdomen. The kick was so severe that the poor man died two days afterwards. The horse was a large awkward creature, which had been spoilt by the natives in their unskilful attempts to break him in. He was for many years attached to the Mission Station at Waimate, and, while there, killed a Maori. He died at last of old age.

A longer, but less doleful, story is connected with the next horse which arrived in the Province. The Chief Surveyor found it very rough and laborious work to travel on foot over the settlement, especially as he had to wade through rivers and swamps at the peril of his life. He therefore requested Captain Liardet to procure him a horse; the Captain promised to do so, and commissioned Captain King, who was about to proceed to Sydney for the purpose of buying live stock, to get a horse for Mr. Carrington. We presume that Captain King was not much of a judge of horse-flesh, nevertheless, the horse was duly purchased, together with the necessary harness, and shipped on board the barque Jupiter, bound for New Plymouth. After a very stormy passage of a month's duration, in which many of the cattle died, the vessel arrived and was made fast to the moorings then newly laid down. The Chief Surveyor's horse was landed, stabled, fed, and groomed, and when sufficiently recovered, was saddled and bridled for use. No longer would the Chief Surveyor run the risk of cramps, rheumatism, or drowning, by wading through the snow-fed rivers of the settlement. Fallacious hope! the brute was full of wickedness, and after three attempts to ride him, his master gave him up in despair. Some months afterwards Mr. Wicksteed thus addresses Colonel Wakefield concerning the animal :—"The horse purchased by Captain King for the Chief Surveyor, at Captain Liardet's orders, I have sold to Mr. Creed, the Wesleyan Missionary, for £39, and his saddle and bridle for £5. The animal, with his saddle and bridle, cost £79, and I was sorry to lose £44 by him, but he was aged, had bad tricks, and was constantly in danger of breaking his legs in the woods. He never was fairly worth £40, and Captain King was cheated when he purchased him. If I had kept him he would have cost the Company £40 per annum." The story of this animal may be extended a little further. The Board of Directors of the New Zealand Company sat in solemn conclave upon him as appears from the following minute:—"Mr. Carrington's claims, as stated in Mr. Wicksteed's letter of 17th May last, have much surprised the Court. He is certainly not entitled to a horse, an indulgence not granted to the principal surveyors at either Wellington or Nelson, and you will please retrench from his allowance the sum (stated to be about £70), expended in the purchase and keep of that animal."

The following letters describe the state of the settlement towards the close of the year:

Messrs. Aubrey to a Gentleman at Plymouth, England.
"Port Nicholson, August 12th, 1842.

"We came overland from New Plymouth to ascertain whether or not it was possible to drive cattle back from Port Nicholson; we have now determined to make the trial, and are going to take four working bullocks there on our own account, but hope to get some one to join us. We are well aware of the difficulties we should have to encounter, for it took us a fortnight to walk here, and I assure you the road is none of the best, and we expect to take a month to return. We have been seven months without letters from England. Wellington is a large town compared with New Plymouth, and the land valuable. Bullocks are now worth from £20 to £30 each, which is a reasonable price. At present there are but four at New Plymouth, which are daily hired at £2 per day."

These young men returned to Taranaki overland, but sent their bullocks by sea.

On 30th September the first anniversary of the arrival of the Amelia Thompson was celebrated. In the day there were boat races, foot races and wrestling matches; in the evening the first ball was held in the hospital, a small imported building, which then stood on the beach under the Kawau pa, but afterwards stood for thirty years at the corner of Brougham and Devon streets, and was used as a shop for the whole of that period. The event was also celebrated by a display of fireworks. Captain King had a small flock of merino sheep, and Mr. Devenish had one of southdown which he had carefully reared from a few he had obtained from a vessel. A subscription for the erection of a Wesleyan chapel had been satisfactorily commenced.

A Taranaki Settler to Thomas Woollcombe, Esq.
"New Plymouth, September 28th, 1842.

"I can now give you the most cheerful account of our dear little settlement, to which we are becoming more attached every day. The recent appointment of Mr. Wicksteed as Agent has been attended with the happiest results; people are now beginning to resume their entire confidence in the good intentions of the Company.

"At the Huatoki we have several excellent wooden and cob houses building and built. A new bridge has also been erected over that river. A miserable lock-up has also been built, the expenses of which have not yet been paid by the Government, and I suppose never will be. We have two public houses, 120 raupo and cob huts, and four large wholesale and retail stores, viz., Capt. Davy's, Mr. Dorset's, Mr. Baine's, and Mr. Richard Brown's. On Devonport Hill there are three or four Maori whares and a cluster of immigrant's houses. We have seven or eight master carpenters, who have their hands full of work and complain that they cannot get journeymen; four blacksmiths, and thatchers, hedgers, and ditchers, who get from five to ten shillings per day.

"On the banks of the Henui we have several houses, amongst them my own, and a substantial bridge over the river on the Devon line. A tremendous cutting through a high bank on the east side of the river, which is just completed, takes you along as fine a road as a man can desire, to the banks of the river Waiwakaiho. On each side of the road are the houses of the early emigrants, who have nearly all bought four or five acres of ground each. At present the river is crossed in a ferry-boat, but Messrs. Edwin Brown and Goodall have contracted to build a suspension bridge for £500, and if they can procure the chains in Wellington it will be finished in four months. The road, as far as the river Waiongona, would now be in a forward state, but the landowners have all the laborers in their employ. About six miles along the Waitara road are situated the farms and clearings of the brothers Bayly, Messrs. Flight and Devenish, Pearce, Paynter, Edgcombe, and a few others. At the Waitara Mr. Goodall is clearing extensively. To return to the suburban district. Capt. King and Mr. Cutfield have cleared about 70 acres and built a capital house and farm buildings upon their estate. Norice has built a capital thatched house and has cleared about three acres which I am ploughing for him. To the northward, Mr. Chilman has partly cleared and fenced a 50 acre section belonging to Mr. Blank, who let or sold nearly all his land at the average rate of £20 per acre, and then left the Colony to abuse us at Sydney. Distin has a house and clearing in the same direction, but more easterly. Across the Waiwakaiho Capt. Davy and myself are clearing and putting in crops. Added to all these clearings we have nearly 40 acres of garden ground this year, and have established a Horticultural Society."

The Rev. Samuel Ironside, Wesleyan Missionary, thus speaks of the return of the Ngatiawa from captivity in Waikato :—" Waikato hearing of the sale of lands at Taranaki by those whom they deemed their slaves, were very angry, and resolved to come down in force, and utterly destroy the remnant there. But there were many sincere Christians in Waikato, chiefly under the care of Rev. John Whitely, at Kawhia, and the Rev. James Wallace at Whaingaroa. These Christian natives opposed the design of their heathen relatives, and farther, resolved to give freedom to their Taranaki slaves, and escort them back to their native place. At the annual meeting of the Wesleyan ministers stationed in and near Waikato, in May, 1842, I was directed to go with these Christian natives on their errand of mercy. I went on this journey attended by some hundreds of

Waikato natives, Christian and heathen. At Mokau we left all signs of population behind us, and for sixty miles travelled through a silent country. On nearing New Plymouth the few inhabitants, not over twenty, took alarm, hurried into their canoes and paddled off to their rock, leaving the food cooking in their iron pots on the fire. It was only after considerable persuasion that they ventured to come ashore. We spent two or three days in discussion, and at length, the Waikato natives receiving a large portion of the purchase money for the country, and firing off their guns in memory of their dead there, and in token of their rights, returned home leaving the poor Taranaki people in peace."

In the winter of 1842 the contract for erecting a bridge over the Waiwakaiho river was let to Messrs. E. Brown and Goodall. These persons erected a suspension bridge, utilising for this purpose the chain cables of the ship Fifeshire, wrecked in Nelson. Unfortunately they used pukatea piles for the suspension of the chains, and this being a soft and perishable wood, the structure was a complete wreck in five years after erection. In October Bishop Selwyn and Chief Justice Martin visited the settlement. A cutter and a surf boat, iron fastened, had been built in the settlement, the cutter at an expense of £200, and the boat of £104. Another large surf boat, copper fastened, was in course of construction. The expenditure in salaries at this time was great; the Chief Surveyor received £350 per annum; First Assistant, £290; Second Assistant, £290; Third Assistant, £250; Fourth Assistant, £200; Fifth Assistant, £170; 15 men, £80 each; total £2,750. The total charge for surveys for the year ending March 31st, 1842, was £6,025. 3s. 0d. The department was now subjected to the following reduced scale: Chief Surveyor, £350, as before: First Assistant, Mr. Octavius Carrington, £290, as before; Third Assistant, Mr. Rogan, £200; 6 men at £80, and one boy at £40 per annum; total, £1360.

On the 19th November the Blenheim arrived from Plymouth, having left that port on the 1st July. She brought 159 souls, 49 of whom were cabin passengers. By this vessel came Mr. Parris and family, Mr. Smart and family, Mr. and Mrs. Murch, Miss Chilman, and Mr. George Duncan.

December 31st, 1842. The cutter built in the settlement had been sold for £200 at Wellington; the launch of the Oriental had also been sold. A lock-up had been finished at an expense of £57 13s. 2d. Heretofore prisoners had been confined in a small wooden cabin. Mr. Copps had been sent to Mokau to examine the district, and reported two large veins of coal sixteen miles up the river on the lower side of a rapid, and another vein above the rapid; also, the existence of limestone forty miles up the river.

During the month a person made application to the Agent for the possession of a town section which he had purchased, but which some natives were fencing in for the purpose of planting potatoes. On the 23rd Mr. Wicksteed proceeded to the spot with 20 men, and the natives having refused to give up the land, he directed the men to remove the fence. They did so, but the natives replaced it as it was removed. Mr. Wicksteed then retired, promising the natives to return on the following morning. On the morning of the 24th Mr. Wicksteed again appeared at the place with his men, and again had the fence pulled down, when one of the natives, a son of the chief E. Rangi, brandished a tomahawk over the Agent's head. The Maori was taken into custody, and being brought up before the Resident Magistrate, was bound over to keep the peace. Captain King wrote to the Colonial Secretary, complaining of the illegality of Mr. Wicksteed's conduct in this affair. In exonerating himself Mr. Wicksteed replied :—" The representative of the Government here, Capt. King, except where the possession of his own land is in jeopardy, gives me the least possible assistance. Once, when the natives took possession of part of his property, I had great difficulty in preventing the arrest of a number of Maoris who had come to my house under a safe conduct from Mr. Carrington—a breach of faith which might have produced the worst consequences."

CHAPTER XIII.

THE EVENTS OF 1843.

ON 23rd January, 1843, the Essex, 392 tons, Captain Oakley, arrived from Plymouth, bringing two sons of Colonel Aubrey in her cabin and 114 immigrants. She was the last vessel despatched from Plymouth to New Plymouth, and excepting military settlers during the war, no such number of immigrants arrived at one time in the settlement for a period of thirty-one years.

On 20th February, Captain Cooke left Wellington for New Plymouth with a herd of seventy head of cattle and a large flock of sheep. They defiled along the beach followed by their owner, two or three stockmen, and Richard Barrett, some mounted and some on foot. Mr. Cooke had been spending the anniversary of the Colony at Wellington, and Mr. Barrett had been giving his evidence before the Court of Land Claims.

On the 25th, the officer administering the Government, Lieutenant Shortland, arrived in Taranaki roadstead, but would not land or permit any of the official persons with him to leave the Goverment brig. The Resident Agent went off to the vessel and had a long conversation with his Excellency, who informed him that he considered the Taranaki district to have been fairly purchased from the Chief of the Taranaki tribe, the real owner of the land.

Mr. E. J. Wakefield started overland for Taranaki on horseback and overtook Mr. Cooke with his sheep and cattle on the road, but afterwards got again behind them. Both intended to reach the settlement by the road through the forest on the east of Mount Egmont. Mr. Wakefield was much struck with the appearance of the country as he entered the bush track. We quote from his journal :—

" After all the beautiful spots and districts which I had already seen in New Zealand, I was struck with the surpassing beauty and luxuriant productiveness of the country hereabouts. Just after entering the wood, which is at first like an immense shrubbery, with occasional large trees, the abundance of the crops in the existing native gardens, the rankness, and yet softness of the grass which had sprung up in the old deserted patches, surrounded with flowering shrubs, amidst which singing birds were chasing each other, all combined with the genial weather, although it was approaching to the middle of winter, to remind me touchingly of Shakespeare's sweet picture of the perfection of agriculture—

" ' Earth's increase and foyson plenty,
Barns and garners never empty,

Vines, with clustering branches growing,
Plants with goodly burden bowing,
Spring come to you at the farthest,
In the very end of the harvest.
Scarcity and want shall shun you
Ceres' blessing so is on you.'

"A long trudge through the forest, of which the trees increased in size as we advanced, presented but little variety till we emerged on the picturesque broken country which stretches northward from Mount Egmont at a distance of ten or twelve miles from the coast (Kairoa). We had slept two nights in the bush, and on the third we reached a hut in a small cultivation on the northern edge of the forest. The journey had proved very tedious from the extraordinary number of gullies and streams we had to cross. Among these were the Patea and several of its tributaries which take their rise in the side of Mount Egmont. After passing them we came to those which join to swell the Waitara.

"We had passed about half way in the bush the skeletons of two horses. These had belonged to Mr. Cooke and his stockman. On his journey with the herd of cattle he had expected to find the road open. On being disappointed he left his horse, being guided by the natives through the forest along the line which the road was to take. His cattle and sheep were in the meanwhile feeding on the rich pasture of the coast of Cook Strait. He directed his stockman to take the horses back, and drive the cattle along the coast; but the stockman left his horse too, and also came through the forest to New Plymouth. When he got back again both horses were dead of starvation.

"Descending from the broken country we found ourselves on the plains of New Plymouth, which are almost entirely covered with fern. Scattered groves of timber and gentle undulations from the plain into the valleys of the watercourses and their tributaries, diversify the view agreeably. At length we got into a line of road through the fern. One or two strong wooden bridges over the streams, and three or four neat houses and fields in various directions, soon told of the neighborhood of a European settlement. We crossed the Waiwakaiho river by a rough suspension bridge in process of erection, of which the chains were supported on the round trunks of four large trees; then some smiling gardens, neatly hedged and ditched; a forge, a row of laborers cottages, some cob houses in various stages of progress, and we reached the house of Mr. Cooke, who had invited me to come and find him out. From thence to the mouth of the Huatoki river the houses and gardens thicken apace; and there a little nucleus of dwellings form the town.

"The population of New Plymouth seemed a particularly happy set of people. As they are little troubled with politics I saw very few of them in the town, which is a dull place, except to look at as you can imagine. But on going to their little farms a mile off in one direction, or two miles in another, I found them hard at work, delighted at the fertility of the soil which they were turning over, with hardly a complaint to make, and spending homely English evenings round a huge farm-house chimney; rising early and not long out of their beds after their tea and pipes."

At this date the wages of the laborers in the employ of the Company were reduced to sixteen shillings per week, and preparations were also made for still more important reductions as will appear by the following letters :—

"The Resident Agent to George Cutfield, Esq.
"New Plymouth, March 24th, 1843.
"Sir :—I beg to inform you that instructions have been received from the Court of Directors of the New Zealand Company, which instructions have been communicated to me by the Principal Agent, to discontinue, as far as practicable, the issue of stores and rations, and to abolish the Storekeeper's Department. I am also instructed to discharge in future the duties of Immigration Agent myself. You will please therefore to take notice that after the close of the next quarter your employment under the Company as Storekeeper and Immigration Agent will cease.—I have the honor to be, &c.,
"JOHN TYLSON WICKSTEED,
"Resident Agent."

"The Resident Agent to F. A. Carrington, Esq., Chief Surveyor.
"New Plymouth, March 31st, 1843.
"Sir :—As the quantity of land now surveyed and ready for selection in this settlement greatly exceeds the present demand, and will probably prove sufficient to meet any sales which may be made for a considerable time, I am instructed by the Principal Agent of the New Zealand Company to give you notice in pursuance of the terms of your engagement, that your employment as Chief Surveyor of the Company in this settlement will cease on 31st March, 1844.— I have the honor to be,
"JOHN TYLSON WICKSTEED."

At this date Nairn's Mountain Road was finished. In April the Waiwakaiho Bridge was finished and tested.

On May 29th, the barque Thomas Sparks, Captain Sparks, arrived from London, via Nelson, bringing Messrs. John and Charles Hursthouse, John Smith, their families, and other passengers. Her passage occupied six months, but a considerable portion of that time was spent at the Cape of Good Hope, whither she put in for repairs. The passengers by this ship introduced the Cape Acacia to the settlement, which proved useful as a shelter to gardens in exposed situations.

In June laborers' wages were reduced by the Company to eight shillings per week. There was a considerable importation of sheep and cattle, and twenty pairs of oxen were at work. The Waiwakaiho Bridge partially broke down through the failure of a portion of the ironwork.

On 17th June, a fatal collision with the natives, headed by Rauparaha and Rangihaeata, took place at the Wairau river in the Nelson district. In this affray twenty-two Europeans were killed, and five wounded. Among the killed were: Captain Arthur Wakefield, R.N., uncle to Colonel Wakefield; H. A. Thompson, Esq., Police Magistrate of Nelson; G. Richardson, Esq., Crown Prosecutor; and Captain Howard, late of the 12th regiment. The affray arose out of an attempt to arrest the two chiefs on a warrant for arson. In consequence of this affair the Acting Governor issued the following Proclamation :—

"By his Excellency Willoughby Shortland, Esquire, the officer administering the Government of the Colony of New Zealand and its Dependencies and Vice-Admiral of the same, &c.

"Whereas it is essential to the well being of the Colony that confidence and good feeling should continue to exist between the two races of its inhabitants, and that the owners of the soil should have no cause to doubt the good faith of Her Majesty's solemn assurance that their territorial rights would be recognised and respected. Now therefore I, the officer administering the Government, do hereby publicly warn all persons claiming land in this Colony in all cases where the land is disputed or denied by the original native owners, from exercising acts of ownership thereon, or otherwise prejudicing the question of title to the same, until the question of ownership shall be heard and determined by one of Her Majesty's Commissioners appointed to investigate claims to land in New Zealand.

"Given under my hand and issued under the public seal of the Colony of New Zealand at Government House, Auckland, this twelfth day of July, in the year of our Lord, one thousand eight hundred and forty-three,

"WILLOUGHBY SHORTLAND,
"The Officer Administering the Government."

The following reports of the Resident Agent give interesting details of the affairs of the settlement at this period :—

"Mr. Wicksteed to Colonel Wakefield.
"New Plymouth, July 31st, 1843.

"Sir :—During this month the settlers have been annoyed by constant rumors of a hostile visit from some Waikato chiefs. Those who have announced this intention profess friendly feelings towards the Europeans, and I am convinced that if suffered quietly to occupy certain lands on the Waitara there would be amicable intercourse between the two races. It is, however, so desirable to prevent an irruption of the Northern tribes—whose chief has sold all his claims in this part of New Zealand to the Company—that, while I concurred with Captain King, the chief police magistrate, in declaring that the Europeans would not interfere in a native quarrel, I have nevertheless, in common with almost all the principal settlers, shown a marked sympathy towards our own natives, and aided them in constructing a new pa; at the same time we have let the Waikatos clearly understand, that to bring war into this settlement would almost inevitably produce a collision with the white population, who had taken precautions to defend themselves. In fact, the magistrates have sworn in about 250 special constables, most of whom have arms of some description, and some of them being old soldiers or Preventive Service men, know how to use them. The guns and ammunition belonging to the Company I have placed in Captain King's hands for the public service.

"These precautionary measures have had the double effect of making the settlers easy, and of postponing, at least for a while, the visit of the Waikatos, who dread the hostility of the whites. In fact the principal object of their movement would be to obtain for themselves the advantages of the European connection which are enjoyed by the resident Maoris, almost all of whom have till very lately been slaves to the Waikatos. Their former slaves have now a much better supply of blankets, tobacco, and double-barrelled guns, than they have or can hope to procure, except from intercourse with the European settlers.

"I have had some trouble with Maoris, not Waikatos, at the Waitara. A number of men belonging to Kapiti appeared lately among the Waitara people, and in conjunction with a chief, who lives some miles up the river, stopped a party of surveying men who were cutting a line preparatory to making a 'road. They were not armed and used no violence, but sat down in the road to the number of about 188, including men women and children, and quietly declared that they would not allow the white men to occupy any land at the Waitara. When the assistant surveyor and some of the white settlers attempted to reason with them they said 'You are all Wicksteed's slaves, and we will not listen to you.' As soon as I heard of this occurrence I withdrew all the Company's men from the Waitara, wishing at present to avoid collision with the natives; and the more especially as the Government has prohibited us from taking effectual measures, directing us to apply for aid in all similar circumstances to the Chief Police Magistrate, who is utterly powerless. I do not think that the settlers will be molested, and stopping the road is of little consequence.

"I have authorised Mr. Wellington Carrington to remain at the Waitara to take care of the Company's property there, and have requested him to afford every assistance to the settlers which his knowledge of the Maori language, and considerable influence with the natives, may enable him to give.

"Although the circumstances above mentioned indicate a disturbed state of things, I am happy to inform you that in reality they seem to make but little impression on the settlers, who enjoy the advantage for the most part of living near to one another, and of a good understanding with nearly all the natives. They do, however, complain, and justly so, of the inability of the Government representative to afford that protection which they claim as British subjects. The Chief Police Magistrate has not a single gun, sword, or weapon of defence; and his position in a time of peril is pitiable.—I have the honor to be, &c.

"JOHN TYLSON WICKSTEED."

On August 27th F. A. Carrington, Esq., late Chief Surveyor, with his family, left the settlement in the Deborah, bound to Wellington. To prevent all the silver from going out of the settlement, Mr. Richard Brown took £100 worth for the Resident Agent's draft on Colonel Wakefield.

The Resident Agent to Colonel Wakefield.
"New Plymouth, August 31st, 1843.
"Sir :—By the abolition of the office of Chief Surveyor a saving of upwards of £400 per annum will be effected. Mr. Nairn, also, who acted as superintendent of the workmen on the roads, at a salary of £3 per week, has been discharged. I was enabled to effect this reduction by the success of an experiment which has relieved the Company of the greatest part of the cost of employing the laboring immigrants. Finding that I could not get rid of them, even by sending them twenty-two miles inland, where they had little or no shelter, but that the men returned at the end of the week, many sick, and all of them miserable and discontented, I offered to the landowners to pay 6s. a week to the married men, and 2s. to the unmarried, provided they would pay the amount wanting to make up the Company's wages of 16s. and 8s. per week. This proposal was acceded to, and about 50 laborers are now employed in agriculture, within a reasonable distance of their homes, having the opportunity of using their overtime in cultivating their own gardens.

"As this is a dull season of the year for mechanics, many have applied to me for the same privileges as the laborers have obtained; but I adhere to the rule of paying and employing those only who would be destitute without such aid, excluding all who have had the opportunity of saving money when wages were higher. The refusal has subjected me to the fiercest storm of menaces and abuse I have as yet had to encounter in New Plymouth.

"Such an impulse has been given to the process of preparing land for cultivation by the above mentioned measure, that I fully anticipate a natural, instead of a forced increase in the demand for labor, arising from the necessity of saving the larger crops which must be produced. This is the fairest prospect I can discern of a complete relief from the 'Company's laborers.'

"The proclamation recently issued by the acting Governor, prohibiting the exercise by the settlers of any act of ownership on land

claimed by the natives, is used as a not unreasonable excuse for non
payment of instalments due on land purchases, and acts as a bar to
future sales. The Maoris, stimulated by this document from head-
quarters, have given Capt. King, Chief Police Magistrate, notice to
quit, and threatened to burn down the house of Mr. Creed, Wesleyan
missionary, unless he yields peaceable possession of the same to the
native claimant. I have no fear that these threats will be put in
execution, but they create annoyance and uneasiness. In my opinion,
the decision of Mr. Spain, whose name has become a bye-word, would
only be respected where favorable to the natives.
"All apprehension of a hostile visit from the Waikatos has
disappeared.
"Seven vessels have, within the last few days, arrived and been
discharged in the roadstead.—I have the honor to be,
"JOHN TYLSON WICKSTEED."

September 30th. The settlement is reported to be in a flourishing
condition. Capt. Davy had entered into contracts for the erection of
a malt house and brewery. A flour mill was in course of erection.
A party of natives had cut away a large quantity of timber from a
section on the banks of the Waiwakaiho, the property of Captain
Bulkeley, for whom Capt. King was agent. Capt. King endeavored
to stop the devastation, but the natives treated him with ridicule and
defiance.

The Bishop of New Zealand had sent a message announcing the
appointment of Mr. Bolland, nephew of the late Judge, to be the
clergyman of the Episcopalian church in New Plymouth. To defray
the cost of his maintenance and the erection of a church at New
Plymouth, the Bishop proposed that the settlers should make
contributions "in kind," and in labor, the value of which he would
furnish in money. Mr. Bolland was to be expected at the close of
the next month, and it was proposed to let him have the residence of
the late Chief Surveyor. On the 26th October the ship William
Stoveld arrived from London, via Nelson. She brought about forty
tons of merchandise, chiefly for Capt. Davy. Mr. Law, a passenger
by the Phœbe, who had purchased and commenced to cultivate a
suburban section on the east side of the Waiwakaiho, was visited by
some Maoris, one of whom menaced him with a tomahawk, but Mr.
Law, a strong and resolute man, used him so roughly that he was
glad to fly, and the visit had not been repeated. The Waiwakaiho
bridge had been repaired.

On the 23rd December the barque Himalaya arrived, bringing us
settlers Capt. Creagh, lady and five children ; two sons of Capt. Davy ;
Messrs. Thatcher, Watt, Low, Crooke, and several steerage passengers.
She left Plymouth on the 7th September, and touched at St. Jago and
St. Paul's.

GOVERNOR FITZROY.

In December, 1843, Captain Robert Fitzroy, R.N., arrived at

Auckland, in H.M.S. North Star, to take the reins of government, in the room of the late Governor Hobson. Captain Fitzroy was probably selected for the post on account of his having given evidence concerning New Zealand before a Committee of the House of Commons in 1838; his knowledge of the country having been obtained while employed on a hydrographic survey of its coasts in H.M.S. Beagle. His ridiculous landing in Auckland is thus described by Dr. Thompson:—"A gentleman connected with the Native Department carried a pole surmounted with a crown of flax (Phormium), from which waved the New Zealand flag, and Captain Fitzroy, excited by the occasion, cried aloud when stepping on shore, 'I am come to do you all the good I can.' The crowd of fifty persons replied to this noble sentiment with a cheer, and the commanding officer of the company of soldiers in attendance shouted 'quick march,' immediately the two drummer boys and the fifer of the guard of honor struck up 'The King of the Cannibal Islands,' to which appropriate air his Excellency marched to Government House. Next day a curious scene occurred at the levee. The Colonial Office had given Captain Fitzroy files of a New Zealand paper, famous for abusing Acting Governor Shortland, to read during the voyage, and when the editor of that paper was presented at Government House, the Governor informed him that he highly approved of the principles of the 'Southern Cross.' This speech, which was equivalent to announcing in the Government Gazette that the Colonial Secretary was an arrogant fool, caused Mr. Shortland to resign his office, and Dr. Sinclair, a surgeon of the Royal Navy, who had acccompanied Captain Fitzroy to explore the natural history of the country, was appointed Colonial Secretary in his stead." Governor Fitzroy quickly proved to be a mere tool in the hands of Mr. Protector Clarke and the missionaries. The result of his policy was the almost complete ruin of Taranaki, the crippling of the other settlements of the Company, a disastrous war in the North, and the serious financial embarrassment of the Colony. After performing an incalculable amount of mischief, he was superseded in the government by Governor Grey, in November, 1845.

Captain, afterwards Admiral Robert Fitzroy, Superintendent of the Meteorological Department of the Board of Trade, was born in 1805. He entered the Navy at the age of 14, was made lieutenant in 1824, served on the Mediterranean and South American stations, and at the close of 1828 was appointed to take part as commander of the Beagle in the Government expedition for the survey of the coasts of South America. In 1831 he was charged with the conduct of a second scientific expedition to South America, in command of the Beagle. Mr. Darwin accompanied the expedition as naturalist. The valuable scientific results of this voyage, which occupied five years, were published in Darwin's well known 'Journal of a Voyage round the World,' and in a separate narrative by Admiral Fitzroy. In 1841 Admiral Fitzroy entered Parliament as member for Durham, and two years later he was appointed Governor of New Zealand, a post which he held till 1846. In the subsequent portion of his life he was greatly distinguished for his patient researches in meteorology, and his admirable practical application of the new science to navigation. As Superintendent of the Meteorological Department of the Board of Trade he rendered important services by the establishment of his system of storm warnings and forecasts communicated to the principal ports of Great Britain; which, though of so recent a date, no doubt contributed to the acknowledged decrease in the rate of deaths of British sailors. His latest publication was the 'Weather Book,' containing the explanation of his method of forecasts and the chief results of his studies and observations. He was a fellow of the Royal Society, and of the Royal Geographical Society, and a correspondent of the French Academy of Sciences. At the time of his death he was engaged with Le Verrier and other foreign men of science in establishing a European system of storm signals. Mental overwork and excessive wear and tear of brain and nerves undermined his health and destroyed his powers, and, in a state of extreme depression or derangement, he committed suicide by cutting his throat, at his residence, Upper Norwood, 30th April, 1865.

CHAPTER XIV.

EVENTS OF 1844.

AT the commencement of the year there was a great scarcity of food in the settlement; musty biscuits which had lain a long time in store were in request, and to sustain life some of the poorer settlers had little else but small potatoes. The reason assigned by Mr. Wicksteed for this state of affairs was that the coasting traders refused to sell flour where they could not dispose of draperies, and that the New Plymouth merchants imported their drapery goods direct from England.

Mr. Wicksteed to Colonel Wakefield.
"New Plymouth, Jan. 30th, 1844.

"Sir:—The settlers have been engaged in saving the grain crops, planting potatoes, and breaking up ground for autumn sowing. I have much pleasure in stating that notwithstanding some wheat has been damaged by smut, and barley by caterpillars, the result of the harvest is very satisfactory. Where due precaution has been taken in preparing both the seed and the soil, the yield has been very large; in one instance from 55 to 60 bushels per acre. From the exertions now in progress for next year's crops, we may safely anticipate that upwards of 100 tons of wheaten flour will be available for home consumption, which, when added to the considerable quantities of barley bread used by the Devonshire and Cornish laborers, and the profusion of vegetables, will render the settlement almost independent of a foreign supply of flour.

"The natives have continued to cut down the bush and timber on Mr. Cooke's section, and have extended their devastation to Mr. Marshall's, adjoining Mr. Cooke's. I have made repeated attempts to stop their progress, but they can safely disregard the warnings and menaces of those who are prevented by the Government from acting in self-defence. The settlers are anxiously awaiting the Governor's reply to the address and memorial recording their grievances and praying for redress, which Messrs. Cooke and Thatcher have taken overland to Auckland for presentation to his Excellency. Mr. Taylor, the Church Missionary at Wanganui, who has recently visited New Plymouth, used his utmost endeavors to save Mr. Cooke's property from destruction. Mr. Whiteley, also Chairman of the Wesleyan Missionaries, has written an earnest letter to deter them from farther depredations, but apparently without effect. It is, indeed, a general opinion, confirmed by my own observation, that the missionary influence with the natives is rapidly on the decline. These proceedings of the natives have somewhat alarmed the settlers by the Himalaya, whom I have difficulty in persuading that an alteration for the better is at hand. Captain Creagh, who was disposed to act with spirit as a farmer, has been turned off the land he selected ; but I hope yet to fix him in a spot where he is less likely to be molested. I have given notice that after the 9th of February the Company's allowance to agricultural laborers will be reduced from 6s. to 3s. per week ; an anonncement which has provoked a threat of personal violence against myself, but I am not deterred by such conduct from carrying into effect a retrenchment which can now be fairly made.— I am, etc.,

"J. T. WICKSTEED."

Mr. Wicksteed to Colonel Wakefield.
"New Plymouth, March 2nd, 1844.

" Sir :—The reduction of the Company's allowance to laborers from 6s. to 3s. per week has been submitted to with less opposition than I anticipated ; and the entire abolition of this payment will soon be effected. I am confident that under the peculiar advantages of the settlement, the allowance has been highly advantageous to the Company, as well as to all classes of settlers. There appears to be every disposition on the part of the farmers and land owners to extend their agricultural operations to the utmost of their ability, the result of this year's harvest having been on the whole very satisfactory. In various directions clearing is going on, and the holders of superior grain obtain high prices for their seed. I am informed that Captain Davy, who is employing more capital than any other settler, will retain nearly all his crop of wheat for his own autumn sowing. Captain Creagh is clearing a section of land between the town and the Sugarloaves, and Mr. Thatcher, also a passenger by the Himalaya, is similarly employed. No molestation from natives is apprehended in the district where these gentlemen have commenced farming, but at Te Hua, in the neighborhood of Mr. Cooke's section, the Maoris are still clearing and burning. Two flour mills are at work on the Huatoki, within five minutes walk of Mount Eliot. In one of them Italian stones are used ; in the other, stones cut out of the trachytic rocks on the sea beach. The Star of China, from Sydney, and the Deborah, from Launceston, have supplied the settlement with about fifty tons of flour, which is now selling at the moderate price of £17 per ton. I bought five tons on the Company's account at £15, to prevent an advance of price by combination among the very few holders during the ensuing winter. With the assistance of the Deborah, the heavy buoy which was laid down two years ago by the Timandra, has been brought ashore for examination, and replaced by the buoy last sent from England. The first buoy appears to be perfectly sound, but it was completely incrusted by mussels and other shell-fish, and requires fresh painting. It is my intention to use it for a second set of moorings, to be laid down as near the shore as practicable, for the accommodation of small vessels under 250 tons burden. When this is accomplished I think there can be no reasonable demand for farther outlay to improve the roadstead. The moorings and the boats will be sufficient for the purposes of this

agricultural settlement for a long period of time. No accident worth mentioning has occurred in the roadstead to vessels, boats or human beings since May, 1842, when the term of my agency commenced.—
I have the honor to be,

"J. T. WICKSTEED."

Mr. Wicksteed to Colonel Wakefield.
"New Plymouth, March 22nd, 1844.
"Sir:—I have the pleasure to report the safe arrival of the barque Theresa from London direct. She left the Channel on the 29th November, and reached New Plymouth on the 19th instant. She brings eighteen passengers for this settlement, including some farmers who have bought land in England. The day of the Theresa's arrival and the two following were extremely fine; but owing to bad arrangement of the cargo, the sickness of the Captain and the inefficiency of the crew, not more than twenty tons have been discharged, and we have with difficulty obtained two boat-loads per day, instead of eight. This morning the wind is from the N.W., and the work of discharging the vessel has been suspended, which makes me the more regret that advantage was not taken of the calm weather. Stricter attention to the loading of the vessels in England would be very desirable on all accounts.

"One death occurred in the Theresa, that of a steerage passenger for Wellington, John Bray, who was drowned at sea on the 23rd of February.—I have the honor to be,

"J. T. WICKSTEED."

Poor John Bray had been emptying the brine out of a pork tub through the lee gangway, after which he took a broom and attempted to sweep the steps outside the bulwarks, on which some of the salt had lodged. In a lurch of the ship he lost his balance, fell across a brace and from thence into the sea. The ship was immediately brought to, and a boat was lowered, but the unfortunate man was lost.

Mr. Wicksteed to Colonel Wakefield.
"New Plymouth, April 1st, 1844.
"The arrival of the barque Theresa was reported in my despatch forwarded by the overland mail. I there mentioned that the work of unloading the vessel had been suspended by the weather; and I now regret to add that during an equinoctial gale, the buoy parted from the moorings, the 'bridle,' or chain, which connects the buoy to the chains attached to the anchors, having been broken. The buoy has been preserved, and I hope the disaster may be repaired without much expense or loss of time. In the meanwhile I have the satisfaction to state that the Theresa rode out the gale in perfect safety; also that after an interval of two days southerly weather, she also endured another gale at a different anchorage. At the commencement of the first gale I directed Mr. Watson, the beach master, to board the Theresa with a good boat's crew, which was

afterwards reinforced by another party of seven, every able-bodied seaman on board the Theresa having refused to work, and only resumed duty when the vessel having discharged her cargo started for Nelson.

" The newly arrived settlers are much pleased with the country, and others who had not purchased land in other settlements, remain or intend to return to New Plymouth.

" There is now a small surveying corps engaged in opening up a very splendid district, about three miles and a half east of the Devon Road, to which a line has been cut through a nearly level country between the rivers Mangoraka and Waiongona. The road made by the natives behind Mount Egmont comes into this district, which is the same you admired so much on your last visit to New Plymouth. In the course of a few days, notice of selection will be issued, when the late purchasers will have the option of choosing their sections out of a large extent of excellent land at a moderate distance from the town, and approachable by good roads.—I have the honor to be,

"J. T. WICKSTEED."

On the 27th May, the Bella Marina, 600 tons, Captain Ashbridge, arrived from London *via* Hobart Town. She brought Messrs. F. U. Gledhill and Bateman as passengers, and the latter, after landing his goods and appointing an agent, departed again to Tasmania for the purpose of purchasing live stock.

[EXTRACT.]
Mr. Spain to Colonel Wakefield.
" Land Claims Office,
" Wellington, April 16th, 1844.

" Sir :—I have the honor to inform you that it is my intention to leave this place on Thursday next for Manawatu, Wanganui, and Taranaki in order to settle the native claims in those districts ; and I have to request the attendance of yourself to meet the Protector of Aborigines in order to carry out the arrangement you have made with his Excellency the Governor for that purpose.—I remain, &c.
" WILLIAM SPAIN,
" Commissioner."

Mr. Spain and Colonel Wakefield reached Taranaki overland. The Colonel, in a dispatch to the Secretary of the Company thus writes :—

"The journey from Wanganui occupied us ten days in consequence of some bad weather, and the swollen state of the streams. The Waimate plain, which I have before described, was covered with a thick coat of fine grass. The Commissioner and his party expressed their admiration of its qualities as the finest field for flocks and herds they had seen in New Zealand.

" The Commissioners Court opened at New Plymouth on the 31st of

May, when a large assemblage of natives took place. Richard Barrett's evidence was interpreted, word for word, to about 300 of them. After several days occupied in examining witnessess, whom I called in favour of the Company's claim, and one against it, who completely broke down, Mr. Clarke declined to call any more evidence. On the 8th June, Mr. Spain pronounced judgment as follows :—

Mr. Commissioner Spain's Award.

" I, William Spain, Her Majesty's Commissioner for investigating and determining titles and claims to land in New Zealand, do hereby award, that upon the payment by the New Zealand Company of two hundred pounds sterling to His Excellency the Governor of New Zealand, to be applied for the benefit of the resident natives of New Plymouth or Taranaki in the Northern Division of New Zealand in any way His Excellency may think necessary to promote their interests, the Directors of the New Zealand Company of London, and their successors are entitled to a Crown Grant of a block of sixty thousand (60,000) acres of land, situate, lying, and being in the district or settlement of New Plymouth or Taranaki in the Northern Division of New Zealand : Which said block of land commences on the north side of the Sugarloaf Islands, and extends in a northerly direction to a place called Taniwha, and which said block of land is more particularly set forth upon the accompanying plan, saving and excepting as follows :—All the pas, burying places, and grounds actually in cultivation by the natives, situate within any part of the before described block of land hereby awarded to the New Zealand Company as aforesaid, the lands of the pas to be the grounds fenced in around their native houses, including the cultivation or occupation around the adjoining houses, without the fence, and cultivations on those tracts of country which are now used by the Aboriginal Natives of New Zealand since the establishment of the Colony. And also excepting all the native reserves equal to one-tenth of the sixty thousand acres hereby awarded to the said Company, part of which said native reserves have already been chosen and are marked yellow upon the said district hereinbefore referred to, and the remainder of the reserves are to be chosen according to the rate of one choice in ten, as fully explained to the Resident Agent of the New Zealand Company in my letter to him under date, the 13th June, 1845, forming enclosure No. 7 of this report : And also excepting all that piece of land containing one hundred acres reserved by the natives at the time of sale to the New Zealand Company, for the Wesleyan Mission Station, which said piece of land is delineated and set forth upon the said plan of the district and also upon the plan herewith enclosed, No. 10 : And also excepting all that piece of land containing eighty acres, and all that piece of land containing one hundred acres, being sections 23 and 37, which have been reserved for Richard Barrett, his wife and children, which said two pieces of land are delineated and set forth upon the said plan of the district, and also upon the plan herewith enclosed, No. 11 : And also excepting any portions of land within any part of the block of land hereinbefore described, and hereby awarded to the said Company, to which private claimants have already or may hereafter prove before the Commissioner of Land Claims a title prior to the purchase by the New Zealand Company."

This decision of the Commissioner, as might be expected, was satisfactory to the settlers, and the reverse to the Maoris. So threatening was the aspect of the latter, that messengers were sent off to Auckland to report to the Governor the state of affairs. The Governor, immediately on receiving the news, dispatched a competent person (Mr. Maclean), with special instructions, overland to Taranaki, and himself embarked on board H.M.S. Hazard and hastened thither. The Bishop also repaired to the scene of difficulty with the utmost celerity, travelling from Auckland by Kawhia to Taranaki in eight days; while Mr. Whiteley, the Wesleyan Missionary at Kawhia, preceded them. On the 3rd of August a large meeting of English and natives assembled at Mount Eliot to hear the formal decision of the Governor, who informed the assembly that he did not take the same view of the question as Mr. Commissioner Spain, and that he should not confirm the award of that gentleman, however carefully and conscientiously it had been weighed and delivered. On points of law, especially the law of New Zealand considered with reference to national laws in general, authorities might differ, without prejudice to the opinion of either, but it was for him, the Governor, to decide. He would immediately cause farther investigation to be made as to the various claimants to particular portions of land. He would then endeavor to make special arrangements with those claimants, and he would allow, in all their integrity, the claims of those of the Ngatiawa tribe who were not parties to the sale of 1840. As time would be required for these additional enquiries, he would now return to Auckland and the Bay of Islands, where his presence was imperatively wanted, and would again visit Taranaki in about two months to adjust this land question satisfactorily. Meanwhile he recommended and urged upon all parties the exercise of forbearance and conciliatory conduct. After promising the natives that they should not be dispossessed of their lands, and instructing their Protector, Mr. Maclean, how to proceed, the Governor, with the Bishop, embarked on board the Hazard on the 5th of August and proceeded to Auckland. On the 8th of November the Governor again landed at New Plymouth from H.M.S. Hazard. This time he had some difficulty in assembling the natives, but by the 25th they were got together in the town, when he declared the whole of the settlement forfeited, and induced the natives to accept £350 in goods, money, and animals, as a full compensation and completion of payment for a block of land at and around the town, containing about 3,500 acres. The consequences of this insane act were crushing.

After all the excellent speeches at Plymouth, after all the hopes that had been excited, after thousands of pounds had been spent, and hundreds of simple-hearted people had left their homes, traversed the seas, and established themselves in the wilderness, the settlement was diminished to the dimensions of a nobleman's park. What was perhaps the most unjust part of the business was that the £350 paid to buy back the township and a small block of land behind it was taken from the New Zealand Company. By this act was laid the foundation of quarrelling and bloodshed. To it is to be attributed the deaths of Rawiri and Katatore, and also the Taranaki war. For years the settlement pined under this almost overwhelming affliction, and the only wonder is that it was not entirely broken up. As soon as the Governor's decision was made known the exulting Maoris commenced a series of persecutions upon all the settlers who were living outside the lines of the reduced settlement. One by one they sorrowfully came in, abandoning their newly reclaimed fields, which soon reverted to a state of nature, containing here and there a thorn or some other very hardy British plant to prove to another generation that Britons had made an attempt to cultivate that part of the wilderness. If the Governor had felt that the manumitted slaves should receive payment for their share of the land, it was within his power to have ordered payment to be made to them. He, however, did not so act, but chose rather to give back the entire settlement to the natives, and then re-purchase with the funds of the Company the township and its suburbs. To injury the Governor added insult; when the simple-minded Devonshire and Cornish peasants attempted to remonstrate with him and plead the cause of their families, he told them they were all trespassers and deserved transportation. Years after this transaction, when discussing the events of 1844 over the winter's evening fire, the conclusion universally come to by the settlers was that Governor Fitzroy was insane, and the fact of his afterwards dying by his own hand seems to show that that conclusion was not far from the fact. Not only ought the decision of Mr. Commissioner Spain to have been accepted, armed as he was both with Imperial and Colonial jurisdiction in the matter, but there are strong grounds for believing that the Company's claims ought never to have been brought into his Court.

Governor Fitzroy to Colonel Wakefield.
"Wellington, August, 1844.
"Sir:—I take the earliest opportunity of informing you that it is not my intention to comply with the recommendation of Mr. Commissioner Spain regarding the New Zealand Company's purchase of land in Taranaki, and that I shall cause a further investigation to be made as speedily as possible. A large number of natives would be set aside by Mr. Spain, namely those who were absent, or in captivity, at the time their lands were said to be sold, whose claims I am bound to recognise and maintain.—I have the honor to be,"

It is remarkable that the above letter bore no signature.

Mr. Wicksteed to Colonel Wakefield.
"New Plymouth, August 4th, 1844.

"Sir:—It is impossible to get off a nearly completed despatch about the Governor's proceedings. At first he was dreadfully unpopular, having partially set aside Spain's award, maintaining the right of absentees and slaves to compensation, attacking the Company, and positively abusive to me. But in private converse the Bishop and I brought him round, and he is now very civil and full of fair promises. But I fear we shall have to pay altogether £500 of the Company's money. He says that will do, and I really think that it would have been next to impossible to have obtained peace with the natives without some payment. He is to come here by the 1st of October and settle the affair himself. In the meanwhile any small sum which I may pay to get rid of present and pressing difficulty is to go as part of the future payment. I suspect nearly all the land we actually want will have to be paid for even on his own showing.—Yours most truly.

"J. T. W."

[Extract from Report of Mr. Forsaith, 10th July, 1844.]

"On the 17th of May we left Wanganui and Wellington through Waitotara, Otihoe, Manawapou, Waimate, Kaupokonui, Otumatua, Waiaua, Warea and Hauranga to New Plymouth, at which place we arrived on the 29th. The following day Mr. Clarke and myself visited the different settlements as far as Waitara, to request the attendance of the natives at the Commissioners Court. On the 31st the Court opened, and the investigation was continued without any material interruption until the 6th of June. On the 8th the Court again opened, when the Commissioner notified the nature of his decision upon the case, which was an award in favour of the Company of all the land described in the chart which was exhibited, excepting some reserves which were specified, lying between Ngamotu on the South and Te Taniwha on the North.

"When I interpreted Mr. Spain's decision some considerable excitement was at first manifested among the natives, who strongly objected to it; but this ebulition of feeling subsided, and they refrained from all further expressions of discontent, except signifying their intention of appealing to His Excellency. On the 31st the Victoria arrived, and Mr. Spain, accompanied by Colonel Whitmore and Mr. Protector Clarke embarked, and about 4 p.m. the brig again made sail. I, according to my orders received from the brig, resumed my journey Northward, and arrived at Auckland on the 8th instant, having left New Plymouth on the 24th ultimo."

[Extract from Report of Mr. Protector Maclean.]

"Taranaki, August 5th, 1844.

"I have the honor to acquaint you that, in pursuance of your instructions of the 16th July I proceeded on my journey to Taranaki on the 18th, calling at the station of the Rev. J. Whiteley, Wesleyan

Missionary at Kawhia, who accompanied me to New Plymouth, at which place I arrived on the 28th. On the 29th that gentleman went with me to visit the natives at their different residences in the neighborhood of Ngamotu, where we found a considerable degree of excitement and bad feeling existing among them, arising principally from portions of their land having been occupied by the Europeans without the consent of the real owners, who were in captivity at the time the purchase was effected by the New Zealand Company from a small party of natives, whose claims I am given to believe were but to a limited portion of the lands now claimed by the Company. I then took an opportunity of informing them that His Excellency was coming to remain at this settlement for a few days, and that he would hear their causes of complaint. They then assured me that whatever their former resolutions might have been, they would be peaceable and not disturb the settlers till they saw His Excellency and made their case known to him. I am happy to inform you that His Excellency's arrival here, and his late interview with the natives, has produced a most salutary effect in quelling their excited feelings; and I am in hope that an amicable arrangement will be entered into with regard to their lands. When I have had further intercourse with the natives and am more acquainted with the different portions of the land they dispute, I shall be enabled to report to you more fully upon the matters to which my attention has been directed in my instructions."

[Extract of a Letter from Rev. J. Whiteley.]

"August 15th, 1844.

"On receiving your letter of July the 16th, together with one from His Excellency, requesting me to accompany Mr. Maclean to Taranaki, I immediately prepared for the journey, and in a few hours after that gentleman arrived at my house we were on our way. I first, however, despatched a messenger with a letter to the chief Haupokia Te Pakaru, desiring him to follow me as soon as possible, as I believed that his presence and influence in Taranaki would, in the present state of affairs, be most beneficial. We arrived at New Plymouth on the 30th ult., and in passing through the suburbs endeavored to see and converse with all the natives we could meet. The next day, accompanied by the Rev. Mr. Turton, we visited the settlements, and had a long conversation with the natives of Mangoraka, who are stated to have been the most dissatisfied and troublesome. On Thursday I was glad to hear that Haupokia had arrived at Waitara, and I arranged to spend the next day in private and friendly conversation with the different parties of natives at their respective settlements. At dawn of day, however, the Governor's ship appeared in sight, and leaving Mr. Maclean to arrange with the resident natives, I rode off with Mr. Turton to bring up Haupokia from Waitara, and the other natives from different localities. Some objected to go at all to meet His Excellency; and others were for putting it off until after the Sabbath on account of food. On arriving at Waitara, however, and requesting Haupokiu to attend at once, he instantly complied, and his example influenced all the rest, so that on Saturday morning we had the satisfaction of seeing all the natives present before His Excellency."

[TRANSLATION.]

Wiremu Kingi Whiti and other Ngatiawa Chiefs to Governor Fitzroy.

": Taranaki, June 8th, 1844.

" Friend Governor :—Salutations ! Great is our love* to you ; this is our speech to you. Listen to us respecting this land, respecting Waitara. Our hearts are dark by reason of Mr. Spain's words. Indeed the Europeans are wrong in striving for this land which was never sold by its owners, the men of Ngatiawa.

" Now, when the Ngatiawa tribe went to Kapiti they left some men behind on our lands, who were surprised by the Waikatos, and some of them led away captive, who having arrived at Waikato were afterwards returned by the Waikatos to Waitara to dwell there. Others came back from Kapiti. We love the land of our ancestors ; we did not receive any of the goods of Colonel Wakefield ; it was wrong to buy the land which belonged to other men. There are many chiefs to whom this land belongs who are now at Waikanae and Arapaoa. It was love for the land of our forefathers that brought us back to those lands. Friend Governor our thoughts are that those lands were never settled by the Waikatos ; and when we embraced Christianity, we learnt the rules of the Gospel and to dwell in peace.

" This also is the determination of our people ; Waitara shall not be given up ; the men to whom it belongs will hold it for themselves. There was not a single man of the Ngatiawa tribe who received the payment of Colonel Wakefield. These are the only men who took the payment—the men of Ngamotu and Puketapu, and they had no right in Waitara. The Ngatiawa are constantly returning to their land, on account of their attachment to the land of their birth—the land which we have cultivated and which our ancestors marked out and delivered to us.

" Friend Governor, do you not love your land—England—the land of your fathers, as we also love our land at Waitara ? Friend, let your thoughts be good towards us. We desire not to strive with the Europeans, but, at the same time, we do not wish to have our land settled by them ; rather let them be returned to the places which have been paid for by them, lest a root of quarrel remain between us and the Europeans. Friend Governor, be kind to the natives. The places which have been justly purchased by the Europeans, let them have them, that your judgment may be just.

" This is not from us only, but from all the Ngatiawa, though the greater part are absent. From Hakopa, Tipene, Te Wataraui,

Tutarahaina, Paturoi, Te Wareraka, Tamete Tirauran, Hirini Mangonui.
"By us, by all the men at Waikanae and Warekauri.
"Written by me, Wiremu Kingi Whiti."

The writer of the above letter signed the deed known as the Queen Charlotte's Sound Deed, which purported to convey a large territory to the New Zealand Company. He states that not a single man of Ngatiawa received payment for the land from Colonel Wakefield, yet he acknowledges that Ngamotu and Puketapu received payment. Now, Ngamotu and Puketapu are but hapus or families of the iwi or tribe of Ngatiawa.

[Extract from Mr. Forsaith's Report to Governor Fitzroy.]

"Taranaki, 22nd October, 1844.

"Again the Taranaki captives, released by the Waikatos from the purest and best of motives, have assumed a position of importance which can hardly be tolerated by these powerful chiefs, their former masters; and, in some instances, the emancipists have so far forgotten their obligation and the respect due to their former conquerers, as to ridicule the poverty and destitution of their present circumstances. I mention these matters because they afford a key to the interpretation of the sentiments of the Kawhia and Ngatimaniapoto Chiefs, which were formally conveyed to me on the eve of my departure, and which appear to me to involve principles bearing an important relation to the Taranaki land question, the successful settlement of which is so great a desideratum, and which your Excellency is now endeavoring to effect. I shall give these sentiments as nearly as possible in the same words in which they were delivered to me by the Chiefs, without comment:—' You are going to Taranaki; listen to our parting words. That land is ours. We claim it by right of conquest, and some part of it by possession. We have power to enforce our claim if we choose, but our inclination is for peace, not war. The Governor who is dead professed to buy the interests of the Waikatos in the lands of Taranaki, and paid Te Wherowhero for them. Te Wherowhero had a perfect right to sell his own or his tribe's interest, but not ours. He was not the principal man in subjugating Taranaki, many were before him; we do not recognise his sale. We might insist on our right to a payment equal to that of Te Wherowhero, but we are not so very anxious about that, as we want Europeans. You have told us that the Governor will do all in his power to send them to us; now, we will wait a reasonable time; if they come, well; if not, we must go to them. We hold the late Governor's permission to settle on any of the lands at Taranaki, provided we do not go south of Urenui. We sent the present occupants of Taranaki home to the land of their fathers, and we did so from the influence of Christian principles, but we did not send them back to assume the airs of superiority they have done, or to molest the Europeans. They have Europeans, but do not know how to treat them, while we who would treat them well, cannot get them. We are therefore determined in the event of no Europeans coming to us, to go back and resume our rights. We shall not go in hostile mood, though we shall go prepared to resist opposition. If kindly received and treated with respect by our former captives, we shall simply arrange for our joint occupation of the land. But on the contrary, if opposed we shall take the matter into our own hands, and settle the disputes with the Europeans in our own way. Go and tell the Ngatiawa that the Waikato Chiefs remind them that the land is theirs, and advise them to settle their dispute with the Europeans, or the Waikatos will settle it for them."

Mr. Wicksteed to Colonel Wakefield.

"New Plymouth, August 31st, 1844.

"Sir:—In separate despatches I have noticed the principal events of the month, namely, the arrival of the Governor at New Plymouth, with an account of his proceedings, and the arrival of the Raymond on the 29th inst., with the intelligence of the suspension of the Company's operations. It only remains for me to state that your instructions relative to the discharge of persons in the Company's employment at New Plymouth have this day been carried into effect. Mr. Carrington and Mr. Rogan, with the surveying men, Mr. Watson, beachmaster, Mr. Wellington Carrington, stationed at the Waitara, with the boatmen and a few persons employed upon the roads, have been discharged. Mr. Chilman, whose services as clerk to the Resident Agent and clerk of the Land Office are indispensable, is the only officer retained besides myself. Mr. Octavius Carrington continues to reside at the Surveyor's house, taking care of the maps, instruments and other property of the Company there. He has promised to afford, without pay, the usual assistance in explaining boundaries, showing plans, and so forth, in the hope, which I have partially encouraged, of being again employed in the Company's service. For the present he and Mr. Rogan waive the claim they have for a year's notice prior to dismissal. I have made a temporary arrangement with Mr. Watson for the use of the boats. He is to have them without rent for six months, on condition of keeping them in thorough repair, and at all times affording at moderate prices the accommodation to settlers and vessels visiting New Plymouth hitherto afforded gratuitously by the Company. At the end of the six months, when the success or failure of the experiment may be ascertained, a new arrangement may be entered into, or the same terms continued. The Company will not, under any circumstances, be again saddled with the cost of a boat establishment.

"These necessary changes have been effected quietly, without anger or remonstrance from any of the parties interested, though it will be easily believed that they have spread gloom over the settlement. I trust, however, that the prospect of an abundant harvest, of a successful whale fishery, and the development generally of the resources of the country, will soon restore the spirits of the settlers.

8

It is certain that they are very much better able to endure the withdrawal of the Company's expenditure now than last year. Almost every person in the district has a comfortable house and garden. All might have them; and it is calculated that at least £4,500 which last year went out of Taranaki for flour alone, will this year be retained. This, and other facts of an encouraging nature, it is my constant habit to present to the settlers. Twenty tons of oil, and more than a ton of whalebone from R. Barrett's whaling establishment, have been shipped in the Urgent for Sydney. The business of salting pork for exportation has been commenced, and will probably be carried out to some extent. The Taranaki pork is of the very best quality. It is now retailed at 3d. per pound. The weather has been remarkably fine and favorable to the growing crops.—I have the honor to be, etc.,

"J. T. WICKSTEED."

Mr. Wicksteed to Colonel Wakefield.
"New Plymouth, November 9th, 1844.
"Sir:—His Excellency arrived yesterday evening in the Hazard, which vessel immediately sailed for Kapiti, to return next week and convey the Governor to Auckland. Immediately after landing, and before I received your despatch, which unaccountably was not delivered to me till the middle of the day by Mr. Secretary Hamilton to whom you had entrusted it, His Excellency, with Captain King and Mr. Forsaith, called upon me to enquire what amount of money I could put into his hands for the purpose of treating with the natives, at the same time expressing his own readiness to advance an equal sum. I replied that until the question of title was so settled as to enable one to collect debts and to effect sales, I was not prepared to expend any more of the Company's funds in payment of the natives, but that if His Excellency could himself make such a settlement I would pay the amount he advanced, provided it did not much exceed the sum he formerly named, £350 to £500. The Governor thought that on these terms he should probably succeed in his negotiations with the natives, so far as the actual settlers are interested; but he would not undertake to secure the property of the absentee owners. This is the present state of the question; of its progress, if any is really made, you will be advised by the earliest opportunity. In the meanwhile, you may rely upon my not entering into any engagement by which the interests of the absentees will be sacrificed, or the Company deprived of the advantages of Mr. Spain's award, in the event of any proceedings being taken against the Company in England, on the plea that the land sold was not fairly purchased in the first instance from the natives. I think that a great point will be gained if the actual settlers are secured from molestation by the Maoris; and that thereby the whole question will be virtually set at rest. At all events nothing more will be paid except in exchange for a substantial benefit. I hope you will think that so far I have acted in compliance with the spirit of your despatch,

though I had not seen it at the time the Governor called upon me. His Excellency this morning had a long interview with the laboring people, who complain of low wages and want of employment during the few weeks preceeding the harvest; evils, as I took care to assure the Governor, arising solely from the delay in settling the land question, which has prevented several capitalists from commencing agricultural operations. His Excellency promised to send a vessel in the course of next month to take about twelve miners with their families to Auckland, whence they might proceed to the Barrier Island, and obtain work in the copper mines. The other laborers and artisans he recommended to remain at New Plymouth, and promised them present employment in some public work at 2s. per day for five days in the week. He complained of the number of men he had on his hands at Nelson, Wellington and this place, in consequence of the Company's 'failure;' especially when the low condition of the treasury compelled him to reduce Government salaries one half. His Excellency might have said, as regards New Plymouth at least, that want of money forced him to suspend payment of their entire salaries, as even the constables wages are many weeks in arrear. How the Governor will find the means of dealing with the natives and paying the laborers it is not easy to comprehend. He has already offered his debentures to almost every gentleman in the place at ten per cent. discount, but nobody will take them. It is not believed that any net revenue will be derived from the tax of one per cent. on property and income, and therefore that the security for the redemption of the debentures does not exist. His Excellency intends to visit the Waitara on Monday, and to talk to the natives on Tuesday.—I have the honor to be,

"J. T. WICKSTEED."

[EXTRACT.]

Colonel Wakefield to Mr. Wicksteed.

"Wellington, November 30th, 1844.

"Sir:—The proceedings of the Commissioner's Court in June last made you fully acquainted with the purchase of the land by the Company in February, 1840. In the month of October of the following year Governor Hobson set at rest, as he thought, the right of preemption vested in the Crown, and the conflicting interests between the Company and other purchasers, by the publication in the 'Government Gazette' dated October the 13th, 1841, of a letter to me, as the Agent of the Company, enclosing a schedule in which the block of land at New Plymouth is especially included. The decision of the Commissioner that the whole block claimed by the Company was fairly and fully purchased from the natives by proving our fulfilment of the conditions subject to which Governor Hobson engaged on behalf of the Crown to issue a grant of such land, places us in a position to call upon the local Government to fulfil its pledge. The completion of the scheme of the Settlement, and the engagement of the Company with the public as well as in the interests of the actual settlers, are dependent on the fulfilment of Governor Hobson's engagement. And as a measure calculated to quiet the minds of the natives, agitated as they have been by the colonisation of their country, the delays of the Court of Claims, and the ever changing measures of the present Governor, none could be more effective and just. The Company's purchase was made from all the natives resident in the block, the remnant of a tribe of two thousand souls, which removed ten years ago to Cook Strait in fear of their northern neighbors.

"I have lately had authentic accounts of a meeting in Queen Charlotte's Sound of six hundred of these emigrants, who determined upon returning to the New Plymouth block of land, upon the ground that they have more right to it than the returned slaves from the Waikato, whose claims the Governor has allowed. The district south of the Sugarloaf Islands which the Company also purchased, but the claim to which was not brought by me before the Commissioner, in consequence of its having become thickly inhabited by its former owners, who have returned to it since the European settlement was established between it and their enemies, will not alone be re-inhabited. From the Sugarloaf Islands to the Waitara your settlement will be overrun with its former occupants, induced to return thither more by the recognition of the Governor of their claims to *utu*, than by any patriotic feelings. Already numerous individuals who have received payment from the Company under the Commissioner's Award for land in this district are amongst you, and are the most urgent for compensation for their claims in your settlement. I may instance Moturoa, who received £200 in March last for his pretended rights here. It is probable that it is unknown to the Governor and Mr. Maclean that these men have already received compensation, and since Mr. Spain and Mr. Clarke are no longer parties to the adjustment of claims in your district, I know of no one there who can recognize similar claimants. Neither the Wesleyan Missionaries, Messrs. Whiteley, Skevington, and Turton, nor the Sub-Protectors, Maclean and Forsaith, to whom the adjustment of the Maori claims seems to be entrusted, can be cognizant of the Commissioner's proceedings in other districts that bear on the question. The encouragement thus held out to the present resident natives of Waikanae, Queen Charlotte's Sound, Port Nicholson, and other parts of the shores of Cook Strait, to the number of 1200 men, to return to the neighborhood of Mount Egmont, will, it appears to me, be productive of ruin to the colonists, and may hereafter convert the New Plymouth Block into the battle field of the New Zealand tribes. I have the honor to be, etc.,

"W. WAKEFIELD."

Mr. Wicksteed to Colonel Wakefield.
"New Plymouth, 23rd Nov., 1844.
"Sir:—Since I had the honor of writing to you on the 9th inst., His Excellency the Governor has been employed in negotiations with

the natives for a final purchase of a portion of the block of land, the whole of which the Company is entitled to under Mr. Commissioner Spain's award. The land in question lies between a road cut behind sections owned by Captain Davy on the north side of the Waiwakaiho river, and the southern boundary of the Mission Station near the Sugarloaves, extending inland to a line cut beyond the sections occupied by Captain King, Mr. Hursthouse and others. I hope by the next opportunity to send you a separate map of this block, but in the meanwhile can inform you that it embraces nearly all the land in what may be called the Home District, excluding part of that owned by Mr. Smart, and the sections belonging to Messrs. C. Brown, Candish, Broadmore and Barrett. The Governor having failed in his attempt to purchase the Mangoraka and Waiongona District from the very troublesome chief Katatore, proposed to remove the settlers within that district to the Block above mentioned, or to carry them to some other part of the Island— Whaingaroa, Kawhia, or the country nearer Auckland—making an allowance at the rate of one-half, two-thirds, and three-fourths of their outlay, respectively, during the first, second, and third years of their occupation. The sum required to meet this engagement has been computed to amount to £1,345 11s. 8d., the total estimated outlay being £2,402 19s. 1d. The settlers were to defray the expense of inland removal of their crops, houses, etc. The disinclination to leave the settlement was universal; but no final decision has yet been given as to the removal within the Home Block. It is, however, most improbable that more than two or three will accept the Governor's offer, both because the loss on removal of property would be great, and the quantity of land within the block barely sufficient, although increased by the belt round the town, and four sections of Native Reserves, which the Governor has placed at my disposal for the purpose of effecting this arrangement. The chief inducement for removal is the Crown title and protection of property, which the Governor has unreservedly and repeatedly promised to those within the Home District. I enclose copies of a communication received yesterday from the Governor, and my reply of this day's date, from which you will obtain an outline of the plan which His Excellency has determined to pursue. I have as yet no reply to my request for a distinct and written engagement to give a Crown title and protection, but I understand that both will be forthcoming.

"In my reply to His Excellency's letter, you will perceive that I expressly repudiate any liability on the part of the Company to an additional payment beyond £500, which was the outside sum the Governor assured me would be required, when on his last visit to Taranaki. I have also, during the negotiation with the natives, protested against payment of those absent at the time of the sale, and repeatedly against additional *utu* to those who then received so much, and who are now the most troublesome and importunate for more compensation. The Governor will not listen to anything against the claims of absentees, but he has often appeared to acquiesce in the justice of my remonstrance against giving more to those who according to His Excellency's own opinion must have already been greatly overpaid, inasmuch as they were deemed owners of a very large district instead of a fraction of it; yet a few minutes afterwards the Governor will act as if there never had been any previous transaction, and the whole business is recommenced. I consider the Company's property taken as cash by the Government as on the whole fairly valued. It comprises many articles now utterly useless to the Company, and constantly becoming less valuable by wear and tear. Although the quantity of land now about to be secured to the Company and settlers is very small—only about 3,800 acres—it comprises most of that to which the natives have attached the highest value, and I have reason to believe that little difficulty will be experienced in acquiring large additions to it. Already several offers are made; but having found land for the immediate wants of the actual settlers, it is not my intention at present to appear ready to purchase more. In the meantime, it is not impossible that the extraordinary and most arbitrary proceedings of the Governor may be checked by the interference of the Home Government. Nothing, you may be assured, but pressing necessity has induced me to accede so far to the Governor's proposition. The amount of the additional payment now being made in blankets, guns, tobacco, cattle, and so forth, is about £300. His Excellency appears to treat his brother Commissioners of Native Reserves and to deal with that property in the same slashing manner which he adopts towards the Company's officers and the Company's land. I have mentioned his making over to me four Native Reserves within the Home Block, and you will observe in the last paragraph but one of the enclosed copy of His Excellency's letter, that the Trustees of the Native Reserves are to obtain land in future by small purchases from the natives. Thus it would seem that, as regards Taranaki, the whole scheme of the Native Reserves is annihilated; for in future, the Trustees, not the Company, are to purchase land out of non-existent funds. The natives have been signing the Deed of Sale this day, and the Governor is to take his departure in the Hazard for Auckland on Monday next. I had hoped to have forwarded to you by this mail a statement of the conclusion of the affair, but this will not be effected before Monday, if then.—I have the honor to be, etc.,

"J. T. WICKSTEED."

[Enclosed in the last Letter.]

Governor Fitzroy to Mr. Wicksteed.

"New Plymouth, Nov. 22nd, 1844.

"Sir:—Under the present difficult and very critical circumstances of this settlement I am obliged to take unusual measures for the assistance of the settlers here, and for the tranquillity of the Colony in general—measures of which I must bear the whole responsibility; and I now call upon you as the Resident Agent of the New Zealand Company to aid and assist me to the utmost of your means. The circumstances to which I principally refer are, the suspension of payment by the New Zealand Company; their defective title to the land in this neighborhood; and the consequent distress prevailing in this settlement. The measures I am about to take, or have already taken with the view of diminishing the evil effects of such a state of things, are the following :—(1.) To secure the rightful possession of a small block of land about the town, sufficient for the present occupation of the settlers, by completing that small part only of the purchase said to be made by the New Zealand Company. (2.) To remove outlying settlers from distant locations to land within the boundaries of such a block. (3.) To remove settlers from Mangoraka or that neighborhood within four months from this date; unless, within that time, the free consent of the native owners of the lands on which those settlers are now resident be obtained for their occupation of them. (4.) A valuation of the outlay or expenditure on such lands, respectively, has been completed, and an allowance will be made by the Government on account of the New Zealand Company to each settler so removed, to enable him to establish himself in a nearly equivalent position on other land given him in exchange. (5.) Settlers so removed to be allowed to choose unoccupied land within the boundaries of the said block, exchanging acre for acre outside the Town Belt, or one acre within the Belt for two acres of other land. (6.) To enable you to effect such changes more readily, the whole of the Town Belt, including spaces intended for parks, will be placed at your disposal for this purpose only. (7.) Reserves, hitherto intended for the natives, within the said small block, and not required for their present use or occupation, will likewise be placed at your disposal for the above mentioned purpose alone. (8.) To enable you to complete purchases of land outside the boundaries of the aforesaid small block, the Crown's right of pre-emption will be waived, in favor of the New Zealand Company only, throughout the whole extent of the large block of land already surveyed by the Company, and said to contain about 60,000 acres. (9.) To enable you to make payments for the several portions of land to be purchased or of which the purchase is to be completed, the Government will advance funds from time to time, on such satisfactory security as the New Zealand Company's property may afford. (10.) A survey having been held at my desire on the New Zealand Company's boats, stores, cranes, and storehouse, as shown in the enclosed documents, I am ready to accept these effects for the purposes of Government, at the valuation annexed in the accompanying Report of Survey, as an equivalent for so much sterling money advanced by Government.

"More land may be obtained by small purchases from the proper owners from time to time; and in a similar manner land for the future benefit of the natives themselves may be obtained by the trustees of Native Reserves.

"By adopting these measures I believe that the settlement will be

beneficially concentrated, and that prosperity will gradually follow.—
I have the honor to be, etc.,

"ROBERT FITZROY, Governor."

The Company's property alluded to in the above letter was valued at £382 17s. 0d., and was handed over to Captain King for the Government. It consisted of the storehouse, boats, oars, cranes, studs, capstan, flagstaff, two cannon, muskets, rifles and other ammunition.

[EXTRACT.]
Colonel Wakefield to Mr. Wicksteed.

"Wellington, 13th Nov., 1844.

"I can imagine no other reason than the haste which is apparent in your negotiations for your omitting to protest in the strongest terms against the ungrounded assumption of the Governor that the Company's title to land in the neighborhood was defective, and that that combined with the suspension of payment by the Company was the cause of the distress prevailing in the settlement. I consider it due to the character of the Company to record my unqualified contradiction of such statements, and to repudiate any tacit admission of their truth. The land in question has been solemnly awarded, after a lengthened and patient investigation into its sale and purchase, by a Commissioner appointed under the Queen's Sign-Manual, to be the property of the New Zealand Company. The assumed distress amongst the laboring population is, I am assured by yourself, of trifling amount, and entirely caused by the interference of the Governor with Mr. Spain's Award, deterring landowners from employing hands; and the suspension of payment by the Company has no reference to the settlement of New Plymouth, where none of its servants' salaries are in arrear, where its expenditure on other objects had nearly ceased before a cessation of outlay on its part became a measure of policy calculated to secure justice from the Home and Local Governments, and where an absolute debt to the Company to a considerable amount for sales of land will be sacrificed by the accomplishment of Captain Fitzroy's designs. I must also protest against the delusive promises held out to settlers and laborers to abandon the settlement for the neighborhood of Auckland.—I have the honor to be, etc.,

"W. WAKEFIELD."

[EXTRACT.]
Mr. Wicksteed to Colonel Wakefield.

"New Plymouth, Jan. 2nd, 1845.

"The delay of Captain Fitzroy in returning to New Plymouth to settle the Land Question had annoyed all parties. The Maoris especially were insolent and troublesome, marking out very narrow boundaries of the land they intended to give up to the Europeans; who first were to be confined to the seaside of the Devon line, then to be allowed to progress towards the Belt, or, in the event of large *utu* not being forthcoming, to the south side of the Huatoki. The settlers in the Home District, Captain King, Captain Davy, Mr. Chilman, the cottagers at the Henui, and others were irritated by the violence and threats of the natives. The settlement was in a very feverish and excited state when Captain Fitzroy arrived with his plan for breaking it up.

"J. T. WICKSTEED."

CHAPTER XV.

THE HISTORY OF THE ESTABLISHMENT OF VARIOUS RELIGIOUS DENOMINATIONS IN TARANAKI.

THE ESTABLISHMENT OF A BRANCH OF THE CHURCH OF ENGLAND.

THE establishment of the Church of England in New Zealand dates from Christmas Day, 1814, when the Rev. Samuel Marsden, Senior Chaplain of New South Wales, preached the first sermon at the Bay of Islands. This inaugural labor of that excellent minister was followed by the services of the agents of the Church of England and Wesleyan Missionary Societies. The missionaries located themselves among the Maoris, and confined their ministrations to that race, consequently when the Colonies were founded there was a lack of spiritual instructors for the Europeans. The Company sent the Rev. J. F. Churton to officiate at Wellington, but he speedily left his post for Auckland, to the great disgust of the Company's settlers.

On the 20th of March, 1840, an Association was formed in London, under the title of The Church Society for New Zealand, having for its object the procuring for New Zealand a bishop and an associated body of clergy, and the erection and maintenance of churches and schools for the Colonists and Natives. The Earl of Devon, Viscount Sandon,, Viscount Courtenay, Lord Ashley, Dr. Hinds, Archdeacon Hall, Rev. S. Hawtrey, and others of equal note were members of its committee. To endow the proposed bishopric the Church Society and the New Zealand Company came to the following arrangement: —The Company agreed to set apart for this object 4,000 acres of land in the vicinity of its chief settlement at Wellington, and the Society agreed to pay to the Company at the end of twelvemonths £2,000 as the price of half the land set apart, with the understanding that the Company should make its customary rebatement on land purchases for the purpose of conveying the bishop and his suite to the Colony. After this the Society memorialised the Archbishop of Canterbury for the appointment of a bishop. The Archbishop forwarded the memorial to Lord John Russel, who, in reply, under date July the 6th, 1840, stated that he was unable to do anything in the matter, because Her Majesty's Government had repeatedly and distinctly refused to recognise the body associated under the title of the New Zealand Company. The Society, however, obtained from the Company a land order for 4,000 acres, and despatched Mr. John Tylson Wicksteed, in the London, as their agent, to make an early selection. In the course of the following year the Government granted a Charter to the Company and determined to found a bishopric in the Colony. At the recommendation of the Archbishop of Canterbury, Lord John Russell nominated the Rev. George Augustus Selwyn, Curate of New Windsor, to the office of Bishop, and he was accordingly consecrated at Lambeth on the 17th of October, 1841. Dr. Selwyn was of the high church school, and was possessed of high mental and physical endowments. Indeed, as men judge, he appeared to be specially fitted for the office he was destined to fulfil.

On Wednesday, the 17th of November, a very numerous meeting of the inhabitants of Windsor, and the gentry and clergy of the neighborhood, was held at the Town Hall for the purpose of witnessing the presentation of a splendid Service of Communion Plate, purchased by subscription, to the Right Rev. Dr. Selwyn, the Bishop of New Zealand. The hall was completely filled. The service, which cost nearly £300, consisted of six pieces—A large flagon with modelled and chased wreaths of olives, corn, and passion flowers, on the body and cover, and palm branches and leaves on the body on one side, and on the other the Christian monogram IHS and the glory; in the four compartments of the foot were introduced double seraphs with clouds, and the lip was supported by the figure of an angel, the handle being richly modelled and chased to correspond with a chased cross on the cover; two richly chased chalices which corresponded with the flagon; one large salver with shaped moulded edge, divided by bold gothic shapings into compartments, in which were placed alternately wreaths and doves, with the monogram and glory in the centre to match the flagon ; two patens with moulded shaped edges, on high feet, with seraphs and the glory in the centre. The plate bore the following inscription :—" Presented to the Right Reverend Father in God, George Augustus, First Bishop of New Zealand, by the inhabitants of Windsor, Berkshire, England, as a mark of their high esteem, regard, and gratitude. A.D. 1841.—John Banister, Mayor."

The Bishop sailed for Sydney in the ship Tomatin, on Saturday, the 11th of December, 1841, and arrived in Auckland from Sydney in the brig Bristolian, on Monday, the 30th of May, 1842. Young, strong, and full of zeal, he speedily made the tour of his great diocese, visiting all the mission stations, preaching to all the tribes, addressing the whalers, and bringing to their remembrance truths which they had not heard for many a day. Homely and forcible were his addresses to these rough men. You labor hard, said he, and procure barrels of oil in exchange for barrels of rum. No distance was too great for the Bishop to travel ; where the Maoris went he ventured to follow ; and no river was too broad, too deep, or too rapid for him to cross. Furnished with a pedometer he measured distances, and after his tour he published an itinerary in which distances were given with sufficient accuracy.

"On the 10th of October, 1842," says the Bishop in a letter to a friend, " I left Wellington on foot, accompanied by several natives who carried our tents, beds, food, clothes, and books, and set out on a land journey to New Plymouth, one of the principal settlements of the Company, which is situated to the north of Cape Egmont, the western extremity of New Zealand, and near the Sugarloaf Islands. After a few days journey I was detained by a slight inflammation in my heel and was obliged to rest, while some of the natives went forward to procure me a horse. I was encamped near the river Wanganui, on some low sand hills, with three of the natives as my companions. My little tent was pitched in the hollow of the sand hills, and my native attendants made themselves comfortable round a large fire, under a little hut, which they soon constructed of drift wood and coarse grass. You would be surprised with the comparative comfort which I enjoy in my encampment. My tent is strewn with dry fern or grass; my air bed is laid upon it, my books, my clothes, and other goods lie beside it; and though the whole dimensions of my dwelling do not exceed eight feet by five, I have more room than I require and am as comfortable as it is possible for a man to be when he is absent from those whom he loves most. I thus spent October the 17th, the first anniversary of my consecration, in my tent on the sand hills; and while in that situation I was led naturally to contrast my present position with the very different scenes in England last year. I can assure you the comparison brought with it no feelings of regret; on the contrary I spent the greater part of the day, after the usual services and readings with my natives, in thinking with gratitude on the many services and blessings which have been granted to me in the past year. Indeed, in looking back upon the events of the year; upon my happy parting with all my friends, my visit to the Bishop of Australia, my voyages—eight in number—my favorable reception in every town in my diocese, my growing friendship with the natives, who hear me in every part of the Country, and receive me with characteristic cordiality; all from an inexhaustible subject of joy and thanksgiving, which sometimes fills the heart with joy and overflowing. Here," he afterwards adds, " my favorite text came into my mind, ' The lot is fallen unto me in a fair ground; Yea, I have a goodly heritage."

The Bishop organised an institution for the education of his clergy. In a letter dated November, 1842, he says:—" Our institution at Waimate will probably consist of a small college for candidates for Holy Orders, under the care of the Rev. Thomas Whytchead; a collegiate school under the direction of a competent master, assisted by the young students of the college; and a native boarding school for the education of native children selected from the different mission stations. By putting our plan of life upon a collegiate system, and by the aid of a good extent of land, formerly the farm of the Church Mission, I hope to be able to make the whole institution support itself without much assistance from home." A little later the Bishop writes:—" Next door to our own house, which is the college, is the collegiate school, which has not yet been opened, but will probably be set on foot after Easter. The premises have hitherto been used as the missionary school, and are very complete for the purpose. The cathedral library is established at Kirikiri, two miles from this place, in a fine stone building partly used as a store. I have just completed the arrangement of the library, so that the goodly presents of my numerous friends are all accessible ; and a beautiful sight they are. It is enough to cheer the heart to see such a body of sound divinity collected in this most distant of the dioceses of the Church of England; add to this the private feeling of knowing that every one of the books is the gift of some friend, whose heart, and whose prayers are with us. One of the chief advantages of the Waimate is, that we have a spacious church close to the house. It is built entirely of wood, painted white, and gives a very English look to the village. In the interior we have a stone font, an altar cloth and cushions, a pulpit, and beautiful large books, all the gifts of different friends in England. Here I held my first confirmation, at which 325 natives were confirmed. A more orderly, and I hope impressive, ceremony could not have been conducted in any church in England ; the natives coming up in parties to the communion table and audibly repeating the answer—'*E wakaoetia ana e ahau*, (I do confess).' It was a most striking sight to see a church filled with native Christians, ready at my first invitation to obey the ordinances of their religion. On the following Sunday 300 native communicants assembled at the Lord's table, though the rain was increasing. Some of them came two days' journey for this purpose. My Windsor communion plate was used for the second time on this occasion. The natives were much pleased when they were told that it was a present from my congregation in England, and seemed to enter fully into the spirit of the gift."

On the Bishop's appointment to his diocese, he was informed by the New Zealand Company that they would make certain liberal grants towards the endowment of the church in their various settlements, provided the Bishop would meet these grants by equal contributions on the part of the church. The sum given by the Company towards the endowment of the church in Taranaki was £500. Early in 1844 the Bishop appointed the Rev. William Bolland, whom he had recently ordained at Waimate, to be minister at New Plymouth. The young clergyman was full of zeal, but he lacked the robust and well-knit frame of Bishop Selwyn. Horses were scarce in those days, yet the services of the church were regularly conducted in a temporary building in town and also at Mangoraka. On Sundays the slim figure of the young clergyman might be seen hasting along the very rugged roads, assisted by a *taiaha*, to fulfil his clerical appointments. To the poor he was a true friend. Soon after Mr. Bolland's arrival steps were taken towards the erection of a substantial church. A committee was appointed consisting of Rev. W. Bolland, and Messrs. Thatcher and Wicksteed, who undertook to receive from the settlers contributions either in cash or produce. Mr. Thatcher being by profession an architect, designed the building in the Gothic style, and gave his professional assistance to the work. Mr. Wicksteed, under date Jan. 31st, 1845, thus writes to his Chief :—" Most of the materials for the erection of a church in New Plymouth are collected. The settlers have paid up nearly all their contributions, and the building will be completed in the course of three or four months. The Bishop provides a sum equal to that contributed by the settlers. His Lordship has also given instructions for building out of his own funds a small wooden chapel at the Henui." The first stone of the sacred edifice was laid on the Reserve fronting Marsland Hill on the 25th March, 1845, and the church was consequently dedicated to St. Mary. On the 29th September, 1846 the new church was opened without ceremony. Indeed, to this day it has not been ritually consecrated. It was built by the local masons and carpenters, the materials being the trachytic rock from the sea beach, and rimu or red pine timber from the forest. The cost of erection was £800, of which the Bishop paid one-half out of funds at his disposal for church building purposes, and the settlers contributed the remainder. During the war the church was twice enlarged, at a very considerable expense, and was furnished with an organ, and the roof has recently been slated. Notwithstanding the delicacy of his frame, Mr. Bolland on one occasion undertook the journey to Auckland and back, overland, a task sufficiently arduous to try the strongest constitution. In the autumn of 1847 Mr. Fisher, the Superintendent of the Bishop's College, arrived at Taranaki, and took up his abode at Mr. Bolland's house. When he left Auckland fever prevailed both there and at the College. The fever poison was evidently latent in his system when he arrived, for he shortly afterwards sickened, and the fever ran its course. Mr. Bolland was then attacked, and, in the absence of a medical man, was treated by Mrs. Bolland and a well-intentioned lady, the wife of one of the principal settlers. After languishing a few weeks, a son was born to him; he took the infant in his arms, thanking God, and blessing it, after which he expired, to the grief of the entire settlement, and the inconsolable sorrow of his young widow. He was buried in the church yard, a short distance from the east window, and for several years his grave was constantly bedecked with flowers. It is now marked by a stone bearing the inscription:—" Sacred to the Memory of the Rev. William Bolland, who departed this life May 29th, 1847, aged 27 years. Blessed are the dead that die in the Lord."

The death of Mr. Bolland having left the Episcopal Church at Taranaki without a minister, Mr. Turton, of the Wesleyan Mission, proffered his services to the Bishop, but the Bishop refused to accept them. After an interval of some months, the Rev. Henry Govett, B.A., son of the incumbent of Staines, Middlesex, a descendant of the Rev. W. Romaine, a popular Calvanistic divine of the last century, and one of the Bishop's candidates, was appointed to the vacancy. With the exception of an interval of three years, 1856–9, during which he paid a visit to England, Mr. Govett has continued to labor diligently among both the races in this province. In 1855, Mr. Woollaston, then a Catechist, but now a minister of the Episcopal Church in Melbourne, officiated at Bell Block. He was much beloved by the settlers, and would doubtless have made an excellent clergyman, but,

on account of his objecting to qualify himself for ministering to the
Maoris, the Bishop refused him a permanent appointment. During
Mr. Govett's absence the Rev. Mr. Lally officiated in town, and the
Rev. G. Bayley at Omata. On the resignation of Mr. Bayley the
Rev. Henry Handley Brown, Rector of Burton Pedwardine, and
Vicar of Howell, Lincolnshire, England, was appointed to Omata.
Mr. Brown and family arrived from England in the barque Eclipse,
Capt. Elliot, on 4th March, 1859, and has up to this date (1877)
acted as the laborious coadjutor of Mr. Govett. In August, 1859,
Taranaki was constituted an Archdeaconry, and Mr. Govett was
appointed Archdeacon. In 1874 the Rev. Mr. Kennedy was
appointed to Patea. From his own purse Bishop Selwyn erected in
1844 a chapel at the Henui village. In 1872 this chapel was put
into a state of thorough repair. In 1848 a wooden church was erected
at Omata, on a plot of land given for the purpose by Mr. Wicksteed.
This having decayed, a new church in that district was opened on
February 14th, 1875. In 1854 a substantial timber church was
erected at Bell Block, and in 1859 a church was erected in the Barrett
Road. In January, 1875, Mr. Walsh was appointed Curate of
Waitara, and on the 16th October, 1877, a church was opened at
Inglewood. In districts where there are no churches, divine service
is held in school rooms and block houses.

THE ESTABLISHMENT OF THE ROMAN CATHOLIC CHURCH IN TARANAKI.

In the year 1836, Pope Gregory XVI, appointed J. B. Pompallier
Roman Catholic Bishop of New Zealand, and the Lyons Association
for the Propagation of the Faith furnished him with money. In the
year 1838 he landed in the North with several priests, and took up
his abode at Karorareka in the Bay of Islands. Since then French
missionary priests have established themselves in various parts of the
Islands, both among the Maori and European inhabitants, and at the
time we write there are three Roman Catholic Bishops in the Colony;
one in Auckland, one in Wellington, and one in Dunedin, Bishop
Redwood of Wellington being of New Zealand birth. Taranaki
has never been regarded with favor by the Roman Catholics of
England or Ireland. One or two families who came with the early
settlers soon left the district for Sydney for the sake of their
children; those that remain are chiefly the families of soldiers who
have fought in the wars of the Colony. The district was for several
years visited annually by the Rev. Father Pezant, who traversed on
foot the whole distance between Wanganui and Taranaki. Although
a grant of a town section in New Plymouth was made to the Catholic
Mission by the Provincial Government, and was supplemented by a
donation of an adjoining section by Mr. Richard Brown, a New
Plymouth merchant, no attempt was made to build a chapel till the
year 1856, when one or two companies of the 65th Regiment were
stationed at New Plymouth in consequence of the Puketapu feud
which was then raging, many of whom were catholics. At that
time a collection was made, not only in Taranaki, but also in

Wellington and other places, and from the funds so obtained a small chapel was erected on the Mission land in Courtenay Street, New Plymouth. Until the outbreak of the Maori rebellion in 1860, no resident priest was stationed in the district, but at that time the Rev. Father Tressallet was sent thither. He soon perceived as the war proceeded, and fresh troops were poured in, that the chapel was too far from the town for the soldiers to attend. He therefore commenced a new subscription and succeeded in purchasing an acre of ground in Devon Street, nearly facing Queen Street, and upon it he built a larger chapel, which was subsequently added to and enlarged by the Rev. Father Pertuis, who succeeded Father Tressallet, and also by the Rev. Father Rolland, a most energetic and exemplary Priest in the performance of his duties under fire in the field of battle to the wounded and the dying. Had the funds at the disposal of Father Rolland been equal to his desire, a thriving Catholic community would most probably have been established in the district. Father Rolland was succeeded by Father Biusfeld, shortly after whose arrival the war ceased and the troops were withdrawn. The ill-judged abandonment of the Military Settler System by the Government reduced the trade of the province to its lowest ebb, and the Catholic community now scattered over a large extent of forest country, and numbering about 800, is composed almost entirely of discharged soldiers, who have taken up land under the land regulations, with their families. At the time we write the Rev. Father Lampilia is the resident Priest at New Plymouth, and efforts are being made under his direction for the erection of a chapel at Inglewood.

THE ESTABLISHMENT OF THE WESLEYAN METHODIST SOCIETY IN TARANAKI.

Shortly after the formation of the Church Mission in New Zealand, the Wesleyan Missionary Society sent out agents to the country, who established themselves on the shores of the fine harbor of Wangaroa in the North. Being driven from thence in 1827, a successful re-establishment was effected at Hokianga. By an arrangement the Church missioned the East Coast and the Wesleyans the West Coast. As soon as the agents of the Plymouth Company took possession of the land situate between Ngamotu and Waitara, and under the ægis of the Europeans the fugitive Ngatiawa began to return to their homes, Mr. Creed was sent down and established himself on a fine section of 100 acres at Ngamotu, reserved for the use of the mission. Mr. Skevington, another missionary, was at the same time stationed among the Taranaki and Ngatiruanuis at Waimate.

In 1842, the Wesleyan settlers, aided by a grant of £10 from the Company through its agent, Captain Liardet, erected a temporary church on the hill in Brougham Street South. Refusing to admit Captain King and Mr. Wicksteed for the purpose of holding a horticultural show within it, they were ordered to remove the building, having erected it before the survey was completed in what afterwards proved to be a public road. Mr. Groube, the Independent Minister, had begun the erection of a small sand-stone chapel at the corner of Courtenay and Liardet streets, but was unable from want of funds to finish it. The Wesleyans took it off his hands, completed it, and worshipped in it for many years. When the Episcopal Church was closed, which happened every fourth Sunday, in order that the clergyman should devote that day to the Maoris, the two congregations used to mingle in harmony in the Wesleyan Chapel.

In 1844, Mr. Creed was succeeded by the Rev. Henry Hanson Turton, a young, clever, handsome man. In its policy with the natives the Government required the assistance of Maori linguists, and such, unless they were missionaries, were scarce in those days. Mr. Turton was employed in much secular business with the Maoris, by Governor Fitzroy, which did not result in the spiritual improvement of either himself or people.

In 1848, Governor Grey erected an industrial school on the Mission land at Ngamotu, for the education and training in useful employment of the Maori youth of both sexes. This institution was placed under the care of Mr. Turton. At first it gave some little promise of good, but ultimately failed through the apathy of the Maoris. When parents were requested to send their children to be taught to work they not unfrequently replied by asking how much *utu* they were to receive if they complied. In 1849, Mr. Turton lost his wife through a cold caught shortly after confinement, and buried her with many tears on a hill on the Mission land.

Mr. Skevington having died suddenly at the District Meeting in Auckland, was succeeded at Waimate by the Rev. William Woon. Mr. Woon was a native of Truro in Cornwall, a man of gigantic proportion, possessing a trumpet voice, but withal as gentle as a child. He was sent out to Tongatapu in 1830 as a missionary printer, but the climate affecting his health he was removed to the north of New Zealand, where he resided during Heki's rebellion in 1845. Great demands upon his charity were made by the wounded rebels who were brought to his house for surgical aid. Mr. Woon received much ill-treatment from the people of Waimate. After enduring many insults from the very cowardly and ungrateful people among whom he labored, he obtained his superannuation, after a service of twenty-three years, and retired to Wanganui, where he died in 1858, aged fifty-two years. He has had no successor.

In 1856, in consequence of the alarming state of the district, Mr. Whiteley was sent to Taranaki to co-operate with Mr. Turton. In the following year Mr. Turton was removed to Auckland, and was succeeded by Mr. Ironside. In consequence of the increase of settlers, and the presence of troops in the town, the stone chapel became too small for the congregation. In 1856, a fine new chapel was erected diagonally opposite to the old one, and was opened on October the 2nd of that year. In 1859, Mr. Ironside was succeeded by Mr. Fletcher. Since then Messrs. Innis, Reid, Watkins, Crump,

Kirk, Cannell, Smith, Russell, Hammond and Isitt have ministered in the district. The Society has at various times been assisted by lay preachers, several of whom have gone to their rest. Thomas Skinner and William Edgecombe labored among the Maoris; Sergeant Marjouram, of the Royal Artillery, among the troops; and Messrs. Hooker, Rawson, and Veale among the settlers. During the war the church was considerably enlarged and schools erected. In 1864, the building formerly used as an Independent Chapel was purchased and removed from Devon Street East to the Cutfield Road, and there used as a Wesleyan Chapel. In 1875 it was removed to the Waitara and opened in March. In 1876 a chapel was erected at Inglewood. The Wesleyans perform their part with other denominations of Christians in the evangelisation of the district, holding Sunday services in various localities between Tataraimaka and Tikorangi. Very recently a minister has been appointed to Patea.

THE ESTABLISHMENT OF PRIMITIVE METHODISM IN TARANAKI.

The angularity which characterised early Methodism gave way to the abrading influence of time, prosperity and education. Time toned down its fiery zeal; prosperity—the result of obedience to its precepts—elevated its members among the gentle and respectable of society; and education taught them that intense earnestness could exist beneath a peaceable demeanour. In some districts of England, lying remote from the centre of national life and progress, this modification of early Methodism was looked upon as a declension from its original stand point, and a relapsing into worldliness. In the year 1801, some zealous Wesleyan·Methodists in the Staffordshire potteries proposed a day's praying upon Mow Cop, a high hill on the borders of Staffordshire and Cheshire. The proposition was not carried out till 1807. On the 31st of May of that year, under the leadership of Hugh Bourne, of Bemersley, a Camp Meeting was held on the "Cop" or Mount, the Wesleyan Methodist authorities treating this, and similar meetings as decidedly irregular, Hugh Bourne and his friends seceded and established the Primitive Methodist Connexion in 1810. Primitive Methodism has grown to be the most extensive of all the Methodist secessions. Its government is more democratic than that of Wesleyan Methodism, but in doctrine and church order it is almost identical with it.

There is a Methodist body called Bible Christians or Bryanites, which is not the result of any secession from the Wesleyan Methodists, but grew up as an independent community and adopted the principles of Methodism. Its founder was one William O'Bryan, a Wesleyan local preacher of North Cornwall, who left that body in 1815, and began to form societies on the Methodist plan. In doctrine and order they do not differ from the other Arminian Methodists. They have never been a very numerous body. Many of the early settlers in Taranaki came from North Devon and Cornwall, and were members of the Bible Christian Society. Among them were several local preachers of that body. Shortly after the establishment of New Plymouth, the elder Mr. Veale offered these people a site in the centre of the town for a place of worship. The offer was acccepted, and very speedily a small chapel was built upon it, in which they conducted worship among themselves. Supposing that they needed a leader, they wrote home to the officers of their society requesting that a minister, or to use their own phraseology, a travelling preacher, should be sent out to them. In reply they received a number of queries as to the means they possessed of supporting a minister. While this matter was pending, an event took place which threw this little church into the lap of the Primitive Methodist Connexion. On a Sunday afternoon, September the 1st, 1844, after the afternoon service had concluded in their little chapel, they observed a stranger standing on a chair preaching on the Huatoki Bridge. Mingling with his congregation they soon perceived that the strange preacher taught doctrines in accord with their own religious opinions. The preacher proved to be the Rev. Robert Ward, a missionary sent out by the Primitive Methodist Society, who had just arrived by the ship Raymond, from London. The result was that Mr. Ward, became their minister, and they were absorbed into his Connexion. A plot of land having been given to the Society at the Henui village, a small chapel was there built, and Mr. Ward took up his residence in the neighborhood. Mr. and Mrs. Green followed Mr. Ward and labored in the settlement for some time, during which Mr. Ward paid a visit to some of the other settlements. Mr. Ward set himself to study the Maori language, and as soon as he had mastered it sufficiently to converse with the natives, attempted to preach to them. This aroused a pitiful jealousy, which resulted in the Mangoraka Maoris driving him out of their district by flourishing their tomahawks over his head. When in 1848 the Omata block was opened many of the Henui villagers removed thither, and those among them who were Primitive Methodists erected a small chapel in the district. In 1850, Mr. Ward removed to Auckland, and was succeeded by the Rev. Joseph Long, who won golden opinions from all classes by his affability. Shortly after this minister's arrival the Bell district was opened, and he, with his local preachers held service there in the rush built houses of the settlers till Sept. 22nd, 1855, when the present chapel was opened. Through Mr. Long's exertions a chapel was built at Hurdon, on the Franklyn Road, and preaching services instituted at Mangorei and Tataraimaka. Having fulfilled his term, Mr. Long removed to Auckland on the 24th of January, 1859, and was succeeded by Mr. Ward, who returned to the settlement on the 31st of the same month. During the war Mr. Ward suffered much from being driven to take shelter within the intrenchments and from the alarms consequent on continually expected assaults. In 1862 a large connexional chapel was erected in Queen Street, New Plymouth. In the following year it was considerably enlarged. In 1865, Mr. Ward removed to Wellington, and was succeeded by the Rev. Mr. and Mrs. Waters. They having fulfilled their term were succeeded by the Rev. John Dumbell, who was succeeded by the Rev. Messrs. Standrin and Clover, the present ministers. The settlement owes a debt of gratitude to the plain, but earnest members of the connexion. At their Sunday schools many obtained all the book learning they ever received. When there were no newspapers, and but little literature of any kind in the Province, the Primitive Methodists distributed books in their schools and congregations, and while other denominations devoted a very large part of their attention to the Maoris, these directed all their labors to the spiritual, moral, and intellectual good of their fellow countrymen, the colonists. Messrs. Thomas Bayly, Henry Gilbert, William Bassett, and Edward Moyle, are the persons who have labored longest and most constantly in the cause of the connexion.

THE HISTORY OF CONGREGATIONALISM IN NEW PLYMOUTH.

The Rev. Horatio Groube, son of Admiral Groube, of Dorsetshire, England, a minister of the Congregational body, arrived in New Plymouth by the Timandra, in February, 1842, and for some time conducted divine service in a raupo *whare* in Devon street East, not far from the Huatoki stream. He attempted the erection of a sandstone chapel, but failing to complete it for want of funds, sold it to the Wesleyans. Among the early settlers there were very few Congregationalists, and Mr. Groube in consequence failed to secure much favor as a minister. In 1849 he erected a small wooden chapel in Devon street East, and ministered for eleven years to a small congregation. In 1861, owing to the wretched condition to which he and his family were reduced by the war, he determined to leave the settlement, and he accordingly removed to Melbourne, Victoria. Since his removal the Trustees have sold the chapel to the Wesleyans, who, after removing it to the Town Belt, have finally enlarged and re-erected it at Waitara East, and Congregationalism has ceased to exist in the province.

THE HISTORY OF PRESBYTERIANISM IN TARANAKI.

About the year 1858 the Rev. John Thom, a Presbyterian Minister, came up from Wanganui on a ministerial visit to Taranaki. He was gladly received by the few Presbyterian families in the settlement, and preached acceptably in several of the places of worship. Shortly after the removal of Mr. Groube to Melbourne Mr. Thom came to reside permanently at New Plymouth, conducting divine service in the Independent chapel. Mr. Thom was well adapted for pioneer work, but did not succeed as a stated minister. He did not obtain the hearty co-operation of his congregation. During the war there were a number of young men in the province, Presbyterians by profession, who had come to serve as Military Settlers, but had no intention of residing permanently in the province. Mr. Thom, representing to these fugitives the desirability of a young Presbyterian Minister being stationed in Taranaki, induced them to sign a memorial to the Colonial Committee of the Church of Scotland in

Edinburgh, praying that a minister might be sent to take the pastoral charge of St. Andrew's Kirk in Taranaki. In answer to this memorial, the Rev. Robert Ferguson Macnicol, of Oban, who had recently left the University of Glasgow, was ordained by the Presbytery of Lorne, in Argyleshire, Scotland, in June, 1865, and he shortly afterwards embarked at Glasgow in the ship Robert Henderson, with his young wife for his distant field of labor, arriving in New Plymouth, viâ Otago, on 23rd November, 1865.

On the young minister's landing in the settlement, he found to his surprise and vexation that St. Andrew's Kirk had no existence, except in the imagination of those persons who had memorialised the Colonial Committee of the Church. Some of the old and substantial Presbyterians, however, rallied round the young minister, and by dint of great exertions succeeded in erecting a place of worship in Devon street. The first stone was laid with Masonic ceremony early in 1866, and the building was opened for Divine worship in November of the same year by the Rev. David Bruce, of Auckland, who preached from the text "Let us not be weary in well-doing, for in due season we shall reap, if we faint not." Mr. Macnicol's congregation was never very numerous, but it managed to pay the interest on the church debt, and to allow the minister £150 per annum, which was supplemented by an annual grant of £150 from the Colonial Committee. As the excitement and expenditure attendant upon the war gradually ceased, the province sank into a state of great depression. The peace was fitful and disturbed, and there was no security that hostilities might not at any time be renewed. As a climax to the depression of the settlement, the Home Government withdrew all the troops, and the settlers lost thereby not only their protection but also the pecuniary aid they afforded by their presence. As the prospect of supporting a minister became more and more doubtful to the Presbyterians, Mr. Macnicol was induced to accept a call made to him by the congregation of St. James', Auckland, the ministerial office having become vacant by the removal of Mr. Hill to the Thames. Mr. Macnicol left New Plymouth for his new charge on the 29th January, 1869, and was succeeded in the following February by the Rev. Thomas Blain, of the Ulster Presbytery. Mr. Blain left for New South Wales in July of the same year, and the ministry devolved on Mr. B. Wells, a member of the congregation, who conducted divine service gratuitously, till June, 1872, when the church made a call to the Rev. M. S. Breach, of Kaipara, the present minister. During Mr. Wells' lay ministry the church debt was cleared off.

The Rev. John Thom, after memorialising the Colonial Committee, left Taranaki for New South Wales, where as a laborious pioneer he succeeded in founding several churches. His last station was on the banks of the Richmond river, and there, while in the act of ferrying a friend across the water, his boat was accidentally upset, and he was drowned.

HISTORY OF THE BAPTIST CAUSE IN NEW PLYMOUTH.

On the 12th of March, 1868, the foundation stone of a Baptist Church was laid on the section situated at the corner of Gill and Liardet streets, New Plymouth, by the Rev. John Whiteley. In the stone was placed a bottle containing a piece of parchment bearing the following inscription:—"On the 11th March, 1868, the foundation stone of this chapel, intended for the Baptist Denomination, was laid by the Rev. John Whiteley. The building is held in trust by Josiah Flight, William Bayly, T. G. Billing, Richard Hart, and George Hoby." The building was in due time completed, but up to this date it has never been opened for Divine service.

CHAPTER XVI.

THE EVENTS OF 1845-48.

THE promised re-purchase of the rural lands of the settlement did not take place. We may reasonably suppose that the Governor was very anxious that such a transaction should occur, moreover, his finances were in a deplorable condition, and the natives having got their ancestral lands into their possession held them with a firm grasp. The Fitzroy Block now formed the settlement; many of the Europeans who had taken up their lands at Mangoraka were permitted to hold them at the sufferance of the Puketapu hapu, but eventually they were all driven into the Fitzroy Block. In February an excellent wheat crop had been reaped. On Capt. King's farm the produce, after accurate measurement, was ascertained to be at the rate of 60 bushels to the acre. Mr. Day had gone to Sydney in the Slaines Castle, for the purpose of procuring cattle. At a meeting of the employers of labor it was agreed to pay farm laborers 12 shillings per week, partly in cash and partly in wheat at 6 shillings per bushel. Messrs. White and Gillingham's saw mill was completed, and it was expected that their flour mill would be soon at work. A large body of natives had assembled at the Mimi to resist an expected attack of the Ngnatiruanui. The expected collision did not take place, and they had returned home in peace. In March the Slaines Castle came in with a quantity of English goods. Fears were entertained both by Europeans and Maoris that an attack would be made on the district by the Ngapuhi tribe. A number of special constables were sworn in. In April the Paul Jones sailed for Adelaide, with 18 despairing settlers, among whom were Mr. and Mrs. Yems, whose loss was much deplored. In May two small exports of flour were made in the vessels Carbon and Richmond. Coal was reported to have been found on suburban section No. 12, on the West side of the town, and specimens of nickel have been dug up in the same locality. Mr. Gledhill had commenced the manufacture of leather. The Maoris had committed several robberies at Mangoraka, and had attempted to violate a little girl, the daughter of a settler. A church had been erected by the Maoris at Mangoraka, the materials for which they had stolen from the settlers. The Governor had refused to send troops, because he considered New Plymouth to be a place inaccessible both by sea and land, and consequently a place where troops could not be kept. The overland mail to Auckland had been stopped. In July a dreadful storm occurred at Kawhia, during which the schooner Richmond was lost on the Kawhia bar, and all hands perished. She was manned by Spencer, Frederic Aubrey, and some other young gentlemen connected with the settlement who led a free life among the natives on the coast. The vessel is said to have been under-manned and badly found. She was to have been refitted at Wellington. A suspicious fire occurred at Mangoraka which destroyed a barn and wheat stack, the property of Mr. William Bayly.

In September the land in cultivation was 1,106¼ acres, of which 635¼ were in wheat, and 128½ in barley. It was estimated that the surplus produce for export in the coming autumn would be 267 tons of flour, 1600 bushels of barley, a quantity of salt pork and other articles. On the 30th the Rev. Mr. Bolland returned overland from Auckland, bringing the joyful intelligence of the appointment of a new Governor in the place of Governor Fitzroy. Mr. Bolland had performed the entire journey of 200 miles in six days. In October Messrs. Broadmore and Lethbridge had nearly completed a saw mill which they had constructed with part of the machinery brought out by Mr. Charles Brown. The Carbon arrived with the intelligence that Captain Grey had been appointed Governor. In November the Maoris were all busy strengthening their pas, an attack by Waikatos having been threatened. In December wages were high and labor scarce.

SIR GEORGE GREY, K.C.B., D.C.L.

Sir George Grey was born at Lisburn, in Ireland, the 14th April, 1812. His father, Lieutenant-Colonel Grey, fell at the siege of Badajoz during the Peninsular War, just three days before the birth of his son. Being intended for the military profession he was educated at Sandhurst, where Mr. Ligar, formerly Surveyor-General of the Colony, and the lamented Colonels Nixon and Austen, who fell in the war, were his contemporaries. At Sandhurst Sir George laid the foundation of that vast and accurate learning for which he is so justly celebrated. Eventually Sir George joined the 83rd Regiment, and was first brought prominently forward in the year 1837, when, being then a Captain, he commanded an expedition which was undertaken to gain information as to the state and resources of the interior of Australia. In this expedition Captain Grey and his party suffered extraordinary hardships from want of water, and from the attacks of the natives. There is little doubt that the success of the expedition and the preservation of the lives of the men composing it were the fruits of the energy, prudence, and foresight of its leader. On the death of Mr. Spencer, the Governor of Adelaide, Captain Grey, as the officer commanding the troops, assumed the reins of government, and so well did he administer the affairs of that little Colony that the Imperial Government appointed him to be the Governor of it.

In 1845 the Honorable East India Company's ship Elphinstone, which had been sent from Bombay to South Australia with despatches, conveyed Captain Grey to Auckland. The mismanagement of Governor Fitzroy had involved the Colony in troubles of every sort. The Treasury was bankrupt, and war was being feebly waged by a weak and faint-hearted commander against the natives in the north. Practically assuming the command of the troops in the field Captain

Grey directed all the operations against the enemy until the war in the North was brought to a triumphant conclusion by the siege and storming of Ruapekapeka. Disturbances took place both at Wellington and Wanganui, but the natives being treated with a judicious mixture of rigor and diplomacy, peace was restored in those districts. Moreover, a potent lesson was taught the so called friendly natives by the kidnapping of the double-dealing Rauparara, at Porirua, on 23rd July, 1846. On the institution of the Civil Order of the Bath in 1848, Captain George Grey was made a Knight Commander, and when invested with the star of the order at Auckland, Tomati Waka Nene and Te Puni were the chosen esquires of the newly made Knight. Sir George deserved both the civil and military decorations, for he accompanied the soldiers in all their expeditions against the natives. Sir George, so far as he was able, satisfactorily settled the land claims of the dispossessed settlers of New Plymouth. In 1847 Sir George established Pensioner Settlements around Auckland. In 1846 the Imperial Government expressed its willingness to grant a Constitution to New Zealand, but Sir George Grey caused the grant to be deferred for five years, owing to the unsatisfactory state of the native mind. At length, in 1852, when Heke, Kawhiti, Pomare, Taniwha, Rauparaha, and Rangihaeata were dead, he consented, and by Act of the Imperial Parliament a representative constitution was given to the Colony. Early in 1853 the Constitution was proclaimed in New Zealand. After ruling New Zealand for eight years Sir George Grey obtained the Secretary of State's permission to return to England, and he left New Zealand on 31st December, 1853. Having made some valuable contributions to literature by translating the traditions, cosmogony, chants, and Karakias, or mysteries of the Maoris, the University of Oxford conferred on him the degree of Doctor of Civil Laws. Shortly after his arrival in England he was appointed Governor of the Cape of Good Hope. In 1861 Sir George Grey was again sent to New Zealand. The natives were then in rebellion, and it was thought that by his skill they would be quickly pacified. He was again proclaimed Governor on 2nd October, 1861. At first Sir George tried his old method of diplomacy with the natives, known as the "sugar and blanket policy," but he soon discovered that it had lost its efficacy, and he was, by the massacre of an escort of the 57th Regt. at the Wairau, near Tataraimaka, on 4th May, 1863, reluctantly compelled to permit General Cameron to commence hostilities. Then followed the destruction of the power of Waikato. The hand of the corrector was, however, stayed too soon, and the rebel prisoners were treated in a weak and ridiculous manner, the result of which was an unnecessary prolongation of the war and an unnecessary waste of blood and treasure. At length the spirit of the rebellion being crushed Sir George Grey again left New Zealand for England on the 7th of October, 1868. After staying a year or two in England he returned and took up his abode at the Kawau island, in the Hauraki Gulf, near Auckland, which is his property. Here he amused himself by acclimating valuable birds and animals, and by collecting rare and valuable books.

After spending a few years in seclusion at the Kawau, Sir George Grey accepted the office of Superintendent of Auckland, and entered the House of Representatives as member of one of the Auckland Electoral districts. In the House he distinguished himself by his ultra-democratic opinions and by his opposition to the abolition of Provincial institutions. On the defeat of the Vogel-Atkinson Ministry in October, in 1877, he became Premier of the Colony.

Sir Grey is the author of "Journals of Discovery in Australia," "Polynesian Mythology and Traditions of New Zealand," "Proverbial Sayings of the Ancestors of the New Zealand Race," and other works on New Zealand.

EVENTS OF 1846.

January.—In consequence of the attempt of the millers to raise the charge of grinding wheat from sixpence to ninepence per bushel, a company was formed for the purpose of erecting a Union Mill.

February.—The grain crops were never so abundant, nor so free from blight. Working bullocks and cows were in demand.

April.—Mr. Broadmore had to pay the Maoris *utu* for every tree he cut down for his mill. Governor Grey abolished the Maori Protectorate, and appointed Mr. Maclean, the Protector, Inspector of a small body of armed police.

May.—Prices Current : Clearing fern land, £3 per acre ; clearing timber, £8 to £12 per acre ; working bullocks, £35 ; cows, £14 to £20 each ; pigs supplied by the natives to the butchers at 1d. to 1½d. per lb. Retail Prices : pork, 3d. per lb ; mutton, 6d.; beef, very seldom in the market, 6d. to 8d. per lb.; Taranaki beer, 2s. per gallon ; potatoes, 1s. 6d. per cwt.; fowls, 1s. 6d. per couple ; sawn board, 12s. per 100 feet superficial ; limestone, delivered from Massacre Bay at £1 per ton. Statistics : Land sold and selected 14,000 acres ; land surveyed, but unsold, 11,000 acres ; minimum price of suburban land, £2 5s. per acre ; rural land, £1 5s. per acre ; 95 suburban sections remained unsold and 800 town sections, the minimum price of the latter being £12 10s. The European population was 1,200, and there was an excess of males over females.

May.—The roads were in a very bad condition owing to the unusually wet weather ; subscriptions were being made for putting them in repair.

June.—The Marianne, from Nelson to Auckland, with emigrants, called and took away Mr. and Mrs. William Edgecumbe, who came out in the Amelia Thompson.

July.—400 Waikatos visited the settlement and stayed a fortnight. There was great feasting during their stay. They sold a number of pigs to the settlers. Mr. Maclean's force contributed much to the maintenance of peace.

Despatch from the Secretary of State to Governor Sir George Grey.
"Downing Street, 2nd July, 1846.
"Sir :—I have received Governor Fitzroy's despatch marked

Separate, the 29th of October last, enclosing a copy of a letter addressed to the Colonial Secretary by the principal agent of the New Zealand Company. Captain Fitzroy states that letter to have been forwarded by him as it might be required for reference in connection with the arrangements made at New Plymouth.

"From that letter it appears that Colonel Wakefield adverting to the arrangement entered into by the Company with the Government in the year 1840 for the purchase of land in New Plymouth, and to the award of Mr. Commissioner Spain, which had been overruled by Captain Fitzroy, had refused to accept on the part of the Company the Title Deeds to 3,500 acres of land at that settlement.

"I cannot but express my great surprise and regret at not having been placed by Captain Fitzroy in possession of a full report of the course which he pursued in this case, and of his reasons for that course. I, however, indulge the hope that you may have found yourself in a condition to give effect to the award of Mr. Spain in the case of the Company's claims at New Plymouth, and in any case I rely on your endeavors to gain that end so far as you have found it practicable, unless, indeed, which I can hardly think probable, you may have seen reason to believe that the reversal of the Commisioner's judgment was a wise and just measure.—I have, &c.

"W. E. GLADSTONE."

August.—Mr. Williams, farm bailiff to Captain Davy, shot himself at Barrett's Lagoon. Mr. Copps the surveyor died. Fifty tons of whale oil ready for exportation.

September.—The Madras, from London viâ Nelson, arrived, bringing Mr. and Mrs. Green of the Primitive Methodist Mission. Her goods for New Plymouth were transhipped on board the vessel Fanny Morris then in the roadstead.

October.—The Ralph Bernal arrived from Auckland. Captain McLaren purchased all the oil remaining at the whaling station, and a quantity of flour, biscuit, salt pork, and hams for his homeward voyage.

November.—Constabulary Barracks built in Courtenay Street. The Carbon arrived with Mr. Ryan and family. Mr. Ryan brought a quantity of goods from Sydney with the intention of opening a store.

December.—The police collected the statistics as follows:—Land in cultivation: wheat, $838\frac{1}{2}$ acres; barley, $132\frac{1}{4}$ acres; rye, 3 acres; oats, $74\frac{1}{4}$ acres; potatoes, $132\frac{3}{4}$ acres; turnips, 57 acres; maize, 1 acre; grass, 153 acres; flax, $\frac{3}{4}$ acres; fallow, $122\frac{1}{4}$ acres; total, $1,515\frac{1}{2}$ acres. Live Stock: Horses, 22; mules, 2; horned cattle, 363; sheep, 571; pigs, 702; goats, 96; total, 1,696. Population: males, 586; females, 502; total, 1,088. A plan for a hospital, to cost £700, had been sent to New Plymouth by the Governor, who had purchased as a site for it five acres of land in the Town Belt, near the Henui river, being part of the land taken by William Edgcumbe for land at Mangoraka under Governor Fitzroy's arrangement.

Sometime during this year Mr. F. Dillon Bell and Mr. Wellington Carrington ascended Mount Egmont, and discovered Bell's Falls.

EVENTS OF 1847.

January 30th.—The Elora arrived from London direct, bringing Mr. Pestel and a quantity of goods, among which were two threshing machines. The overland mail to Auckland was re-established.

February 23rd.—Died at Moturoa, Richard Barrett, whose name has been often mentioned in connexion with the early history of the Province, and who rendered signal service to Colonel Wakefield, Dr. Dieffenbach, Messrs. Carrington and Cutfield, in the purchase, survey, and establishment of the settlemement.

About 9 a.m., on the 26th, H.M.S.S. Inflexible came smoking up from the Southward towards the anchorage, and being the first steamship seen in the roadstead, excited much surprise among the natives and the New Zealand born children of the Europeans. At 10.30 a.m. His Excellency Sir George Grey landed, accompanied by Colonel Wakefield, the old Ngatiawa chief Te Puni, and other natives of his tribe from Wellington. The object of His Excellency's visit was the adoption of some conciliatory measures for the obtaining of more land for the settlement, and for this purpose he had an interview with the Ngamotu and Puketapu *hapus*. High talk was indulged in on both sides, the natives expressing their determination to sell no more land, and the Governor threatening to recognise the claims of Waikato as the conquerors of the district. Wi Kingi, who had come in the steamer from Waikanae, professedly to further the Governor's plans, was very insolent. His Excellency had proposed a site for a hamlet for Kingi and his people on the north side of the Waitara, laid out in streets with plots for cottages, gardens, church, school-house, minister's residence, and small farms, on condition that the *hapu* would consent to his purchasing the land from thence to the Mokau for the Europeans. Kingi objected to this and told the Governor that he did not need his assistance, that he would erect his pa himself and build it where he pleased, and when he pleased, without asking permission of anyone. Governor Grey, who was much annoyed at this speech, replied :—"Tell him, that I say he is to remain at Waikanae, and that I will now place him under guard, and that if he dares to remove to Waitara without my permission I will send the war steamer after him and destroy all his canoes."

On the 6th of March His Excellency embarked for Nelson. The result of this was the issue of the following :—

Instructions from Governor Grey to Commissioner Maclean.

"March 5th, 1847.

"(1.) Mr. Commissioner Spain reported that the New Zealand Company were entitled to a Crown Grant of a block of 60,000 acres of land lying within certain defined limits.

"(2.) The Governor (Fitzroy) did not take the same view of the question as Mr. Spain and would not confirm that gentleman's award;

on the contrary, in November, 1844, he sanctioned a totally new purchase of a small block of land of 3,500 acres, by the Agent of the New Zealand Company, and he made certain promises to the natives which have induced many of them to return to lands which they state they understood Captain Fitzroy to guarantee to them in permanent possession. On these lands they have now extensive pas and cultivations included in the block awarded by Mr. Spain.

" (3.) Thus on the one hand the New Zealand Company claim the rights (if any) which they may have acquired under Mr. Spain's award; while on the other hand the natives claim the disallowance of that award by the Governor, the rights which the late Governor promised to maintain to them in all their integrity, and the fact of their present occupation of the land under the sanction of the Governor.

" (4.) It is proposed to evade, in as far as practicable, the various difficulties which have arisen under these conflicting circumstances, by in the first place reserving to the several tribes who claim land in this district tracts which will amply suffice for their present and future wants; and secondly, resuming the remaining portion of the district for the European population, and where the extent of the land so resumed has been ascertained, to determine what price shall be paid to the natives for it; this amount not to be paid at once, but in annual instalments, extending over a period of three or four years, at the end of which time it may be calculated that the lands reserved for the natives will have become so valuable as to yield them some income, in addition to the produce raised from those portions of them which they cultivate.

" (5.) Every effort should be made to acquire for the European population those tracts of land which were awarded to the New Zealand Company by Mr. Spain; and where blocks are reserved for the natives within these limits, portions of land of equal extent (if possible), must be purchased without the limits for the New Zealand Company.

" (6.) If possible the total amount of land resumed for the Europeans should be from 60,000 to 70,000 acres; a grant of this tract of land will then be offered by the Government to the Company.

" (6.) The price paid for any portion of the land should not exceed 1s. 6d. per acre, and the average price should be below this amount. The greatest economy on this subject is necessary.

" (8.) No time must be lost in completing these arrangements.

" (9.) Two surveyors and parties upon the most economical scale must be engaged for this purpose. The police should as far as practicable be employed on it.

" (10.) This arrangement should be carried out in the first instance with those parties who have given their assent to it, including the natives who have offered a tract of land for sale to the south of the Sugarloaves.

" (11.) Where land without the block awarded by Mr. Spain is newly acquired, and required for immediate use by the Company's settlers, sections must be surveyed for them.

"(12.) Those natives who refuse to assent to this arrangement must distinctly understand that the Government does not admit that they are the true owners of the land they have recently thought proper to occupy.

"(13.) Mr. Maclean is intrusted with the conduct of these arrangements, but in all matters of importance he must consult Captain King, and acquaint him with the steps which he proposes to take.

"(14.) In reserving the blocks intended for the natives, the surveyed lines of the Company should in as far as practicable be observed, but whenever there is a necessity for a departure from this course the lines must be run as Mr. Maclean thinks proper.

"G. GREY."

March.—Messrs. Gillingham and E. Davy made an unsuccessful attempt to ascend the mountain.

April.—A quarrel took place among the Puketapu hapu respecting the boundaries of lands lying between Waiwakaiho and Waiongona. The Tataraimaka Block was purchased at the rate of three halfpence per acre. Capt. King and Mr. Cutfield were desirous of obtaining a lease of this block at the rent of £12 per annum, with power to purchase 300 acres for £120. If the lease were granted they proposed placing 200 head of cattle upon the block. Tataraimaka at this time was a beautiful shrubbery, which 20 years previously was all in a state of cultivation. In old times it possessed a very strong pa, capable of holding a very large garrison, which was called Pukeporoporo. The purchase of Omata from the Taranaki tribe was expected to be soon completed. May 29th died the Rev. Mr. Bolland, the first Episcopal minister of the settlement. His premature death was universally regretted.

May 1st.—An Ordinance for establishing a court for the recovery of small debts came into operation. On Mr. Bulkeley's section at the Waiwakaiho the natives claimed 41 out of 50 acres, but Governor Grey refused to interfere in the matter, as Governor Fitzroy had allowed the claim. Mr. Maclean was authorised to purchase the Grey Block.

August 31st.—Mr. Frederick Dillon Bell arrived from Nelson by the Catherine Johnson to supersede Mr. J. T. Wicksteed in the office of Company's Agent.

September 9th.—Bishop Selwyn arrived in the Undine, but only remained ashore for a few hours. The Comet arrived from Sydney with cattle. A great quarrel arose between the Puketapu hapu and the Ngatitairi hapu of the Taranaki tribe about a Taranaki girl whom some of the Puketapu had abducted and carried into the forest. Puketapu determined to attack the Omata chiefs when they came to town to receive payment for their land. By a piece of strategy the Omata chiefs led Puketapu to suppose that they would come into town on a certain day, but they deceived them by coming in on a different day. They signed the deed on that day, received the first instalment of the payment, and then danced the war dance, but while so engaged Puketapu stole out to Omata and burnt the pa. There were two whaling parties at this time in the settlement, but this season they had only succeeded in capturing one small whale. On the 14th Lieutenant Collinson, R.E., and Corporal Henderson, R.A., came up the coast from Wanganui and visited Waitara and Kawhia, but the object of their visit did not transpire. Most probably it was of a military nature. Dr. Wilson, of Wanganui, paid a visit to the settlement, and was so pleased with it that he determined to settle here if he could get his Wanganui land exchanged for land at New Plymouth. He thought he should be able to induce Capt. Campbell and other friends to follow his example. The remaining portion of the Waiwakaiho bridge gave way and the whole became a total wreck. Between the Henui and the Waiwakaiho there were many cases of fever. Mr. Carrington was engaged surveying a road to Omata. Mr. Hulke, of Wanganui, purchased the Union Mill.

September 22nd.—A small block of land containing 3,560 acres, situate about nine miles from New Plymouth, was purchased from the natives for £150. The Omata Block containing 12,000 acres was purchased for £400, or 8d. per acre. The Grey Block was also purchased for £390. The payment for these blocks was, according to the Governor's instructions, to be made by instalments.

October.—£50, due to the Ngamotu hapu for some of their land included in the Fitzroy Block, was paid. The sum had been owing to them since 1844. The hapu expressed its willingness to sign the deed conveying the Grey Block, and to receive the first instalment of the payment. More than 1,000 acres of the best land in this block were to be reserved for the natives. The settlers had a great desire for the re-purchase of the lands at the Waitara. Negotiations were being made for the purchase of a block of 10,000 acres at £390, or 10d. per acre. The cutter Sarah Berry called and took away several working men to Auckland. A meeting of settlers took place, Capt. Cooke in the Chair, to memorialise the Government for compensation for the loss of their lands through the reversal of Spain's award by Governor Fitzroy. The natives of the district were quiet, but a letter had been received from a Waikato chief named Te Kareno, acquainting the authorities of intrigues which were being carried on in the north by Rauparaha, and particularly of his recent attempt, at a meeting of the Waikato tribes, to unite them in a war of extermination against the tribes of the south, between Port Nicholson and the Sugarloaves. Te Wherowhero opposed the plan, but the Ngatipawas, the Ngatimarus, and the Ngatimatems, together with some of the Waikatos themselves, were all for war and were prepared to follow Rauparaha. Private and reliable information from Auckland stated that Rauparaha was incessantly, though secretly, laboring to stir up the northern tribes to avenge his captivity.

November.—In accordance with a promise of Colonel Wakefield 34 acres of land were allotted to the old whalers out of section No. 13.

John Wright received 10 acres, Simon Crawley 4 acres, William Bundy, 4 acres, Robert Sinclair 4 acres, James Bosworth 4 acres, and James Robinson 4 acres. The Inspector of Police reported that the police had cut a road through the Omata Block, which had cost the Government but 3s. per chain. The forest was reported to consist of Rata, Hinau, Rimu, Pukatea, Karaka, and Koromiko trees. Evidence of Puketapu intrusion were evident, and marks had been set on trees to indicate where distinguished warriors had fallen in battle. The Edward Stanley came in from Wanganui with goods belonging to Dr. Wilson and Mr. Hulke. Mr. Maclean had been to the Waitara, but had been unable to repurchase any of the lands in that district. Mr. Devenish returned from Wellington overland with 22 head of cattle. His bullocks sold at from £26 10s. 0d. to £36 10s. 0d. per pair, and his heifers from £10 10s. 0d. to £17 10s. 0d. each. He was 21 days coming up, and had but 1 horse and one white man as an assistant.

THE EVENTS OF 1848.

In March Sir George Grey revisited New Plymouth and specially advised Mr. Bell, the Company's Agent, to enter into negotiations with a portion of the Puketapu hapu for the purchase of the land lying between the Mangati and Wataha streams, now known as Bell Block. The land was offered by Rawiri Waiaua and others, but the sale thereof was violently opposed by Katatore, Parata Te Huia, and their followers. After the preliminary negotiations had taken place, a day was named in which to commence cutting the boundary lines in order to try the right of the disputants, Parata, Katatore, and the other hostile men, who immediately cut lines as boundaries to their own lands, and then prepared to resist by force the determination of the others to sell theirs. Mr. Bell took out with him the whole of the friendly party to work, numbering nearly sixty men. The battle began at the first line, and at some places the ground was fought for inch by inch. The natives only used their fists, sticks, and the backs of their tomahawks; anything like a sharp edge was most carefully let alone, and it was wonderful to see the amount of battering they endured without really using their deadly weapons. The end of it all was that in a few days the whole of the lines were cut, and afterwards *tangis* and feasts caused a speedy oblivion of the hard blows that had been exchanged. Wi Kingi made a claim upon a portion of this block, and was invited to be present when payment was made. He accordingly came, but no portion of the *utu* was allotted to him by the Puketapu, for he had no claim. Shortly after this transaction Mr. Bell left the settlement, and was succeeded as Company's Agent by Mr. William Halse.

In April a great migration of natives from Waikanae to Waitara took place. They were chiefly of the Ngatiawa tribe, and had either left their birth place to assist Rauparaha in his wars, or had fled from the Waikatos in their Southern raids. The number of souls who took part in this movement was 587, viz., 273 males, 195 females,

HISTORY OF TARANAKI. 145

and 119 children. They were conveyed from Waikanae to Waitara in one vessel, four boats, and forty-four canoes, and twenty men and one woman travelled overland on horses. The reasons for this migration were—(1) The love the people bore to their native place ; (2) They had sold Waikanae, a conquered district, to the British ; (3) Wi Kingi, who was related to the Tainui, had obtained Te Wherowhero's consent to return. When preparations were first made for this migration the Government was alarmed and seriously thought of seizing the canoes and boats prepared for the journey. But on Wi Kingi promising to settle on the north bank of the Waitara, the expedition was suffered to depart. When the people reached Waitara Kingi pretended that he was afraid of settling on the north bank of the river, because some Ngatimaniapotos had cultivations there, so he obtained permission of an old chief named Tamati Ruru, the father of Teira, to settle near to the South head of the river, and there he quickly erected a very large and strong pa.

During this year the Omata Block was opened, the Grey Institution —an industrial school for young Maoris on the Wesleyan Mission Farm at Moturoa—was inaugurated, and a new bridge constructed in the Devon Road over the river Henui. On the 17th September Colonel William Wakefield died at Wellington, and on the 17th, 18th, and 19th of October severe shocks of earthquake were felt.

THE WAIKANAE MIGRATION IN APRIL, 1848.

Where intending to settle.	Tribe.	Name of Canoe.	Principal Men in Canoe.	Men.	Women.	Children.
North of Waitara	Ngatimama	Takahurihuri	Rangikatatu	5	5	1
,,	,,	Nangaroa	Kurihanga	2	2	2
,,	Ngatimutanga	Tokekure	E Ru	3	3	2
,,	,,	Poterangi	Kotuka	5	6	6
,,	Puketapu	Marutangata	Katekamotakirau	6	2	2
,,	,,	(Vessel)	Te Ponga	20	21	1
,,	Ngatirahiri	Kairuru	Te Nirihana	9	5	5
,,	,,	Mohia	Ko Ongiongi	7	8	2
,,	,,	Karurukiterangi	Tutawa	9	7	1
,,	,,	Kiriorakau	Areuu	9	8	5
,,	,,	Kakaniwa	Governor Grey	4	3	1
,,	,,	Kaikaka	Nicodemus	6	3	3
,,	,,	(Boat Kaitonu)	Tekahinga	6	5	2
,,	,,	Wakarangi	Te Kaokao	13	7	4
Waitara	Manukorihi	Taupaki	Te Heke	4	4	1
,,	,,	Piritahataha	Maika	5	2	2
,,	,,	Maroro	Tararau	6	5	3
,,	,,	Wikitoria	Enoka	5	4	4
,,	,,	Marohopa	Tamati	5	8	1
,,	,,	Oropi	Te Rangui	6	7	6
,,	,,	Tipapa	Koane	3	3	5
,,	,,	Tiarora	E Kaumu	5	1	0
,,	,,	Taumamata	E Pero	6	5	4

THE WAIKANAE MIGRATION—Continued.

Where intending to settle.	Tribe.	Name of Canoe.	Principal Men in Canoe.	Men.	Women.	Children.
Waitara	Manukorihi	Kaupahanui	Wi Kingi	3	8	3
,,	,,	Konenuku	Maruiratimutu	6	4	4
,,	,,	Ko E Au	Poko Pomate	4	1	1
,,	,,	Konotekateka	WR Taupinga	4	1	0
,,	,,	Apupu	Panua	2	2	3
,,	,,	Maketu	Takaratahi	3	3	1
,,	,,	Pukawa	Kewai Tumihaka	4	3	1
,,	,,	Heu Heu	Hapimana	3	2	2
,,	,,	Hupipaipa	Wirihana	3	2	3
,,	,,	Rauparaha	Ihaia te Waripa	3	3	4
,,	,,	Aratotara	Heke	5	10	3
,,	,,	(Boat)	Te Teira	2	2	3
,,	,,	(Boat Louisa)	Kauriri	3	4	2
,,	,,	(Boat Prince Albert)	Albert	3	5	2
,,	,,	Tamakaikau	Ramera	2	1	0
,,	,,	(On horses)		20	1	0
Between Waitara and New Plymouth	Puketapu	Waikaane	Martin Luther	9	4	4
,,	,,	Okatarewa	Patekita	6	3	1
,,	,,	Pawakawa	Henry	6	4	4
South of New Plymouth	Taranaki	Kekenui	Horopapera	5	3	0
,,	,,	Ruapairoa	O Hua	5	6	0
,,	,,	Maratuahu	Haia	4	4	3
,,	,,	Te Naru	Petua	4	3	2
,,	Ngatiruanui	Harawangi	Herewene	3	4	4
,,	,,	Te Raho	Paura	2	2	2
,,	,,	Tu Puruatainui	Rewiti	3	3	3
,,	,,	Rongotekateka	Orumene	2	2	1
			Total	273	195	119

```
Total Persons   ...   ...   ...   ...   ...   587
  ,,  Vessels   ...   ...   ...   ...   ...     1
  ,,  Boats     ...   ...   ...   ...   ...     4
  ,,  Canoes    ...   ...   ...   ...   ...    44
  ,,  Horses    ...   ...   ...   ...   ...    21
```

CHAPTER XVII.

THE EVENTS OF 1849.

FROM 1844 to 1848 the settlement experienced its deepest depression; not even in the midst of the war did its position seem so utterly hopeless as then. But after that period the darkness seemed to brighten a little. In 1849, the town consisted of a few small stores on either side of the Huatoki Bridge, a few cottages at Devonport, as St. Aubyn Street was then called, and a few around the church. There was the lingering remnant of a Maori pa on Mount Eliot, near the flag staff, and a thickly peopled pa called the Kawau at the seaward end of Currie Street. Within a radius of 500 feet of the Huatoki Bridge all was a ferny wilderness. At Omata the settlers had just commenced clearing. Beyond the Waiwakaiho all was wilderness except Davy's, Smart's, and Nairn's farms, near the east bank of the Waiwakaiho, and Captain Cooke's at the Hua, and Wills' at Mangati. In order that the Pakeha should never return to the lands on the east of the Waiwakaiho, Parata te Huia, Katatore, and other turbulent natives erected a carved pole on the east side of the river, beyond which the white people were not to settle. This year the road from Puketotara to Mangorei was cut, and the first settlers went out to that district. The only draught horse in the settlement at this time was Lightfoot, the property of William Richards, but Dalby's bullock Redmond, who would suffer himself to be harnessed into a cart with shafts, assisted in performing the little cartage at that time required. It frequently happened that the little town ran completely out of some commodity. Once there was no salt to be had, and sea water had to be evaporated in order to obtain that necessary article. Now there was a tobacco famine. The times were duller than they would otherwise have been by reason of the partial failure of the wheat crops through excessive wet, and by many of the Puketapu natives insolently refusing to permit the completion of the purchase of Mangati, or, as it was afterwards called, Bell Block, because the whole of the money was not paid at once, and more especially because in a quarrel in town, Richard Brown, a merchant, had nearly cracked the skull of a Maori named Witana Rangiora. As the Huatoki Bridge was the most central and public spot in the little town, a black board was erected upon its rails, and upon this board all proclamations and advertisements were posted. Some of these were sufficiently ludicrous. For instance, a jocular parson of the period had a pony for sale, and the advertisement upon the bridge ran thus :—" For Sale. That redoubtable pony POMPEY, possessing all the admirable and characteristic qualities of horse, ass and mule. For particulars apply at the Mission House."

On the 4th of May, 1849, the New Zealand Company agreed to

grant compensation in land to those settlers who had been deprived of their holdings by the arbitrary act of Governor Fitzoy in 1844.

On the afternoon of Saturday, the 18th of August, a gun was heard at sea, and to the joy of the whole community, an English barque was seen approaching the Sugarloaves. A volunteer crew was soon procured, and one of the surf boats put off with Mr. Webster, the Custom House Officer; Mr. Watson, the Pilot; and others. The barque proved to be the Cornwall, 580 tons, chartered by the New Zealand Company—which having come to an understanding with the Government had recommenced operations—and commanded by Captain Dawson, formerly commander of the Amelia Thompson and Slaines Castle, who had brought some of the first immigrants to the settlement. Captain Dawson had called to land Mr. Charles Brown, who had returned from England with a large quantity of hardware, and a few other passengers, but the greater part of the immigrants were bound for the new settlement of Otago. Captain Dawson was hospitably received by his old friends who came out in the Amelia Thompson. Unfortunately the children in the Cornwall were suffering from measles, and the disorder was communicated to the settlement.

The Cornwall was followed by other ships chartered by the Company, and a number of respectable settlers were added to the little community.

Donald Maclean, Esq., to Captain King, R.N., Resident Magistrate.
"New Plymouth, 19th October, 1849.

"Sir:—In compliance with your instructions that the original deeds for lands purchased from the natives in this district should be forwarded by the next mail to Auckland, I hereby do myself the honor to hand them over to you for transmission. If you deem it advisable I shall order a small wooden or tin case, in which they may be placed for greater security. For reference at the settlement, copies and translations of the several deeds are duly entered in a book I am keeping expressly for that purpose. I should have sent the deeds, as you suggested, direct to the Colonial Secretary, but on after consideration it occurred to me that documents of such importance had better be examined and passed through your hands as the resident representative of the Government. The deeds are:—

"No. 1, November. 1844—Conveyance of the Fitzroy Block.

"No. 2 May 11th, 1848—Conveyance of a block of land between the Timaru and Katikara rivers at Tataraimaka.

"No. 3, August 30th, 1847—Conveyance by the Taranaki tribe of the Omata Block of 12,000 acres.

"No. 4, October 10th, 1847—Deed of the resident Ngamotu natives conveying their claims to the Grey block of 9,770 acres.

"No. 5, April 12th, 1848—Deed by absentee natives of the Ngamotu tribe residing at Wellington and Cook Strait, relinquishing their claims to the Fitzroy and Grey blocks of land respectively.

"No. 6, November 24th, 1840—Deed of conveyance by the

Puketapu natives for lands situate near the Hua, in the occupation of John George Cooke, Esq.

"No. 7, November 29th, 1848—Deed by the Puketapu natives conveying about 1,500 acres of land.

"I shall feel much obliged by your acknowledging the receipt of the foregoing documents.—I have, &c.

"DONALD MACLEAN."

The Fitzroy block, mentioned in Mr. Maclean's letter, contained 3,500 acres; the Tataraimaka block 3,500, to which by a subsequent purchase was added 500 acres; the Omata block 12,000 acres; the Grey block 9,770 acres; Bell block 1,500 acres.

Donald Maclean, Esq., to Captain King, R.N., Resident Magistrate.

"Taranaki, November 23rd, 1849.

"Sir:—I have the honor to acknowledge the receipt of your letter of yesterday's date enclosing a copy of a letter from Mr. Richard Brown, complaining that Major Lloyd who intends purchasing some sections of which Mr. Brown is agent, was molested by Peter and other natives residing at Waireka. On the 19th instant I gave notice to the Waireka natives to relinquish all their cultivations on the above sections, which they agreed to do, offering on the 22nd instant to dispose of their old fencing on the abandoned cultivations to Major Lloyd. Major Lloyd declined the offer, and from what I can learn from that gentleman he referred them to Mr. Brown, while he himself proceeded with his work on the section. Peter threatened if he were not paid for the fencing he would set fire to it, removing a fire-stick from Major Lloyd's fire as if to carry his threat into execution. He did not, however, interfere with the fencing, but set fire to a few straggling sticks which accidentally burnt a small quantity of dry fern. I rebuked Peter, who is usually a quiet native, for such conduct towards a stranger who could not understand the nature of his demands for *utu* for fencing on land fairly purchased, and he expressed his sorrow for what had taken place, stating that he and the rest of the Waireka natives would forthwith abandon all their cultivations and fencing on Major Lloyd's section.—I have, &c.,

"DONALD MACLEAN."

CHAPTER XVIII.

FROM 1850 TO 1855.

DURING the year 1850 the New Zealand Company gave their Charter back to the Crown. The season was a wet one, but the settlers at Mangoraka and Omata were busy clearing bush and cropping with wheat. On Friday morning, 2nd August, the cutter William and James, from Manukau, drifted ashore in the little bay on the east side of Paritutu, the great Sugarloaf, and became a wreck, Eliza Bishop, a passenger, being drowned. On the 14th October, 1850, Charles Macdonald, aged 13, one of the passengers by the Cornwall, was injured by the overturning of a bullock cart near Seccombe's Brewery in the Carrington Road, and died early the next morning. He had been struck by a projecting screw on the rail of the cart, on the occipital bone. In October the ship Eden arrived from London with several respectable settlers. In November Caroline Freeman, a half caste, aged 7 years, died in consequence of severe burns, accidentally received.

During the year H.M.S.S. Acheron, engaged on hydrographical service, anchored in the roadstead for the purpose of enabling her officers to ascertain by trigonometrical admeasurement the altitude of Mount Egmont. The result of this survey was the assigning of a height of 8,270 feet to the mountain.

In 1851 gold was discovered in New South Wales, and a large demand for potatoes sprang up. Ships chartered by Messrs. Willis and other London Shipping Agents now began to make regular calls at the settlement, bringing goods and passengers, and the demand for land became more and more urgent.

On the 4th of August, 1852, the Taranaki Herald, the first newspaper published in the province, was started by Mr. William Collins. In 1852 Captain King, R.N., on account of his age and increasing infirmities, resigned his post as Resident Magistrate, an appointment he had held from the early days of the settlement, his commission as Justice of the Peace being signed by Governor Hobson, and published in the Government Gazette of September 29th, 1841. He was succeeded by Mr. Josiah Flight, formerly of Lyme, Dorsetshire, England. In February, 1852, Elizabeth Crann was found drowned in the Waiwakaiho river.

Early in 1853 the Constitution was proclaimed. In 1846 an Act to make farther provision for the government of the New Zealand Islands passed both Houses of the Imperial Parliament. The Charter was to come into operation in January, 1848. To this Charter Governor Grey, influenced by Bishop Selwyn and Chief Justice Martin objected, and the result of this objection was an Act passed in May, 1848, suspending the Charter and intrusting the Governor with the power of granting or withholding representative institutions upon any basis suitable to the Colony. In virtue of this law Governor Grey assembled the Legislative Council, which had been instituted in 1840, and passed a Provincial Councils' Ordinance which gave to the provinces of New Ulster and New Munster, provinces defined by the Constitution Act of 1846, an Executive and Legislative Council composed of officials and nominees. In 1852 an Act, giving to the Islands a Representative Constitution, passed both Houses of the Imperial Parliament. The Act was as follows:—"There was to be a General Government, conducted by a General Assembly composed of a Governor appointed by the Crown; a Legislative Council of ten members, increased in 1857 to twenty members, appointed by the Crown for life; and a House of Representatives, consisting of from twenty-four to forty members, elected for five years by the people. The franchise to include all British subjects twenty-one years of age, having £50 freehold estate, £10 household in town, or £5 household in the country. The General Assembly to have the power of making laws for the government of the Colony, which must be in accordance with the laws of England. A Civil List of £16,000 to be provided for without power of alteration, except with the Sovereign's sanction. The expense of collecting the revenue and payments for land to be first provided for; all the remaining revenue to be under the control of the General Government. All money votes to be brought forward by the Governor. The Sovereign has the power of vetoing all Acts within two years, and the Governor of reserving Acts for Her Majesty's approval. The natives to be under the laws of the Colony, but the Sovereign to have the power of purchasing land from the natives. £7000 of the £16,000 on the Civil List to be spent in native purposes, and the remainder in paying the salaries of the Governor and Judges. The Colony was to be divided into six provinces, viz., Auckland, Wellington, New Plymouth, Nelson, Otago and Canterbury. Each province was to be ruled by a Superintendent elected by the people; the Governor to have a veto on the election. There was to be a Council for each province composed of members elected for four years, the franchise to be the same as for the General Assembly. The Provincial Council to have the power of making all laws for the government of the province with the exception of customs, high courts of law, currency, weights and measures, port duties, marriages, crown and native lands, criminal law, and inheritance. The Governor to have the power of vetoing all laws within three months. The Sovereign to have the power of establishing municipal corporations, subject to the approval of the Provincial Council."

On the 4th of March Governor Grey, by proclamation, reduced the price of the waste rural lands of the Crown to an upset price of 10s. per acre.

On the 17th of July, 1853, the election of the first Superintendent took place at the old Court House in Devon street. There were three candidates for the office; Charles Brown, William Halse, and John Tylson Wicksteed, and Charles Brown was elected and drawn in triumph through the town by a troop of enthusiastic young men. Prior to this the following gentlemen were elected members of the Provincial Council :—George Cutfield, R. Chilman, Robert Parris, George Rutt Burton, Thomas Good, Samuel Vickers, and Isaac Newton Watt. Mr. Watt was chosen Speaker, and Mr. Chilman Provincial Treasurer. Mr. Christopher William Richmond was chosen Clerk to the Council and Provincial Attorney, and Mr. Charles Batkin Private Secretary to the Superintendent. The first session of the Provincial Council was opened at the Old Court House, Devon street, on Tuesday morning, 16th September, 1853, at 11.30 o'clock, and by a provisional arrangement of the Governor Provincial institutions were supported by two-thirds of the Customs duties of the Colony.

In 1853, five years after the payment of the first instalment of the purchase money, and after very much opposition, the Government ventured to open the Bell Block to the settlers. On the evening of the 29th May, James Foreman, a fine young man, fell into the Mangatuku stream in Brougham street, and was drowned.

On the last day of the year 1853 Sir George Grey left Auckland for London, and Colonel Wynyard, C.B., of the 58th Regt., the senior military officer in the Colony, and newly elected Superintendent of the province of Auckland, assumed the administration of the Government.

On 1st January, 1854, at half-past 8, p.m., a severe shock of earthquake was felt in New Plymouth. The afternoon had been hazy, and a remarkable round cloud, which sent out a long tail-like streamer, hovered near to the peak of the mountain. On the 6th of February Mr. G. S. Cooper was appointed Sub Commissioner for the purchase of lands in New Plymouth.

The Chief Commissioner to the Honorable the Colonial Secretary.
"Land Commissioner's Office,
"Taranaki, 20th Feb., 1854.

"Sir :—I have the honor to report to you, for the information of His Excellency, the officer administering the government, that the negotiations at present in progress with the natives for the acquisition of land at this settlement, are of such a complicated nature, involving conflicting interests of different tribes who are at variance with each other respecting their claims, that I apprehend it will yet take some time either to effect a satisfactory purchase or enable Mr. Cooper to go on with fresh negotiatious. Another cause of delay arises from the fact that the natives are busily engaged with the wheat harvest, and any interruption of their labors would not only be a serious loss to themselves, but would also affect the Europeans who employ many of them to secure their crops. In the meanwhile, however, the surveys of Reserves in the Waiwakaiho Block are carried on, and I am in hope that most of these difficulties which have delayed the occupation by settlers of that purchase, and which I am engaged with Mr. Cooper in arranging, will soon be adjusted. The purchase of the land in question has been greatly complicated by a league which has been entered into by the Ngatiawa, Taranaki, and Ngatiruanui tribes, by which they have solemnly bound themselves and each other to put a stop to all sales of land to the North of the Bell Block, or South of Tataraimaka; and so much political importance do they attach to this, that, in order to give greater solemnity to the covenant, and by way of rendering it as binding as possible on the parties, a copy of the Scriptures was buried in the earth with many ceremonies, thereby, as it were, calling on the Deity to witness the inviolabilty of their compact. It is therefore a matter of the utmost importance to the interests of the Province that every exertion should be used without delay, not only to obtain possession of the lands at present unaffected by this league, but also to endeavor by every possible means to induce the natives to break through, or, if possible, entirely put an end to the ill-advised compact they have made.

"To facilitate the acquisition of land to the south of the settlement I have deemed it advisable to secure the services of Mr. Wellington Carrington, a surveyor, to assist in effecting arrangements for this purpose, in order that his professional services, and any influence he may possess over the natives, with whom he is connected by marriage, may, under the urgent necessity for acquiring land, be made temporarily available for this object.

"I feel most anxious to proceed to Auckland, and shall not delay an hour longer in this place than I can avoid; but I fear that my leaving abruptly at present would prove injurious to future negotiations, on the result of which the prosperity of the Province depends. I beg to enclose for His Excellency's information copies of letters that have been received by me from his Honor the Superintendent, and the Resident Magistrate on the subject. His Excellency will no doubt be informed by his Honor the Superintendent of this Province that an Ordinance has been passed in the Provincial Council to authorise the raising of a loan of £5,000, in the event of such a sum being required for the purchase of land from the natives.—I have, &c.

"DONALD MACLEAN,
"Land Commissioner."

The Same to the Same.
"Land Commissioner's Office, Taranaki, 7th March, 1854.

"Sir :—I have the honor to report to you for the information of His Excellency, the officer administering the Government, that after numerous meetings with the majority of the native tribes of this Province, an arrangement has been effected for the purchase of a block of land contiguous to the settlement and estimated to comprise from 12,000 to 14,000 acres of fine open agricultural land. The growing opposition to the sale of any of their land; their knowledge of its increased value, and of the extreme urgency of the Europeans to obtain it; their apprehension of never being allowed to repurchase any part of what they once alienate; the fear that they should thereby lose their distinctive national character and standing and be reduced to a state of slavery and indigence—has encouraged a combined and systematic opposition by those tribes to the cession of their territory.

"From the decided minority of natives in favor of a sale it has become a most difficult matter to acquire any land in this Province, and consequently it has been found necessary, after due consideration by His Honor the Superintendent, and the officers of the General Government at this place, to accede to their lowest demand of £3,000, which was paid subject, however, to conditions which I shall presently notice. The most interesting feature in this transaction, and the only one which I considered justified my assenting to so large a payment was, that the natives agreed, instead of having extensive reserves which would monopolise the best of the land, to repurchase out of the block they have sold one thousand pounds worth of land with a pre-emptive right of selection at ten shillings per acre. I have every reason to expect that this arrangement will be most important in its results by giving the natives a security of tenure they never previously enjoyed, by removing all apprehension as to 'their inability to repurchase from the Government, by leading them to take an interest in the political institutions of the country by being qualified to take part in them, by introducing a feature in their mode of living which must improve their circumstances, while it dispenses with the necessity that existed under their former precarious tenure and custom of living in confederate bands in large pas, ready at a moment's notice to collect and arm themselves either for defence or depredation. Nor are these the only advantages to be gained from the introduction of this system; another most important one is, that it will lead without much difficulty to the purchase of the whole of the native lands in this Province, and to the adoption by the natives of exchanging their extensive tracts of country at present lying waste and unproductive for a moderate consideration, which will be chiefly expended by them in repurchasing land from the Crown. The natives have entered into the spirit of this arrangement with greater readiness than might be at first expected, and instead of having reserves of several thousand acres they have been satisfied with three hundred acres round their pas; they have also deposited the thousand pounds with Mr. Cooper for the repurchase of the additional land they may require—and the arrangements for the survey of those lands and the settlement of natives on them are now in progress, so that the land may be thrown open for European selection with as little delay as possible.

"I am glad to add that the several meetings with the natives at which the claims of district tribes to the Taranaki mountains were discussed have terminated, notwithstanding considerable excitement, without any disturbance, and this notice is due to the natives, since upwards of twelve hundred of them representing conflicting interests were collected in town.—I have, &c.,

"DONALD MACLEAN,
"Land Commissioner."

The result of the purchase of the Hua and Waiwakaiho block proved unsatisfactory. In order to obtain the conseut of Wi Tako, a great partizan of the King movement, and other powerful chiefs residing in Wellington who had an interest in the block, it became necessary to make large reserves of the best of the land. Then Henry Puni, a son of the great Ngatiawa chief Te Puni, seized a large portion of the open land from the sea coast to the south of the Devon Road, including the ancient pa Rewarewa, at the mouth of the Waiwakaiho river, which was at one time garrisoned by a thousand men, and successfully resisted a fierce and powerful attack of the southern tribes. On the Mangaone Hill, Puni erected a strong pa and bid defiance thereby to the pakeha. Inland of this seizure and of these reserves the other Maoris exercised their pre-emptive right of purchase, after which the only land left for the settlers was the very broken district above the junction of the Waiwakaiho river with its numerous tributaries. The repurchase of the lands by some of the natives, and the possession of a Crown Title to them, led to no beneficial results. The holders of these lands never cultivated a tithe of them, shirked all their duties as land owners under the Crown, refused to pay highway rates, and ultimately sold their lands to the settlers and spent the money in intoxicating drink.

In May, Ihaia and Tamati offered some land at Waitara for sale.

On the 13th May, Harihanu, a Maori, killed another Maori named Aperahama, by striking him on the head with a hammer at Katatore's pa, Kaipakopako. No legal proceedings were taken in the case.

The first session of the General Assembly of New Zealand was opened at Auckland by Colonel Wynyard, the officer administering the Government, on the 27th May, 1854. The Representatives of Taranaki in that Assembly were—in the Legislative Council: Major J. Y. Lloyd—in the House of Representatives: for the town of New Plymouth, Mr. F. U. Gledhill; for the Grey and Bell district, Mr. T. King, and for Omata, Mr. W. Crompton.

On the 3rd July, Simon Crawley, whaler and boatman, escaped from the Colonial Hospital while suffering from delirium tremens, and drowned himself in the sea on the Henui beach.

On the 14th September, Joseph Cassidy, a discharged soldier, in a fit of jealousy killed Mary Rodgers, a widow, residing at Omata, by stabbing her with a knife. Cassidy was removed to Auckland for trial, and being found guilty, was reprieved on the ground of insanity. He shortly afterwards died worn out with remorse and fear.

Towards the close of the year a Church Missionary clergyman and a catechist conjointly published a Maori tract against the selling of land to Europeans, and comparing the latter to Ahab who coveted the vineyard of Naboth, the Jezreelite.

On the 3rd January, 1855, Richard Eaton was drowned in the endeavor to get some sheep across the Waiwakaiho river. On the 23rd, at 9.15 p.m., a severe earthquake occurred, which did much damage to chimneys and sandstone buildings. On the same day

William Holloway, in endeavoring to catch a goat, fell over a cliff at Omata and was killed. On the 25th the ship Josephine Willis, Capt. Canney, arrived from London, and reported having felt the shock of earthquake at sea. On Saturday evening, February 10th, Mr. Thomas Bayly's house was accidentally burned down. About this time much dissatisfaction was expressed in the Provincial Council at the refusal of the natives to give up the seaward end of the Hua and Waiwakaiho Block which had been purchased by Mr. Cooper. They took advantage of a promise of reserves made at the time of purchase, which was not defined by writing or plans. One of the earliest enactments of the Provincial Council was that of the " Public Works Ordinance," by which provision was made for the repair of the roads. Since the cessation of the operations of the New Zealand Company very little had been done to the streets of the town or the country highways, and most of the rivers were unbridged. The first election under this Ordinance was that for the district of the town of New Plymouth, which took place at the Old Court House, Devon street, on Saturday, 17th February, at 4 p.m. About 18 persons were present and Mr. I. N. Watt was called to the chair. The meeting decided that a uniform rate of 5s. should be levied on all sections, and chose Messrs. H. L. Redhead, G. Y. Lethbridge, and W. Brooking, Commissioners. In March, at a public meeting it was determined to memorialise the Queen on the unprotected state of the settlement in the midst of the Puketapu feud which was then raging. On the 25th H.M.S. Pandora arrived, bringing Acting Governor Wynyard, Capt. Travers, and Mr. J. White, Maori Interpreter. After personally investigating the unsettled state of the district His Excellency re-embarked on the 10th of April. On April 19th a schooner designed by Mr. Cutfield, and built at Moturoa in front of Barrett's farm, by Messrs. Rundle, Clare, and others, was launched and named by Miss Anna Rundle the "Taranaki." On June 3rd the ship Cresswell arrived from London, bringing Mr. E. J. Cudd and the Kelly family. In August the whole of the male adult population were sworn in as special constables, and a strict account of arms was taken. On August 19th the ship Duke of Portland, Capt. Seymour, arrived from Auckland with 250 rank and file of the 58th Regiment, ten officers, 13 non-commissioned officers, three drummers, detachments of Artillery and Sappers, and several field pieces. On September 6th the Duke of Portland arrived from Wellington with 210 non-commissioned officers and men of the 65th Regiment. The crown of Marsland Hill was levelled for the erection of barracks of galvanized iron which had been brought from Melbourne. During the process of levelling human bones were found, and a coffin containing a skeleton which had fair hair attached to the skull. Naval buttons were found in the coffin, from which it was supposed that the skeleton was that of some Naval Officer who had died off the coast, and whose body had been brought ashore for burial. In September a pastoral letter of Bishop Selwyn was published in the settlement, and gave great offence to many of the settlers on account of the charge of greed which it brought against them as regarded their desire to obtain more land, and the special pleadings and apologies it made on behalf of the Maori land leaguers.

On the 27th October Governor Gore Brown arrived in the S.S. Zingari on a visit to the settlement. On Nov. 5th Mr. Christopher William Richmond was returned to the House of Representatives for the Town of New Plymouth, in the room of Mr. F. U. Gledhill who had resigned. On Nov. 5th the ship Egmont arrived from London, bringing the Upjohn family.

On Dec. 25th a portion of the 58th Regiment left for Auckland by the Ocean brig, the Regiment being ordered to England, having completed its term of service. During this year the Taranaki natives cut a line about ten feet broad across the northern face of the ranges adjoining Mount Egmont, which they call Iringanui, but the Ngatiawa Ponakai; faces were cut on all the prominent trees along the line. These people were so superstitious as to believe that the retention of these ranges would preserve them from the encroachments and dominance of the Pakehas. The Public Works Ordinance of this year was a mild measure of the Provincial Council for promoting the repair of roads and the erection and maintenance of bridges. It provided merely for an optional road rate.

CHAPTER XIX.

THE PUKETAPU FEUD.

THE Puketapu were one of the most powerful families of the whole Ngatiawa tribe. They took their name from that remarkable hill on the sea coast in the broad and beautiful bay which is situated between the rivers Waiwakaiho and Waiongona. Sheltered by reefs the bay abounds with fish during the summer months, and the reefs themselves yield a harvest of molluscs. The land around the hill is very fertile, and on the hill a dense littoral vegetation grows. Here, according to tradition, the beautiful crimson veronica once flourished. From some unknown cause the hill was named Puketapu, the sacred mount, and on it the great pa of the hapu once stood. The shepherd boy seeking some stray ewe occasionally meets with some relic of its inhabitants in the shape of a stone ear-drop or axe. Possibly, like Jeshurun, this family waxed fat and kicked by reason of the fruitfulness of their inheritance. They formed part of the army which Rauparaha led against the Southern tribes, and Colonel Wakefield in his journal speaks of the difficulty he experienced in dealing with them in Cook Strait. After their return from the South they were in a state of degeneracy, most of their great chiefs had fallen in battle, and their places had been taken by inferior men. It was by the unremitting opposition of these people that the settlers were driven from the Mangoraka district, and the settlement reduced to the smallest limits. These remarks, however, do not apply to the whole, for there were chiefs and others among them who were amicably disposed towards the Europeans. The most notable friendly Puketapu Chief was Rawiri Waiaua, *i.e.*, David the Porpoise, a well-proportioned man, mild of disposition, profusely tatooed, who was in the habit of paying visits to the town on a gray horse, wearing a white hat and green spectacles. By this chief's influence the Bell Block came into the hands of the Europeans, and now he was pressed by the Sub Land Commissioner to sell more land in the same district, land being greatly in demand through the influx of substantial settlers, and the high price of farm produce, brought about by the recent discovery of gold in Australia. This had the effect of dividing the Puketapu hapu into two parties; the anti-land-selling-leaguers, headed by the chief Waitere Katatore, and the land-sellers under the leadership of Rawiri Waiaua. Early in the morning of the 3rd of August, 1854, Rawiri and a party of his followers went out with billhooks to cut a line for the purpose of marking the boundaries of a piece of land they intended to sell to the Europeans. While they were engaged in the work they were met by an armed party under the command of Waitere Katatore, who fired upon them, killing four persons, mortally wounding Rawiri and another, severely wounding four, and slightly wounding six. In proof of the murderous nature of the attack, out of twenty-six persons composing Rawiri's party, sixteen were hit. Arrangements were made as quickly as possible after the affray to convey the wounded to the hospital. Paora's case was hopeless, so that nothing could be done for him, and he could not bear removal. Rawiri had received a ball in his side which had passed upwards and out through the breast bone. The natives were in too great a state of excitement to remove him the day he fell, and the settlers were afraid to interfere in the quarrel. All, therefore, that could be done for him was to put a tent over him. The news of the encounter quickly spread among the natives, and by noon an armed party had collected from the Hua and Tairutu. These first visited Katatore's pa at Kaipakopako and fired a volley into it, after which they proceeded to the scene of the encounter where they buried the dead and encamped for the night. The next morning Paora expired, and after his interment Rawiri was conveyed in a litter to the hospital, but medical skill was of no avail in his case, for he expired at half-past one on the morning of the 6th inst. Then pas were strengthened, roads were tapued, and preparations were made for conflict. The Government was appealed to for the purpose of executing the law against the murderers. It was argued that Rawiri was a British subject, was in the Commission of the Peace, and was performing an act of friendship to the Europeans when he fell. But His Excellency Colonel Wynyard was afraid to interfere, and the feelings of Rawiri's friends were soothed to some extent by the influence of the Rev. John Whiteley, Mr. Maclean, William Nero, an influential Waikato chief, and others. The murderer, Katatore, either out of fear or remorse, suddenly turned his back upon the league, and offered to sell some land to the Government. In November, 1854, just three months after the death of Rawiri, another tragical event took place at the Mamaku pa, on the west bank of the Waitara. A young native named Rimene, who had been residing with the Puketapu and Waitara natives, committed adultery with the wife of Ihaia, the chief of the Mamaku pa, and when taxed with it confessed the crime. At the instigation of Ihaia a Maori named Hori approached Rimene as he was sitting in the pa, presented a gun to his breast, and killed him. Ihaia was friendly with the Europeans and willing to sell them land, the committal of this act was therefore taken advantage of by the anti-land-selling-leaguers to pick a quarrel with him. Rimene, besides being a member of the Ngatiruanui tribe, was related to that of Taranaki. Accordingly Wi Kingi, of Waitara, artfully represented to these tribes that the killing of Rimene was not on account of his crime of adultery, but because he had been for some time a follower of Katatore. By this means the death of Rimene became mixed up with the land quarrel, and the consequence was that on the 20th of December the Mamaku pa was besieged by three hundred and eighty warriors of the Ngatiruanui tribe. Ihaia erected elevated platforms at the angles of his pa for sharpshooters, and lined his stockade with bundles of green flax for a defence against musket balls. The friendly portion of the Puketapu sympathised with Ihaia, and before the action Wi te Ahoaho, commonly called by Europeans Sam Puketap, a considerable chief, entered the Mamaku to take part in its defence. Ihaia and his people fought bravely, but they were out-numbered by the Ngatiruanui. Seeing that he was hard pressed, Ihaia's Puketapu friends made a diversion in his favor, and he retreated to Mahoetahi. Ihaia had six killed and five wounded, and the Ngatiruanuis had five killed and ten wounded.

After making some attempt to renew the contest on the 22nd, and threatening to return home coastwise through New Plymouth, the Ngatiruanuis on the 25th, Christmas Day, quietly commenced their march homewards by the mountain road through the bush. These people had not been home long before a report was circulated among them that Ihaia had desecrated the graves of their slain at Waitara. This caused a great ferment, and threats were made of returning to annihilate Ihaia, but these were not carried out at that time. The relatives of Rawiri were loud in demanding the Government to punish Katatore for the murder of their chief and relative, but the Government was not strong enough to enforce the law, therefore Mr. Maclean, the Rev. Messrs. Whitely and Turton, and several Waikato chiefs were sent to appease their wrath. Finding that the Government would do nothing in the matter, the chief Arama Karaka, the relative and successor of Rawiri, came up from the south with his followers to avenge his relative's death. The east end of Bell Block and the Puketapu beyond, now became a battle-field. For months Maoris armed and clad in gaily colored shawls used to go out to fight every morning with great regularity. The sounds of the musketry could be plainly heard in town and at Mangorei. Ihaia joined his force with that of Arama Karaka, and the latter gave him a piece of land at Puketapu, on the Devon Road, and near to the Te Arei Road, on which Ihaia built a pa to which he gave the name of Ikamoana, sea-fish. Wi Kingi, Katatore, and some detachments of Ngatiruanui formed one party, and Arama Karaka, Ihaia, and Mahau and their followers formed the other. Considering the number of persons engaged, and the quantity of cartridges exploded, few casualties occurred. Sometimes a skirmish took place among the hedges of the settler's farms, and occasionally bullets pierced their houses, but no Pakeha was injured. At length a truce was made in 1856 after sixty Maoris had been killed, and one hundred wounded.

In 1855, the settlers of New Plymouth petitioned the Government for military protection. Mr. Maclean advised that block-houses should be built, the Militia called out, and that other steps should be taken for the defence of the settlement.

In August and September, 1855, detachments of the 58th and 65th Regiments, with two twenty-four pounder guns, landed at New Plymouth under the command of Major Nugent of the 58th Regiment. These were shortly afterwards followed by Colonel Wynyard, accompanied by Tamati Waka Nene, Te Whero, and Te Puni. The result of this visit was a ratification of the neutral policy to which we have alluded.

In July, 1857, Ihaia and Mahau offered the land at Ikamoana and Waiongona for sale, and in August following Katatore offered 40,000 acres for sale. The land-leaguers were astonished at this proceeding of their once staunch adherent, and wrote letters to him saying how dark their hearts were by reason of his apostacy. Katatore continued to press the land upon the Government, and the Government took preparatory steps towards the purchase, ignoring the offer of land by Ihaia and Mahau. Then Ihaia determined to destroy Katatore. In order to carry out his plan he caused Katatore to be made merry with drink in New Plymouth on Saturday, the 9th January, 1858, and as the old chief turned up the Wills Road, at Bell Block, to proceed to Kaipakopako, he was killed with his relative Rawiri Karira, by an ambuscade headed by Tamati Tiraurau, the brother of Ihaia. Katatore was not only the open enemy of the Mangoraka settlers, never resting till he had expelled them from their homes, but the arch scoundrel secretly planned a general massacre of the settlers, and nothing but extreme endurance and moderation on their part preserved them from this end. Nevertheless, the atrocious manner in which he was destroyed, filled every one with horror.

Report from Assistant Native Secretary Halse, to the Native Secretary.
"New Plymouth, January 11th, 1858.

"Sir,—I have to report to you that Katatore was killed last Saturday under very atrocious circumstances. On his return from town towards sundown, with three natives, all on horseback, he was waylaid by Tamati Tiraurau and a party of five natives—four Ngatirahiris and one belonging to Mahoetahi—on one of the main roads of the Bell district and shot. His relative, Rawiri Karira, fell at the first shot and was literally hacked to pieces.

"Tamihana pushed on, but Katatore dismounted, and whilst leading his horse up the cross road towards the Huira, was overtaken and pierced with several bullets, then beaten about the head with the discharged guns—three of which were broken over him—and finally mangled with tomahawks.

"The plans laid for Katatore's death were Ihaia's, as he has admitted to Mr. Parris; but they were so well kept by the natives concerned that nothing was known of them until they were effected. Even Katatore, who received a warning on the road from Mr. Hollis, who had observed armed natives remaining in one spot, had no thought of being attacked. Ihaia was observed watching him about town during the day under an assumed desire for reconcilliation, and he followed him out of the town. I am of opinion that that attack must have been meditated for some time, as on the first occasion of his moving out unarmed he has been killed. It may be attributed partly to revenge for Rawiri Waiaua's death, and

11

jealousy that Katatore, after all their efforts to punish him for it, should be in a position to offer land for sale when Ihaia's offer was rejected.

"I am quite unable to venture an opinion on the probable consequences of this unfortunate business. I fear it will lead to serious native troubles. Wiremu Kingi of Waitara occupied the Tima pa yesterday, and will aid the Kaipakupaku natives. The latter intend to attack the Ikamoana at once, rather than remain prisoners in their own pa. Hone Ropiha, the Assessor, met Katatore in town on Saturday, and was quite ignorant of Ihaia's plans.

"In conclusion, I deem it my duty to observe that Tamati Tiraurau, who resides in a well furnished wooden house in town, and is remarkable for his intelligence and extensive mercantile transactions with the settlers, was especially prominent for his ferocity in this attack. He dragged Rawiri off his horse, when mortally wounded by the first volley, and seizing him by the hair of his head, with the most fiendish gesticulations, as witnessed by two of the Bell Block settlers, first hacked his body and then his head and face to pieces. —I have, etc.,

"HENRY HALSE."

After the death of Katatore the followers and allies of that chief laid siege to the Ikamoana, and in less than a month brought Ihaia to great straits. Ihaia had not then the aid of Arama Karaka, for that chief, worn out with anxiety, had died in January, 1857. On the night of Saturday, February 6th, 1858, Ihaia quietly evacuated his pa and retreated to the Karaka, a pa near to a ford of the river Waitara, in the midst of groves of the beautiful *corynocarpus laevigata*. Early on Sunday morning the friends of Katatore entered the Ikamoana and made a great fire in the midst of it, in which they consumed all Ihaia's agricultural implements, ploughs, harrows, winnowing and threshing machines. The pigs were caught, and after their eyes were dug out with pointed knives, they were thrown alive into the fire. The poultry were also caught and thrown into the flames. All that Sunday morning the work of destruction went on till the Ikamoana and all that it contained was utterly consumed. Having driven Ihaia from the Puketapu territory, Katatore's friends followed him to the Waitara, and there laid so close a siege to him that he and his people were in danger of perishing for want of food. The Europeans sympathised much with Ihaia, because, in spite of all his atrocities, he had been friendly and true to them, but they were powerless to help him in his distress. At last the Rev. John Whiteley and Mr. Commissioner Parris, out of compassion to him, persuaded his enemies to permit him to escape. They consented to do so, and Ihaia fell back upon the river Mimi, where he received contributions of food from the Europeans, and built a pa at a place called Papawera, on a fine district of land called Te Kaweka, close to the south side of the river. Respecting the evacuation of the Karaka pa Mr. Parris thus wrote to the Colonial Secretary under date December 21st, 1860:—"When Ihaia, Nikorima and their party were besieged in the Karaka pa at Waitara, and were in a most miserable plight, Mr. Whiteley suggested to me that I should try and arrange terms of peace on the following basis, namely; that the besieged should be allowed to vacate the pa, and that the besiegers should then destroy it. I availed myself of the suggestion, and obtained the consent of Ihaia and Wiremu Kingi, the former to leave the pa, and the latter to destroy it, and not to follow them any farther; and shortly after, in the middle of the night, Ihaia's party took a loud farewell of their pa, but their places were immediately occupied by his Wanganui and Mokau allies. They thus tried to take advantage of arrangements which I had attempted to make for their preservation, and, but for my opportune arrival and discovery of the ambush, would probably have succeeded." No excuse can be offered for this act of treachery, but it will appear less atrocious when we remember that Ihaia's enemies declared their intention of roasting him alive if he should fall into their hands.

Mr. Cooper, shortly after the death of Rawiri, was transferred to another Province, in order to remove as much as possible all sources of irritation from the quarrelling natives on the part of the Government. Messrs. H. Halse and J. Rogan performed the duties of Commissioners temporarily. At length, in August, 1857, Mr. R. Parris was permanently appointed Commissioner of the District.

IHAIA KIRIKUMARA.

This celebrated warrior chief, and ally of the British, died of consumption accelerated by hard drinking, at the Wakatete pa, on the east bank of the Waitara river, on 9th July, 1873, and was interred in the burial place of his people at the Karaka on the 11th of the same month.

Ihaia was a chief of the Otaraua hapu of the Ngatiawa tribe. His early days were spent in captivity in the Waikato country, but in 1842-3 when, by the interference of the Missionaries, the Waikato tribe manumitted its slaves, he, with the rest of the captives, was permitted to return to the home of his fathers on the banks of the Waitara. Ihaia played a very prominent part in the Puketapu feud, which raged in the settlement from 1854 to 1860, the particulars of which have already been given. During the rebellion Ihaia occupied a prominent position among our native allies, and was present with the British troops and settlers in several engagements. In stature he was below the ordinary standard of his race, and his physiognomy was of so mild an appearance that from it no one would have suspected the true character of the man. One who knew him well declared that he was neither true to his race, his tribe, or to the British.

On July 15th, 1860, Ihaia, in conjunction with his friend Tamati Tiraura, wrote a letter to the New Plymouth settlers, from which we give the following extracts:—

"Friends:—Formerly we, the Maoris, lived alone in New Zealand; we did wrong one to another, made war on one another, we ate one another, we exterminated one another. Some had deserted the land, some were enslaved, the remnant that was spared went to seek other lands.

"Now this was the arrangement of this Ngatiawa land. Mokau was the boundary on the north, Ngamotu the boundary on the south; beyond were Taranaki and Ngatiruanui.

"All was quite deserted; the land, the sea, the streams, the lakes, the forests, the rocks, were deserted; the food, the property, the work, was deserted; the dead and the sick were deserted; the landmarks were deserted.

"Then came the Pakeha hither by sea from other dwellings—they came to this land and the Maoris allowed them—they came by chance to this place—they came to a place whose inhabitants had left it. There were few men here—the men were a remnant, a handful returned from slavery.

"And the Pakeha asked, 'Where are the men of this place?' and they answered, 'They have been driven away by war; we few have come back from another land.' And the Pakeha said, 'Are you willing to sell us this land?' And they replied, 'We are willing to sell it that it may not be merely barren; presently our enemies will come, and our places will be quite taken from us.'

"So payment was made; it was not said, 'let the place be simply taken,' although the men were few; the Pakeha did not say 'let it be taken,' but the land was quietly paid for.

"Now the Pakeha thoroughly occupied the purchase made with their money; and the Maoris living in the house of bondage, and those that had fled, heard of it; they heard that the land had been occupied, and they said, 'Ah! ah! the land has revived, the men have revived, let us return to the land.' So they returned. Their return was in a friendly manner. The thought of the Pakeha was, 'Let us dwell together, let us work together.'

"The Maoris began to dispute with the Pakeha. When the Governor saw it he removed the Pakeha to one spot to dwell. Afterwards the Pakeha made a second payment for the land, and afterwards a third; then I said, 'Ah! ah! very great indeed is the goodness of the Pakeha, he has not said that the payment ceases at the first time.'

"My friends the Pakeha, wholly through you this land and the men of this land have become independent; do not say that I have seen this your goodness to-day for the first time, I knew it formerly. At the coming here of Governor Grey, I was urgent that the land might be surrendered and paid for by him; that we might live there together, we the Maori and the Pakeha. And my urgency did not end then, but continued throughout the days of Governor Grey till the death of Rawiri. The death of Rawiri was owing to obstinacy about the land. Rawiri was killed for his friendly disposition towards the Pakeha. My interference on the occasion of the death of Rawiri was because I thought him a man more favorable to the Pakeha, a man whose opinion was like my own; if he had been evil disposed towards the Pakeha, then I should not have interfered; if he had been a parent or a relative, I should not have interfered. But, however, Rawiri and the rest are dead; it was by God that they were made chiefs of the land, and I was urgent that the land should be a payment for their deaths. By the obstinacy of Katatore he became a payment. If he had yielded, the land would have died, he would have been spared.

"Although after his death all the hapu gathered to overthrow and kill me, I was urgent for the sale of the land. Although my pa the 'Karaka' was besieged, and I was besieged, that I might be killed, when I earnestly prayed God that I might be saved, I urgently wrote to the Governor that he would purchase the land. However, I arrived at Mimi—I know that the Governor is a parent to me—I was urgent at that time about the sale in my letter to the Governor; although my word at that time did not influence him, what was that to me? my urgency was fixed in my heart. Although peace was renewed to me, I did not say through this peace I shall be preserved; but I consider that my security is from the Pakeha. And at this day I know that my security is great, for the Pakeha is a bulwark for me against destruction.

"IHAIA KIRIKUMARA,
"TAMATI TIRAURAU,

"Waitara, July 15th, 1860."

CHAPTER XX.

THE EVENTS OF 1856-58.

GOVERNOR GORE BROWN.

COLONEL WYNYARD, after administering the Government of the Colony for twenty months, was superseded by Colonel Gore Browne, who landed in Auckland on the 4th of September, 1855, and took the oaths of office on the 6th of September. Colonel Sir Thomas Gore Browne, K.C.M.G., son of Robert Browne, Esq., of Morton House, Buckinghamshire, England, and brother of the Bishop of Winchester, was born in 1807. Entering the army at sixteen he served many years with the 28th Regiment, acted as aide-de-camp to Lord Nugent, Lord High Commissioner of the Ionian Islands, and was for some time Colonial Secretary. In 1836, Major Gore Browne exchanged into the 41st Regiment, and served during the occupation of Afghanistan. After the massacre of our troops at the Khyber Pass, the 41st joined General England, and advanced to the rescue of General Nott and his troops. During that war Major Browne held the command of the 41st, and also commanded the reserve at the disastrous battle of Hykulzie, and by forming a square when the van of the army had been broken, was enabled to repulse the enemy and cover the retreat. He held command of the regiment at the battles of Candahar, Ghuznee, Cabul, and during the march through the Khyber Pass, where he commanded the rear, and under General McGaskell at the storming of the hill fort at Issaliff, the most daring action during the war. Major Gore Browne's gallantry and humanity were praised in the general's despatches, which were quoted in both Houses of Parliament, and for his services he obtained a lieutenant-colonelcy, and was made C.B. On his return with his regiment from India, he exchanged into the 21st, which he commanded until made Governor of St. Helena, in 1851. From St. Helena he went in 1855 to New Zealand. On the breaking out of the Maori war in the last year of his government, Colonel Gore Browne showed a vigor which was essential in resisting the land-league and the Maori King movement, the outcome of the feeble rule of his predecessors. In 1861, having completed his term of office, he was succeeded in the government of New Zealand by Sir George Grey, and he himself succeeded Sir Henry Young as Governor of Tasmania. He resigned the last-mentioned office in January, 1869, when he was created a Knight Commander of the Order of S.S. Michael and George. Sir Thomas was appointed Governor of Bermuda in 1870. He is now in England, and still takes an interest in New Zealand, being a Director of the National Bank, and of some other mercantile institutions connected with the Colony.

Colonel Gore Brown arrived towards the close of the first session of the General Assembly. He prorogued that body on the 15th of September, declaring his intention of carrying on the Government by responsible advisers.

In the session of 1856, under Mr. Stafford's Ministry, some important measures were passed for obtaining loans for the redemption of the New Zealand Company's and other debts. Money was also voted for the promotion of steam communication. The great event of the year however, was the Maori King demonstration at the Waikato. Dr. Thomson thus relates the circumstances attending this movement:—

"The Anti-land-selling League formed in 1854 had acquired extensive ramifications. At a meeting of several influential chiefs of the League near the residence of Iwikau, on the Taupo Lake, in December, 1856, it was decided, not however without opposition, that Tongariro should be the centre of a district in which no land was to be sold to the Government, and Hauraki, Waikato, Kawhia, Mokau, Ngatiruanui, Wanganui, Rangitikei, and Titi o Kura, the circumference; that the Queen should not be prayed for; that roads should not be made within this district; and that a king should be elected to rule over the New Zealanders, as the Queen and Governor did over the settlers. In imitation of the Constitution Act, this meeting was called the Maori General Assembly, and was to be held annually."

The Rev. J. Morgan, in a letter addressed to the Select Committee of the House of Representatives on Waikato affairs, thus speaks of this movement:—

"The origin of the King movement was, first, a land league to prevent the sale of land by aboriginal owners to the Government, or the private sale of such land to individuals of the European or Pakeha race; secondly, a desire to stop the rapid advance of European colonisation; thirdly, a desire to introduce a code of laws suited to their own requirements; fourthly, and chiefly, a desire to establish first in the Waikato, and afterwards gradually in all Maori districts, an independent sovereignty over all Maori and European residents in such districts. Many of the aboriginies saw with fear the rapid advance of European colonisation and the earnest desire of the Pakeha to obtain possession of their lands. They also noticed what they considered the confined bounds to which some tribes who had sold land were reduced. As the promoters of the league knew there were many tribes favorably disposed to the sale of land and European colonization, they felt that their league would be powerless unless they could unite the various tribes of Waikato, and afterwards other districts under one chief or king whose flag when received, even by the minority of any tribe in any district, should cover all lands in such districts, and prohibit the sale thereof to Europeans. The aborigines also feared, as their own numbers were being so rapidly diminished by death, that unless European colonization could be arrested the white settlers would in a few years greatly outnumber them, and that then the Treaty of Waitangi would be set aside, and their lands seized by the English Government."

In February, 1856, the ship Josephine Willis, bound for New Zealand, was sunk in the English Channel by collision with the s.s. Mangerton, and Captain Canney and most of the crew and passengers drowned.

On the 13th of March the first stone of the new Wesleyan Church was laid by the Resident Magistrate, Josiah Flight, Esq., the services on the occasion being conducted by the Rev. S. Ironside and the Rev. J. Long.

On the 15th of March the remainder of the men of the 58th Regiment left in the s.s. Zingari for Auckland, and in the same month new moorings for vessels were laid down in the roadstead; and the barracks on Marsland Hill were finished and the troops removed into them.

On the 16th of August, Mrs. Jones of Bell Block was drowned in the Waiwakaiho while crossing the flooded stream in a bullock cart.

The year 1857 commenced with the excitement consequent on an election. Mr. Charles Brown's term of office having expired, the election of a Superintendent of the Province took place on the 13th of January, when Mr. George Cutfield was returned. Just prior to the election, the Taranaki "Herald" in one week changed from the advocacy of the return of Mr. Brown to that of Mr. Cutfield, and Mr. Pheney failing to concur in the change was dismissed by the proprietor, in consequence of which the friends of Mr. Brown started the Taranaki "News," the editorship of which was given to Mr. Pheney.

In May, the second session of the Maori Parliament met on the banks of the Waikato river, and was attended by 200 natives. The flag given by William the Fourth to the united tribes at the Bay of Islands was hoisted by one of the party, bearing the inscription, "POTATAU, KING OF NEW ZEALAND," and the Union Jack by another party. Several days were spent in discussion, during which Iwikau Te Heuheu demanded total separation between the two races, the erection of a native custom-house at Kawhia, and the ultimate expulsion of the settlers from New Zealand. The old Waikato chief, Potatau Te Wherowhero, a pensioner of the British Government, was asked to accept the royal office, and although he declined it yet he was hailed King of the Maoris. Prayers were offered up for his safe guidance, arms were presented in his honor by a body of drilled men, his flag was sent over the land to obtain the allegiance of the distant tribes, £57 was collected to uphold his dignity, and £100 to establish a printing press. By a Government Gazette the Governor, by the advice of his responsible Ministers, relaxed the "Arms Ordinance" by which the natives obtained permission under certain circumstances to buy guns and powder.

Two events of importance to the settlement took place in the Parliamentary session of 1868; the one was the alteration of the name of the Province from New Plymouth to Taranaki, and the other the passing of the "Public Debt Apportionment Act," a measure of considerable moment in the history of the Province, and therefore here given *in extenso*.

"The 21st and 22nd of Victoria.—An Act to apportion among the provinces of the Northern Island the sum of £180,000 to be raised for the extinguishment of native title; and to make the provincial revenues of the several provinces chargeable, in exoneration of the revenue of the Colony, with specific portions of the public debt. [Passed 21st August, 1858.]

"Contents:—Preamble. (1.) Apportionment amongst Provinces of Northern Island of fund for extinguishment of native title. (2) Sums raised for such extinguishment to be charged against the Provinces for which it is raised. (3) New Plymouth to be allowed £20,000 out of fund for extinguishment without charge. (4) New Plymouth receipts for land sales to be made up to £2,200 per annum. (5) Apportionment amongst Provinces of Southern Island of the charge of £200,000. (6) Auckland relieved from annual charge of balance of refund. (7) Interpretation. (8) Short title.

"Whereas, under and by virtue of the Act of Assembly entitled 'The New Zealand Loan Act, 1856,' the general revenue of the Colony is or will become charged with the repayment of the principal sums to be borrowed under the said Act, amounting in the whole to the sum of £500,000, and with interest thereon at the rate of four per centum per annum, and with a further payment at the rate of two per centum per annum on the amount of such principal sums, for the purpose of providing a sinking fund for the liquidation of the said debt.

"And whereas, by the said Act it is provided that the money to be borrowed under the authority thereof shall be applied as follows, namely: First, the sum of £200,000 in liquidation and full discharge of the debt then due to the New Zealand Company, and towards the repayment of such sums as the Province of Auckland should have paid towards liquidation of the said debt; secondly, any sum not exceeding the sum of £120,000, in payment of any public debt of the Colony which should be due on the 1st day of January, 1858; thirdly, any sum not exceeding the sum of £180,000 for the purpose of extinguishing the right of the aboriginal inhabitants to lands in the Northern Island of New Zealand.

"And whereas, the said sum of £200,000 has been fully raised and began to bear interest on the 1st day of January, 1858.

"And whereas, it is expedient to provide, as between the several Provinces of the Northern Island, in what proportions the said sum of £180,000 shall be applied for the extinction of the rights of the aboriginal inhabitants to lands within the bounds of the several Provinces thereof, that the Provincial revenues of the several Provinces shall be chargeable in exoneration of the revenue of the Colony with specific portions of the said sums of £180,000 and £200,000.

"And whereas, in consideration of the limited extent of land over which the title of the aborigines to lands within the Province of New Plymouth has been extinguished, and on other grounds, it is also expedient to make special provision respecting the charge of such extinguishment within the Province; and to make temporary provision for making good to the same Province the deficiency in its land revenue in any year in which the same shall not amount to the sum of £2,200.

"And whereas, it is expedient that the sum of £911 8s. 9d., being the principal money secured by certain outstanding debentures issued under an Ordinance of the Lieutenant-Governor of New Zealand and the Legislative Council thereof, Session VII, No. 22, entitled 'An Ordinance to authorise compensation in Colonial debentures to be made to certain claimants to land in the Colony of New Zealand,' should be charged against the Province of Auckland in exoneration of the general revenue of the Colony.

"And whereas, in pursuance of the provisions of the 'New Zealand Loan Act,' 1856, and of resolutions of both Houses of the General Assembly, to the effect that a refund ought to be made to the Province of Auckland of such sums as should have been contributed from its revenues towards the liquidation of the New Zealand Company's debt, the sum of £32,973 9s. 3½d., being the balance of the said sum of £200,000 remaining after the discharge of the said debt, has been paid, or is in course of payment, to the Treasurer of the said Province on account of such refund.

"And whereas, after making the said payment of £32,973 9s. 3½d, and after charging against the Province of Auckland the said sum of £911 8s. 9d., there will remain payable into the Treasury of the said Province on account of the said refund a balance of £11,151 10s. 1½d.

"And whereas, the said balance of the said refund is payable out of monies raised under the 'New Zealand Debentures Act, 1866,' but will ultimately be charged against the said sum of £120,000.

"And whereas, it is expedient that provision be made for relieving the Provincial revenue of the Province of Auckland from any part of the annual charge of such part of the said sum of £120,000 as shall be applied in discharge of the said balance.

"Be it therefore enacted by the General Assembly of New Zealand in Parliament assembled, and by the authority of the same, as follows :—

"1. The sum of £180,000, part of the said loan of £500,000 to be raised under the 'New Zealand Loan Act, 1856,' shall be applied for the extinguishment of the rights of the aboriginal inhabitants to lands within the present limits of the Provinces next hereinafter mentioned in the following proportions, that is to say, within the Province of Auckland there shall be applied for the purpose aforesaid five-tenths of the sum of £180,000; within the Province of Wellington three-tenths of the said sum; and within the Province of New Plymouth two-tenths of the said sum.

"2. As between the Colony on one part and the Provinces of Auckland, Wellington, and New Plymouth respectively, on the other part, the principal sums raised from time to time out of the said sum of £180,000 in order to be applied as aforesaid within the limits of any one of the said Provinces, and the annual charge in respect of such principal sums, shall be primarily charged upon the Provincial revenue of such Province, in exoneration of the ordinary revenue of the Colony.

"3. Provided always that the Provincial revenue of the Province of New Plymouth shall not be so chargeable until after the sum of £20,000 in the aggregate shall have been raised in order to be applied as aforesaid within the limits of the said Province, and then shall be chargeable only with the principal of such sums as shall for the time being have been raised in excess of the sum of £20,000, and with the annual charge in respect thereof.

"4. Commencing on the 1st day of July, 1858, and until the sum of £20,000 in the aggregate shall have been raised as aforesaid, and expended within the limits of the said Province of New Plymouth, there shall be annually payable into the Treasury such a sum as, together with the gross proceeds during the year, of the sale, letting, disposal, and occupation of the waste lands of the Crown, within the said Province, will amount to the sum of £2,200.

"5. As between the Colony on the one part, and the Provinces of Nelson, Canterbury, and Otago, respectively, on the other part, the principal sum of £200,000, part of the sum of £500,000, raised under the 'New Zealand Loan Act, 1856,' and the annual charge in respect thereof, shall, on and after the 1st day of January, 1858, be primarily charged upon the respective Provincial revenues of the said Provinces in exoneration of the ordinary revenue of the Colony, in the following proportions, that is to say, upon the Provincial revenue of the Province of Nelson the principal sum of £45,000 together with the annual charge in respect thereof; upon the Provincial revenue of the Province of Canterbury the principal sum of £77,500 together with the annual charge in respect thereof; and upon the Provincial revenue of the Province of Otago the principal sum of £77,500 together with the annual charge in respect thereof.

"6. In order to relieve the Provincial revenue of the Province of Auckland from the annual charge of the balance of £11,151 10s. 1½d, payable to the Treasurer of the said Province as aforesaid, the said Province, shall, as from the 30th day of June, 1858, be annually credited in account with the Colony, with such a sum as will suffice to throw such charge exclusively upon the Provincial revenues of the other Provinces of the Colony.

"7. In the construction of this Act, the expression 'Provincial Revenue' shall import the moneys payable under the Acts of the Assembly respectively intituled 'The Surplus Revenues Act, 1858,' and 'The Land Revenue Appropriation Act, 1858,' into the Treasury of the Province with reference to which such expression is used; and the expression 'annual charge,' used in reference to any principal sum raised under the Act of Assembly intituled 'The New Zealand Loan Act, 1856,' shall include both the interests thereon, and the annual payment of two per cent. for providing a sinking fund for the liquidation thereof.

"8. The short title of this Act shall be 'The Public Debt Apportionment Act, 1858.'"

The Act was amended in 1861 on account of the boundaries of the Provinces of the Middle Island being defined, and their former assumed boundaries altered; but it left the provisions of the original Act relating to the Provinces of the North Island intact.

This Act was the ratification of a compact made in 1856 between the representatives of the North Island on the one part, and the representatives of the Middle Island on the other. By it the North, in consideration of certain sums of money paid to it, was to permit the Middle Island Provinces to hold entire possession of their waste lands, and to devote the proceeds of the sale thereof to their several Provincial Treasuries. The sums of money paid to the North were, however, ridiculously incommensurate with the privileges granted to the South, and it was afterwards very truly said concerning the transaction by an hon. member in the House that by it the North sold its birthright to the South for a mess of pottage. By this compact alone Taranaki existed as a Province up to 1875. For nearly 20 years after the compact her land fund was *nil* through the natives refusing to sell their waste lands, and on the guaranteed £2,200 per annum she supported her Superintendent and Provincial Officers up to the period of the abolition of provincial institutions.

In February, 1858, the Taranaki Militia were called out for training, Charles Brown, Esq., being appointed the captain. Each man was served with an old smooth-bore musket, a bayonet, and belts and pouches of ancient date. The drilling was performed by old soldiers of the 65th Regiment, under the superintendence of Major Lloyd, who had settled at Omata. This officer was eventually superseded by Lieutenant Stapp of the 58th Regiment, who had seen active service with his regiment in the North during the native rebellion, and as a volunteer in the Crimea. This duty was felt as very irksome by the settlers, most of whom had never handled a musket or a ball cartridge in their lives, but it was patiently submitted to by the majority.

On the 27th of July, 1858, at Singapore, on his voyage from Melbourne to Hongkong, died William Dawson, of Tarbert, Argyleshire, Scotland, commander of the barque Cornwall. When in command of the Amelia Thompson he landed many of the early settlers at New Plymouth in September, 1841. On his return voyage the vessel foundered in a storm off Madras and several hands perished. He afterwards revisited New Zealand in the Slaines Castle, which was taken up as a transport by the Colonial Government during the rebellion at the Bay of Islands, and finally visited the Colony in the barque Cornwall in 1849.

In December, two fatal occurrences took place at Omata. On the 22nd, Francis Henry Newsham, a lad eight years of age was killed by falling from a horse, and being dragged hanging from the stirrups of the saddle ; and on the 30th of December, John Wright, an old whaler, and the oldest inhabitant of the Province, committed suicide at Pataweke, the district near Moturoa given by the New Zealand Company to the members of the original whaling fraternity. Wright was a very quiet man, and like most of his class reticent concerning his antecedents. He carved his name in large and deep letters on the south side of the island of Mikotahi, and affixed the date October 18th, 1829. As he carefully kept this inscription legible till his death, it may be assumed that it was the date of his arrival at Ngamotu. He fought with Barrett and the Ngamotu hapu of the Ngatiawa tribe, in the defence of the Ngamotu pa against the Waikatos in 1832. He was buried by Mr. Whiteley at the Waitapu burial ground at Moturoa, a spot where lie the families of Barrett and other traders and whalers of the pre-colonial time, and some of the early colonists.

By the " Roads and Bridges Ordinance, 1858," road rates were made compulsory in the settled portion of the Province.

" Colonial Secretary's Office,
" Auckland, 17th December, 1858.

" It is hereby notified for general information that from and after the 1st day of January, 1859, the Province of New Plymouth will be called the Province of Taranaki, in accordance with the provisions of the ' Province of Taranaki Act, 1858.'

" HENRY JOHN TANCRED,
" In the absence of the Colonial Secretary."

CHAPTER XXI.

THE EVENTS OF 1859.

ON the 1st of January the Puketapu natives went into New Plymouth to receive payment for the Tarurutangi Block. This was the piece of land concerning which the chief Rawiri lost his life. For a block of 20,000 acres the Government paid the owners £1,400. Preparations were at this time making for the erection of a bridge over the Waiwakaiho river, a work which was much needed, several valuable lives having been lost in attempts to ford the stream. The river has its sources high up on the peak of the mountain, and when flooded comes down with great impetuosity. A sapper and miner, named Jones, designed the structure from an engraving published in the Illustrated London News. The contractors for the building were Messrs. Brooking and Rundle.

PROCLAMATION.

"In pursuance of the authority in me invested by the 'Militia Act, 1858,' I, Thomas Gore Brown, Governor of the Colony of New Zealand, do hereby make and ordain the following Regulations respecting the training and exercise, arms and accoutrements, clothing and equipments, of 'a Company of Volunteers enrolled in the district of Taranaki, under an order in Council dated the thirteenth day of January, One Thousand Eight Hundred and Fifty-nine.

"1. The Company shall be called 'The Taranaki Volunteer Rifle Company,' and shall consist of one Captain, two Lieutenants, four Sergeants, four Corporals, and ninety-two Privates.

"2. The arms will be a rifle and bayonet, with accoutrements to be issued by the Adjutant to each volunteer, the value of which, for determining the amount to be paid in case of loss or damage, is hereby fixed at 'six pounds six shillings.

"3. The Company shall be divided into the following local sub-divisions, viz., the Town, Grey, Omata, Bell, and Hua, and each volunteer shall belong to such one of the sub-divisions as he shall think fit.

"4. Drill shall be local and general. The several sub-divisions shall meet for local drill as follows:—The Town—at some place within the Town of New Plymouth or Town Belt; the Grey—at some place within the Grey Block; the Omata—at some place within the Omata Block; the Bell and Hua—at some place within the Bell or the Hua Block. Such places of meeting and the times thereof to be from time to time fixed by the Captain of the Company.

"5. The general drill shall be at such times and places as the Captain of the Company shall from time to time fix for that purpose, subject to the approval of the Governor.

"6. Provided always that the time required for attendance on

general drill shall not exceed forty-two hours within the year.
"Given under my hand at Government House, at Auckland, this thirteenth day of January, One Thousand Eight Hundred and Fifty-nine.
"T. GORE BROWNE."

On Saturday, the 12th February, the nomination of officers took place as authorised by 3rd Clause of the Order in Council dated 13th January, 1859, as follows :—
"All officers of Companies will be appointed by the Governor, and names for that purpose are to be submitted to him for his approval by the Company to which they are proposed to be appointed."

The election terminated as follows :—For Captain, Isaac Newton Watt; 1st Lieutenant, James Hirst; 2nd Lieutenant, Robert Chisenhall Hammerton.

The New Zealand Government Gazette of 25th February, notifies the following appointments by the Governor :—Isaac Newton Watt to be Captain; James Hirst to be 1st Lieutenant; Robert Chisenhall Hammerton to be 2nd Lieutenant, in the Taranaki Volunteer Rifles; Commissions to date from 12th of February. Also, the appointment of Christopher William Richmond as a member of the Legislative Council.

On Sunday, the 6th March, H.M.S. Iris, 26 guns, Captain Loring, C.B., arrived at Port Eliot, New Plymouth, having on board His Excellency the Governor, attended by Captain Seward, Private Secretary. His Excellency left the frigate under a salute, and on landing was received by the Officer commanding the troops and a guard of honor. A salute was fired by the Royal Artillery when His Excellency reached the shore. On Tuesday, the 8th March, a meeting of the Moturoa, Town, Waiwakaiho, Puketapu, and Waitara natives was held in a paddock adjoining the residence of the Land Purchase Commissioner. It was less numerously attended than many former ones, the muster of the Waitara natives being particularly small. Shortly after 11 o'clock His Excellency the Governor, attended by his Private Secretary and Mr. Maclean, the Chief Land Purchase Commissioner, arrived on the ground and was welcomed by the assembled natives, the whole rising up to receive him, with the exception of William King and some few of his followers.

The principal Chiefs then paid their respects to the Governor.

Tahana, a native assessor, opened the proceedings by acknowledging the benefits conferred on the natives by the introduction of Christianity and European customs, and expressed the desire of himself and his tribe to have British law established among them.

Mr. Maclean, on behalf of His Excellency, spoke as follows :—
"The Governor wished them to understand that the Queen regards equally all her subjects; that all her Governors have had and would have the same instructions, viz., to do their utmost to promote the welfare of her subjects without distinction of race. The missionaries

had imparted to them the blessings of Christianity and translated the Bible for their use. It was not in the power of man to confer any other gift which would bear comparison with that of the Bible ; but out of consideration for the natives His Excellency had caused an abstract of English law to be translated into Maori. He had no wish to enforce this law ; on the contrary, it would only be put in force in those districts where the people were wise enough to desire it, and prepared to carry it into effect by themselves. One tribe in the North had already desired to have English law, and a Magistrate had been appointed to instruct them how to put it into practice. They were now engaged in doing so with every prospect of becoming a prosperous people and uniting themselves with the Pakeha. This tribe was the Ngapuhi. The Governor had but two subjects on which he desired to speak particularly to the tribes living near Taranaki, and they were—First, in reference to criminal offences ; second, in reference to land. He wished these subjects to be considered separately, and as having no sort of reference to each other. The tribes in the vicinity of Taranaki had greater advantages than most others, as they were much intermixed with the Pakeha, and ought to profit by their intercourse with them. If they chose to live peaceably and cultivate their land they would grow rich and multiply, instead of which they were constantly at war with each other, and their numbers were decreasing. Their disputes were almost always about matters of little or no importance, or about land which was not worth quarrelling for. Had His Excellency the Governor been in New Zealand when Katatore slew Rawiri, he would have had him arrested and brought before the judge, and if the judge had sentenced him to be hanged, he would have caused him to be hanged. He had not thought proper to arrest Ihaia, because though the murders to which he was a party were horrible and disgraceful, yet they admitted of some extenuation, inasmuch as they were committed in retribution for the murder of Rawiri. All this, however, now belonged to the past, but for the future he had determined that every man, whether he were Maori or Pakeha, who should commit any violence or outrage within the European boundaries, should be arrested and taken before the judge, and the sentence of the judge, whatever it might be, should be carried into effect. He was determined that the peace of the settlers should no longer be disturbed by evil doers, and that those Maoris who were not content to live in peace among the Pakehas had better go elsewhere. In reference to the second subject, the Governor thought the Maoris would be wise to sell the land they could not use themselves, as it would make what they could use more valuable than the whole, but that he would never consent to buy land without an undisputed title. He would not permit any one to interfere in the sale of land unless he owned part of it, and on the other hand he would buy no man's land without his consent."

Tahana again addressed his tribe, approving of that portion of His Excellency's speech declaring that if murder were again committed the murderer should be arrested and tried by British law. He then supposed a case of a native policeman or assessor, himself for instance, shot while arresting a murderer, and inquired who would avenge him. He stated that if he were assured of the support of His Excellency, as he knew His Excellency would receive the support of the Queen, he could hereafter single-handed arrest offenders.

Te Teira, of Waitara, then stated that he was anxious to sell land belonging to himself, and that he had heard with satisfaction the declaration of the Governor referring to individual claims, and the assurance of protection that would be afforded by His Excellency. He minutely defined the boundaries of his claim, and repeated that he was anxious to sell. He then rapidly asked if the Governor would buy this land. Mr. Maclean, on behalf of His Excellency, replied that he would. Te Teira then placed a parawai or bordered mat at the Governor's feet, which His Excellency accepted. This ceremony, according to native custom, virtually placed Teira's land at the Waitara in the hands of the Governor.

Hemi Huku then followed, and stated his desire to dispose of land at Onaero, but in consequence of violent opposition his offer was not entertained.

Piripi, a relative of Ihaia, then offered his land at Waitara; his right to sell was denied by Te Teira, Te Waka, of the town, and several of the Waitara natives, who asserted that his land was forfeited by reason of the murder of Katatore by his relatives.

Paora then informed the Governor that Te Teira could not sell the land he had offered without the consent of Waiteriki, and himself, as they had a joint interest in a portion of it.

Te Teira replied to Paora, and was immediately followed by William King, who expressed his determination not to give the land up.

Kipa, of the Waiwakaiho, then expressed the satisfaction which the Governor's speech afforded him, and proposed that henceforward British law should not prevail beyond the Waitaha or eastern boundary of Bell Block.

Matiu, of the Hua, wished to address His Excellency on the King movement, but was informed that another opportunity for so doing would be afforded him.

The Assembly then separated.

The flourishing condition of native agriculture in 1859 may be gathered from the following statistics :—In the Waitara, Huirangi and Ngatimaru districts there were 894 acres of land in cultivation by Maoris, who were in possession of 82 horses, 380 horned cattle, 690 pigs, 36 carts, 30 ploughs, 12 harrows, and 4 threshing machines. In the districts of Waiongona, Mangoraka, Ikamoana and Kaipakupaku, 405 acres of land were in cultivation, and the people possessed 49 horses, 111 horned cattle, 248 pigs, 27 carts, 32 ploughs and 15 harrows. In the Mangati, Te Hua and Waiwakaiho districts, 608 acres were in cultivation, and the people possessed 53 horses, 144 horned cattle, 258 pigs, 28 carts, 26 ploughs, 12 harrows and 3 threshing machines. At Puketotara and Pukenui, 45 acres were in cultivation, and the people possessed 17 horses, 41 horned cattle, 14 pigs, 5 carts, 5 ploughs and 2 harrows. At Ararepi, Ratapihipihi and Moturoa, 109 acres were in cultivation, and the people possessed 17 horses, 16 horned cattle, 16 pigs, 14 carts, 9 ploughs and 4 harrows. The total number of acres in cultivation in the native districts was 2,061, and the Maoris possessed 218 horses, 692 horned cattle, 1,226 pigs, 110 carts, 102 ploughs, 45 harrows and 7 threshing machines.

On the 2nd of April a band for the Volunteer Rifles was formed, Mr. Manley undertaking to teach the members gratuitously for twelve months. His Excellency gave a donation of £5 towards the purchase of instruments.

The Government Gazette of the 5th of April notified that His Excellency the Governor had appointed Charles Stapp, Esq., junior Captain of the Taranaki Regiment of Militia, Charles Brown, Esq., being the senior Captain.

Steps were taken at this time for the enlargement of St. Mary's Episcopal Church, New Plymouth, and the Provincial Council were busy with a Bill for consolidating the town.

On Thursday, the 18th of August, the new Waiwakaiho bridge was formally opened by His Honor the Superintendent, and a public luncheon given on the banks of the river. In the evening a subscription ball to celebrate the event took place at the Masonic Hotel, the garrison band performing by permission of Colonel Murray. At three o'clock on the following morning some late wassailer, in a state of intoxication, set fire to the Council Chambers and Government Office in Courtenay Street. The buildings were burned down and all the Provincial records destroyed.

On the evening of the 29th of August there was a very splendid display of Aurora Australis.

On November the 29th, £100 was paid to Teira on account of his land at Waitara.

On December the 1st, the Tarurutangi Block was offered for sale.

PROCLAMATION,

" By George Cutfield, Esq., Superintendent of the Province of Taranaki.

" Whereas by an Ordinance of the present Session of the Provincial Council of Taranaki, entitled ' The Town of New Plymouth Consolidation Ordinance, 1859,' it is among other things enacted that it shall be lawful for the Superintendent, with the approval of the Provincial Council, to alter and contract the boundaries of the Town Site of New Plymouth, and to declare such alteration and contraction by proclamation in the Government Gazette of the Province. Now therefore, I, the Superintendent of the Province of Taranaki, do hereby proclaim and declare that the boundaries described in the Schedule hereto shall be taken to be the boundaries of the Town of New Plymouth.

"Given under my hand at New Plymouth, this 16th day of December, one thousand eight hundred and fifty nine.

"G. CUTFIELD,
"Superintendent.

"J. C. Richmond,
"Provincial Secretary."

[Schedule Referred To.]

"On the North, the sea at high water; on the East, the Henui River; on the South, Lemon Street to Watson Street, along Watson Street and the North boundary of Native Reserve No. 14 to Hobson Street, along Hobson Street to Gilbert Street, along Gilbert Street to Gardner Street, thence in a direct line to Fillis Street, along Fillis Street to the boundary of the Military Reserve, along the South boundary of the Military Reserve to Down Street, along Down Street to Dawson Street, along Dawson Street to Fulford Street, along Fulford Street to the Cutfield Road; and on the West the Cutfield Road."

WIREMU KINGI WHITI RANGITAKI.

The natives who in old time resided in Auckland and occupied Mount Eden as their principal fortification, assert that they came to New Zealand in a canoe named "Tainui," high tide, by which name the tribe is called to this day. The remnant of these people now reside at Raglan. The Tainui is said to have come in company with the canoe "Arawa." The people of the Arawa first discovered land. Tainui then parted company with Arawa for some time, but they met again at Whaingaparoa, and having there quarrelled about a whale the Arawa went along the East Coast, and Tainui went into the Tamaki river, where the people observed sea-birds coming from the west. This led them to suspect that there must be a sea coast in that direction, and searching they discovered the Manukau river. They then dragged the Tainui across the portage and launching it in the Manukau waters near Otahuhu, proceeded out of the harbor and coasted along southwards to Kawhia. Here part of the people landed and settled, and the remainder returned to Mount Eden, and took possession of the Auckland district.

There is in the Wellington province a portion of a Waikato tribe called Ngatiraukawa. A quarrel of two brothers near Maungatautari, in Waikato, was the cause of the tribe fighting. The defeated section retreated to the south, and located themselves in the present home of their descendants. It was in the war of these brothers that the ancestor of Wi Kingi came from Waikato to Waitara, and took a wife from the youngest female branch of the family of Te Teira, and lived with her at an old pa called Manukorihi, on the north bank of the Waitara. This old pa was abandoned in 1826, but up to that time Wi Kingi's relatives lived there and were the last to leave, hence his hapu or branch of the Ngatiawa are called to this day Manukorihi, which signifies the singing bird. Up to 1826, Wi Kingi's relatives had never cultivated the north side of the Waitara but once, and that cultivation was allowed for the following reason :—A number of canoes manned by Ngatiawa went out of the Waitara on a deep sea fishing expedition, when they were caught by an unexpected squall, and all swamped but one, and the people drowned. The other was driven to the Sugarloaves, where the crew effected a landing, and according to Maori custom remained for some time at the place of their deliverance. The people of Manukorihi mourned the loss of the fishermen, believing them all to be dead, but Wi Kingi's ancestors hearing of the escape of one canoe's crew, crossed over the river, and cleared a spot of land for the survivors of the disaster. The escaped men then came back to the Waitara, and were permitted by Te Teira's ancestors to live for one season on the clearing on the south side of the river, near to the spot where the Kuhikuhi pa was afterwards built. Keretawhangawhanga, the father of Wi Kingi, lived at the Manukorihi pa, and there early in the present century Wi Kingi was born. Just before the siege and taking of Pukerangiora by the Waikato, Wi Kingi went to Kapiti and put himself under the protection of Rauparaha, at Mana. The reason of this was that Rauparaha was descended from the Tainui migration, and was consequently related to Wi Kingi. Hence when the Waikato intended to attack Pukerangiora they sent word to Wi Kingi to leave the district, and he obeyed and saved himself and family by so doing.

In 1839, when Colonel Wakefield visited Cook Strait for the purpose of buying land for the New Zealand Company, Wi Kingi, who was then called E Whiti, or the shining one, sailed in the Tory from village to village in Cook Strait to persuade the Ngatiawa to sell their lands at Taranaki in order that he and they might return to the north of the Waitara and dwell there in the security afforded by the presence of the white people, and upon reserves which were promised to be set apart for such purposes. The name of E Whiti is the first signature upon the deed of sale known as the Queen Charlotte Sound Deed. A year or two after this he went to Ngapuhi, where he had a dispute with Kati, the younger brother of Potatau, about the land. Kati said to Wi Kingi, "That land Taranaki will be sold to the Governor." Kingi replied, "Then I will sell the Waipa Valley as a payment for my slain," alluding to an encounter which took place between the Ngatiawa of Taranaki and the people of Waipa. On Kati's return from the north he repeated what had passed between himself and Wi Kingi to the old chief Potatau. Soon afterwards Potatau went to Kapiti with Governor Hobson, and on one occasion thus addressed His Excellency :—" Friend, listen to me, Taranaki is mine ; my hand holds it : I wish to sell it to you." The windows of the room in which this conversation took place happened to be open, and some papers which had been lying on the table had been scattered by the wind. The old chief collected them, and placing them upon the table put a weight upon them, and addressing the Governor, said :—" This is like Taranaki ; if I press the Taranaki people they will remain quiet. See, O Governor, when I put a weight upon them they are still, they cannot move." It was probably just prior to this last occurrence that Wi Kingi was baptised by the Rev. Octavius Hadfield, the present Bishop of Wellington.

In 1846, when Rauparaha and his fighting general, Rangihaeata, were in rebellion at Wellington, Wi Kingi took up arms on the side of the British.

In 1847 Kingi visited Taranaki with the Governor in the Inflexible, and afterwards, with upwards of 500 Ngatiawa, began to make preparations for a return from Cook Strait to Waitara. Having sold the land at Waikanae, which he held with others of his tribe by right of conquest, he proposed to the natives of Ngatiruanui and Taranaki to give them allotments of land at Waitara with the avowed object of helping to prevent further sales of land to the Pakeha. The origin of Wi Kingi's opposition to the sale of land may be learned from the following statement of Mr. Maclean :—

" In the years 1848 and 1849, when negotiating the purchase of land at Rangitikei and Manawatu, several of the Ngatiruakawa tribe of Otaki publicly stated at meetings held at Te Awahou, that they had, by the advice of their missionary, formed a league against the sale of land."

Wi Kingi having received an invitation from Potatau, the great Waikato chief, to return to Waitara, said to Teira :—" Let us return to Waitara ; you take one side and I will take the other, as Waikato gives us permission to return." He pretended to be anxious not to act in opposition to the Government, but pressed on Major Richmond, the officer of Waikanae, the sale of the district, his anxiety on this head being caused by the scarcely concealed intention of the Ngatitoa tribe to seize on Waikanae the moment he left it. The Governor hearing that canoes were being built at Porirua for the migration, sent peremptory orders that they should be dismantled, and if necessary seized and destroyed ; and these orders, and a memorandum recorded by the Superintendent, show clearly that at that time it was seriously in contemplation to prevent the migration by military force. But Sir George Grey, desirous of trying a last effort to come to terms with Kingi, made a further proposal of certain conditions on which he would permit him to sell Waikanae and come up to Waitara. The basis of this proposal was that Wiremu Kingi should settle on the north bank of the Waitara, and should relinquish all pretensions to any land on the south bank. The exact terms of the agreement were as follows :—

" Upon all pretension being at once relinquished to all lands on the south of the Waitara, the Government will, without further inquiry into such pretensions to these lands, admit that from the prompt settlement they are making of this question the natives are entitled to such compensation as may be agreed on between themselves and the officers of the Government. The Government will then also recognise and permit them immediately to dispose of their claims at Waikanae and Totaranui for such compensation as may be agreed upon."

Kingi agreed to these terms, and an offer made to the Government at the end of 1847 was kept in abeyance till all the claims should be ascertained. Under these circumstances the Government no farther opposed the return of Kingi to Waitara, and the migration took place in 1849. On reaching the Waitara he went to reside at his ancestral place near to the Manukorihi pa. But as some of the Waikato, under Rewi and other chiefs, were then cultivating land in the vicinity, and Kingi being in fear of an invasion from that tribe, he asked permission of Tamati Ruru, Teira's father, to build a pa upon the south bank of the river, in what is now the township of Raleigh, which permission was granted.

In the summer of 1849-50, Kingi had a large and strong pa erected, his flotilla of boats and canoes were drawn up near to it, and he had extensive gardens for a considerable distance along the south margin of the river. Kingi after his return maintained an insolent demeanour towards the Europeans, and rejected all overtures made to induce him to part with the land or to remove to the north bank of the river. Governor Grey on one of his visits to New Plymouth spent a whole night with him in endeavouring to bring him to terms. Kingi cultivated the friendship of Katatore, a Puketapu chief, who resided at Kaipakopako, a determined opponent of the Pakeha.

Shortly after the discovery of gold in Australia in 1851, a great demand for potatoes arose; the demand culminated in 1856 when potatoes to the value of £19,000 were exported from New Zealand. Kingi and his people grew large quantities of these useful tubers on the alluvial soils of the Waitara, and selling them to the merchants in town, became richer than ever they were in their lives. In 1854 these people possessed, in addition to considerable sums of money, 150 horses, 300 head of cattle, 40 carts, 35 ploughs, 20 pairs of harrows, 3 winnowing machines, and 10 wooden houses. In the same year the seeds of the anti-land-selling-league, sown by Kingi at Waikanae in 1847, began to grow. According to Mr. Taylor, Matene Te Whiwhi, on his return from a political visit to Taupo and other places, wrote a letter to the Ngatiruanui and Taranaki natives, calling a meeting at Manawapou; there the natives erected a very large building, the largest perhaps which has ever been made by them, being 120ft. in length by 35ft. in width. This was named Taiporohenui, or the restraining of the great evil, i.e., selling land to Europeans; and there all the great chiefs from Wellington to the Waitara, a distance of nearly 300 miles, assembled. Five hundred were present, and much speaking and bad spirit were displayed. The result was a determination to sell no more land to the Government, and to hinder any one who felt disposed to do so. In token of their determination to carry out this arrangement to the fullest extent, a tomahawk was handed around to each person and afterwards buried with a copy of the New Testament beneath the floor of the house called Taiporohenui. A few months after this the Puketapu feud commenced, and Taranaki became a scene of strife and blood-shedding. Ihaia having been driven to the Karaka pa on the banks of the Waitara, and closely besieged until he was on the verge of starving, the late Rev. John Whiteley and Mr. Parris prevailed on Kingi to permit Ihaia to vacate the pa without molestation. Kingi agreed to do so, and Ihaia with loud lamentations left the pa in the night, but he also left behind a armed party of his allies hidden within the pa, so that Kingi and his followers might be slaughtered when they came to take possession of the fortress. Mr. Parris having become aware of this piece of treachery, warned Kingi of it and saved him from destruction. In one of his encounters with Ihaia, Kingi thus addressed his Taranaki allies:—" Men of Taranaki, be strong ! Be brave and capture Ihaia, Nikorima, and Puhere, as payment for the tapu, of Taranaki and Umuroa. Then we will stretch out their arms and burn them with fire. To prolong their torture let them be suspended over a slow fire for a week, and let the fire consume them. Like the three men of old whom Nebuchadnezzar commanded to be cast into the fiery furnace, even as it was with Shadrach, Meshach, and Abednego, shall it be with Ihaia." On Tuesday, March 7th, 1859, a meeting of natives was held in a paddock adjoining the residence of the Land Purchase Commissioner, New Plymouth, at which His Excellency Governor Brown, Wi Kingi, Te Teira, and other natives were present. After the Governor had addressed the meeting Te Teira came forward and offered his land at Waitara for sale to His Excellency. In doing so he placed a *parawai* (worked mat), at the Governor's feet, which His Excellency accepted. This ceremony, according to native custom, virtually placed the lands in the hands of the Governor. Wiremu Kingi, before addressing the Governor, said to his people, " I will only say a few words and then we will depart," to which they assented. He then said, " Listen, Governor ; notwithstanding Teira's offer, I will not permit the sale of Waitara to the Pakeha. Waitara is in my hands. I will not give it up ; *e kore, e kore, e kore*—I will not, I will not, I will not. I have spoken." Then making use of an insulting expression towards His Excellency, he turned to his people and said, " Arise, let us go." Whereupon he and his followers abruptly withdrew.

Wiremu Kingi to the Governor.

" Waitara, 25th April, 1859.

" Sir :—Salutations to you. Your letter has reached me about Te Teira and Te Retimana's thoughts. I do not agree to our bed-room being sold I mean Waitara, for this bed belongs to the whole of us ; and do not you be in haste to give the money. Do you hearken to my word. If you give the money secretly you will get no land for it ; you may insist, but I will never agree to it. Do not suppose that this is nonsense on my part : no, it is true, for it is an old word ; and now I have no proposal to make, either as regards selling or anything else. All I have to say to you, O, Governor, is that none of the land will be given to you, never, never, till I die. I have heard it said that I am to be imprisoned because of this land. I am very sad because of this word. Why is it? You should remember that the Maoris and Pakehas are living quietly upon their pieces of land, and therefore do not disturb them. Do not also say that there is no one so bad as myself. This is another word to you, O, Governor. The land will never, never, be given to you, not till death. Do not be anxious for men's thoughts. This is all I have to say to you.—From your loving friend,

"WIREMU KINGI WHITI."

In December, 1859, a native called Waitere, from Rangitikei, an active agent of the King movement, called at Waitara on his way to the South, and left secretly a King's flag with a native called Erueti, a miscreant, who at one time proposed to murder Mr. Parris, and who did a great deal of mischief in the district. As soon as Wi Kingi found that this flag had been left there, he accused those who sanctioned the transaction with acting treacherously to him, and finding some of his own people favorable to it he threatened to leave the district. This caused a division in the party, and Wi Kingi left the Waitara, and went to live with Te Ito, near the Waiongona, while the other party retained the flag, bearing thereby allegiance to the Maori King, and set about preparing a flagstaff. Two old men, Tamati Ruru, and Rawiri Raupongo, declared they would lose their lives rather than allow the flagstaff to be erected on their lands.

On Tuesday, 29th November, 1859, Mr. Parris paid Te Teira and others an instalment of £100 for their lands at Waitara. On the preceding Friday Mr. Parris went to Waitara and informed Wi Kingi of his intentions, who on the 29th came into New Plymouth with a party of about thirty to oppose the payment. In the presence of a large number of Europeans Mr. Parris put the following questions to him and received the corresponding replies, calling the Rev. John Whiteley to be witness :—

Q. Does the land belong to Teira and his party.
A. Yes, the land is theirs, but I will not let them sell it.
Q. Why will you oppose the selling of that which is their own.
A. Because I do not wish for the land to be disturbed, and although they have floated it, I will not let it go to sea.
Q. Show me the justice or correctness of your opposition.
A. It is enough, Parris, their bellies are full with the sight of the money you have promised them, but do not give it to them; if you do, I will not let you have the land, but will take it and cultivate it myself.

On Monday, 20th February, 1860, Mr. Parris, with Mr. O. Carrington and Mr. Hursthouse, of the Survey Department, and one of the armed police force, proceeded to Waitara for the purpose of surveying the block of land sold by Te Teira and others to the Government. Arrived at the land to be surveyed, a party of 70 or 80 native men and women were found assembled, some of whom attempted, without success, to hinder the unpacking of the instruments, but when the chain was thrown out they effectually prevented any use being made of it. The obstruction was managed in the least objectionable way possible. The Maoris laid hold of the middle of the chain and so disturbed the measuring, and the surveying party finding it vain to persist farther, forthwith returned to town. Subsequently a communication from the authorities was made to Kingi, giving him twenty-four hours to apologise for the obstruction offered by his people, and to notify the relinquishment of his opposition to the survey. To this Kingi returned an answer to the purport that he did not desire war; that he loved the white people very much, but that he would keep the land. On the 22nd of February the Proclamation of Martial Law was published by Colonel Murray. It was published both in the English and Maori languages, and extended over the whole Province. On the 1st of March the Governor arrived from Auckland with extra troops, and immediately sent a message to Kingi requesting that, to prevent misunderstanding, he would come into town and learn the Governor's intention, and offering him a safe conduct. After a long conference with the Governor's messengers he said he would either come or send his final decision to the Governor the next day, but on the following day he sent a letter declining to come. On the 5th March the troops were marched down to Waitara and occupied a position on the disputed block. On the 13th and 14th Te Teira and his party pointed out the boundaries of the land. On the night of the 15th a pa was built by Kingi's people on the disputed block. The next day they pulled up the survey pegs and burnt them. On the 17th March the conflict began. Kingi being no warrior himself, fell to the rear, and his relative, Hapurona, became his fighting general. Kingi and his general wrote to Waikato for help, and their letter was immediately responded to by the arrival of Te Wetini Taiporutu and other men of note at the scene of conflict. After the war had been carried on for twelve months, Kingi's party and their Waikato allies met with a signal defeat at the Huirangi redoubt, upon which Hapurona submitted to the British, and signed articles of peace on the 8th of April, 1861. At this time Wi Kingi was safe in Waikato. After the peace Kingi returned and lived for ten years a secluded life in the inland native district of Ngatimaru. After this long seclusion he ventured to town and was present at a native gathering and feast, after which he went to Parihaka, a Taranaki stronghold, 33 miles south of New Plymouth, and took up his abode with the Chief and Prophet, Te Whiti, who teaches the Maoris that they are Israel, and the British Pharaoh and the Egyptians who enslave Israel. Since then Wi Kingi has been living at Ngatimaru, near the head waters of the Waitara. In the prime of his life Wi Kingi was about six feet three inches in height, and proportionately stout. His physiognomy was heavy and disagreeable, and his character that of a blusterer and a coward.

CHAPTER XXII.

THE TARANAKI WAR.

WE now approach the most eventful period in the history of Taranaki, when the artizan was called from his workshop, the shepherd from his pastures, the husbandman from the fields, and the bushman from the forest, to hold the land for the British Crown, and to repel the hordes of Maoris who came from all quarters to endeavor to drive the pale-faced Pakeha into the sea from whence he came. The change from the avocations of peace to the pursuits of war was not entered into without very serious thoughts as to the nature of the struggle that would have to be made. So far as the settlers were concerned there was no alternative to engagement in the strife. The Governor had come to the conclusion with his Council that it was necessary for the interests of the Colony, and also as a matter of justice that the land-league should be broken up, and that the *imperium in imperio*, established in the person of the Maori King should be subverted, and accordingly the district was placed under martial law. The settlers were led to understand that hostilities would be resorted to should Kingi continue contumacious, and they instinctively proceeded to New Plymouth to seek protection for their families. The pioneers who had witnessed the war dances of the Maoris in the early days of the settlement, who had received every kind of insolence short of personal violence from the Puketapu hapu after its release from Waikato slavery, and had witnessed the internecine feud of that family, who had been compelled to submit to the exactions and robberies of the Taranakis, and to cultivate the most broken and heavily wooded portions of the district, while all around them lay thousands of acres of fine fertile, level, and open land in a state of nature, felt how necessary it was for the sake of ultimate peace and prosperity to plunge into the war, and let the tyrannical barbarians learn once and for ever the royalty of the Pakeha race and the majesty of their laws.

The following document shows the feelings and intentions of the Government with regard to this subject at the commencement of the year 1860:—

[Extract from the minutes of the Executive Council, held on Wednesday, 25th January, 1860.]

" Present: His Excellency the Governor, the Honorable the Officer Commanding the Troops, the Honorable the Colonial Secretary, the Honorable the Attorney-General, the Honorable the Colonial Treasurer, the Honorable Mr. Tancred.

" The Governor submits to the Council the question of the completion of the purchase from the native chief, Te Teira, of a certain block of land, situated in the Province of Taranaki, at the mouth of the Waitara, on the South and left bank, as a preliminary to which a survey of the land is necessary.

"The Council, after a full consideration of the case, advise:

" 1. That Mr. Parris be instructed to have the land surveyed in the ordinary manner, and to take care that the native chief William King, is indirectly, but not officially, made aware of the day on which the survey will be commenced.

" 2nd. Should William King or any other native endeavor to prevent the survey, or in any way interfere with the prosecution of the work, in that case that the surveying party be protected during the whole performance of their work by an adequate Military Force under the command of the Senior Military Officer; with which view power to call out the Taranaki Militia and Volunteers and to proclaim Martial Law be transmitted to the Commanding Officer at New Plymouth.

" 3rd. That when the survey shall have been completed, the Officer Commanding at New Plymouth, shall, until further instructed, keep possession, by force if necessary, of the said land, so as to prevent the occupation of, or any act of trespass upon it by any natives.

" 4th. That the Civil Authorities at New Plymouth be instructed to assist and co-operate, by every means in their power, with the Military Authorities in carrying out these instructions, and the Honorable Colonel Gold, and the Honorable C. W. Richmond are to give the necessary directions accordingly.

" F. G. STEWARD,
" Clerk of Executive Council."

Mr. Richmond to Mr. Parris.
"Office of Minister of Native Affairs,
" Auckland, 25th January, 1860.

" Sir:—I have the honor, by the direction of His Excellency the Governor, to inform you that His Excellency with the advice of the Executive Council, has determined that the survey of Te Teira's land at Waitara shall be proceeded with without further delay.

"The survey is to be commenced in the first instance without any display of force, by a surveyor attended only by an ordinary survey party—all being unarmed - you yourself being present on the ground, or not, as may seem expedient.

"You are to take care that the intended commencement of the survey is publicly known; and in particular that Wiremu Kingi and his party are made fully aware of it, and of the firm determination of His Excellency to complete the purchase. You will, however, avoid any official or formal announcement which might wear the aspect of an irritating challenge to the opposing party.

"Should resistance be made to the survey, the survey party will quietly retire; and you are then to intimate to Lieutenant-Colonel Murray that the assistance of a Military Force has become necessary.

"Military possession of the Block will thereupon be taken and kept by the Forces under the command of Lieutenant-Colonel Murray, who has received instructions upon this subject, and the survey is to be prosecuted under the protection of the troops.

"As regards the payment of Te Teira's purchase-money before commencing the survey, or at any subsequent time, you are to use your discretion. The Sub-Treasurer at New Plymouth has been instructed to make the necessary advances on your requisition.

"The Governor relies upon your tact and firmness in the execution of the difficult service entrusted to you, hoping that matters may be so conducted as to obviate the necessity of resorting to force, but feeling at the same time that it is impossible for himself as Her Majesty's Representative to withdraw from the position which he had deliberately assumed in reference to this affair.—I have, &c.,
"C. W. RICHMOND.
"R. Parris, Esq., New Plymouth."

The summer had been fine, and the settlers were busy harvesting their grass seed and other early crops assisted by a goodly number of natives from the South, when on Saturday, the 18th of February, the following notice was published by His Honor the Superintendent:—

PUBLIC NOTICE.

"Superintendent's Office,
"Saturday, 18th February, 1860.
"All persons are earnestly requested not to visit Waitara on Monday next, as a surveying party will proceed there on that day for the purpose of surveying the new block of land, and the presence of private individuals on that occasion would cause irritation among the natives.
"GEORGE CUTFIELD,
"Superintendent."

On Monday, the 20th, Mr. Parris, with Mr. Octavius Carrington and Mr. W. Hursthouse, of the Survey Department, and one of the armed police force, proceeded to Waitara. They were met at various parts of the road by parties of natives, but no obstruction was offered to their progress. Arrived at the land to be surveyed, a large number of natives, men, women, and children, were found assembled, and a party, apparently appointed for the purpose, attempted to obstruct the unpacking of the instruments, without success, but when the chain was thrown out and taken by Messrs. Parris and Carrington they effectually prevented their making any use of it. The obstruction was managed in the least objectionable way possible; there was no noisy language, and no more violence was used than was necessary to prevent the extension of the chain. They laid hold of the middle of the chain, and so disturbed the measuring, and the surveying party, finding it vain to persist farther, forthwith returned to town. Subsequently a communication from the authorities was made, giving the Waitara chief twenty-four hours to apologise for the obstruction offered by his people, and to notify his relinquishment of his opposition to the survey. To this an answer was received to the purport that he, Wiremu Kingi, did not desire war, that he loved the white people very much, but that he would keep the land, and that he and the Government might be very good friends if the survey were relinquished.

On the 22nd of February the following notice was published and posted in every district :—

PROCLAMATION.

" By His Excellency Colonel Thomas Gore Browne, Companion of the Most Honorable Order of the Bath, Governor and Commander-in-Chief in and over Her Majesty's Colony of New Zealand and its Dependencies, and Vice-Admiral of the same, etc.

" Whereas active military operations are about to be undertaken by the Queen's Forces against natives in the Province of Taranaki in arms against Her Majesty's Sovereign Authority.

" Now, I, the Governor, do hereby proclaim and declare that MARTIAL LAW will be exercised throughout the said Province from publication hereof within the Province of Taranaki, until the relief of the said district from Martial Law by public proclamation.

" Given under my hand and issued under the Public Seal of the Colony of New Zealand at Government House at Auckland, this Twenty-fifth Day of January, in the Year of our Lord, one thousand eight hundred and sixty.

" By His Excellency's Command.
          " E. W. STAFFORD.
  " God Save The Queen.
" Published 22nd February, 1860.
          " G. F. MURRAY,
   " Lieutenant-Colonel Commanding Troops,"

HE PANUITANGA.

" Na te Kawana Colonel Thomas Gore Browne, Tino Rangatira, aha, aha, ua te Kawana o tenei Koroni o Niu Tireno tenei Panuitanga.

" Ko te mea, meake ka timata nga Hoia o te Kuini ta ratou mahi ki nga Maori i Taranaki, e tutu ana, e whawhai ana, ki to te Kuini mana.—Na, ko ahau tenei ko te Kawana, te panui te whakapuaki nui nei i tenei kupu, Ko te Ture whawhai kia puta inaianei ki Taranaki, hei Ture tuturu tae noa ki te wa ka panuitia te whakarerenga.

" I tukua e taku ringa, i whakaputaia i raro iho i te Hiri Nui o te Koroni o Niu Tirene, i Akarana, i tenei ra i te rua tekau ma rima o Hanuere i te tau o to tatou Ariki, Kotahi mano ewaru rau e ono tekau.
         " THOMAS GORE BROWNE, Kawana.

" Na te Kawana i mea
  " E. W. Stafford,
  " Kai tuhituhi o te Koroni
    "Tohungia E. Te Atua Te Kuini."

NOTICE.

"It having become necessary to issue the Governor's Proclamation placing the district under Martial Law, I deem it advisable in order to prevent unnecessary alarm among the settlers to assure them that should events lead to actual collision with the natives that due notice will be given to enable them to provide for the safety of their families.

"G. F. MURRAY,
"Lieut.-Colonel Commanding Troops.
"Taranaki, 22nd February, 1860."

Shortly after the publication of this proclamation the country settlers began to move into New Plymouth. The little town had not room for half of them, much less for their goods. Many contented themselves with taking the most portable of their valuable goods and leaving the rest to fate. Others more wisely took their perishable goods to town and buried such as were not likely to be seriously damaged by the earth. The parting from the domestic animals was in many cases painful; pet lambs ran bleating after those that fed them as if foreseeing the horrible troubles that were coming on the land. Many of the domestic cats went wild and preyed upon the rats, mice and birds, but some lingered about the deserted houses till they perished with grief and starvation. The dogs fared much better, for they all accompanied their masters and appeared to thoroughly enjoy both the military parades and the actual engagements. Seeing the settlers crowding into town, an old Maori woman cried out in one of the streets, "Ah, you are leaving your houses and I shall shortly be applying a firebrand to them," and then she chuckled, gleefully anticipating the mischief she was about to indulge in. All the dwelling-houses, warehouses and some of the places of worship were filled with fugitives and their effects.

On March 1st the s.s. Airedale arrived from Auckland with Governor Browne and suite, accompanied by Colonel Gold, a military staff, and 200 rank and file of the 65th Regiment. The same day H.M.S.S. Niger anchored in the roadstead.

THE COMMENCEMENT OF HOSTILITIES.

On Monday morning, March 3rd, at four o'clock, the troops of the garrison of New Plymouth to the number of over 400 officers and men, ordered for the occupation of Teira's land at Waitara, under the command of Colonel Gold, left the town with a long train of baggage and provision waggons, escorted by an armed body of mounted settlers, by the Devon line, and passed over the Waiwakaiho bridge and through the Hua and Bell districts, to the site of the Ikamoana pa, when they branched off to the left, pursuing a line about equidistant between the coast and the Devon line, where the country is more open. The troops after refreshment encamped on high ground, the site of an old pa commanding the coast line of the disputed land. The s.s. corvette Niger was lying off the mouth of the river when the troops arrived. During the following night a pa was built by the natives across the Devon line, but was found deserted on the arrival of an escort from town with the following letter :—

"To the Chief who obstructs the Queen's Road—
"You have presumed to block up the Queen's road, to build on the Queen's land, and to stop the free passage of persons going and coming. This is levying war against the Queen; destroy the places you have built; ask my forgiveness and you shall receive it. If you refuse, the blood of your people be on your own head. I shall fire upon you in twenty minutes from this time if you have not obeyed my order.
"T. GORE BROWNE,
"Camp Waitara, 6th March, 1860."

The following notice was posted at the Militia Office :—
"New Plymouth, March 5th, 1850.
"The natives of the Kawau pa having left it at the request of His Excellency the Governor, the pa is in charge of the Garrison of the town, and must with all the property it contains be respected by all persons accordingly.
"(By Order) C. STAPP."

On the same day was published the following Gazette notice of promotions :—
"His Excellency has been pleased to make the following promotions and appointments in the Taranaki Militia :—
"Lieut. H. Richmond to be Capt., *vice* Watt, resigned.
"Ensign J. H. Armstrong to be Lieut., *vice* Richmond, promoted.
"Thomas Good to be Ensign, *vice* Armstrong.
"W. B. Messenger to be Ensign, *vice* Blackett, resigned.
"Lieut. Chevalier, 65th Regiment, to act as paymaster.
"Charles Des Voeux to command the Volunteer Mounted Force.
"Alexander King to be supernumary Lieutenant, and to act as Aide-de-Camp to the Officer Commanding the Forces."

On Friday, March the 9th, twenty marines, thirty blue jackets, the first and second lieutenants, a midshipman, an assistant surgeon, and a gunner, with a 12-pounder howitzer were landed from H.M.S.S. Niger, and encamped on Mount Bryan, a hill on the east side of New Plymouth, which was temporarily re-named Fort Niger.

On Friday evening, March the 16th, it was reported to the officer commanding the forces that Wiremu Kingi's natives had erected another pa on the land purchased from Teira. Early on Saturday morning, the 17th, Mr. Parris was sent to ascertain whether or not it was within our boundaries. It was found to be two chains within the boundary, and about four from the Devon line. Soon after it was reconnoitred by one of the mounted escort, who reported that it was a very strong pa with double palisading, ditch and galleries.

A letter was addressed to the natives by Colonel Gold ordering them to move off the Queen's land, and warning them of the consequence of refusal. This they would not even receive.

Subsequently Colonel Gold resolved to destroy the pa with rockets and 24-pounder howitzers. At half-past twelve, three companies of the 65th Regiment, under the command of Colonel Gold, assisted by Lieutenant-Colonel Sillery, Captains Paul and Barton, 65th Regiment, and six subalterns; six sailors from H.M.S. Niger, under Lieutenant Wells, with a rocket tube; two sergeants and seventeen men of the Royal Artillery, with one 12-pounder and two 24-pounder howitzers, under Lieutenant McNaughten; nine sappers and miners, under Lieutenant Mould; and twenty mounted volunteers under Captain Des Voeux. This force passed along the Waitara Road within range of the pa unmolested, when Lieutenants McNaughten and Mould were despatched with the mounted escort to find a suitable position for the guns and rocket tube. They fixed upon a little mound at the distance of 750 yards from the pa, from whence, as soon as the artillery and troops reached the position, a fire was opened, upon which the natives danced the war dance, hoisted their fighting flag, and returned the fire from the three faces of the pa. From the pa being placed in a hollow at the head of a gully, at first a few of the shells and rockets fell short, but the range was ascertained and the practice was excellent, the shells and rockets exploding in the pa and raising clouds of dust and smoke. After a short time it was found that the distance was too great. The Mounted Volunteers were extended on the right to threaten the enemy's line of retreat, and soon exchanged shots with some natives stealing up the gully to the pa, one of whom was wounded in the back and was toppled over. The guns moved to within three hundred yards of the inland face of the pa and with the rocket tube kept up a smart fire, making good practice and carrying away the flagstaff. The troops then took ground to the left, and the guns were fired at long intervals, when the enemy having ceased for more than an hour to reply to our fire it was supposed he had deserted the pa. Under this impression two or three of the volunteers made a dash at the flag, reached the palisade and were tugging away at it when a volley was fired from every face of the pa; the two at the palisade escaped unhurt with about two-thirds of the flag, but the third, who was galloping up, received a dangerous wound, fell from his horse, and after crawling a short distance was gallantly carried beyond the reach of fire by a sailor of the Naval Brigade and a private of the 65th Regiment. About this time two privates of the 65th Regiment were also badly wounded, one of whom afterwards died.

The guns soon silenced the fire of the pa, and finally took up a position within 200 yards of it. Night now approached and the gun ammunition was expended, the skirmishers were called in, and the troops formed in close column, the escort was despatched with the ammunition waggons to the camp, entrenchments were traced by the

Engineer officer, and the trenches soon formed, where under cover of the guns the weary soldiers lay down under arms. During the whole of this time the enemy kept up a smart fire from rifles, of which he had several, and musketry, and bullets were flying about the ears of the troops like hail. The natives at dark having come out of the pa, the escort returning with the ammunition was under fire for ten minutes, but providentially escaped uninjured, and having completed their mission were ordered back to camp, and ran the gauntlet by creeping slowly along the road and under cover of their horses. The supperless soldiers remained in the trenches all night. Shortly before day-break the enemy fired three guns, and is supposed then to have vacated the pa.

At early dawn on the 18th, the guns and skirmishers advanced nearer to the pa, the sappers throwing up an earthwork in their front; the fire was opened, under cover of which another breastwork was completed within fifty yards of the stockade. The shot soon reduced to splinters the palisading at the south end, and through the breach Lieutenant McNaughten coolly entered, followed by the troops, who were chagrined to find the pa abandoned. The pa was somewhat in the shape of a capital L, about 110 feet long and 33 feet wide. The ditches were five feet wide, and four feet deep, and were covered with a framework of split timber, and about two feet of earth and fern in layers on the top. These communicated with chambers worked out of the solid red earth, and were snugly lined with fern. In them fragments of shells, whole shells used as solid shot, and grape shot were found scattered about, also two spears, a bugle, two mats, with a supply of potatoes, melons, prepared maize, dried mutton-fish, and other food sufficient for several days consumption. As it is positively known that there were not less than 80 men in the pa when it was attacked, it may be assumed that the casualties were numerous.

THE DEFECTION OF MANAHI.

On Friday, March the 23rd, news was brought to town of the defection of Manahi and his people at the Native Reserve called Ratapihipihi, on the Barrett Road. This old chief and his people had but recently sworn allegiance to the British, and were armed for their defence.

On the following day news arrived that several hundred natives of the Taranaki and Ngatiruanui tribes were on their way to Ratapihipihi, and that the advanced guard numbering 70 men had already arrived and danced the war dance. It was reported that they intended to create a diversion in favor of Wi Kingi by menacing the settlement in that direction. In the evening, at about 9.30 o'clock, 250 troops from the camp at Waitara marched into town, bringing three field guns with them.

On Sunday, the 25th, at 4 a.m., 130 Taranaki Rifle Volunteers and Militia, with 200 men of the 65th Regiment, under Lieutenant-Colonel Murray, marched to Ratapihipihi, the natives having already commenced to kill the settlers' cattle and sheep and to commit other depredations. The Volunteers, led by Major Herbert, formed the advance, and proceeded in skirmishing order under Captain Stapp within range of the rebels before they were observed. An order on no account to engage the rebels in the forest having been issued before the expedition started, the skirmishers fell back upon the troops in good order without provoking attack. The plan for this particular service was well laid, and would have cut off the natives and placed them between the fire of the troops and militia, who were to have reached the enemy by different roads.

On Monday, the 26th, firing was heard at Ratapihipihi, and was supposed to be salutes by the enemy welcoming the arrival of reinforcements. The enemy, with the intention of encompassing the town, commenced to build a pa on Burton's Hill, on the Barrett or Mountain Road. The volunteers and militia were busily engaged in erecting small stockades, digging rifle pits, and in strengthening the Kawau pa. The Niger arrived from Manukau with 30 men of the 65th Regiment. The Rev. Mr. Wollaston reported the death of Sarten. From the first his wound was considered mortal, the ball that struck him having entered near his left hip, passed through his body, and was cut out from his right breast. 500 Taranakis and Ngatiruanuis arrived at Hauranga.

On Tuesday, the 27th, intelligence was brought into town that Wi Kingi's natives were about to build two large pas, one on Teira's land, and the other outside the boundary. They were to be near to one another, and were to be built of puriri. About five o'clock intelligence was brought to town of the murder of three settlers at Omata. The victims were Mr. Samuel Ford, a saddler and merchant of New Plymouth; Mr. S. Shaw and Mr. H. Passmore, farmers of Omata. These persons while on their way to different parts of the block were shot down by natives concealed behind a furze hedge near to the Primitive Methodist Chapel, and were afterwards tomahawked. Mr. Ford was on his way to see some sheep on Mr. Grayling's farm, and had that morning ridden out to Moturoa with Mr. George and purchased six of his bullocks. Mr. Ford proceeded from Moturoa towards Omata alone, and on passing the stockade was by several persons warned not to go on. Mr. H. Passmore was out with his bullocks and cart for the purpose of obtaining some puriri fencing. His bullocks were both shot in the head and the yoke was taken off and thrown into the hedge. Shaw accompanied Passmore, and was supposed to have been going to his farm to milk his cows. Information was given to the men at the stockade by Mr. W. Gilbert, who, as he was riding along the road, saw a body lying on the ground, and at once galloped back and gave the intelligence. A party then proceeded to recover the bodies, and on arriving at the spot found three corpses lying within a few yards of each other, and they also saw a native in the act of taking off Mr. Ford's coat. They fired at the native but missed him, and he ran off. Ford and Passmore appeared to have died instantaneously, but Shaw had evidently struggled for some time. Passmore and Shaw were tomahawked about the head. Two boys named Pote and Parker were reported missing.

ENGAGEMENT AT WAIREKA

On Wednesday, the 28th, news arrived in town that the two boys, Parker and Pote, had been found by the Rev. H. H. Brown, dead and dreadfully tomahawked. No. 10 Company of the 65th Regiment, commanded by Colonel Murray, 25 blue jackets, under Lieutenant Blake, and 102 volunteers and militia proceeded to Omata with the intention of rescuing the Rev. H. H. Brown, his family, with other settlers who still remained out in that district. Before the departure of the volunteers and militia they were addressed by the Governor, who expressed a hope that they would do their duty. About noon two signal guns, fired from Marsland Hill, brought all stragglers from town, and Captain Cracroft, from the Niger, with 60 blue jackets and marines, and a 24-pounder rocket-tube and rockets. The troops proceeded along the road, and the volunteers and militia went by the beach, and proceeded inland diagonally from Paritutu towards the Waireka stream at Omata. They were engaged as soon as they came within range of the enemy, who came down from the hill on the south-west side of the stream to meet them. After the departure of the troops, volunteers, and militia from town, the Niger's men took up a temporary position near to the boat house, and an officer went to the truck of the flagstaff on Marsland Hill. As soon as he perceived that the engagement had begun he ran down Brougham Street without his hat, and with his cutlass at his shoulder, and at once led his men off to the scene of action. Intelligence soon arrived in town that Sergeant Fahey of the militia was killed, the gallant Captain Blake severely wounded, and that the volunteers were hotly engaged and were running out of ammunition, and were surrounded until succoured by the soldiers and sailors. The excitement in town was intense. When night closed in the soldiers returned, and also a party of the blue jackets with some of the wounded. It was then learned that the blue jackets under Captain Cracroft, after firing a few rockets into it, had gallantly stormed the pa on Jury's Hill, and killed many of the inmates and captured the rebel flags. About 8 p.m. the sailors came in bringing into town the flags, and were heartily cheered by the people. The volunteers were said to be surrounded by the Maoris, but to have possession of Jury's house near to the beach; it was also said that their ammunition was expended. A mixed volunteer force was despatched to their rescue at 11 p.m., but they had not long gone when great cheering announced that the forces had met each other.

Mr. Wellington Carrington, who resided at the time at Tapuae, and counted the Maoris as they passed his house towards Omata, gave the following particulars respecting them :—

"First hapu, Nga Mahanga, headed by Kingi Parenga and

Paretene Kopara, numbering 66, struck off into the bush at Tapuae and went on to Ratapihipihi; this was on Saturday, the 24th of March.

"On the 27th, 64 natives of the Patukai hapu, headed by Paora Kututae and Aperahama passed on. This party went along the main road and settled themselves at Ratanui, a little above Mr. Jury's house.

"On the 28th, 200 went along the main road; they were the Ngatituwekerangi, Upokomutu, Ngarangi, Ngatihau and Ngatihaumia hapus, headed by old Hori Kingi, the head man of the whole Taranaki tribe, Wi Kingi Matakatea, Arama Karaka, and several other chiefs of lesser note. Those that I have mentioned were the whole of the Taranaki tribe engaged in the insurrection.

"In the afternoon of the 28th, 130 Ngatiruanui natives of the Ngaruahine hapu passed along the main road, and joined the others at Ratanui. They had hardly taken off their pikaus when the action commenced."

At Major Lloyd's farm, Waireka, the battle was fought by the Nga Mahanga, headed by Kingi, Paretene and Perere, the best fighting men of the tribe. The first was wounded, the two latter were killed. On Jury's farm the battle was fought by Ngatiruanuis, headed by Te Hanatau, the head chief of the tribe, who was killed. The main body was posted behind the pa they had erected at Ratanui, and a number were also in Mr. Armstong's turnip field. Old Paul was killed when the pa was stormed and the colors taken. From that time the whole of the hapus became thoroughly disorganised, and early next morning commenced their retreat. However, they carried off most of their dead and all their wounded. The road between their pa and Poutoko was strewed with all sorts of plunder. The number of dead positively ascertained is 17. This includes the principal chiefs, but more men of note fell and were buried at Omata. There were 450 more Ngatiruanui and some Ngarutu natives coming up, but meeting the broken taua at Warea and Kapoaiaia, they remained for a time at those places. Taking 330 as the number of the Taranakis who came up, and allowing 100 as the number of those who remained neutral, we arrive nearly at the strength of the tribe, 430. Adding 130 Ngatiruanuis to the 450 who were on their way up, we get 580 as the strength of the Ngatiruanui and Ngarauru tribes, which makes a grand total of 1,010 natives capable of bearing arms between New Plymouth and Wanganui.

The following is a translation of a notice posted at Omata by the rebels:—

"Listen! Listen! all the tribe. The road to our minister must not be trodden upon; also the road to his friends,—James who is from Kihi; to Emmanuel who is a Portuguese, to his children and wife; to Touet and his wife and children, who are French; let the thought of these three tribes be light to their farms, to their property; let it be light, because the word has gone forth from Paratene, Hoani,

and Kingi Parenga to those people that we must strictly preserve them. Let there be no mistake ; with us the three tribes of Taranaki, Ngatiruanui and Ngaraura ; let it be light. That is all from
"PARETENE,   From "KINGI,
"HOANI,   "PORIKAPA."

The following are the official reports of the engagement at Waireka :—
"Lieutenant-Colonel Murray to the Major of Brigade.
"New Plymouth, 20th March, 1860.
" Sir :—I have the honor to report for the information of the Officer Commanding the Forces in New Zealand, that on the 28th instant I proceeded agreeably to orders in command of a force, as per margin, to Omata for the purpose of rescuing some European families stated to be in the hands of the rebel natives assembled in considerable force at that village.

"The plan of operations was, that Captain Brown, in command of the militia and volunteers, should proceed by the beach, keeping the sea coast, and passing in the rear of the natives, who had built a pa on the Waireka Hills,—whilst I should proceed by the main road with a view to dislodge a party of rebels reported to have taken up a position at a spot called Whaler's Gate, for the purpose of cutting off the communication between Omata and the Town. In the meantime, Captain Brown, should he succeed in recovering the European families, was to join me at or near this spot. On reaching the spot named, I found the road clear and no trace of natives anywhere near, accordingly I moved on leisurely with a view to sooner meeting Captain Brown ; but on reaching the top of a hill about a quarter of a mile on the side of the Omata stockade, the sound of rapid firing, about two miles off and towards the sea, made it evident that the volunteers were hotly engaged. I accordingly pushed on to the stockade, when I dispatched Lieutenant Blake, R.N., with his men, supported by a subdivision of the company, 65th Regiment, under Lieutenant Urquhart, with orders to proceed in a direct line to the assistance of Captain Brown's party, whilst I continued along the road with the remainder of the force to a lane about a quarter of a mile beyond the stockade, which leads from the road down to the sea. About half way down this lane I turned into the fields and formed line of skirmishers, with the intention, also, of proceeding to the assistance of the volunteers, &c. The rebels, however, showed such a disposition to get round our left, and so cut us off from the main road, that I was obliged to abandon that intention, and manœuvre to prevent it, keeping up a fire whenever they gave us an opportunity, as they were covered by a wood and deep ravine, out of which we attempted to dislodge them with rockets. I ultimately took up a position in the lane so as to secure the main road ; and the natives seeing us retire came down through the wood and ravine, but such an effective fire was kept up wherever they showed themselves that they retired to the bush again. Considering my force, however, too small to keep our communication open, should they attack us in force, I recalled Lieutenant Blake's party and Lieutenant Urquhart's, particularly as the day was so far advanced and my orders were to return by dark. I continued to occupy this position until it became absolutely necessary to return, keeping up a frequent fire of rockets on the pa and any groups of rebels we observed. It became necessary, however, to detach Lieutenant Urquhart a second time to drive back the rebels, who were attempting to get up on our right, and between us and the volunteers, which, having accomplished, he rejoined me in time to return. I beg to add that nothing I can say could adequately describe the steadiness and gallantry of both officers and men composing my little force. I have but one regret in reporting that I was early deprived of the very able assistance of Lieutenant Blake, H.M.S.S. Niger, who was severely wounded.

"I enclose returns of casualties. I have received no report of Captain Brown's proceedings, who was too far off for observation, apparently in a gully, with the natives about him.—I have, &c.

"G. F. MURRAY,
"Bt. Lieutenant-Colonel, 65th Regt.,
"Commanding Garrison.

"The Major of Brigade, Taranaki.

[Force engaged.]
"Royal Navy—3 officers and 25 men. 65th Regiment—4 officers and 84 rank and file. Names of Officers—Lieutenant Urquhart, 65th Regiment; Lieutenat Whitbread, 65th Regiment; Surgeon White, Lieutenant Blake, R.N., H.M.S. Niger."

"Captain Cracroft, R.N., to Colonel Gold.
"H.M.S.S. Niger, New Plymouth, 28th March, 1860.

Sir:—In compliance with your requisition, I landed the force noted in the margin at 2 p.m. this day, and, at your request that I should advance to the support of Colonel Murray, who was represented to be hard pressed by the natives and short of ammunition, I proceeded to the Omata blockhouse, from which post I was enabled to obtain a good view of the country and of a pa constructed on the crown of a hill about a mile beyond, which displayed flags, and from which a continued fire of musketry was kept up upon Colonel Murray's force on my right, with whom I immediately communicated.

"It was now about half-past five, and as there was only half-an-hour's daylight left, I determined to attack this pa at once. I accordingly planted the 24-pounder rocket tube about 700 yards from it, and after a few discharges the men stormed this pa under a heavy fire in the most gallant style, William Odgers, leading seamen, doing duty as my coxwain, being the first man in it; and having captured the flags and destroyed everything living in the trenches, as far as could be ascertained in the dark, I returned to the blockhouse.

"In performing this service I am thankful to say that there were only four men wounded, which may be in some measure accounted for by the rapidity of the attack, taking the enemy completely by surprise, and giving no time for the usual Maori tactics, while the increasing darkness also favored our small force and prevented a good aim being taken by their sharpshooters. It is difficult to estimate the numbers opposed to us, nor could their exact loss be ascertained. Sixteen dead were counted inside the intrenchments, and several were lying in the road outside.

"After a short rest at the blockhouse I returned to town, placed the wounded in the military hospital, and re-embarked my men, as I did not consider the ship safe without them at this exposed anchorage.

"I cannot speak too highly of all engaged in this affair, and I should wish to recommend to your notice three of the volunteers, who accompanied me from the blockhouse and pointed out the road to the pa.

"I beg to enclose for your information the surgeon's return of casualties, and I have, &c.,

"P. CRACROFT,
"Captain and Senior Officer,
"At New Zealand.

"The Honorable Colonel Gold,
"Commanding the Forces in New Zealand.

[Force engaged.]
"Lieutenant A. J. Villiers; Mr. Smith, acting mate; Mr. T. Gassiott, third mate; Mr. J. Carslake, third mate; Dr. W. Patrick, surgeon; Mr. W. H. Hyatt, assistant paymaster. Officers 7, seamen 43, marines 10: total 60, and a 24-pounder rocket and tube."

"Captain Brown to Major Herbert.
"New Plymouth, 29th March, 1860.

"Sir:—I have the honor to report what took place yesterday, from the time I left the town with the force under my command at half-past one, till my return at half-past twelve this morning.

"The officers and men who accompanied me were:—

"Captain and Adjutant Stapp, Militia; Captain H. A. Atkinson, Volunteer Rifles; Lieutenant McKechney, Militia; Lieutenant McKellar, Militia; Lieutenant Hirst, Volunteer Rifles; Lieutenant Hammerton, Volunteer Rifles; Second Lieutenant Webster, Volunteer Rifles; Second Lieutenant Jonas, Volunteer Rifles; Ensign Messenger, Militia. Rank and File: Militia 52, Volunteer Rifles 98.

"After a quick march of about two hours we reached the stream Waireka, where it runs on to the beach. We here perceived that the natives were rapidly running down from their pa, about a mile off, on the Waireka hill, to meet us. We were, however, able to get into position without difficulty on the high land in the following manner, under Captain Stapp's direction :—

"A Company of Volunteers, under Captain Atkinson, were thrown forward, and reached the high ground on the south side of the Waireka, driving back the natives; but greater numbers of the enemy coming on both flanks, Captain Stapp, who had joined and taken command, ordered a retreat on position No. 1, shown in the enclosed tracing made by the Provincial Surveyor, the position consisting of a house, stacks, and furze and rail fences on level ground on the brink of two gullies running out on the beach. From this point Captain Atkinson was moved on to No. 2, to cover the rear of the main body. Lieutenant Hirst with his Company occupied No. 3, and was joined by Lieutenant McKechney and myself, when I pushed Lieutenant Hirst forward to endeavor to occupy the bush in the Waireka gully, under cover of which the natives were swarming, and followed myself. Lieutenant Blake with a party of the Niger's men having thrown themselves in advance by another route, I directed Lieutenant Hirst to turn his attention to the natives on the lower and open part of the Waireka gully, whence they were annoying Captain Atkinson's party as well as our own. Lieutenant Hirst having done some execution, passed across the gully by No. 2, to Captain Stapp at No. 1. The natives soon made us aware that they possessed pieces of long range, against which our muskets were of no use, and I had to fall back on the scanty cover at No. 3, where I had not been long when Lieutenant Urquhart, 65th Regiment, with some 25 men joined me, as also some stragglers of the Naval Brigade, and some volunteers from the Omata Stockade, under Lieutenant Armstrong, Militia, and Lieutenant McNaughten, R.A. With their assistance we drove the natives out of sight into a straggling and slight line of cover in the gully that runs into the Waireka, and as I perceived the intention of the natives was to intercept our line of retreat to the Omata Stockade by occupying the cover of flax between Nos. 3 and 4, I requested Lieutenant Urquhart to leave me a few men, and with the remainder occupy No. 4, thus placing the natives creeping along the gully between two fires, and securing our communication with the Omata Stockade; to my surprise and regret Lieutenant Urquhart had not many minutes occupied No. 4 before I saw him and his men retire, recalled, as I am informed by Colonel Murray, by his orders. The position commanded my own, was uncommanded by any other, had open and level country between it and the Omata Stockade, and had excellent cover of flax at the edge of the position to seaward. When the natives saw them retire they called out 'Kia hohoro, Kia hohoro,' and boldly ran along the open part of the gully to the cover on the North side of the Waireka, bringing themselves under the murderous fire of Captain Atkinson, which dropped them in twos and threes about the ground. At this time finding my position untenable and valueless to the natives, I ordered our wounded and dead to be carried to Captain Stapp's position. These consisted of one of the marines of H.M.S.S. Niger, wounded in the head and since dead, one militiaman shot through the neck, and Sergeant Fahey of the Stockade at Omata shot dead, the first and last were shot by the same native, who was himself shot by Mr. P. Wilson with a fowling piece.

"I then sent my men to join Captain Stapp, while I went to see Captain Atkinson, who joined me in going to see Captain Stapp and conferring with him; when I saw the extensive defences we should have to maintain at this place and their weak nature, I was of opinion that the whole force should be concentrated at No. I. Captain Stapp and Captain Atkinson differed with me, and considered that No. 2 ought to be maintained to the last. I gave way to their opinions, and am happy to say their judgement proved correct, as Captain Atkinson from his position killed at least two-thirds of the natives that were killed. We then proceeded at No. 1 to make our position defensible by throwing up breast works of sheaves of oats and fencing, so as to enable us to enfilade our position. While thus employed we became aware of the diversion effected in our favor by the attack on the pa by Captain Cracroft, R.N., and his Naval Brigade, and which I considered enabled us to retreat after dark unmolested. Had my men been concentrated at No. 1, I would have endeavored to ascertain what had taken place at the pa with a view of joining Captain Cracroft; but under the circumstances, very few charges of ammunition being left, and believing that the retreat of our wounded by No. 4, the shortest route, would be open after dark, in consequence of the diversion effected, I determined to remain in our positions till the moon had set, when Captain Stapp took charge of the advance to No. 4, followed by the wounded, and thence on to the Omata Stockade. I told off the men by fours, and marched from No. 1, one four just keeping the other in sight; when the last four had left No. 1, I went to Captain Atkinson and directed him to follow with his men and eight men of the 65th who had been left with us, and who did us gallant service, also three men from the Naval Brigade and the party from the Garrison of the Omata Stockade.

"After resting a short time at the Omata Stockade, and reinforcing that post with 20 men, we resumed our march to Town, passing the Whaler's Gate without seeing anything of the support, which, according to my instructions, I was to expect there. We reached Town unmolested at about half-past twelve at night, bringing with us also the dead and all the wounded but two, who were left at the Stockade.

"Where every one behaved so well it would be invidious, not to say impossible, to recommend particular officers or men for particular notice. I will, therefore, limit myself to commending the gallantry and coolness of Captains Stapp and Atkinson, of Lieutenant Urquhart, 65th, and of Private Inch of the Volunteers, who shot two natives after he had himself received a wound across his chest. The casualties are as follows in my Detachment:—

"Killed—Sergeant Fahey, Militia.

"Wounded—Lieutenant Hammerton, Volunteer Rifles; Private W. Bayley, Militia; Private J. Climo, Militia; Private J. Hawken,

Volunteer Rifles; Private Inch, Volunteer Rifles; Private Messenger, Volunteer Rifles; Private W. Oliver, Militia; Private Rawson, Volunteer Rifles.

"I am happy to state that the wounded, though not all out of danger, are all doing well.

"I have carefully estimated the number of the enemy killed at not less than thirty, besides wounded.—I have, &c.,

"CHARLES BROWN,
"Senior Captain of Taranaki Militia.

"Major Herbert,
"Commanding Militia and Volunteers."

The village of Omata at the time of the war was situated at the junction of two roads at the foot of the Waireka Hill, and a little westward of the present church and school house. After the battle it presented a very sad appearance. In the centre lay a pair of fine working bullocks, dead and swollen, and near to them a dead horse. These animals were the property of the men who were murdered just prior to the battle. The houses had all been sacked, all the windows had been broken by the butt end of guns being driven through them, and such domestic articles as the rebels were unable to carry away were wantonly broken and scattered about. The children's dolls were derisively hung up by the neck on the fences. The curtains and calico linings of the houses had all been carefully taken away to serve as bandages for the wounded.

Much indignation was felt at the conduct of Colonel Murray in withdrawing his men at sunset, and leaving the volunteers to their fate, and men wondered why the advantages which had been gained were not followed up. On the day after the battle the Niger steamed down the coast and shelled the native settlement at Warea, after which armed parties went out and obtained as much of the crops as possible, and the natives commenced pillaging the farms and burning the houses of the settlers.

On Sunday, April the 22nd, three Companies of the 65th Regiment, with one brass howitzer and some artillery men, started on a reconnoitring expedition to Wareatea, and returned a few days afterwards without seeing any natives or effecting anything. In the meantime Hapurona had been strengthening his position at Waitara, and his garrison had been reinforced by a number of Waikatos.

NARROW ESCAPE OF MR. PARRIS.

A number of Taranaki and Ngatiruanui natives, who were on a visit to Potatau, the Maori King at Waikato, being desirous at this time to return to their homes, the Waikato chief, Rewi, went to the Rev. Mr. Morgan of Otawa, and expressed a desire to see Mr. Parris on the road, as his people were about to escort the Taranaki and Ngatiruanui deputations towards their homes. Mr. Parris accordingly started for the north on Friday, the 11th day of May. On reaching Urenui he was informed that the natives were expected to be between

Tongaporutu and Mimi, but on arriving at Pukekohe he unexpectedly came upon the whole party, finding them seated behind the breakwind away from the pa. A Ngatiruanui chief having been the first to observe Mr. Parris, rose and shook hands with him, for which he afterwards received the censure of the whole of his tribe. The natives of Pukekohe—Nikorima's people—seeing Mr. Parris approach waved to him with their blankets to keep off from the war party. Mr. Parris at once rode to the pa, when he discovered that there had been no communication between the two parties. Here he remained a little time. The pa natives, according to custom, put out some potatoes and other food for the war party, after which some of the latter rose and said :—" This white man Parris has arrived and entered the pa, and therefore we suppose the pa belongs to him ; in consequence thereof the food is *tapu*"—i.e. not to be accepted or eaten by them. This produced a discussion which ended in the Waikatos declining to agree with the others. The Ngatiruanui and Taranaki ate nothing but dry karaka berries brought by them from Waikato, but the Waikatos partook of some food from the pa. Wetini, a Mokau chief, entered the pa and informed Mr. Parris of the state of feeling amongst the natives being against him, advised him to be cautious, and added that the Mokaus had endeavored to keep the party back. Mr. Parris asked Wetini if he had any objection to return and to invite the heads of the Waikato party to come and speak with him. He consented, but said it would lead to nothing. He went and remained away fully an hour, during which time Mr. Parris recognised Hone Pumipi, a Kawhia chief, among the party. Mr. Parris asked a native of the pa to go and see if Hone would come and see him. Mr. Parris saw Hone submit the proposal to the natives, after which he came towards the pa accompanied by a body guard of four men armed with guns. Hone approached the side of the pa, and addressing Mr. Parris, said :—" I have come because you have sent for me, but the people are *pouri*," evil disposed. Mr. Parris observing an indisposition on Hone's part to converse— probably owing to the presence of the armed natives—said, " I merely sent to see you and ask you how you are." Upon which one of the guard said " Let us return," and they returned. As soon as they rejoined the party the Ngatiruanui and Taranaki rose and fired off their guns, and started for Urenui, some few miles nearer town. The Waikatos remained. Shortly afterwards the head of the Waikato party, Epiha, came to the pa to see Mr. Parris, and made the following disclosure. He commenced with a regular scolding :—" You are foolish : you have brought your body upon us without sending a messenger or a letter to let us know you were coming ; if we had met you on the march you would have been shot dead without our being able to save you. As it is you are dead." Mr. Parris interrupted him to explain that it was in consequence of being requested by Mr. Morgan and Rewi to meet the party that he had come, and he asked Epiha to explain what he meant by saying he was dead. Epiha replied, " It has been proposed to murder you.

Shortly after your arrival this morning Erueti—one of Wi Kingi's natives—came to us Waikatos and said when he saw you his flesh shook, and that he was going to Urenui. Epiha asked, 'What for?' Erueti answered, 'to wait for Parris's return.' Epiha said, 'What to do?' Erueti replied, 'To finish him.' Epiha observed, 'We have not come from Waikato for any such thing as murder, and if you determine to do it we shall leave at once and return to Waikato.' Eureti was displeased and left for Urenui with three others—Hori, Paori and Taimona, all of Kaipakopako." This occurred before the Taranakis and Ngatiruanui started for Urenui. A long and anxious conversation ensued as to the course to be taken, which ended in Epiha stating that he would wait for Mr. Parris at Urenui and see him safely across.

After Epiha left it was arranged with Nikorima that a party of ten of his natives should accompany Mr. Parris as far as Waitara. Night was now setting in, and as the party approached Urenui they sang out to warn Epiha, who was across the river. In ascending the cliff the natives were found assembled near the top, the party halted, and Mr. Parris was asked to come to the front. A row of armed natives was on each side of the path. As soon as Mr. Parris had got clear of the armed men, Epiha ordered a halt, and requested the ten natives who had accompanied Mr. Parris from Pukekohe to return to their pa. This they refused to do, and as it threatened an unpleasant discussion Mr. Parris entreated them to return, as he threw himself entirely on the Waikato. Hone Pumipi thereupon stepped forth from the crowd and said, "Parris, I'll take charge of you." As Hone said this a man in a flax mat forced his way forward and rubbed noses with Mr. Parris. Hone observing this seized the stranger by the chest and forced him back, when he explained, "This is my white man," and he proved to be a brother of Teira, of the Waitara. The situation was one of extreme peril. A large body of natives hustled Mr. Parris, and amongst the crowd, though they could not be distinguished in the starlight, were many of the conspirators.

The chiefs Epiha and Hone now called out to them to stand clear of the Pakeha, and the dark mass of Maoris fell back. It was communicated to Mr. Parris that the ambush party had gone on to Onaero. An armed party of Waikatos then fell in, a native on each side of Mr. Parris grasping him by the hand, besides a rear and an advanced guard; and in this way Mr. Parris was conducted to Waiau, about five miles, in the darkness of the night. On arriving at Onaero where the road passes through a piece of bush the party halted, one native remarking, "This is the spot in which they said they would kill him." Double files were here placed around Mr. Parris, and the whole were directed to keep close together. From Waiau to Waitara the road was on the beach. At the former place Mr. Parris was required to join in a clever extempore prayer for the King, the Queen's and his own safety. After which Mr. Parris separated from his preservers.. Epiha, in reply to the acknowledgments made to him, told Mr. Parris not to attribute his deliverance to him, but to God; that he would yet meet him as an enemy by daylight, but that; he (Mr. Parris), had seen that he would not consent to his being murdered.

The Waikato escort was estimated at 150 natives, the Taranaki and Ngatiruanui deputation at 50.

The Government apprehending the serious nature of the conflict in which they had become involved, sent pressing requests to the Australian Colonies for troops and warlike stores. In response to these requests the City of Sydney steamer arrived in the roadstead with H.M.S. Cordelia on the 16th of April, bringing of the Royal Artillery 1 captain, 2 corporals, 3 bombardiers, and 39 gunners; of· the Royal Engineers, 1 corporal and 5 privates; of the Commissariat Department, Deputy-Assistant Commissary Dunn; of the 1st Battalion of the 12th Regiment, 2 captains, 2 subalterns, 1 staff officer, 7 sergeants, 2 drummers, 9 corporals, and 117 rank and file; with two 24-pounder howitzers, two 9-pounder guns, and six mortars, and a large amount of ammunition.

On Tuesday, the 24th of April, the City of Hobart arrived with 230 officers and men of the 40th Regiment.

A strong stockade, well garrisoned, was maintained at Omata, and another at Bell Block, and temporary guard rooms were constructed on the Race course and elsewhere. Every night a cordon of sentinels kept watch around the town, many of whom were without any shelter, and the weather proved very wet. Naval Camps were also established in various parts of the town, and a strong force guarded the port, flagstaff, and the boats.

CAPTAIN RICHARD BROWN.

Richard Brown was born in Dublin in 1804, and was brought up and educated in that city by an uncle. In his youth he was employed in a mercantile house in Hobart Town, Tasmania, and at the age of 20 paid a visit to the Bay of Islands, and to the islands of the Pacific Ocean, in a Tasmanian whale ship. Shortly after the foundation of New Plymouth he came hither, and after conducting a coasting trade for some time ultimately became a merchant in the town, having for his place of business a long low warehouse near to the boat sheds.

In 1847 he had a quarrel with the natives about a horse, and striking one on the head with a heavy whip handle he nearly paid for his temerity with his life, for the natives came into town in large numbers, danced the war dance, and demanded that·he should be given up to them. For his safety the authorities confined him in the town prison, around which the natives kept watch all night. In the morning the natives were pacified by the prisoner's consenting to give up the horse as *utu* for the damage he had done. For some time after this Mr. Brown engaged in whaling, employing a shore party at Moturoa, under the leadership of Robert Sinclair. Next he added to his business the profession of land agent, and eventually he super-added to it that of editor of the "Taranaki Herald." When the war broke out he received a commission as Captain of the Native Contingent, and proved himself to be an intrepid officer.

On Saturday, May the 26th, 1860, Captain Brown left the camp at Waitara for the purpose of seeking a straying horse. Riding along the beach towards New Plymouth, on reaching the ford of the Waiongona river he was surprised by three of Wi Kingi's natives, one of whom, a young man named Tawatihi, who had recently been in Captain Brown's employment, sprang out of a bush and fired at him. The first shot struck Captain Brown's revolver-cartouch-box and glanced off, the next penetrated his thigh, and the third passed through his left side and lodged in his body. After the first shot Captain Brown's horse swerved, and the succeeding shots struck him as he was turning. Captain Brown galloped back to the camp, and being observed to drop out of the saddle, was carried to the camp in a fainting state. Here he lingered, suffering with great patience and resignation, till the 21st of August, when death brought him release. Captain Brown was a person of education and of polite manners, a clever improvisatore, and convivial, but sober in his habits. He was singularly reticent as regarded his antecedents and business transactions. He was strictly just and pleasant in his dealings, but there was an inner intrenchment in his nature that was impenetrable and a fire in his eye that forbade too close an acquaintance. To a certain extent he lived and died a mystery. Dying intestate and without legal heirs his estate was escheated.

BATTLE OF PUKETAKUERE.

After the ineffectual demonstrations made by several expeditions to the South the British remained inert, waiting for the rebels to renew hostilities. Very many of the settlers' wives and children were removed to Nelson, where they were received with much compassion. The militia and volunteers aided the military and the blue jackets in guarding the town from the attacks which were constantly threatened by the enemy. Such of the natives as professed friendship with the British were armed, supplied with rations, and furnished with serge blouses marked with a large white bull's-eye on the back to prevent their being taken for rebels. The service of this contingent was of but little use to the British, on account of the ill-disguised sympathy of many of its members with their countrymen in rebellion. In the meantime house-burning and the plunder of cattle, horses, and sheep was going on in the country districts, and Hapurona was at work strengthening his position on the edge of the table land overlooking the Waitara Valley, between the Devon Road and the site of the present township of Raleigh, and receiving daily reinforcements from Waikato.

At length, on Saturday, the 23rd of June, a reconnoitring party of the 40th Regiment were fired upon from the enemy's works at Puketakuere, and the officer in command determined to make preparations for an attack on the pa. The enemy's works consisted of two stockades, one erected upon an entrenchment of an old pa. They stood upon a ridge formed by two small gullies, which met a little below the pa, and opened on to the swampy ground in the Waitara valley, forming a sort of long Y with the stalk towards the river, and the stockades in the fork.

On Wednesday, June the 27th, Major Nelson marched the troops from the camp in three divisions. The main body consisting of the grenadier and light company of the 40th Regiment, under Captain Richards, and 60 blue jackets under First Lieutenant Battiscombe of the Pelorus, with the Artillery, approached the pa by the direct road from the camp, and at 7 a.m. the guns were brought to bear and the men extended on the seaward side of the pa, the smaller gully behind them and it. With this division were Major Nelson and Captain Seymour of the Pelorus. A second division of about 50 men, under Captain Messenger, was posted on the flat of the Waitara to cut off the retreat on that side, and a third, under Captain Bowdler, passed along the river bank and attempted to take the pa in the rear. The natives, from their position on the edge of the plateau, could observe every movement of the troops, while the British could see little but the palisading of the pas and the high fern. The firing of the enemy commenced on the rear of our troops, the natives at the time leaving the pas and seeking the shelter of the gullies in order to pour from thence volleys of musketry on our men.

Shortly after the commencement of the engagement large reinforcements of Maoris poured in from the inland villages of the rebels, who creeping in the fern, fired unseen, but at close quarters with the British, and the main body of the latter overlapping a dangerous gully, was exposed to a terrific fire from numerous rifle pits within it.

When the attack was planned it was arranged that Colonel Gold, with a large force and two 24-pounder howitzers, should co-operate with the Waitara force by proceeding from town and attacking the rebels from the plateau on the edge of which these works were situated. Had he done so the fortune of the day would have been the reverse of what it proved to be; but the Colonel after reaching the Mangoraka considered the river too high for the troops to cross, and marched back to town, leaving Major Nelson to do the best he could. The fire at this engagement was said by veterans to have been hotter than that at Feroszeshah and Sabraon, and a soldier of the Crimea declared it to be hotter than the attack on the Redan. The natives, as was their custom, used double-barrelled guns and loosely fitting balls, and in loading jerked the charge down the barrels by striking the butt of their pieces on the ground. So much pressed were the British at last that it was only by a timely discharge of canister shot that a retreat was effected. Finding that his expected reinforcements did not appear, Major Nelson ordered the retreat to be sounded, and the men withdrew, sadly harassed by the enemy, and by the swampy nature of the ground. So hasty was the retreat that many of the dead and wounded were left on the field, and quantities of ammunition were shot out of the carts into the fern to facilitate the flight.

Captain Seymour had his leg broken by a bullet, and Lieutenant Brooke of the 40th Regiment was barbarously killed in a swamp after surrendering his sword to the enemy. Three or four of the wounded men crept through the fern to the camp during the afternoon, and another was brought in after dark, after having crawled on one knee for four hours through the fern, the other knee having been shattered by a shot. One man escaped by swimming the river, and two others were drowned in attempting to do so.

"Major Nelson to Major of Brigade.
"Camp Waitara, 27th June, 1860.

"Sir:—I have the honor to inform you, for the information of the Colonel commanding, that, in reference to your letter of yesterday's date, I moved out this morning at 5 o'clock, with the detail noted in the margin, to attack the new pas on the mounds of the South-East of the camp, and returned from thence at 11 a.m.

"The attack was commenced by the Artillery at 7 a.m., at a range of 400 yards to the North-West of the pas. A breach was, however, not made in the large pa of a sufficient size to justify me in ordering the men to assault it.

"During the time the Artillery was playing on the pa, large bodies of Maoris were seen advancing from the rear and occupying in extended order a ditch and a bank, about 400 yards in advance of our right flank, from which they kept up a constant fire.

"Seeing there was no means of entering the pa, I immediately ordered an advance towards the ditch and bank just mentioned, which was made in a most continued and gallant manner until the men reached a deep ravine with an intrenchment behind, and which they found it impossible to pass, it being defended by two, if not more, large bodies of Maoris, who were almost entirely concealed behind it, and another entrenchment in rear; as well as the very high fern.

"Here a desperate and destructive fire was opened upon us, and gallantly returned.

"Our skirmishers being far fewer in number, and exposed in a much greater degree than the enemy, I deemed it desirable to direct them to join the main body; and our ammunition being nearly expended, I withdrew the whole of the men, and returned to camp in regular order.

"I regret to report that the casualties have been numerous, but when, as it is supposed, the whole of Wi Kingi's natives came down to support the Waikatos in the pas, the whole amounting to about 700 men (foremost among whom was a European, who was shot dead), it cannot be considered that the number is great in proportion to the number opposed to us.

"Among the deaths I have to lament that of Lieutenant Brooke,

40th Regiment, who fell in the noble discharge of his duty, and 29 non-commissioned officers and men of the different corps.

"Among the wounded, Captain Seymour, R.N., severely, and 33 non-commissioned officers and men of the different corps.

"I enclose a return of casualties.

"The loss of the rebels, from personal observations, must have been very great.

"I cannot speak too highly of the gallant bearing of the officers and men of all arms engaged, and I should particularly beg to mention the valuable services rendered by the several officers in command, viz.: Lieutenant McNaughten, R.A.; Lieutenant Battiscombe, R.N.; Lieutenant Morris, R.M.A.; Captains Bowdler and Richards, 40th Regiment.

"I would also desire to express my sense of the very valuable services of Captain Seymour, R.N., who was so good as to accompany me, and afforded me every assistance until he was severely wounded.

"I feel much indebted to Assistant-Surgeon B. Stiles, 40th Regiment; Assistant-Surgeon Edwards, R.N.; and Mr. J. N. Murray, Surgeon (attached to the 40th Regiment), for the very efficient services they afforded to the wounded in the field.

"The best thanks are due to Lieutenant Mould, R.E., who attended me, and to my Staff-Officer Ensign and Acting-Adjutant Whelan, Detachment 40th Regiment,—I have, &c.,

"THOMAS NELSON,
"Major 40th Regt.,
"Camp, Waitara.

"P.S. 5 p.m. I have just visited the wounded in the whares and hospital tent. There are five dangerous cases; the remainder are doing as well as could be hoped for.

"T. N.

[Force engaged.]

"Royal Artillery, two 24-pounder howitzers, 1 officer, 1 sergeant, 19 men; Royal Engineers, 1 sergeant, 6 men; Naval Brigade, 4 officers, 50 blue jackets; Royal Marines, 1 officer, 10 rank and file; 40th Regiment, 10 officers, 245 men."

On July the 7th, the s.s. Airedale brought from Auckland 104 men of the Royal Engineers and 64th Regiment, and two breaching 56-pounder guns.

On the 8th, H.M.S.S. Cordelia came in from the Manukau, bringing Commodore Loring and 200 more blue jackets and marines from the Iris and Elk, also the Victorian Government s.s. Victoria. The Victoria's men only were landed and took up their quarters at Fort Niger.

On the 23rd, H.M.S. Fawn arrived with 112 officers and men of the 12th Regiment, and on the 24th the City of Hobart arrived with the head-quarters of the 40th Regiment, consisting of 11 officers and 233 men, under the command of Colonel Leslie.

DEATH OF HUGH CORBYN HARRIS.

On June the 29th, Hugh Corbyn Harris, a Taranaki Volunteer, on service at the Waitara Camp, went out to the swamp in front of the camp unarmed, accompanied by two soldiers, who were also unarmed, for the purpose of getting firewood. Arriving at the swamp, some natives who had been lying in ambush rushed upon him, and placing a musket to his head shot him through the temple. The soldiers who were with him made their escape, and alarmed the camp. A party of soldiers immediately turned out, and the natives took to flight, leaving the bullocks and cart of the deceased. This young man was of exemplary character, the hope of his parents, and highly esteemed by a large circle of friends. The body was taken by boat to New Plymouth for interment.

At this date a party, consisting of 200 men of the 12th and 40th Regiments, with Artillery and Engineers, under the command of Major Hutchins of the 12th Regiment, started from New Plymouth for the purpose of taking up a position on Waireka Hill, in order to check the advance of the southern natives.

On August the 3rd, H.M. Colonial steam sloop Victoria, Captain Norman, arrived from Melbourne, bringing General Pratt, C.B.; Lieutenant-Colonel Carey, Deputy-Adjutant General; Lieutenant Foster, R.A., A.D.C.; Deputy-Inspector General of Medical Department, J. Mouat, C.B.; Captain Pasley, R.E., and 50 men of the 40th Regiment.

DEATH OF JOHN HURFORD.

On August the 3rd, news was brought into town that on the previous day John Hurford, an old settler and a farmer at Omata, had left the Omata stockade to visit his farm, and had not returned. It afterwards was discovered that he had called at the newly formed camp at Waireka, and left there accompanied by three Artillerymen. It appeared also that after many hours absence two of the Artillerymen had returned by different routes to the camp, and reported that they had encountered a party of natives while searching for pigs on Hurford's farm, who had fired at them, and being unarmed they separated, and took to flight, and had great difficulty in finding their way back to camp. After an interview between Captain Burton in command of the Militia at the Omata stockade, and Major Hutchins in command of the camp at Waireka, it was arranged to send a guard of ten men from the camp with a party of Militia in search of the missing men. In the course of the afternoon this detachment returned, bringing with them the body of Gaffney, the Artilleryman, which they had found in a gully near to Hurford's house, mutilated to a frightful extent about the head and body with a tomahawk, but without any gunshot wounds. They were not able to find the body of Hurford, but had no doubt about his fate.

On Sunday, the 5th, another party went out, and after a long search found Hurford's body among some bushes. The unfortunate man appeared to have been shot in attempting to escape, and had fallen down a steep bank into the bushes. The ball had struck him in the region of the heart, and his death must have been instantaneous. There were no other marks of violence about his person. He left a wife and large family, who were at that time refugees in Nelson.

The town of New Plymouth was now entrenched in triangular form, the sea coast being the base, and Marsland Hill Barracks the apex, one side of the triangle being Liardet Street, and the other Queen Street. There were gates on the lines at the junction of Devon and Liardet Street, and at the junction of Devon and Queen Street. A strong redoubt around the Port flagstaff was held by the blue jackets, and Fort Niger was also held by the sailors, besides which there were blockhouses at the Henui, on the racecourse, on the hill on the Carrington Road, and on the hill in Young Street, west of Dawson Street.

On Saturday, the 4th, the town presented a scene of great confusion, arising out of an alarm that the natives were in force on the Mangorei Road, near to the old Colonial Hospital, and were marching on the town. The alarm was sounded, and the guns from Marsland Hill thundered out the preconcerted notice to all persons outside to hasten into the town. Crowds of women and children were to be seen hurrying up Marsland Hill—the face of which seemed to be covered with them, while the men were falling in under arms. The confusion was happily speedily put an end to by further intelligence arriving to the effect that the natives had contented themselves with wrecking several houses, and had then retired across the Waiwakaiho.

The result of this alarm was the following—

PROCLAMATION.

"As it is indispensibly necessary that families should leave town, they must prepare to embark for such place as shall be decided upon.
"By Order,
"R. CAREY,
"Lieut.-Colonel,
"Deputy-Adjutant General.
"August 6th, 1860."

On the 16th, the brig George Henderson, which was being fitted up for taking the families of the settlers to Nelson, was driven ashore northward of the Henui in a gale. A large party of blue jackets, in command of Commodore Loring, followed her course on the beach with a gun and a rocket, and when she grounded lent all possible aid. In town the assembly was sounded, and a large party of Militia and Volunteers were marched to the wreck to preserve it from being plundered by the natives.

On the 20th, Ephraim Coad, an old settler, while proceeding from the wreck towards town, was shot dead on the beach near the mouth of the Henui by an ambuscade. At this time there was continuous skirmishing in the vicinity of the town, and the rebels burned the Henui village, leaving the church and chapel and the minister's house.

About this time, Henry Crann, while searching for his bullocks on the Avenue Road, was shot by a professedly friendly native of Puketotara.

The General Assembly being at this time in session, the native policy of the Government was endorsed in the House of Representatives, Members voting by a large majority in favor of the following resolution, which was moved by Mr. Stafford, the Colonial Secretary:—
"That in the opinion of this House the interference of Wiremu Kingi at Waitara, and his resort to force to prevent the survey of the land, that rendered the measures adopted by His Excellency the Governor indispensible for the maintenance of Her Majesty's sovereignty, and the welfare of both races of Her Majesty's subjects, peremptorily requires a vigorous prosecution of the war to a successful termination."

Early in September the troops were engaged in burning the old pas in the neighborhood of Bell Block, which had been erected during the Puketapu feud, also the pas on the edge of the plateau between Puketakauere and Huirangi, which had been deserted by the enemy. A blockhouse was also erected at Puketakauere. On the other side of the town marches were made to Burton's Hill on the Barrett Road, and towards Waireka, for the purpose of checking the advance of the Taranakis and the Ngatiruanuis.

On the 18th, a large force marched to Kaihihi, which destroyed several pas. The proclamation of the General demanding the removal of all the women and children was not only disobeyed, but in some instances resisted, the women positively refusing to leave their husbands and sons, choosing rather to suffer the miseries of the siege. A proclamation was then made offering a discharge from Military service to all married settlers who were willing to remove with their families to Nelson. To alleviate to some extent the misery of the besieged, a comic paper, under the title of the Taranaki Punch, was commenced. It was chiefly devoted to skits on the Military commanders.

THE ATTACK ON MAHOETAHI.

Mahoetahi is a hill a little to the westward of the Waiongona river, through which the Devon Road now passes. It is of volcanic formation, and is one of a series of small volcanic mounds in the neighborhood which are called collectively Ngapuketurua, and as we have already stated are the sites of the first settlements of the Ngatiawa tribe in the district. Kingi having appealed to Waikato for help, received a powerful reinforcement from that tribe.

Early in November, Mr. Parris received the following letter :—

"To Mr. Parris:

"Friend,—I have heard your word—come to fight me, that is very good; come inland, and let us meet each other. Fish fight at sea—come inland and stand on our feet; make haste, do not prolong it. That is all I have to say to you—make haste.

"From WETINI TAIPORUTU,
"From PORUKORU,
"From all the Chiefs of Ngatihaua and Waikato."

On the 5th of November, news reached town that the Waikatos had crossed the Waitara river in force, and that they would probably be in the neighborhood of Mahoetahi on the following morning. It was at once arranged by General Pratt that a force from New Plymouth, and another from the camp at Waitara under Major Nelson, should march so as to join early in the morning at that place. This arrangement was carried into effect, and on the forces arriving at the spot it was found that the main body of the Waikatos occupied an intrenchment on the crest of the Mahoetahi hill, in which were some entrenched whares.

The detachment of the 65th Regiment, which had formed the advanced guard from town, now formed a line of skirmishers under Lieutenants Bailie and Toker, at the base of the hill, and extended towards their right. This body was commanded by Captain Turner. The Rifle Volunteers continued this extension towards the left, under the direction of Major Herbert; and the 40th Regiment, commanded by Lieutenant-Colonel Leslie, were massed in columns, forming the reserve, while the detachment of the 12th Regiment, under Major Hutchins, which had formed the rear guard during the march, now remained in charge of the baggage and spare ammunition. The detachment of Artillery, under Captain Strover and Lieutenant McNaughten, rendered, as usual, important service.

The whole force was commanded by Major-General Pratt, C.B., who throughout the engagement occupied a foremost place, and was much exposed to the hot and rapid fire of his determined enemy.

The Waikatos commenced the action by firing the first shots from an old entrenched position in the crest of the Mahoetahi hill. This was quickly returned by the skirmishers, and after a short fire the 65th and Volunteers rushed up the hill, and stormed that position. In performing this service they were exposed to heavy flanking fires, but it was not until they had entered the entrenchments that they experienced any loss. Within that confined space a heavy fire from entrenched whares laid low the gallant son of the Rev. H. H. Brown, a volunteer, not 16 years of age, and private F. Rooney, Light Company, 65th Regiment, while further towards the left Mr. Henry Edgecombe, aged 20, also of the Volunteers, received his mortal wound. Here Captain Turner was struck in the face by a musket ball, and Colonel Sillery slightly wounded. A rush was now made on the whares, and the bayonet speedily silenced all further annoyance. This service was accomplished by some 65th men and Rifle Volunteers. Some shells thrown into the raupo swamp caused the Waikatos to quit their lairs, and now commenced the work of extermination, for a detachment of the 40th under Major Nelson, and a company of the 65th, under Lieutenant Talbot, from Waitara (the latter advancing in skirmishing order), came up from the north side of the hill, and the Light Company of the 65th, led on by Lieutenant Urquhart (then forming a flank guard), closing on their centre, together with a good show of Rifle Volunteers. The rebels, who were almost surrounded, then dashed into the swamp, and a hand-to-hand encounter followed, the bayonet and the butt end of the rifle, when the bullet had missed, speedily convincing the brave enemy that the avenger was at hand. They commenced their retreat, still fighting with desperate valour, and in one of these encounters private McGivern met his fate, though not before the enemy had felt the effects of his prowess. They gradually got in the Huirangi road, followed by a part of the 65th, under Lieutenants Urquhart and Talbot, their retreating steps marked by pools of blood, and a storm of shot and shells bursting over and among them. In their terror they threw away their arms and pouches, and any articles of clothing that impeded their flight, and the pursuers followed them to near the Waiongona river, when fatigue alone compelled them to desist, for the day had been intensely hot, without a breath of air.

The *mêlée* in the swamp had been a succession of desperate hand to hand encounters, and many instances of courage were exhibited on both sides. Private Gilligan, 65th, shot one Waikato, and brained another with the butt end of his rifle. Many other daring acts were witnessed, but must remain unrecorded as the individuals could not be identified. But the bayonet played a conspicuous part in the exciting scene.

When all but the dead and mortally wounded Waikatos had disappeared, a reconnoitring party, under Major-General Pratt, composed of 12th, supported by 65th, proceeded to Ngataiparirua, and came in sight of a pa having a red flag flying, but it was speedily hauled down, and a white flag half-mast high succeeded it. The party then proceeded round by Puketakaure, and thence returned to Mahoetahi. In the course of the afternoon, after having buried in one grave some 28 or 29 Waikatos, the main body returned to the town (having left a strong force to retain possession of the field of battle), laden with Maori spoils, in the shape of double-barrelled guns, ornaments, shawls, &c., &c., many battered and bloody, proving that they had not been parted with willingly.

On the force passing the town barrier, loud and continued cheers proved to them that their conduct was duly appreciated by their countrymen. The list of casualties proves who bore the brunt of the day :—65th Regiment, 2 killed, 10 wounded, 1 officer, wounded ; Volunteers, 2 killed, 4 wounded ; 40th Regiment, 1 wounded.

The following is an extract from Mr. Parris' report of this affair to the Native Secretary, dated the 6th of November, 1860 :—

"We left town this morning at 4 o'clock, six hundred strong, under the command of the Major-General, for the purpose of taking possession of Mahoetahi, and on our arrival found it occupied by the rebels. On approaching the pa the enemy opened fire upon us, which was warmly returned, and the seaward end of the pa soon taken. They at last went out of the pa into a swamp, situated on the inland side of the pa, and there remained until Colonel Mould arrived with his party from Waitara, when they were placed between two fires, the cross-firing wounding some of our own men. After they had lost about twelve of their number they ran away, under a heavy fire, along the road leading to Huirangi, and before they got to the Waiongona ford, ten or twelve more of them fell, and among them Wetini Taiporutu. We followed them to Huirangi, and found four on the road nearly dead, and there is no doubt but a great many have got away badly wounded.

"I recommended that the three chiefs, mentioned at the head of the following list, should be brought into town and buried, which the General sanctioned. We have brought in four prisoners badly wounded, one wounded in the leg, and one not wounded, from whom I obtained a list of the names enclosed. I believe there are as many more killed and wounded whom we have not yet found or heard of.

"The following is a list of Waikatos killed :—
"Wetini Taiporutu, Chief of Waikato; Wharangi, Chief of Ngatiapakura; Hakopa, Chief of Ngatikoura; Tamu, of Ngatiruru; Hikaraia, of Ngatihaua; Hakapo, of Ngatikoroki; Heneriko, of Te Urkopi; Wirihana; Wanganui, of Ngatikoriki; Pari, of Ngatihaua; Tamihana, of Ngatikoroki; Harawira, of Ngatihaua; Hirini, of Ngatikahukura; Tamihana, of Ngatiruru; Wharawhara, of Ngatihaua; Hemi Karena, of Ngatiruru; Harawira, of Ngatihaua; Hakopa.

"Besides these there were twelve whose names I have not obtained.
"ROBT. PARRIS,
"Assistant Native Secretary."

On the night after the battle, the soldiers who held Mahoetahi were astonished to hear the Maoris dancing a war dance in token of defiance, and of their determination to be avenged for their loss on the preceding day. Some shots were fired from the hill in the direction of the spot from whence the noise proceeded, but nothing further transpired.

When the news of the affair at Mahoetahi reached Auckland, fears were entertained that reprisals would be made in the north by the Waikatos, and accordingly the Niger and Victoria were sent to fetch 400 troops from New Plymouth for the protection of that city.

In the neighborhood of the Waitara the enemy seemed exasperated at the loss he had sustained. Numbers of Waikatos poured into Kingi's pas, and small marauding parties issued forth to waylay and murder any European they might meet.

THE DEATH OF JOHN HAWKEN.

On the day after the rout of the Waikatos, Mr. John Hawken, who had formerly been in business as a miller at the Blagdon Mill, and afterwards as a butcher at New Plymouth, but during the war had been engaged as contract butcher to the camp at Waitara, left the camp and proceeded towards Mahoetahi on horseback, probably for the purpose of seeking for cattle. As he did not return search was made for him, and his horse was found shot between Mahoetahi and Huirangi, and also a letter which had evidently been taken from his person.

On the 16th, his body was found, lightly covered with earth, about three-quarters of a mile from Mahoetahi on the road to Huirangi. The friendly natives say that a volley was fired at him which wounded him, and brought down his horse, and that before he could extricate himself he was tomahawked by Tamihana, of Kaipakopako.

On the 9th, eleven more bodies of natives were found about Mahoetahi, making the ascertained loss of the enemy to be 45 killed. It was said by the friendly natives that the loss was 71, several having died at Huirangi, and others in the neighborhood in attempting to reach it.

A blockhouse was erected on one of the Ngapuketurua hills, 800 yards in advance of Mahoetahi, which at that time was covered with a dense growth of karaka trees, *Corynocarpus lævigata*, which have long since been felled for military purposes. Not far from this hill is another of a similar character, which was the *tapu* burial place of the chiefs of the hapu, and here during the war several relics were found. The most interesting of these was a trachytic boulder of oval shape, measuring about ten inches by six inches, with the top cut off so as to form a lid, and the centre hollowed out and containing a piece of red ironstone about the size of a man's thumb. This relic is said to be the memorial of the great ancestor of the tribe, who was buried on this hill, and it was the custom when any of his relatives died to uncover the stone, light a fire, and cook food near to it.

DEATH OF JOSEPH SARTEN.

On Tuesday, December the 4th, at 4 p.m., a lad named Joseph Sarten, who was at the Henui on horseback, seeking a bullock, was shot and tomahawked. A boy, named William Northcote, who was riding alongside him, witnessed the whole affair. A volley was fired and Sarten fell, and directly afterwards several natives ran from behind a furze hedge and tomahawked him. Northcote escaped and rode into town with the intelligence, and a party of Militia and Rifles, and the inlying picket of the 12th, with the Mounted Volunteers, proceeded to recover the body. It was found where he fell, in the lane running from the Devon Road past the Henui Church, towards the beach, about midway between the Henui and Waiwakahio rivers. He had received three bullets in the back and sides, and was brutally hacked about the head and legs by tomahawks. The horse was led into town with a bullet through its neck. The mounted men brought the body as far as the Henui, where they met the troops; it was then put into an ambulance cart, and taken to the hospital. The shots in his body and in the horse showed that at least four persons were concerned in the murder, and from the character of the wounds they had evidently been posted within a few yards of where their victim passed. The poor boy was sixteen years of age, and was the second of the family who met a violent end from the rebels, John Sarten, his brother, being the first man who received a death wound in the war. A party of Waikatos were at this time located at Purakau, near Smart's farm, about half-a-mile from the Waiwakaiho river. A dense fog which hung over the district this day was taken advantage of by the enemy for the perpetration of this murder.

The Waikatos in large numbers now began to pour into the pas at Matarikoriko and Huirangi, on the edge of the plateau overlooking the Waitara valley, and leading up to the ancient fastness of the tribe at Pukerangiora.

In order to reduce these, General Pratt marched for the Waitara, where he encamped on December the 27th. The next day, with a force consisting of 1,000 men, with all the appurtenances required for a protracted siege, he advanced towards Kairau, where the enemy in great strength had formed an extensive series of field works, consisting of rifle pits connected with viaducts that led to gullies bordering the dense bush surrounding the Matarikoriko pa.

The following graphic account is from a letter written at the camp, dated December the 31st, 1860 :—

TAKING OF MATARIKORIKO.

"The day we left town (28th), we arrived at Mahoetahi about 7 a.m., and halted for an hour for breakfast, after which we moved on by the road to the left of the blockhouse, and crossed the Waiongona at the prophet's pa, above the junction of the Mangoraka with the Waiongona. Fortunately the river was not too deep, but it would have been too deep the day before, and we arrived at Waitara at 10 o'clock a.m., and encamped near the pa. We got orders to move at 4 a.m. next morning, and got on the road at that hour, passed the site of the old L pa, and arrived at Ngataipariraa at 5.30 a.m., moved on the advanced ground to Kairau, and commenced firing and throwing shells in the gully towards the pa at Matarikoriko. A working party commenced making a redoubt, and after a short time (8.30 a.m.), the natives crept up through the fern and gave us a volley. A sharp fight until 9.30, and then all quiet until 12.30 p.m. A heavy fire was then commenced and continued all day and night. One man of the 65th killed, and 1 sergeant and 3 men wounded; two 40th killed, and 14 wounded; one naval brigade wounded severely. The 65th fell in at 7 a.m., and marched back to camp (Waitara), with the Naval Brigade. Left the 12th and 40th in camp at Kairau, who were engaged with the enemy till 5.30 next morning. All quiet on Sunday.

"The fire all Saturday was most terrific, and well sustained on our side, which kept the rebels well in check. They fired out of rifle pits without showing themselves or taking aim, and the bullets went very high. Our people fired 70,000 rounds of ammunition, and about 120 shell and case shot.

"The Rev. Mr. Wilson went down to them yesterday morning, and there was a truce all day. Mr. Wilson's object was to get them to agree to spare the dead and wounded, and after a good deal of parleying, an agreement has been made to that effect; one old savage fellow (a chief) dissenting, but they will not mind him.

"In going over some of the rifle pits a splendid tomahawk, all bloody, and a pouch, a large knife and pipe were found, and various other articles. Two Maori letters were also found, one from Takerei Terangi to Wiremu Hoeta, Rewi, and others, in which he urges them to spare the women and children. This morning intelligence was received that the enemy had evacuated their pa and position, and two companies of the 65th, and a few of the blue jackets rushed into it, and hoisted the Union Jack—one the Colonel of the 65th had for the purpose. It was well and quickly done. We found the graves of five men, and one buried far down in the gully. A young fellow came over with Mr. Wilson to-day to show his father's and uncle's grave. It has been fenced in. The enemy is determined to fight. The following names were found carved on calabashes—'Namahuta,' and 'Mihi,' and in a rifle pit 'Kopuareti.' 140 men of the 65th have gone to garrison Matarikoriko.

"The Tasmanian Maid left for Waitara with stores, &c., and returned at midnight. The Cordelia also came up, bringing Colonel Carey, D.A.G., Dr. Mouat, and some wounded men, and returned again in the afternoon. Weather continues fine.

"The following is a list of killed and wounded on Saturday and Sunday:—

"December the 29th, 1860.—Killed: 40th Regiment—Private James Chinnery, Private Michael Lehan; 65th Regiment—Private John Cain. Wounded: Royal Artillery—Gunner William Smoker, twice in left leg severely, Gunner Jeremiah Wright, left arm, severely; Royal Engineers—Sapper Johnston, left arm, severely; Naval Brigade—Alfred Broome, A.B., dangerously; 12th Regiment—Private Robert Dye, slightly; 40th Regiment—Sergeant Instructor of Musketry—Patrick Collins, slightly, Private Roger Lyons, dangerously, Private Richard Fitzgerald, severely, Private James Southwell, dangerously, Private John Sullivan, severely, Private Benjamin Greenwood, severely, Private William Caplice, dangerously, Private John McBren, severely, Private Thomas Davy, slightly, Private J. A. Fox, slightly.

"December the 20th, 1860.—Wounded: 40th Regiment—Sergeant F. Thale, severely. 65th Regiment—Sergeant William Speakman, slightly, Private James Haggan, slightly, Private Martin Kinsella, severely.

"Accident.—Private John Weir, 65th Regiment, explosion of rifle, three fingers amputated."

On June the 14th, 1861, General Pratt again advanced towards Huirangi, throwing up No. 2 redoubt, about 570 yards from Kairau, and afterwards No. 3, a three-angled redoubt *en echelon*, and within three-quarters of a mile of the Huirangi rifle pits, from whence he ran the longest sap on record towards the enemy's position at the foot of Pukerangiora.

EXPEDITION TO THE SOUTH.

In the hope of diverting the General's attention from the north, the southern natives again occupied the Waireka and Burton's Hills, forming an extensive series of fortifications and field works so as to command every road, and lock up the British within the town and the stockades. In a very short time they had completed, in a direct line across the country, ten palisaded pas.

On Tuesday, January the 22nd, at about 3 a.m., 40 of the 12th, under Captain Williams and Lieutenant Dudgeon, 10 of the 40th, under Ensign Murphy, and 130 of the 65th, under Lieutenant and Adjutant A. H. Lewis and Lieutenant Chevalier, the whole under the command of Lieutenant-Colonel Young, 65th Regiment, with one 24-pounder howitzer, left town to take part in a combined attack on Waireka hill, a party of 120 blue jackets from H.M.S. Niger, under Captain Cracroft, R.N., having left in boats during the night to land on the coast in rear of the rebels' position. At daylight, firing having been heard in the direction of Waireka, the bugles of the Militia were sounded, and 108 Militia and Rifle Volunteers, under the command of Major Herbert, mustered, and followed by the road taken by the military. Abreast of Mr. Langman's farm, where the furze fences offered great cover to an enemy, the advanced guard observed three or four natives running towards the road to fire at Major Herbert, who was some 200 yards in advance with a few mounted volunteers, with whom he was riding alongside. The rising sun prevented the natives from seeing the approach of the men, who after giving a shout or two, pushed through the fence at every gap, and in skirmishing order, firing as opportunity offered, drove the natives from their cover off the farm, across the road into Mr. Stephenson Smith's and Mr. P. Elliot's farm and finally into the bush, where they were left to themselves. This was evidently a party out for live stock, and but for the check received would have fired into the backs of the horsemen. No further incident occurred on the road.

On reaching the Omata Stockade, where the troops were halted, it was ascertained that they had been fired upon by natives from John Wright's house (near the Whaler's Gate), and Hospital Sergeant Burnett mortally wounded. It is believed the natives suffered some loss from the fire of the troops. Sergeant Burnett died at the stockade. Large parties of natives could be seen crowning the

Waireka hill, and whilst a signal of the whereabouts of Captain Cracroft was anxiously looked for in that direction, a telegram was received from town that the gallant Captain had returned to his ship, owing to a difficulty in finding the proper landing-place. The land force then started homewards, and struck off the Omata Road through W. George's farm to the beach.

On their arrival in town, it was stated that in Mr. George's house was concealed a party of 50 or 60 natives, who probably not deeming it altogether safe to attack so large a force, remained out of sight until the road was clear, and they were seen from a hill top to leave the premises and go in the direction of Ratapihipihi. This party was probably on the look out for the Omata escort, which needed sufficient strength to repel attack. Whilst the force bivouacked at the Omata Stockade, Major Lloyd's house at Waireka was burnt by the rebels, and shortly afterwards Mr. W. C. King's large barn of hay, near the site of his house, burnt last September.

THE ATTACK ON THE HUIRANGI REDOUBT.

The 23rd of January, 1861, was a fortunate day for the settlement, for at its earliest dawn a blow was struck which virtually turned the tide of battle in the favor of the British, and led to the relinquishment of the struggle of Wi Kingi and his allies of the north, for the possession of the Waitara district. Before daylight on the morning of this day, about 140 natives of the Waikato and Ngatiawa tribes, headed by Rewi, Epiha, Hapurona, and others, contrived to creep into the ditch of No. 3 redoubt, which had not been completed on the previous evening. It is said that the officer in command had given orders that the cry of "All's Well" should not be made, and that the greatest silence should be observed during the night. This, with the fact of the men having worked very hard at the entrenchments during the previous day, possibly led the enemy to think that the garrison was tired and asleep, and that the opportunity for attack was favorable. While in the ditch, in the darkness, the rebels were engaged in cutting steps in the embankment with their tomahawks. In the grey of dawn a sentry perceived one Maori—the last of his party—creeping to the brow of the ditch ; he fired on him, and was immediately shot dead himself. The garrison, consisting of the greater part of the 40th Regiment, under Colonel Leslie, met the attack with great promptitude, and a scene ensued which baffles description. Sapper Chubb, striking a match in order to see to lace his boot, revealed himself to a Maori who was posted in the unfinished part of the redoubt, and was shot dead.

Our troops, as fast as they could load their rifles, fired down over the parapet, and the artillerymen, with great coolness, cut short the fuses of the shells, and lighting them pitched them over into the trench with frightful execution. Lieutenant Jackson, 40th Regiment, while in the act of firing at a native over the parapet with his revolver, was shot through the head, and fell mortally wounded. Some of the natives succeeded in getting so far up the parapet that they were bayoneted by the garrison. A soldier in the act of bayoneting a Maori overbalanced himself and fell in the trench among the rebels, but escaped alive; and a Maori on the embankment, transfixed by a bayonet, drew himself up and tomahawked the soldier who had bayoneted him. This sanguinary conflict was prolonged till daylight, when the support came up from Kairau. A party of the 65th, under Colonel Wyatt, attacked the rebels on their right flank, while the 12th attacked them on the left of the redoubt; here they met the rebel reserve who rose out of the fern, it is stated, like a flock of birds. These were charged by the 12th at the point of the bayonet, and those of the natives who could, turned and fled, leaving many behind them. It was all over before 6 a.m., and in the trench of the redoubt and around lay 49 bodies of rebels, 5 only of whom were alive, 41 were buried in a grave between Nos. 2 and 3 redoubts, others were buried by the friendly natives. Thirteen chief men were said to be amongst the slain, but many of the bodies were beyond identification. The wounded natives were all dangerously so. Our casualties were 5 killed and 11 wounded, viz.:—

Killed—Royal Engineers: Sapper George Chubb; 12th Regiment: Private Edward Archer; 40th Regiment: Lieutenant Jackson, Private W. Gilbert, Private Edward Gorray.

Wounded—Royal Artillery: Daniel Bushell, slightly; 12th Regiment: Captain T. E. Miller, slightly, Private Patrick Cahill, severely, tomahawk; Private Edmond Power, slightly; 40th Regiment: Private Henry Wakefield, severely, Private John Officer, dangerously, Private John Mullins, slightly; 65th Regiment: Lance Corporal James Howard, dangerously, Private Edward Smith, dangerously, Private Joseph Robinson, dangerously, Private Samuel Hamilton, severely.

On the same day as this memorable and decisive engagement occurred, the first instalment of the gallant 57th Regiment arrived from India, viâ Auckland. This Regiment had seen active service in the Crimea, and under its brave commander, Colonel Warre, was destined to render very important service to Taranaki in the guerilla warfare which was maintained by the southern natives for years after the capitulation of Wi Kingi's allies at Waitara. The detachment of this Regiment arrived in the ship Star Queen, Captain Barber, from Bombay, and consisted of Major Butler, Captain Brown, Lieutenants Baynton, Husted, Thompson, Cox and Waller; Ensigns Clarke, Murray, and Clayton; Assistant-Surgeon Davis, 16 sergeants and 314 rank and file.

On the 2nd of February, Lance-Corporal Howard of the 65th Regiment died of the wound which he received at the attack on No. 3 redoubt. Before he died he sent for Lieutenant Urquhart, and revealed to him his history. It was reported at the time that he was a son of Sir William Campbell, of Tullicheven Castle, Dunbartonshire, Scotland, but this was afterwards contradicted.

DEATH OF CAPTAIN W. C. KING.

On February the 8th, a profound sensation of grief and indignation was caused in New Plymouth by the murder of Captain William Cutfield King, of the Volunteer Rifles. Captain King had been in the habit of occasionally visiting his estate, known as Woodleigh, situated but a short distance from town, and in sight of the garrison on Marsland Hill, for the purpose of looking after his cattle. On the day in question, shortly after he had reached the place on horseback, he was fired at by a party of Ngatiruanui rebels in ambush, and wounded. Finding that his horse was wounded he dismounted, and was chased by two natives named Hori Kiwi and Hohepa. These two again fired and Captain King fell. His murderers then ran up to him, when he said, "I am badly wounded—leave me." This was answered by Hori Kiwi discharging both barrels of his gun at his head. The whole of the transaction was witnessed from the barracks on Marsland Hill. The Volunteers and Militia hastened to the scene, followed by the military, but they were too late to render aid to their young captain, or to intercept his murderers, who were seen decamping in the direction of Ratapihipihi. Captain King's body was found pierced by six bullets, three through his head, two in his body, and one in his thigh. From the appearance of the wounds in his head it seemed that he was fired at while lying on the ground. The horse was conveyed into town shot in three places, but the saddle and bridle were taken away by the murderers.

Captain King was the only son of Captain Henry King, R.N. He was born in Devonshire, England, and when but twelve years of age came out with his parents and the pioneer settlers in the Amelia Thompson. He had but recently been elected to represent the Grey and Bell districts in the General Assembly, and was a brave and promising man. He was 32 years of age when he fell, and left a young widow and two infant daughters. The only charge against him was one that reflects the highest credit on his memory—he refused to compel some of the females of the settlement to leave their husbands and embark for Nelson.

The General continued to push on his sap towards the position of the rebels at Te Arei. This sap was a work of immense labor, and was a very questionable piece of military strategy, for with the force at his disposal he could have stormed Pukerangiora, and have taken it with less loss than he sustained in extending the sap.

In fourteen days 1,200 yards of this sap, a demi-parallel of 21 yards, and three large redoubts were constructed under a heavy fire. During the extension the enemy frequently removed the sap roller in the night in spite of the vigilance of the sentinels. This piece of impudence was at length stopped by affixing to the roller a live shell fitted with a friction fuze. For the construction of the sap roller and gabions, the supple-jacks of the forest (*Ripogonum parviflorum*) were extensively used, and the friendly natives were employed in the service of procuring them. As an instance of the curious habits of these people, it was stated at the time that in this business the enemy co-operated with the friendly natives, and received a part of the price paid by the British for these canes.

On Sunday the 10th, the General advanced from No. 6 redoubt with the intention of constructing a redoubt about a mile in advance. The force consisted of a party of Royal Engineers under Colonel Mould, a detachment of Royal Artillery under Captain Strover and Lieutenant McNaughten, a detatchment of the Naval Brigade under Commodore Seymour, two divisions of the 12th Regiment under Major Hutchins, 100 men of the 14th Regiment, four divisions of the 40th Regiment under Colonel Leslie, and four divisions of the 65th Regiment under Colonel Wyatt. Four field pieces and two cohorn mortars, and a 24-pounder rocket tube accompanied the force. Lines of skirmishers were thrown out by each corps,—those of the 40th Regiment having the honor to cover the advance—and the whole force was quickly on the route towards Pukerangiora by the avenue through the belt of the forest, which at that period stretched across Huirangi. A few minutes' march brought the men to the open ground on the east side of the belt, and no opposition was offered until they reached a flat thickly covered with fern, situated about 500 yards from the hill on which stood Hapurona's pa. Here they received a sudden, but not unexpected volley of musketry from the natives, who were wholly concealed in rifle pits within short range. The bullets, however, whizzed harmlessly over the men, and the skirmishers returned the fire. The guns and rocket tube were at once brought into position, and the pa, the hills, and gullies around were scoured with shells and rockets. The 8-inch gun also opened fire from the Huirangi redoubt, and threw several shells into the very centre of the pa. This gun was manned by a detachment of the Naval Brigade, whose practice was always excellent. The Maoris, however, held formidable positions. Having long expected the attack they had spared neither labor nor ingenuity in their preparations for defence. Every available spot that a musket could be effectually fired from was entrenched and manned, and their defences formed a semicircle, extending from some ravines of the Waitara valley on the left of the British, to a dense bush on their right. They had also dug trenches around their pa, and the whole ridge of hills in front of the advancing force had tiers of pits, one over the other, from which the enemy fired as from so many little batteries. It was most annoying to the British to be able to see nothing of the rebels but their smoke and fire, and yet to be so near to them as to hear their taunts.

When the firing commenced the site for a new redoubt was selected by Colonel and Captain Mould. The Royal Engineers superintended its erection, and the men of each regiment in the force worked at it under fire with great zeal. The enemy finding he could not interrupt the work, nor silence the guns, endeavored by stratagem to turn the right flank of the British. To effect this he showered a heavy fire from the hills, and while the attention of the British was directed to this, he would open a sudden fire on their right rear from the forest. Every pass was, however, so well guarded by the skirmishers of the various regiments, that the Maoris were always frustrated in their attempts, and cut off every time they attempted to advance upon the British lines.

Several hours of the morning passed before any casualty occurred, but at length Captain Strange, of the 65th Regiment, was struck by a bullet in his thigh, which severed the femoral artery, and although he received prompt medical assistance he died from loss of blood, after several hours agony. In the storm of bullets which fell around the force several narrow escapes occurred. A man of the 65th Regiment had his ear pierced by a ball, and one of the 40th Regiment was touched on the crown of his head by a ball which passed through his cap; six of the working bullocks which dragged the guns were wounded.

About 6 p.m., the fort being nearly completed, a force of 400 men, composed of the 12th, 40th, and 65th Regiments, was left to garrison it, under the command of Colonel Wyatt, and the remainder of the force marched back to their respective camps—not to rest, but to mount guards and pickets until the morning's sun should call them again to labor or to fight.

The garrison of the new redoubt had no tents, and it required all their vigilance to keep the rebels out of it, firing being kept up till the morning.

Early on Monday a division of the 57th Regiment, and two divisions of the 65th Regiment, advanced to the new redoubt, and formed working parties and coverers. The firing was kept up all day, and a corporal of the 40th Regiment was hit within the breastworks. The poor fellow placed his hand on the part of his body where the ball entered, and walking outside the fort sat down and died before his comrades knew that he was hit.

The casualties in this affair were:—Killed: Captain Strange, 65th Regiment, and a corporal of the 40th Regiment. Wounded: 12th Regiment, 2; 40th Regiment, 2; 65th Regiment, 3; Artillery, 2; Militia, 1.

DEATH OF E. MESSENGER.

On Sunday morning, March the 3rd, E. W. Hollis (Sergeant), W. S. Ginger, J. G. Ginger, H. J. Hall, W. Harrison, senior, C. W. Hursthouse, J. E. W. Hussey, C. Messenger, E. Messenger, H. Newland, C. A. Pope, W. Smart, W. B. Walker, privates of the Rifle Volunteers, and H. W. Brewer, a civilian, started from town to Walker's farm, for the purpose of gathering peaches, Sunday being a day when the natives generally retired to their pas. Not finding any peaches at Walker's farm they determined to go to Mr. Hursthouse's orchard for some, and while on the road they passed through a hedge to cross Captain King's orchard at Brookland's in order to avoid a piece of bush directly behind it, and seeing some peaches there commenced to gather them. They had been so employed for a few minutes, when they were startled by hearing a shot fired at the farther end of the orchard, where two of their number were. Thinking it was fired by one of the party, they called out to know the cause, but before an explanation could be given a volley was fired at them by about 30 natives, within ten yards from a ditch immediately behind the trees, but which was concealed by a hedge, severely wounding W. Smart in the back. The Volunteers, including Smart, fired their rifles and ran for cover through the gap by which they had entered, but before they were all through a second volley was fired by the natives, and Edward Messenger fell shot through the head as he faced about to return his fire. On the rest getting outside the gap they halted to recover Messenger's body, and ran round to the front, then after placing three as sentinels to prevent them being surrounded, and despatching one to town for assistance, they gained cover behind a gate, and a few yards of hedge. The rebels thinking the party had gone, rushed to the body of Messenger for the purpose of tomahawking it, and obtaining the rifle and accoutrements of the deceased, but as soon as the foremost man, who was dressed in a friendly native's blue serge shirt with badge, perceived them, he exclaimed "Hallo," fired both barrels of his gun, and in the act of retreating was shot dead by three of the party. At the same time a second native was fired at while in the act of crossing the orchard hedge on the right, and appeared to fall. No more was seen of the rebels after this, and a small party of friendly natives from Fort Herbert, and six men of the 65th Regiment from the Carrington Road Blockhouse, under Lieutenant Bailie, coming to their assistance, Messenger's body was brought out and carried to town. Deceased was 17 years of age, was the best shot of a family of marksmen, and was emphatically a volunteer, being under age for compulsory service, and yet taking part in Waireka, Mahoetahi, and other encounters with the enemy. The attacking natives were 30 of the Ngatiruanui and Waitotara tribes.

DEATH OF LIEUTENANT MCNAUGHTEN, R.A.

On Sunday, March the 17th, the first anniversary of the Taranaki war, at about 3 p.m., Lieutenant McNaughten fell while laying a cohorn mortar at the head of the sap which had been pushed up close to Te Arei. The mortars had been doing great execution among the rifle pits of the enemy during the day, and while this intrepid soldier was standing with a plumb line in his hand, laying one of these pieces, a Maori from the brow of a precipice which commanded the sap fired, and the ball wounded his hand which held the plumb line and then entered his breast. An officer who was near to him exclaimed "McNaughten you are hit," but the Lieutenant smiled, and with his usual calmness replied, "Oh never mind, 'tis but in the hand." These were his last words. He stood, turned pale, staggered backwards, fell and died. The ball had severed the aorta. He fell on the anniversary of the day the Artillery opened fire on Wi Kingi's pa at the Waitara. He fired the first gun, and his death concluded the first chapter of the Taranaki war.

CHAPTER XXIII.

THE TRUCE.

WHEN Wiremu Tamihana te Tarapipi, *anglaice* Thompson, was residing at Ngaruawahia, he received several letters from Bi٠٠op Selwyn, and the late Chief Justice Martin, soliciting his interference for making peace with the tribes at Taranaki. This was during the height of the war, and he paid no attention to them; but the fourth, containing an intimation that the Governor had joined in the request, induced him to make up his mind to interfere. He accordingly started to the scene of conflict, and arrived at Waitara early in March. The result of his arrival was the hoisting of a flag of truce at Hapurona's pa on the 12th of March, and a brief conference, which ended in the renewal of hostilities. On the 19th, Hapurona again hoisted the white flag.

On the 27th, the Colonial s.s. Victoria brought from Manukau His Excellency the Governor, Mr. Weld the Native Minister, Mr. Whitaker the Attorney-General, Mr. Commissioner McLean, and Tamati Waka Nene, the great Ngapuhi chief.

On the 30th, the s.s. Airedale brought from Manukau Major-General Cameron, C.B., and Miss Cameron. Major-General Sir Duncan Cameron's commissions date as follows :—Ensign, April the 8th, 1825; Lieutenant, August the 15th, 1826; Captain, June the 21st, 1833; Major, August the 23rd, 1839; Lieutenant-Colonel, September the 5th, 1843; Colonel, June the 20th, 1854; Major-General, March the 25th, 1859. .He was the President of the Council of Army Education. He served in the Eastern campaign of 1854–55; commanded the 40th Regiment at the battle of Alma, and the Highland Brigade at the battle of Balaklava, and on the expedition to Kertch, siege of Sebastopol, and assault on the outworks on the 18th of June. His decorations are—medal and clasps, C.B., Officer of the Legion of Honor, Sardinian medal, third class of the Medjindie, Knight Commander of the Bath, 1864, Knight Grand Cross of the Bath, 1873, and New Zealand medal. He was made Colonel of the 42nd Foot in September, 1863, and in 1868 became Governor of the Royal Military College at Sandhurst. He was born about 1808, and is of an ancient Scottish Highland Clan.

Hapurona having kept the white flag hoisted, a lengthened *korero* took place, occupying several days. At length Hapurona and a few followers accepted the following terms, the Waikatos agreeing to return to their homes, while Wi Kingi, who was in the Waikato district, refused to give his sanction to them or to meet the Government :—

" Terms offered by the Governor to the Waitara Insurgents.

" HAPURONA AND NGATIAWA :—For twelvemonths you have been

carrying arms against Her Majesty the Queen, and the authority of the law; you have now laid down your arms, and expressed your desire for peace; believing your desire to be sincere, I have come from Auckland for the purpose of stating the terms upon which it will be granted, and upon which Her Majesty's gracious pardon and protection will be extended to you.

"They are as follows:—

"1. The investigation of the Title, and the survey of the land at Waitara, to be continued and completed without interruption.

"2. Every man to be permitted to state his claims without interference, and my decision, or the decision of such persons as I may appoint, to be conclusive.

"3. All land in possession of Her Majesty's forces belonging to those who have borne arms against Her Majesty to be disposed of by me as I may think fit.

"4. All guns belonging to the Government to be returned.

"5. All plunder taken from the settlers to be forthwith restored.

"6. The Ngatiawa who have borne arms against the Government must submit to the Queen, and to the authority of the law, and not resort to force for the redress of wrongs, real or imaginary.

"7. As I did not use force for the acquisition of land, but for the vindication of the law and for the protection of Her Majesty's native subjects in the exercise of their just rights, I shall divide the land, which I have stated my intention to dispose of, amongst its former owners, but I shall reserve the sites of the blockhouses and redoubts, and a small piece of land around each for the public use, and shall exercise the right of making roads through the Waitara district. In conformity with the declaration made on the 29th of November, 1859, the rights of those who may prove their title to any part of the piece of land at Waitara will be respected.

"On your submission to these terms you will come under the protection of the law, and enjoy your property, both lands and goods, without molestation."

THE DECLARATION OF HAPURONA.

"I hereby declare that the terms of peace proposed by the Governor have been read and fully explained to me, and that I understand them thoroughly; and I declare that on behalf of myself and people I agree to abide by and fulfil them.

"HAPURONA PUKERIMU."

"These terms have been read and explained in our presence, and made thoroughly to be understood, this 8th day of April, 1861.

"J. A. WILSON, Missionary, C.M.S.,
"of the District of Auckland.
"MORE,
"DONALD MCLEAN, Native Secretary."

"I, Hapurona, speak for myself, for all these men whose names are

hereunto described, for the women and children."
Here follow 64 signatures.

THE DECLARATION OF PATUKAKARIKI.

"I hereby declare that the terms of peace proposed by the Governor have been read and fully explained to me, and that I understand them thoroughly; and I declare that on behalf of myself and people I agree to abide by and fulfil them.

"WIREMU NGA WAKA PATUKAKARIKI,
"His + Mark."

"These terms have been read and explained in our presence, and made thoroughly to be understood.

"TE WAKA NENE, +
"FRED. A. WELD, Native Minister,
"DONALD McLEAN, Native Secretary."

Similar terms were offered to the Taranaki and Ngatiruanui natives, who after considerable hesitation declared that they would neither accept nor refuse them, but await the result of a conference on native matters at Waikato.

In times of peace Taranaki is one of the most healthy places in the world. In the early days an entire year has been known to elapse without a single death occurring, and the medical men had to cultivate the land in order to live, there being no sickness to require their aid. During the period of hostilities, however, diarrhœa, fevers, and ultimately diphtheria, were fatally prevalent, the latter disease carrying off numbers of young people. And not only did those suffer who remained in the besieged town of New Plymouth, but those who took refuge in Nelson were afflicted almost as severely.

Considerable irritation was felt in the settlement at this time by the arrival from England of a pamphlet containing a letter to the Duke of Newcastle, entitled, "One of England's Little Wars," written by Archdeacon Hadfield, wherein he defended the action of the rebel Wi Kingi, by endeavoring to show that his claim to the Waitara was superior to that of Te Teira, and blamed Governor Gore Browne for plunging the Colony into war.

Early in May, Mr. Cutfield's term of office as Superintendent of the Province being about to expire, he again became a candidate for the Superintendency, in connection with Messrs. J. C. Richmond and Mr. C. Brown. Before the election Mr. Cutfield withdrew from the contest, and on the 23rd Mr. Brown was elected.

In the New Zealand Gazette of the 31st of May, Judge Johnston was appointed to be H.M. Commissioner to determine questions as to the proprietary rights of certain portions of the Ngatiawa tribe lately in arms against Her Majesty, in a block of land at Taranaki, and John Rogan, Esq., was appointed to mark out the boundaries of the same.

On the 3rd of June, the Prince Arthur steam sloop, of the Indian Navy, arrived from Bombay, with 147 men of the 57th Regiment, 42 soldiers' wives and 69 children, and Brevet-Major Hassard, Captain Sir Robert Douglass, Bart., Captain C. J. Clark, and Lieutenants McClintoc, and A. C. Manners.

On the 15th, E. J. Willcocks, Esq., was appointed Registration and Returning Officer, and Registrar of the Supreme Court for the Province, *vice* Ritchie.

On the 25th, Colors were presented to the Taranaki Militia and Volunteers, from the ladies of Taranaki, by Mrs. Colonel Warre, wife of Colonel Warre, 57th Regiment, the ceremony of consecration being performed by the Ven. Archdeacon Govett.

The sum of £25,000 having been voted by Parliament during the session of 1860 as compensation to the Taranaki settlers for the losses sustained by them during the war, Mr. Sewell, the special Commissioner, arrived at New Plymouth to investigate claims, on July the 8th.

On August the 10th, the prospectus of the Bank of New Zealand was advertised in the *Taranaki Herald*, Messrs. T. King and J. J. Looney being the provisional trustees for Taranaki.

News having reached the Colony of the appointment of Sir George Grey as successor to Colonel Gore Browne in the Governorship of New Zealand, a valedictory address was presented to Colonel Gore Browne, signed by the entire male adult population of Taranaki. On the 26th of September Sir George Grey arrived in Auckland from the Cape of Good Hope by H.M. steam corvette Cossack, 20 guns, and was welcomed on shore by Colonel Gore Browne.

On the 1st of October, Colonel Gore Browne and family embarked at Auckland for Sydney in the Henry Fernie, amidst the warmest expressions of respect and esteem from the inhabitants.

On the 16th of November, Bishop Selwyn left New Plymouth for the purpose of reaching Wanganui by the coast track, and in order to prove to the world that the Taranaki and Ngatiruanui tribes were not so bad as the Taranaki settlers represented them to be. The Bishop returned to New Plymouth on the 22nd, and was very reticent as to the results of his journey. From a letter written by Erueti, a chief of Warea, to the Rev. Mr. Reimenschneider, the following particulars of this journey were obtained:—

" When the Bishop got to Moutoti the Maoris sent a young man after him to demand of him his reason for persisting in pursuing his journey southward, when he knew the Maoris had forbidden any Pakehas to pass that way. As the Bishop proved obstinate his bundle and horse were demanded of him in order that he might turn back to town. The Bishop agreed to return, but desired to be permitted to sleep there that night. This was permitted, and the young man left him. The Bishop slept there two nights, and then went on with the horse, but his bundle was detained for his persistence. The Bishop went on as far as Ohaugi, a place fifty miles on this side of Wanganui, and then returned to New Plymouth to catch the steamer. On passing Moutoti his bundle was restored to him."

Much anxiety was felt at this time concerning the spread of thistles over the cultivated parts of the district. The grass paddocks of the forest clearings were infested with this plant to such a degree that scarcely any grass was to be seen in them.

On the 18th of November, a branch of the Bank of New Zealand was opened at Mr. Richmond's stone house, near Mount Eliot, Mr. T. King being manager.

In December, Governor Grey announced a new scheme of native policy. It consisted chiefly in dividing the Colony into Native and European Districts, and in permitting Native Courts of Law, called Runangas, to have jurisdiction in Native Districts. These Courts were ultimately established, and while they entirely failed to cure the Maoris of their rebelliousness, became the object of derision to all who knew anything about them, the most ridiculous farces being performed in connection with them.

On the 1st of January, 1862, the foundation stone of the Primitive Methodist Church, Queen Street, was laid by Josiah Flight, Esq., R.M.

Governor Grey at this time established camps between Auckland and Waikato, and employed the troops in making roads.

On the 14th of January, the Superintendent of Taranaki proclaimed the Public Cemetery Ordinance, 1861, on which basis the Public Cemetery at Te Henui was established.

On the 1st of February, an extract from a speech delivered by the late Canon Stowell, of Manchester, before a meeting of the Douglas Branch of the Isle of Man Auxilliary of the Church Missionary Society, as reported in the *Manx Sun*, was published in the *Taranaki Herald*, and produced considerable indignation. This extract contained the following extraordinary and impassioned statements:—" New Zealand is the brightest gem in the diadem of the Church Missionary Society. Who has brought this trouble on New Zealand? Was it not the grasping, unfair, and oppressive emigrants? How did the civilised settlers treat the natives? Why, in the way that hunters treat wild animals—they hewed them up and cut them down to make way for their boasted civilisation. Alas! alas! that British civilisation should so far forget itself as to allow the aborigines to be cut down and treated like dogs. The emigrants—in many cases the off-scouring and vagabonds of our own country—ought not to be allowed to take advantage of the ignorance of the natives, and oppress them as they have done, to a great extent pillaging their lands from them, and then when the natives turn round to defend themselves they are cried out against as 'rebels' and savages." These were very cruel and unjust words to say against the settlers who had been dispossessed of their farms at Mangoraka by the manumitted Puketapu slaves, and those whose homes had been rifled, farms bespoiled, and blood been shed by the red-handed murderers of Taranaki and Ngatiruanui. Canon Stowell was, however, the victim of ignorance and misrepresentation.

On the 14th of February, the Taranaki Militia was virtually disbanded, and arrangements were made for employing the men in constructing the roads. Mr. F. A. Carrington was appointed Engineering Surveyor for these works. The women and children who had taken refuge in Nelson returned by every steamer, and a number of timber houses were erected for their temporary accommodation by the Provincial Government in St. Germains Square.

On the 16th of May, Mr. Edward Gibbon Wakefield, whose labors connected with modern colonisation, and with the colonisation of New Zealand have already been alluded to, expired at his residence in Wellington, at the age of 66 years. He arrived in Wellington in 1853, just before the Constitution Act was brought into operation, and was returned for the Hutt by an overwhelming majority as one of its representatives, both in the Provincial Council of Wellington and General Assembly.

On the 8th of July, a great native meeting was held at Kapoaraia. The number present was estimated at 600, and consisted of members of the Taranaki, Ngatiruanui, Ngaruru, and Wanganui tribes. The meeting resolved that if the road making were extended beyond Waireka it would be looked upon as a declaration of war. After the meeting was over Mohi Te Reiroa, of Waikato, cried out *Whitiki! whitiki!* "Gird yourselves," when all the Maoris rushed out of the house, put on their belts, seized their guns, and began the war dance. Mohi then took a *taiaha*, and began a most violent harangue, cut down numbers of imaginary Pakehas, and worked himself up into such a state of frenzy that he fell dead. A similar occurrence took place on the 6th of the previous January, at the *runanga* at Whatino, when Hori Kingi Ngatairakaunui, while discussing the same question, fell down dead.

On the night of the 1st of September, the s.s. Lord Worsley was wrecked at Cape Egmont on her passage from Nelson to New Plymouth. From some inexplicable cause the steamer was run ashore in a small bay near to the cape and became a wreck. The passengers, among whom were several ladies, and the crew were safely landed in the enemy's country, but several of the crew escaped with a boat to New Plymouth with the intelligence. At first much alarm was created by the intelligence, it being feared that the Maoris would kill the whole of the shipwrecked people who remained in their territory, but by the good offices of Wi Kingi, of Umuroa, and the prospect of a rich booty from the wreck, the people were spared and sent up to New Plymouth in bullock carts.

On the 7th of February, 1863, H.M. steam corvette Orpheus, 21 guns, was lost on Manukau bar, with 187 of her crew.

On the 4th of March, H.M.S.S. Harrier arrived with His Excellency Sir George Grey, General Cameron, the Hon. Mr. Domett, Colonial Secretary; and the Hon. Mr. Bell, Native Secretary. The object of the Governor's visit was the reinstating of the Province, and to further this object the House of Representatives had recommended that a sum of £200,000 should be raised on the general security of the colony, but as a special charge on the land and ordinary revenue of the Province of Taranaki, for the purpose of compensating the settlers for their losses, and reinstating them on their farms.

Shortly after the Governor's arrival, strange natives were seen in the bush in the neighborhood of the Kent road, passing apparently to the south. When this fact was mentioned to His Excellency he replied that he was assured that these natives had gone southward with the most laudable intention.

As a first step towards the reinstatement of the Province, the Governor determined to take possession of Tataraimaka, which the natives claimed by right of conquest.

On Thursday, the 12th of March, 300 men of the 57th Regiment, under Colonel Warre, C.B., Captains Woodall and Gorton, Lieutenants Brutton, Thompson, Tragett, and Waller, Adjutant Clarke, and Assistant-Surgeon Hope, together with Lieutenant Ferguson and a detachment of the Royal Engineers, paraded under Mount Eliot, and marched off by the South Road towards Omata, preceded by baggage under the charge of Lieutenant Cox. His Excellency the Governor and General Cameron followed. The troops reached Waireka, and encamped. A number of the Taranaki tribe had been for several days at Wairau, a native settlement lying on the coast, between Oakura river and Tataraimaka. The smoke of large fires, supposed to be signals, was seen at Tataraimaka and beyond it after the arrival of the troops. For several days after this the Governor, the General, the Colonial Secretary, and the Native Minister, paid visits to the Camp at Poutoko, and on one occasion delegates from Taranaki proper met them, and informed them that Tataraimaka would not be given up unless the British first gave up the Waitara.

The Governor's intention, however, was to take repossession of the Tataraimaka block, and the natives were well aware of this, for in a conference with Tamihana at Waikato in the previous January the following dialogue occurred :—

Taminana : " O Governor, all the blocks in the neighborhood of Waitara over which the soldiers went you shall retain for the Queen alone; but the determination of Ngatiruanui and Taranaki, as expressed by them, is to continue in the possession of the Waireka and Tataraimaka blocks over which their feet travelled."

The Governor: "Do you hearken; I shall be obstinate about Tataraimaka. After my return to Auckland I shall embark in the steamer, and proceed to that place, and there abide. Now will Waikato go there and join them, or will Waikato go to Taranaki and assist me? O ye sons, you are in error, for I have Tataraimaka in my hands, and my hands shall be strong to hold it."

On the 19th, H.M.S.S. Harrier arrived at New Plymouth with 200 men of the 70th Regiment, under Captains Rutherford, Tovey, and Tighe, Lieutenants Huskisson and Collins, and Ensign Clarke, and Assistant-Surgeon Alston.

On the 21st of March, the Governor in Council recommended the

Provincial Council of Taranaki to pass a Bill for raising, by debentures, the sum of £50,000 for the purpose of partly paying Mr. Sewell's award for compensation for losses sustained by the war, which was accordingly done.

The following Council Paper will set the rather complicated arrangement of this compensation in a perspicuous manner:—

"His Honor the Superintendent of Taranaki.
"New Plymouth, 21st March, 1863.

"Sir:—In reference to the expenditure of the sum of £200,000 to be raised under the Loan Act, 1862, to assist in any measures adopted by His Excellency the Governor in Council for the reinstatement of the settlement and inhabitants of Taranaki, I have now the honor to convey to you the substance of some measures adopted this day by the Governor in Council for the purpose just stated.

"In order to place the settlers of Taranaki, who have been driven from their homes, or suffered losses during the war, in a position to resume their ordinary operations on their farms or elsewhere, and at the same time to provide funds for the execution of measures absolutely necessary for their permanent security, it is proposed that a sum of £120,000 be considered payable out of the £200,000 for settlers' losses; of this sum £30,000 has been already received by the settlers, and Government propose to raise immediately, if possible, the balance of £90,000, and to pay it to the claimants under Mr. Sewell's award. With the £25,000 paid under the former grant of the General Assembly, this will make £145,000 paid out of the total of £189,000 or thereabout, awarded by Mr. Sewell or the Sub-Commissioners on acccount of all classes of the settlers' claims.

"Although there will thus be left a balance of about £44,000 unprovided for out of reinstatement fund, it is to be remembered that the remainder of that fund will be expended on measures for the permanent reinstatement of the Province generally, including the individual colonists who have suffered during the war; but the Government are desirous that the settlers should receive either in cash or in some acknowledgment bearing interest, the full amount awarded for their losses.

"In order to effect this object and to provide for the balance last mentioned, namely £44,000, it is proposed that the Superintendent and the Provincial Council of Taranaki should immediately pass an Act authorising the issue of debentures to the amount of £50,000, payable at any time after the expiration of ten years, bearing interest at the rate of 7 per cent. per annum, and chargeable on the Provincial revenue of Taranaki. This arrangement must necessarily be submitted to the sanction of the General Assembly, but the General Government will at once guarantee the interest of the first five years, reserving for that purpose a sufficient sum from the reinstatement fund.

"If your Honor and the Provincial Council accede to the above proposition, and will pass the requisite Act without delay, the assent of His Excellency will be given to it, and instructions will be thereupon immediately issued for the raising of the first mentioned sum of £90,000.—I have, &c.,

"ALFRED DOMETT."

Early in March the Maori King natives committed two outrages in Waikato. The Governor had determined to build a Court House and Police Station at Te Kohekohe, and carpenters were employed on the work. After inducing the carpenters to leave their work, the natives took possession of the building, and rafted the timber of which it was being erected and floated it down the river.

On the 24th, they went to the premises of Mr. Gorst, a celebrated Maori apologist, who lived at Te Awamutu, and conducted a Maori newspaper, called *Pihoihoi Mokemoke*. Breaking open the printing office they took away the press and type.

On March the 30th, H.M.S.S. Harrier arrived at New Plymouth, from Manukau, with 80 men of the 65th Regiment under Lieutenant Pagan, and 120 men of the 70th Regiment, under Captain Ralston.

On Saturday the 4th of April, the troops moved from Omata. and took possession of Tataraimaka, encamping on Mr. McDonald's farm, but deciding to build a redoubt on Bayly's farm by to the edge of the cliff overhanging the road, near to the Katikara river.

On Sunday evening, the 19th, the Maoris, under the chief Parenga Kingi, threw into the Tapuae river the stones which the soldiers had collected for repairing the road at that spot.

The *Taranaki Herald*, of May the 2nd, gave full particulars of ambuscades which had been laid for cutting off Europeans passing to and from Tataraimaka and New Plymouth, and the Governor was informed of the same, but blinded by the supposition of his own personal influence over the natives he refused to listen to advice or warning.

CHAPTER XXIV.

THE RENEWAL OF HOSTILITIES.

ON Monday, May the 4th, 1863, a party consisting of seven armed men of the 57th Regiment, in charge of a prisoner, left the Tataraimaka Camp for town. Knowing nothing of the warnings which had been given to the Government, they marched on regardless of danger. They had not proceeded far on their way when Dr. Hope and Lieutenant Tragett of the same regiment overtook them on horseback, both being unarmed. The officers passed the party and proceeded onward at a walking pace, about 200 yards in advance, until nearing the Wairau stream, when they came to a sudden halt, and awaited until the party on foot came up to within five yards of them, when a shot was fired from the bush which at that spot slopes downward to the river, and runs parallel to the beach. So sudden and unexpected was the report, that the man Kelly, who alone escaped to tell the tale, turned round and enquired of Sergeant Ellers, who was immediately in front of him, if his piece had gone off by accident. The question was scarcely answered in the negative when another shot brought poor Ellers to the ground, and another Color-Sergeant Hill. In front Dr. Hope was lying in the stream, having fallen wounded from his horse. Private Flynn, on being requested to aid in the defence, stated his inability to do so from a wound which he had received in his arm. Private Banks, the prisoner, was also prostrate on the ground. While matters were in this state, Lieutenant Tragett, instead of riding off and saving his life, dismounted from his horse and joined the three survivors, remarking, as if speaking to himself, "What is best to be done." Florence Kelly replied, "We had better retire firing." The noble officer replied, "We cannot leave our dead and wounded," so he took a rifle and accoutrements to aid in the defence. After continuing the fire for some time and receiving a wound, he gave his white pocket handkerchief to Kelly with directions to place it on his bayonet, and use it as a flag of truce. Kelly obeyed this order, but the call for mercy was unheeded. The little party again opened fire, which was answered with telling effect by the ambuscade, Kelly alone being left alive. A Maori now, in attempting to take Sergeant Hill's firelock, was shot dead by the survivor. Kelly then retreated towards Tataraimaka, but a Maori trying to outflank him, and the strings of his shoes which were of flax breaking, he kicked off his shoes, threw away his rifle and belts, ran for his life, and escaped. The names of the victims of this massacre were :—Staff Assistant-Surgeon William Astle Hope, M.D. ; Lieutenant Thomas Heathcote Tragett, 57th Regiment ; Color-Sergeant Samuel Ellers ; Sergeant Samuel Hill ; Private Edward Kelly ; Private John Flynn ; Private Bartholomew McCarthy, and Patrick Egan.

That night the Militia and Volunteers again mounted picket, and occupied their old posts around the town. What were the feelings of Governor Grey when the real object of the Maoris, whom he supposed to have crept through the bush with "the most laudable intentions," was thus vividly brought before him we cannot say, but General Cameron was heard to say to him that he would not have his men cut to pieces in that fashion with impunity.

THE ABANDONMENT OF THE WAITARA PURCHASE.

On the 11th, the following extraordinary proclamation was issued by the Governor :—

"PROCLAMATION.
"By His Excellency Sir George Grey, K.C.B., &c.
"Whereas an engagement for the purchase of a certain tract of land at the Waitara, commonly known as Teira's block, was entered into by the Government of New Zealand in 1859, but the said purchase has never been completed.

"And whereas circumstances connected with the said purchase, unknown to the Government at the time of the sale of the said land, have lately transpired, which make it advisable that the said purchase should not be further proceeded with.

"Now, therefore, the Governor, with the advice and consent of the Executive Council, doth hereby declare that the purchase of the said block of land is abandoned, and all claim to the same on the part of the Government is henceforth renounced.

"Given under my hand at New Plymouth, and issued under the Seal of the Colony of New Zealand, this 11th day of May, 1863.
"G. GREY.
"By His Excellency's Command,
"ALFRED DOMETT,
"GOD SAVE THE QUEEN."

On the night of the 24th, two militiamen, Ward and Wolfe, were posted together on the edge of the gully near to the Carrington Road Blockhouse, when by a mistake Ward fired at Wolfe and wounded him in the wrist.

On the 29th, as Lieutenant Waller, 57th Regiment, was riding from St. Andrew's Redoubt to Poutoko, he received a volley from a party of natives in ambush, which killed his horse. While disengaging himself from the fallen beast a native leaped out with a tomahawk to despatch him, when Lieutenant Waller shot him with his revolver, and succeeded in escaping to the redoubt.

THE ATTACK ON THE ENEMY'S POSITION AT KATIKARA.

On the 3rd of June, a force under the command of General Cameron marched from New Plymouth by the Great South Road, and received reinforcements at Poutoko and Oakura, and continued its march in silence to Tataraimaka, where it was again reinforced.

At about 6.15 on the following morning the force advanced to the attack, the course taken being to the left of the redoubt over Bayly's farm. After marching about 400 yards the Armstrong battery halted, and was posted on the edge of the ridge overhanging the Katikara river. Fire was immediately opened upon the native redoubt, about 800 yards distant, and directly inland, the 57th at the same time doubling down the valley in single file to attack the rifle pits to the right of the enemy's position. After dashing across the stream and ascending the opposite height, the advance under Lieutenants Waller and Brutton, with their Colonel in command, immediately charged the rifle pits to the right, and drove the rebels from their position above the mouth of the river, thereby opening up the road to the reserves which came rapidly up. Meanwhile the supporting party, under Lieutenant-Colonel Logan, having been fired upon from the redoubt, turned to the left, and running over an open space of 300 yards with fixed bayonets stormed the place, killing every native within it. Captains Shortt and Russell, with their parties, charged the redoubt almost simultaneously, while Ensign Duncan was coming over at another part. The men behaved well and charged impetuously. The natives were at once driven to their holes, and the bayonet then did its work. On the right Colonel Warre's party cleared the rifle pits, and pursued the flying enemy southwards and inland. The General was highly pleased at the gallant manner in which the enemy's works were carried. Twenty-four bodies of natives were taken in carts to the Tataraimaka Camp and buried. Several guns and a fine *taiaha* were taken.

H.M.S. Eclipse was anchored off the mouth of the valley, and threw some shells while the troops were advancing to the attack. The ship lay about a mile from the rebel redoubt, and threw a shell into the middle of the works which killed at least one Maori, for a piece of the fuze was found in one of the bodies.

The loss on the side of the British was 1 private killed and 2 mortally and 2 severely wounded of the 57th Regiment, and 1 private severely wounded of the 70th Regiment.

The most interesting of the spoils taken by the troops on this occasion was the list of tolls which was set up by the rebels near to Te Ika roa a Maui, the great assembly house at Kapoainia, near Warea, but which was afterwards brought up to Puketehe, just beyond Tataraimaka.

The following is a translation of this singular notice :—

" Taranaki. Te Ika a Maui. The house where lie the laws which are in force here of King Matutaera Potatau, near the gate for payment of offences which stands here.

	£	s.	d.
1. Minister of the Gospel	50	0	0
2. Newspaper Mail	300	0	0
3. Maori Disciple of the Governor	200	0	0

4. Wealthy Pakeha—don't let them go through the
   gate, if they do 5 0 0
5. Pakeha Policeman 500 0 0
6. Maori Policeman 5 0 0
7. Maori Assessor 5 0 0
8. If he comes as a Kingite 0 15 0
9. A King's Letter in the Mail 0 5 0
10. A Letter against the Authority of the King ... 1 0 0
11. Letters from Kinsmen Outside 0 5 0
12. Letters Tempting the Tribe 0 15 0
13. Letters not sent by the Mail 1 0 0
14. A Neutral coming as a Pakeha 0 5 0
15. A Preaching Maori Minister 55 0 0
16. Letter Badly Tempting the Tribe, seize it and make
    the bearer pay 0 5 0
17. The above is the Law for the Pakeha Tolls of the
    Maori.

---

1. A Cart of Wheat or other things 0 1 0
2. Things carried on a man's back 0 0 1
3. A Pig carried in a cart 0 0 6
4. A Pig driven 0 0 6
5. A Cow or Horse each 0 0 6
6. There are no rules referring to neutrals outside, but
   a load carried from inside the gate 0 0 1
7. Money of the tribe for purchasing, free
8. The Law of the Maoris inside and outside of the
   gate
9. Do not Steal, O Man (or evade the tolls) if you do
   you will pay 5 0 0

By authority of the keepers of the gate of Matutaera,
                                    KERE, Policeman,
                                    ROPOMA, Policeman.
8th July, 1862.

On June the 25th, Hapurona sent a challenge addressed to the Governor, the General, Mr. Bell, and Mr. Parris. It was written on half a sheet of account paper, and signed by "Hapurona, the General of the Maoris." He said that he and all his people were ready to fight by the light of the sun. He also desired that the troops would go and fight him, stating that if they did not he should have to make them by occupying land at Bell Block. Hapurona had not been in town since the 25th of January, 1862, when he was arrested by the police for riotous conduct in the streets. He was at that time in the receipt of £100 per annum as commandant of the Matarikoriko Blockhouse, which he threw up in consequence of his having been apprehended, or, as he termed it, made a slave of by the police.

On the 27th, H.M.S. Eclipse arrived with the intelligence that the Waikato tribe had risen in rebellion, and that troops were needed for the defence of Auckland. On the same evening she returned to Manukau with detachments of the 40th, 65th, and 70th Regiments. The Governor and General were at this time in Auckland.

The insurrection in Waikato revealed the cause of the renewal of hostilities in Taranaki. The Maoris who crept through the forest at the back of the settlement, as the Governor supposed "with the most laudable intentions," were emissaries from Waikato sent to stir up the rebels to active measures in order to divert the attention of the Government from what was taking place in the Waikato, and it was a fortunate thing for Taranaki that the rebels received a check at the Katikara before the troops were withdrawn to the North.

The policy of the Maoris was revealed by the following letter found by the Bushrangers at Parakamahoe, when that place was destroyed in April, 1864 :—

"Huiterangiora, February 1st, 1863.

"To Parenga Kingi, Minarapa, Hoani, Inaraira, Aperahama Ngatawa, Totaea, to all the runanga of King Potatau. Friends, greeting to you all, the tribes and the people of the canoe of my ancestors. Do you listen, I am living here with the object of your respect—the King. Listen ; Te Ia has been occupied by the soldiers. If the road crosses the Maungatawhiri there will be war ; if the war does not begin here it will begin where you are, at Taranaki. Take care what you do. My word to you is—go carefully. This is what your King says, "Leave it to the men of the canoe (Waikato) to say how it is to be steered, whether to go with the waves or to turn its head towards them. If they say 'put its head to face them,' then do it ; if they say 'give way' then give way.'

"Enough of that. Friends, do not be troubled at what I said to you about the road for the mail—let it be open—and Pakeha travellers let them go to and fro. Be careful in what you do, so as to leave the Governor to bruise the nose of the King's runanga— that the other tribes may see clearly that we are in the right. Enough of that. This is another thing concerning Taranaki ; leave it as it is. Tataraimaka and Waitara, let them both be as they are. If what the Governor says about Waitara is satisfactory, there will be no difficulty about Tataraimaka. The satisfactoriness of what the Governor says must consist of this—the giving back of Waitara into our hands, and then it will be right about Tataraimaka. Leave the Pakehas to begin the war that the Governor's fine words may be laughed at. Enough ; it is finished.

"WIREMU KINGI WHITI."

The southern rebels now established themselves on the north-western spur of the Kaitake Ranges, and on the 27th Colonel Warre, who, in the absence of the General, had been appointed Commandant of the garrison, commenced to shell them with the Armstrong batteries.

On the 30th, Tataraimaka was evacuated for the second time. Bush parties of Volunteers were at this time organised under the command of Captains Atkinson and Webster, for the purpose of attacking the rebels in the forest, and intercepting their communications with the northern and southern parts of the Province.

On the 11th of July, the Governor, by proclamation, threatened the confiscation of rebel native lands.

On Sunday, September the 13th, T. Langman, J. Sole, and W. H. Rowe were attacked by a party of natives on the Frankley Road, and Langman's arm was badly fractured by a ball. This event was followed by skirmishes on either side of the settlement.

On the 15th, at 3 a.m., Captain Russell, with Lieutenant Manners and Ensign Powys, and 75 men of the 57th Regiment, left the Poutoko redoubt, and leaving 25 of his party in the empty redoubt at Oakura, crossed the river, and turning inland a little way up the road from Wairau to Kaitake, planted an ambush in three parties. The men lay in the scrub beside the road till about eight o'clock, when a body of natives approached from Kaitake. They were headed by an old chief, square shouldered, and with grizzled hair, carrying a handsome *taiaha*, who, when he came opposite to Lieutenant Manners' party, seeing tracks on the road shouted *he pakeha!* The old man was immediately shot with such others as were within reach, but the main body of the natives had not come up to the ambush. Seeing what had happened, the rebels at Kaitake and Ahuahu rushed down from the hills in force for the purpose of taking possession of the redoubt in order to cut off Captain Russell's retreat. Their dismay, when they discovered that it was occupied by soldiers, may be easily imagined. Sergeant Hackett hit one rebel at the distance of 300 yards, who fell and rolled down the steep bank. After this the return to Poutoko was effected without molestation. The loss of the enemy was not exactly known, but Captain Russell stated that he saw seven bodies on the ground, and two men wounded, who were led away.

On January the 18th, 1864, at a Skirmish at Sentry Hill, Hone te Horo, an active rebel of the Puketapu hapu was killed, and several other rebels wounded.

DEATH OF MR. PATTERSON.

On Sunday the 28th of February, several settlers tempted by the beauty of the day roamed abroad on a visit to their once happy, but now desolate homes. The first that proceeded on the Frankley Road was one of Mr. Dingle's sons, who was in the habit of daily visiting his father's farm. This morning he found one of the horses entangled in the supplejacks. Having set the animal free, he returned unharmed. A party of four on foot soon followed, accompanied by Mr. George Patterson, on horseback, who passed on some 300 yards in advance. When the four on foot reached the hill near to where Mr. Dingle's house formerly stood, they saw Mr. Patterson wave his hand as a signal for them to return, and at the same time several natives, armed with guns and tomahawks, appeared on the scene and shot Mr. Patterson. The four on foot seeing this, and having but one gun and five rounds of ammunition, retreated towards town, W. Bishop turning and firing occasionally on the pursuers. When the news reached town Col. Warre collected a force and went out and recovered the body, which was found lying on some logs by the side of the road with three bullet wounds in it, one through the heart, and frightfully mutilated with tomahawks. Mr. Patterson's boots and hat were gone, and his horse lay shot and tomahawked. Mr. Patterson was a native of Northumberland, and by profession a steam and civil engineer. He had performed some professional service in Spain, and in Taranaki erected and worked a saw mill. He was a most energetic settler, and was much respected. He left a widow and several young children.

THE REBELS DISTURBED AT MANGOREI.

On the 12th of February, W. Richards, jun., reported that rebel natives were on Mr. T. King's farm at Mangorei. At 2 p.m. two parties of Bushrangers started for that locality, one party going by Ratanui, and the other by the Avenue Road. When the latter party got into the neighborhood of Mr. King's farm, they saw a column of smoke before them in the bush, and about the Mangorei Bridge they found tracks of natives, and marks of sheep having been dragged. The party that went by Ratanui came up about 5 p.m., and then an advance was made. Following the tracks a Maori was seen fishing in the river, and was fired at, but made his escape into the bush apparently unharmed.

Crossing the river an encampment was discovered, which had the appearance of having but very recently been abandoned. Here were eight very large Maori ovens, from some of which meat had just been taken and laid upon branches; some were still unopened, and contained a barrow-load, or more, of mutton each. A number of kidneys had been reserved in a heap uncooked, and these the men appropriated, and conveyed to town for their suppers. Potatoes, kumeras, and apples were also at hand, as well as a quantity of that Maori delicacy, rotted maize. From the fact of twenty skins being found in a neighboring clearing, and from the number of tracks seen, it was judged that a large number of natives intended to partake of the preparing feast.

The camp was about three-quarters of a mile from the Meeting of the Waters, and about 300 yards beyond the site of an old pa, called Papamoa, but on the eastern side of the Waiwakaiho River. The rebels appeared to have intended to stay there for some time, for they had commenced to build whares.

SKIRMISH AT KAITAKE.

On Friday, March the 11th, an alarm was given in town by two settlers, who had been out on the Frankley Road, that the rebels were out in that direction. Bush parties were sent out in pursuit in various directions, and Major Butler, with a company of Volunteers advanced towards Kaitake. Captain Corbett left Pahitere, a singular mount on the east of the Oakura, and made his way with his men to the left of the Kaitake spur, on which the rebels had their stronghold, while Major Butler advanced straight for the spur, with a force consisting of 84 men of the 57th, and a small detachment of the Royal Artillery under Lieutenant Larcom, with a 24-pounder howitzer and a cohorn mortar. On advancing to within 500 yards of the lower pa firing was opened upon the position. The natives replied by a weak and desultory fire, and the British advanced to a rising ground within 200 yards of the pa, and here the gun was again got into position. This had scarcely been done when the enemy opened a heavy cross fire from three different directions. In this predicament there was no choice other than to retreat, and this was effected in good order, the men retiring skirmishing. The greatest number of casualties occurred in the neighborhood of the gun, at which the rebels chiefly directed their fire.

In the midst of the engagement, Antonio Rodiquez De Sardinha, a member of the Royal House of Portugal, and one of the mounted orderlies, displayed great gallantry by conveying two of the wounded men to the rear under fire. Major Butler also manifested cool courage throughout the affair.

The casualties of this engagement were :—Lieutenant Larcom, R.A., wounded severely ; Private Michael Kennedy, No. 1 Company, 57th Regiment, killed ; Privates William Henry, Martin Stagpoole, James Adley, John Chamberlain, and Charles Keane, 57th Regiment, wounded.

On the 20th of March, the villages of Ahuahu and Te Tutu were taken with trifling loss.

THE DEFEAT AT AHUAHU.

On the 6th of April, in compliance with orders, Captain Lloyd of the 57th Regiment left the Kaitake Camp in order to effect a reconnaisance of the site of the Ahuahu Village. At 6 a.m., Lieutenant Cox, with a party of the 57th, and Captain Page, with the Melbourne Volunteers, crossed the Oakura River from the camp on its banks, striking inland by a newly formed road up the river towards the ranges. Here they halted until joined by Captain Lloyd and his party, the force then consisting of one captain, one subaltern, two sergeants, one drummer, and 53 rank and file of the 57th, with Dr. Jones, and one captain, one subaltern, two sergeants, and 41 rank and file of the Melbourne Volunteers; the united numbers making a force of 101. The march was continued as near to the foot of the ranges and towards the south as the broken state of the country would admit, the men having to toil through a dense and luxuriant growth of fern, tutu, and manuka, up one hillock and down another. On a portion of table land, on a rise to the left, a small plantation was met with. Captain Lloyd gave orders that this should be destroyed, handing his sword to Sergeant Anderson for the purpose of cutting it down, and taking in exchange the Sergeant's rifle and ammunition. Whilst this work was proceeding, Lieutenant Cox, with the right sub-division of the 57th, advanced up another rise to a flat piece of land, posting sentinels near to the ruins of a number of whares, which were destroyed by the soldiers on a former occasion. Afterwards six men under Sergeant Anderson fell back as a picket on the outer spur of the range, carefully searching all around, Hemi, the native guide, having reported that he had heard a call, and that the party had been discovered by the enemy.

Captain Lloyd then passed to the front, descending the hill on to a flat near to a series of rifle pits, the men, after an interval, following down the hill, leaving a rear guard of ten men on the look out. The word was now passed to light pipes, and for the men to make themselves at ease, and the soldiers and volunteers began to congregate about the cart road leading to the beach. Ten minutes had scarcely elapsed, when from the thick fern on the spur the natives poured in a volley, wounding one man. Captain Lloyd then leaped into a rifle pit, ordering his men to seek cover as quickly as possible, and open fire towards the enemy, the Captain himself firing as rapidly as he could with the Sergeant's rifle, which he still retained in his possession. After firing for a quarter of an hour the word was given to retire. In the retreat Captain Lloyd with several of the 57th and Volunteers fell.

When it was known in town that some disaster had befallen Captain Lloyd's party, Colonel Warre despatched a force consisting of the Bushrangers, and a large party of the 57th under Major Butler. When the orders came the Bushrangers were on their way to attend the funeral of Sergeant Appleby, of Captain Corbett's Company of Volunteers, who had died of the wound he received at Kaitake. They immediately fell out, got their arms, and proceeded to Oakura, and from thence by Wairau to Ahuahu. Colonel Warre, with an Armstrong gun, went to Hauranga, and from thence by the road to the ranges, and when pretty near to the foot of the spur he ordered two shells to be fired. This had the effect of rousing the men who were still hiding in the fern. Two men where picked up by the Bushrangers, and one by Colonel Warre's party. An advance was then made to the little plateau where the tragic event of the morning took place, and there a fearful scene presented itself. Six bodies were found by the rifle pits, stripped nearly naked and decapitated, and their heads taken away. Another man, whose body could not be found, appeared to have been viscerated, some intestines being found on the ground. The bodies were placed in two carts and covered with fern, and conveyed to town.

The casualties in this affair were :— 57th Regiment : Captain Lloyd, decapitated ; Privates Jeremiah Dooley, decapitated ; George

Sadler, decapitated; Andrew Collins, wounded; Lawrence Cronin, wounded; John Kirby, wounded; P. Murray, wounded; and Isaac Smith, wounded. Militia: Corporal H. Banks, decapitated; Privates James Nagles and H. Bartley, decapitated; John Gallagher, missing; Color-Sergeant George Bentley, wounded; Corporal Robert Stokes, wounded; Privates Francis T. Tomlins, wounded; Edward Whatmore, wounded, and James McKenna, wounded.

About this time the rebels threw off all pretensions to Christianity, and practised fanatical rites called Pai Marire, and called themselves Hauhaus. For some occult purpose the heads of the unfortunate persons killed at Ahuahu were dried after the native fashion, and conveyed from one native settlement to another by these fanatics.

On the 21st, Lieutenant Hirst found the missing man Gallagher on the ranges, decapitated, and part of his breast and one leg cut off.

DEFEAT OF THE REBELS AT SENTRY HILL.

Sentry Hill is a mount near the termination of the Waiongona and Mangoraka Rivers. After the second rebellion of Hapurona, Wi Kingi's fighting general, it was taken possession of by the British, a redoubt formed, and a blockhouse erected on it which was strongly garrisoned.

From an early hour of the morning of Saturday, the 30th of April, the men in the fort heard the rebels shouting and chanting their war songs at Manutahi. The sounds gradually drew nearer, and at 9 a.m. it was evident that the rebels were in force at Waiongona ford, which is nearly opposite to Sentry Hill. Shortly after they were seen by the sentries to be emerging from the bush which lies in the river valley between the ford and the hill, and distant about 800 yards. About 300 of them advanced along the road, and made slowly and steadily for the redoubt. Captain Shortt of the 57th, who was in command, ordered his men, 75 in number, to lie down under the breastwork of the redoubt, and kept the sentry marching to and fro as usual, as if no danger was expected. The rebels advanced till they were about 150 yards off, but then halted as if rather doubtful. Then Captain Shortt gave the word of command, and the men sprang upon their feet, and opened a murderous fire upon the rebels with their rifles and two cohorn mortars. The rebels drew back a little, but stood the fire remarkably well, taking such cover as the high fern and irregularities of the ground gave them. They returned the fire, but only succeeded in hitting Drummer D. Hurley in the shoulder. One rebel came up to the redoubt, and was shot within 20 yards of it. Major Butler came up with reinforcements from Mahoetahi, and ordered a charge, when the last of the rebels ran, leaving 34 dead and wounded, two of the wounded dying shortly afterwards. A flag of truce was then hoisted at Sentry Hill, and a native messenger despatched to Manutahi to tell the natives to come and bury their dead. The messenger found a large number of Ngatiawa, Taranaki, and Ngatiruanui natives there in a great state of grief at the loss they had sustained, but he could not persuade them to come up for their dead. On the messenger's return the flag of truce was hauled down and the Union Jack hoisted.

Among the rebels who fell on this occasion were Parenga Kingi, chief of Taranaki; Manahi, of the Ngamotu hapu of Ngatiawa, whose defection at Ratapihipi at the commencement of the war we have alluded to, and who was concerned in the Omata murders; Tupara Keina (Tubal Cain), chief of Ngatiawa; and Tamati Hone, head chief of Ngatiruanui.

During the time in which the foregoing events were taking place in Taranaki, General Cameron was engaged with a large force in quelling the insurrection in the Waikato, and no sooner were the northern rebels defeated than those around Taranaki began to slink back to the remoter parts of their districts.

In August, the Maori King with some of his chief people came to reside at Hapurona's pa at Te Arei, Pukerangiora.

CAPTURE OF MANUTAHI, MATAITAWA AND TE AREI.

Intelligence was received in New Plymouth on the 7th of October that the Puketapu section of the Mataitawa natives were desirous of making peace, that Wi Kingi's own people had removed to the east side of the Waitara, and that there would be no difficulty in taking possession of Manutahi and Mataitawa. Accordingly, early on Saturday morning, the 8th, a force consisting of 200 men of the 70th, under Major Ryan, two field guns in charge of Captain Martin, R.A., the Bushrangers of Captains Good and Jonas, numbering 100 men, under Major Atkinson, and Captain Mace's mounted men, started northward. At Mahoetahi they were reinforced by 150 men of the 70th, under Major Saltmarsh, the whole being under the command of Colonel Warre, C.B., who was attended by his staff, and also by Colonel Lepper and Mr. Parris. The force halted for a short time at Sentry Hill, while messengers went on to Manutahi, and shortly afterwards Colonel Warre ordered the advance, and in doing so addressed the Bushrangers telling them that as they had been often disappointed he would give them the post of honor that day, although he did not suppose it would be one of much danger. Some friendly Puketapu natives went first to see if the pa was evacuated, but when some of them were within a few yards of it they were fired upon, and retired.

In front of Manutahi there was at that time a plot of open fern land nearly surrounded with forest, and the pa was built at the south end of this where the open land was about 150 yards wide, the two ends of the pa resting on the forest. Colonel Warre divided Major Atkinson's men into two parties, sending one into the bush on the right, and the other into the bush on the left, and ordering the 70th to advance in the open land as a support. The natives in the pa fired briskly as the Bushrangers approached, but finding themselves outflanked on both sides, they broke and fled, and two of them fell as they ran out of the back of the pa, while a third was wounded and escaped.

The pa was of a very singular shape, being, as has been already stated, 150 yards long, but in the shape, of a double concave lens, 20 yards wide in the middle, but expanding in a curve towards the ends. The ditches were deep, the banks high and 12 feet thick, and had it been adequately garrisoned it would have been hard to take.

The loss on the side of the British was but slight—Private Scammel of the Bushrangers being shot through the upper part of the arm while looking through the palisading of the pa; Private Henry Turner had a very narrow escape, part of the socket of his bayonet being shot away, and the end of his revolver preventing the ball entering his hip. He and a rebel had a duel from opposite sides of the palisading.

Leaving the Bushrangers to destroy Manutahi, Colonel Warre went on with Major Saltmarsh's party of the 70th, and the mounted men and friendly natives, to Mataitawa, but no resistance was attempted there. No fortifications were found at this place.

On Tuesday morning, the 11th, at daybreak, another expedition started from Mahoetahi, where it had encamped the night before, for the purpose of taking Te Arei, Hapurona's stronghold. It consisted of 350 men of the 70th, under Majors Rutherford and Saltmarsh, and Captains Backhouse and Ralston, a detachment of Artillery under Captain Martin, Captain Mace's mounted men, and about 100 friendly natives, the whole under the command of Colonel Warre. The force crossed the Waiongona and passed No. 6 Redoubt, where a picket was left, and soon afterwards divided, one party going to the right over the burnt hill and the long hill next to it, and the other keeping straight on till some of the leading files were little more than a hundred yards from the palisading. As the troops advanced the natives were heard going through their *karakias*, and as soon as they had done these they opened fire, and after firing about twenty shots retired to safer quarters. In the meantime the force on the right, led by native guides, crossed the gully between the long hill and Te Arei, and coming up through a piece of bush entered the pa at the back without firing a shot. The pa was strong against an attack in front, having two lines of palisading, with a considerable space between them, in which were two lines of deep trenches, and a high bank which at one time formed part of the old Pukerangiora pa. But at the back the pa was so constructed that an assailant would have been under cover while the inmates of the pa would have had no shelter at all. This is the position which General Pratt endeavored to take by means of advancing redoubts, and one of the longest saps on record, and after losing a number of officers and men did not succeed in capturing it.

In a flat open space at the back of the pa a pole was standing with two circles round it, made by the feet of the Hauhaus in the practice of their Pai marire rites.

After resting awhile the friendly natives, Captain Mace's men on foot, and Captain Backhouse's company of the 70th, under Major Saltmarsh, went over the hill to the village of Pekatu. While yet a long way from this place it was observed, by the help of glasses, that there were four or five natives there performing their religious exercises round another pole. When the British got near to the village the rebels fired off their guns and retired to the little village of Pukemahoe, about 400 yards farther off across a small valley, where they got into the whares and commenced firing again, but after a short skirmish retreated again, taking with them one of their number wounded, as was shown by the blood along the road. They were followed by a few men for half a mile farther, but without effect. The people of this village, before their perversion to the Pai marire fanatacism, were probably of the Roman Catholic faith, for a portrait of St. Clotilde, a Roman Catholic Catechism, in manuscript, and other similar matters were found there. It was situate in the Waitara Valley, not far from the junction of the Manganui. After burning the whares, and picking up a few trifles, the force returned to Te Arei, where a large redoubt was in course of construction, and was shortly afterwards garrisoned by 150 men of the 70th, under Major Rutherford, No. 6 Redoubt being occupied by Captain Page's company of Military Settlers.

On September the 17th, Maxwell Lepper, Esq., late Major in the 14th Regiment, was appointed Colonel of the Taranaki Military Settlers. Mr. Lepper entered the 86th Regiment on 13th August, 1847, as ensign, and became lieutenant, by purchase, on 23rd February, 1849, and purchased his captaincy on 25th September, 1855. In 1858 he went with his Regiment to India. He was present at the siege, storming, and capture of Chandaree, and of the town and fortress of Jhansi, also at the battles of Betwa and Golowlee, the action of Koonch, and the capture of the town and fort of Calpee. Between the 15th and 21st of May, 1858, he was present during the operations before Calpee, and commanded the European infantry in the pursuing columns from Calpee. He was engaged in the battle of Morar, and in the battle before and capture of the town and fortress of Gwalior. He was thrice mentioned in despatches, and was promoted to the brevet of Major. He possessed also a medal and clasp. On the second battalion of H.M. 14th Regiment coming to New Zealand Major Lepper exchanged into it.

In October, the old Taranaki Militia was disbanded.

On the 25th of October, the Governor issued a proclamation offering a pardon to all such persons implicated in the rebellion, other than the persons charged with murdering the settlers, who should surrender themselves and take the oath of allegiance before the tenth of the succeeding December, and cede such territory as might in each case be fixed by the Governor and the Lieutenant-General commanding the forces in New Zealand.

On the 19th of November, General Cameron arrived in New

Plymouth with a reinforcement of the 43rd and 70th Regiments, and ordered the re-occupation of Tataraimaka. The General's stay was short.

On the 28th, Private Hartley of the 70th, who had gone out unarmed from the Mataitawa Redoubt was met in the bush by the rebels and decapitated.

On the 19th of December, His Honor the Superintendent returned from Auckland, whither he had been attending the session of the General Assembly, bringing with him Mr. Doyne, a civil engineer, who had served in the Army Service Corps in the Crimea, for the purpose of obtaining his opinion respecting the formation of a harbor in the Taranaki roadstead. Mr. Doyne was subsequently joined by Mr. Balfour, a marine engineer, in the service of the Provincial Government of Otago, and the two prepared a preliminary report on the subject.

On the 31st of December, Henare Ngatoke, a Urenui native, left Waitara, where he had some cultivations, to go to Kaipikari, a place on a forest covered ridge to the eastward of Waitara. His chief object in going was to see some of the people there, and to let them know of the arrival of Te Rakatau and others from the Chatham Islands. He had some misgivings before starting, for he said to his friends at leaving that if he were not back on the following day they might conclude that he was dead. He went, and on arriving near to Kaipikari he met some of the men of the place unarmed, among whom were his relatives Pitiroi and Te Retiu. When these men saw him they immediately ran for their guns, and fired at him, wounding him in the arm. He fell from his horse and attempted to run, but was fired on again and was killed. After waiting a week for his return, his wife Rina, and an adopted child, in desperation, *whaka momori*, went after him to ascertain what had become of him. On arriving at Kaipikari they were treated with far greater barbarity, being wounded, thrown into a hole and killed. The murderers were some of them the relatives of their victims, and belonged to the Manukorihi, Wi Kingi's own hapu.

In January, 1865, General Cameron, at the request of the Colonial Government, proceeded to attack the rebels at Wanganui, leaving orders at New Plymouth for Colonel Warre of the 57th to operate from Taranaki towards the south. In obedience to this instruction a force left New Plymouth on the 23rd, for the purpose of occupying Te Ngana, on the Hangatahua, or Stony River.

On the same day, Private Frank Roebuck, of the 9th Company of Military Settlers, was wantonly shot dead at the Camp at Mataitawa by a comrade named John Harris, who was afterwards convicted of manslaughter.

On the 2nd of March, the Rev. Sylvius Volkner, of the Church Mission, and formerly assistant to the Rev. J. Reimenschneider, at Warea, was barbarously murdered by the Maoris at Opotiki, on the East Coast, at the instigation of some Pai marire fanatics from Taranaki.

On the 13th of March, General Cameron, having arrived at Patea, ordered the whole of the available force there to march on Kakaramea. The 57th, under Major Butler, led the advance, followed by detachments of the 50th and 68th. When within a short distance of the pa the natives opposed their further march. After a short engagement the enemy was completely routed, leaving 33 dead. The casualties of the British were one killed and three wounded. The soldiers rushed into the pa, and found a quantity of food just cooked. They also found pork, fowls, bullocks, and about seven tons of flour.

On the 19th, a skirmish took place at Kaipikari between some friendly natives and the rebels.

On the 21st, a force embarked at New Plymouth in the s.s. Ahuriri, for Patea, consisting of 158 non-commissioned officers and men of Nos. 8 and 10 Companies of Taranaki Military Settlers, and a company of Volunteer Bushrangers, composed partly of Taranaki Bushrangers and Volunteers, and partly of Military Settlers, raised by Colonel Lepper, all armed with breech-loaders and revolvers, also the following officers :—Captains Brassey and Pennefather, Lieutenants Kirkby and Wilson, Ensigns Dalrymple and Beer, and Assistant-Surgeon Luther. The whole were under the command of Captain Hirst, who had for his subalterns, Lieutenant W. Newland, and Ensign Chapman. The steamer was not able to land the force at Patea owing to the weather, and took them on to Wanganui in order that they might march overland to Patea. The men, however, were detained at Wanganui for some time, and most of them subsequently volunteered for the East Coast, where they were joined and commanded by Captain Stapp, and performed important services.

While the General was operating on the coast he ordered several surf boats to be conveyed to the coast for the purpose of holding communications with steam vessels bringing supplies.

On the 30th of March, a boat was launched at Manawapou to go out and under-run the mooring buoy. In going out of the creek it was struck by three successive seas, and dashed to pieces against the cliffs. The crew fortunately escaped after incurring considerable danger. On April the 2nd, another boat went off from the same place to the s.s. Ahuriri with despatches, and brought ashore some cargo. The crew on landing told Major Locke that there was too much sea on to allow of the boat going off again. Shortly afterwards the steamer Gundagi arrived, and ran up her ensign " Union down." It being thought there was something the matter, at imminent risk the boat went off. All the captain wanted was to land passengers and cargo, and he adopted this *ruse* to induce the crew to launch the boat. Just as the boat left a sea swept the decks of the steamer. The boat succeeded in reaching the surf warp when she was struck by a sea and took a run. Before she could recover herself the chock was carried away, and the next sea turned her bottom upwards. Seven lives were lost. The names of the boatmen drowned were Francis McGuire, and William Graul *alias* Scotty. Of the rest, two were men of the 57th, one of the 50th, and two of the Colonial Transport Corps. On the 12th another accident happened to a surf-boat at the same place, by which three more lives were lost.

DEATH OF JOSEPH HAWKE.

On the 22nd, early in the morning, Major Colville, commanding the Camp at Stony River, directed four mounted men—Baddeley, Hawke, Reynolds, and Clements—to proceed in the direction of Warea in search of some of the Commissariat bullocks that had strayed. The party after crossing the river detected the tracks of the animals, and followed them as far as Mokotunu, where six soldiers, who had left the camp without permission, were fallen in with. One of the soldiers, named Jury, was mounted on a borrowed horse. The united parties then proceeded as far as to Waiwhiriwherua, where they turned up for a mile and a half inland. Seeing some horses they made an endeavor to capture them, but the animals taking fright, started off rapidly towards the forest. Presently two cows and a calf were met with. The cows ran towards the beach, but Hawke and Clement succeeded in making the calf fast by means of a tether line. The calf then got into a swamp, and while the men were occupied in trying to get it out some rebels appeared and fired at them. Hawke fell, and Jury rode inland and was never seen again. The rest of the Europeans, having only three revolvers amongst them, retreated, and reached the camp.

On the following day, Major Colville, with a party of the 43rd, went out to reconnoitre, and found the body of Hawke shot in several places, and with the left eye gouged out. It was conveyed to town and buried with military honors.

On the 22nd, the following force embarked in the s.s. Phœbe for the White Cliffs :—Colonel Mulock (in command), Captains Ralston and Cay, Lieutenants Gilbert and Bally, Ensign Pierson, Lieutenant and Adjutant Fenneran, 8 sergeants, 2 buglers, and 144 rank and file of the 70th Regiment; A.D.C.G. Castray, Assistant-Surgeon Jones, Lieutenant Ferguson, and 2 gunners of the Royal Artillery; Captain Jonas, Lieutenant Free, Ensign Lawson, 5 sergeants, 4 corporals, 2 buglers, and 49 rank and file of the Taranaki Bushrangers, and Mr. Parris. Owing to a storm the Volunteers and Bushrangers were not landed, but were taken on first to Auckland, and afterwards to Patea.

General Cameron did not advance northward of the Waingongoro River, but Colonel Warre took possession of Opunake, expecting the General to join him there.

An explanation of the General's slow advance may be gathered from the following memorandum by Mr. Weld, Colonial Secretary :—

" In reference to certain statements made by Lieutenant-General

Sir Duncan A. Cameron, which have been communicated by the Governor to his responsible advisers, Ministers express their regret that the Lieutenant-General should have thought fit to attribute base and unworthy motives, and a culpable disregard for the lives of British officers and men, to the Ministry of New Zealand, and by implication to Her Majesty's representative in the Colony.

"They believe that having regard to the character of the Colony, which it is their duty to uphold, and to their own, which as public men is the property of the Colony, it is impossible longer to accept assistance so unwillingly rendered. Nor, indeed, can it be hoped that the zeal and energy which alone can secure or lead to any useful results in operations in the field will be displayed by any officer, however distinguished, in support of a cause which is branded by him with such severe reprobation.

"FRED. A. WELD.

"April 8th, 1865."

At this time the Colony was placed in a dilemma. On the one hand it had a savage and unconquered foe to deal with, and on the other an unwilling General, and a demand by Mr. Cardwell, the British Minister, that the troops should be paid for. As a solution of this difficulty, Mr. Weld recommended that the Colonial Parliament should undertake a reasonable liability for troops engaged in the field, and that to the 6,000 Militia and 4,000 Military Settlers then in the North Island, a force of 1,500 Armed Constabulary should be added.

In May, a scheme for the settlement of Tikorangi was published by Major Atkinson. Two companies of Bushrangers were to be formed under Captains Jonas and Armstrong. The men were to occupy the district against the enemy till September, 1866, and were then to receive each 50 acres of rural land and a town allotment. Until put in possession of their land they were to receive 2s. 6d. per day, but after they were put in possession of their land they were to receive rations for six months longer. Afterwards it was found that there was only land enough for one company, and the other had to take land at Patea.

SKIRMISH AT WHATINO.

On the 1st of June, Lieutenant-Colonel Colville, of the 43rd Regiment, went down from Opunake to Whatino, a distance of five or six miles, with an escort of the Mounted Corps. While there some of the men expressed a wish to go a little inland to see what they could in that direction. The Colonel having no objection to their fulfilling their wishes, a small party consisting of Cornet Johnson and six men—J. Johnson, O'Neill, Olson, C. Curtis, J. Hoskin, and A. Harrison—started accordingly. After proceeding about a mile they saw six Maoris, and supposing them to be decoys the party halted. The Maoris then challenged them to come on, in abusive language. The party then put spurs to their horses and rode up to the rebels, who fired one volley at them as they advanced, and another when they closed on them. The revolvers of the British, however, did their work, and soon put the rebels to flight. On the side of the British Private O'Neill fell mortally wounded. Of the six rebels, three were left dead, or dying on the ground, and one or two of the others who escaped were wounded. Besides their wounded comrade, the party brought away three guns and a *mere pounamu*.

On the 13th of June, Colonel Warre proceeded to attack the Taranaki natives in their settlements inland of Warea. With commendable humanity, he first released a prisoner and sent him up to tell them that if they came and met him at Te Puru they would not be hurt, otherwise they must take the consequences. The ambassador was intrusted with the watch of Mr. Edward Stockman, the interpreter, in order that he might not mistake the hour allotted for his ambassage and return. As nothing was seen of the messenger or the people after the appointed time, Colonel Warre proceeded to carry out the plan of attack which he had previously arranged. The force was divided into three parties. The main division, consisting of a detatchment of the 43rd Regiment, under Colonel Colville, and the Bushrangers under Captain Jonas, went up the road from Te Ikaroa; the second division, under Major Holmes of the 43rd, went straight up to Te Puru from Warea, Colonel Warre accompanying it; and the third, consisting of a party of the 70th, under Major Russell of the 57th, went up on the north side of Warea to a village called Ngakumikumi, after destroying which this party joined the centre one. Colonel Colville's party, who were in front, passed through a mile or two of light bush, and then came upon a village, known as Okeanui. A skirmish took place here; some guns and other things were taken, the houses burnt, and the party went on through a mile or more of heavy bush and up a steep hill, when they came all at once upon Nekeua, which was an old pa with a deep trench round it, and had been recently occupied. It was palisaded against an advance from Te Puru, but not on the other side where the bush came right up to the trench. So sudden was the advance of the 43rd and the Bushrangers, that they surprised a native, named Te Meiha *alias* Big Jack, who was quietly looking through a telescope at Colonel Warre's party at Te Puru. At the first shot he jumped down into the gully, leaving his telescope and a loaded rifle behind him. The other natives fled to the bush, excepting two, who ran to the whares and closing the doors fired out through the rush walls at the British. The whares were then set on fire, and one old man was dragged out from the burning huts and saved. In the meantime Colonel Warre had advanced to Te Puru, and found the rebels running round a Pai marire pole; a slight skirmish took place, and the village was destroyed. Colonel Colville, after the destruction of Kekeua, joined Colonel Warre, and the whole force returned to Warea.

At some of the villages whares were found filled with the plunder from the Lord Worsley.

REVOCATION OF THE PROCLAMATION OF MARTIAL LAW.

[Proclamation.]
" By His Excellency Sir George Grey, Knight, &c.

" Whereas by Proclamation, bearing date 25th day of January, 1860, His Excellency Colonel Thomas Gore Browne, the Governor of the Colony of New Zealand, did proclaim and declare that MARTIAL LAW should be exercised throughout the Province of Taranaki from the date of the publication of the said Proclamation within the said Province, until the relief of the said District from Martial Law by Public Proclamation.

" And whereas it appears unto me expedient to Revoke the said Proclamation : Now therefore I, Sir George Grey, the Governor of the said Colony, in pursuance and exercise of all powers and authorities in this behalf enabling me, Do hereby declare the aforesaid Proclamation of the 25th of January, 1860, to be and the same is hereby revoked. And I do further Proclaim and declare that this Proclamation shall take effect on and after the first day of August, 1865.

" Given at Wellington, &c.,
" This first day of July, 1865,
" G. GREY."

ENGAGEMENT AT WAREA.

On Friday, July the 28th, Captain Close of the 43rd Regiment, stationed at the Warea Redoubt, went with a party of 40 or 50 men into one of the forest clearings, inland of Warea, for the purpose of getting firewood, when he was suddenly fired upon by a party of rebels in ambush. Captain Close and Corporal Hanaghan fell mortally wounded, and a private and a native named Hemi, who was with the party, were slightly wounded. The troops immediately opened out in skirmishing order, and drove the natives back. On the following morning, a force of 300 men left New Plymouth for the purpose of chastising these rebels.

On Wednesday, the 2nd of August, a party paraded at Warea, at 3 a.m., consisting of 100 men of the 43rd and 140 of the 70th, under Lieutenant-Colonel Colville and Captain Cay, Lieutenants Bally, Tylden, and Howard, Surgeon Turner, 43rd Regiment, Captain Mace of the Volunteers, and 150 men of the 70th Regiment. The Hon. Captain Harris, Lieutenants Talbot and Langley, and Assistant-Surgeon Grant, 43rd Regiment, also accompanied the force. The party proceeded as far as Kapoaiaia, where it separated into two divisions, that under Major Russell turned inland and took the track for Okea, and that under Colonel Colville proceeded down the coast and turned inland for the purpose of reaching a place called Kairuru, where it was supposed the natives were. It was believed that a track ran from Kairuru to Okea, and the plan was that after Colonel Colville had driven the rebels out of Kairuru, they should be cut off by Major Russell's party. Major Russell reached Okea about 7 a.m., and going to the top of some high hills that commanded the flat, smoke was seen in the dense scrub at a distance of about 500 yards. Captain Cay was at once sent with 60 men to reconnoitre; and after getting through the bush, found himself close to about twenty whares. The natives were completely surprised, and at first made no resistance. Eleven Maoris were bayonetted in the open, and a large number more must have fallen in the dense scrub and in the whares. Five were taken prisoners. The loss the 70th sustained in this place was one man shot dead, and Lieutenant Tylden severely wounded in the hand and face. Captain Cay's party then returned to the reserve with their wounded and prisoners. Whilst Dr. Turner was examining the wounded, the natives exchanged a few shots with the party, and a skirmish ensued, the rebels fighting with determination and aiming with remarkable precision.

After destroying the native position the force retired, but was galled in its retreat by swarms of rebels on its flanks, who sought *utu* for their slain. During the retreat Lieutenant Bally, while in command of the rear guard, fell, a bullet entering his side, and causing almost instantaneous death. The troops retired to camp at 1.30, and during the march three of the prisoners, in attempting to escape, were shot.

Colonel Colville, hearing the firing, forced his way through a narrow track, guided by Minarapa, and having got on the same road as Major Russell had traversed, fell in with six natives, and shot five of them, two of whom were recognised by Minarapa as chiefs. The casualties of the British on this occasion were as follows:—Killed—Lieutenant Bally, Privates Smith, Brown, and Ralph. Wounded—Lieutenant Tylden, severely; Privates Laughton, severely; Royal, severely; Saville, severely; Ward, dangerously; Maley, dangerously.

On the following day, Colonel Colville with his party returned to the scene of the engagement, and burnt some whares, during which the rebels killed Private S. Bolton, one of his outlying sentries.

On the 1st of August, Lieutenant-General Sir Duncan Cameron resigned the command of the Army in New Zealand, and was succeeded by Major-General Trevor Chute. This resignation had become necessary by the strange conduct of General Cameron in remaining for a long time inactive with a force of 10,000 men under his command, writing secret despatches to the Imperial Government, and complaining that the Colonial Government were regardless of the lives of the officers and men of the Army.

On the 9th of August, the Colonial steam transport Alexandra, having sprung a leak by striking on a rock, was beached at the White Cliffs, where she became a total wreck.

On the 2nd of September, the Governor proclaimed peace to all the Maoris who had taken part in the rebellion on the West Coast, excepting the murderers.

On the 4th of September, Mr. H. R. Richmond was elected Superintendent of the Province.

On the 14th of October, the New Plymouth Building Society was established.

On the 20th, Captain Mace, with a small party of the Mounted Corps, was fired on by an ambuscade of about thirty rebels at the three hills between Warea and the Hangatahua River, which slightly wounded him, and struck W. Bullot in the neck, and W. Oxenham in the foot.

On the same day, Major-General Chute arrived in New Plymouth in order to consult Colonel Warre as to a plan of operations.

On the 22nd, before day-break, Colonel Colville, with a force of 83 men of the 43rd, Captain Hon. J. Harris, Lieutenants Langley and O'Brien, and Captain Mace and a party of the Mounted Corps, marched out to chastise the rebeles who had fired on Captain Mace's party on the 20th at the three hills. A skirmish ensued, in which Sergeant Clifford and Private Pratt were killed, and Colonel Colville and Sergeant Dyer were wounded.

On the 9th of December, Major Stapp returned from Opotiki, having resigned the command there to Colonel Lyons, on whose assumption of command the following orders were issued :—

"Lieutenant-Colonel Lyons has much pleasure in publishing the following communication received from the Hon. the Defence Minister, dated Wellington, 13th November, 1865 : ' I am at the same time to request you will convey to Major Stapp the thanks of the Government for the zeal, ability, and discretion with which he has performed very arduous and important duties, from the time he joined the force, and especially since he assuumed the chief command.'

"J. HOLT,
" Captain and Under Secretary."

" In giving over the command of the Expeditionary Force, I feel it incumbent on me to express my thanks to the officers and men composing it for the ready manner in which they have co-operated with me on all occasions in the performance of very arduous duties, and more particularly for the gallantry they have displayed whenever engaged with the enemy. I sincerely regret parting from a force with which I have served for upwards of three months, with great satisfaction to myself, and in doing so heartily wish it every success in the future, whether with the sword or the plough.

"C. STAPP."

At this period the embarkation of the Imperial Forces for England commenced, the first regiments to leave being the 70th and 65th. At the end of the year the Imperial force in the Colony consisted of ten regiments, embodying 10,000 men; the regiments being the 12th, 14th, 18th, 40th, 43rd, 50th, 57th, 65th, and 70th, two Batteries of Field Artillery, with Engineers and Military Train. There were also at this time four ships of war in New Zealand waters, namely: the Curaçoa, Eclipse, Esk, and Miranda.

CHAPTER XXV.

CONFISCATION OF LANDS AND ESTABLISHMENT OF MILITARY SETTLEMENTS.

OWING to the extreme reluctance with which military aid was granted by the Imperial Government to New Zealand during the Native Rebellion, the demand made for payment for the troops, the inactivity of General Cameron and his extraordinary attempts to interfere politically with the Colonial Government, it became necessary for the latter to adopt measures for the pacification of the country. In this emergency, Mr. Domett suggested the establishment of a series of outposts around the unsettled districts, garrisoned by military settlers, who were to combine within themselves the profession of arms and agriculture, and were to receive lands as a recompence for their military service, and pay and rations until they had subdued the enemy around them and firmly established themselves. In order to carry out this project, an Act intituled "An Act to enable the Governor to establish Settlements for Colonisation in the Northern Island of New Zealand," was passed on the 3rd of December 1863, which provided that, " Whenever the Governor in Council shall be satisfied that any Native tribe or section of a tribe, or any considerable number thereof, has since the first day of January, 1863, been engaged in rebellion against Her Majesty's authority, it shall be lawful for the Governor in Council to declare that the district within which any land being the property or in the possession of such tribe or section or considerable number thereof shall be situate, shall be a district within the provisions of this Act, and the boundaries of such district in like manner to define and vary as he shall think fit. That it shall be lawful for the Governor in Council from time to time to set apart within any such district eligible sites for settlements for colonisation, and the boundaries of such settlements to define and vary. That for the purposes of such settlements, the Governor in Council may from time to time reserve or take any land within such district, and such land shall be deemed to be Crown land, freed and discharged from all title, interest, or claim of any person whomsoever, as soon as the Governor in Council shall have declared that such land is required for the purposes of this Act and is subject to the provisions thereof."

Shortly after the passing of this Act, agents were employed to enlist men for military service in the Province from among the gold miners of Otago and Melbourne.

On the 30th of December, 1863, the Choice arrived at New Plymouth from Melbourne *viâ* Lyttelton, with 40 volunteers for this service.

On the 16th of January, 1864, the s.s. Phœbe brought Captain

17

Edward Carthew and 29 volunteers from Otago.

On February the 13th, the ship Gresham brought from Melbourne Lieutenants Pennefather and Sisson, Ensign Roddy, and 420 volunteers.

On the 17th of February, the barque Brilliant brought from Melbourne Lieutenants Kirkby, Clark, Gascoigne and Jackson, Mrs. Kirkby, and two children. These were followed by others at various times.

"PROCLAMATION.

"PROCLAIMING CERTAIN LANDS UNDER THE NEW ZEALAND SETTLE-
MENTS ACT, 1863.

"By His Excellency Sir George Grey, K.C.B., &c.

"Whereas by the New Zealand Settlements Act, 1863, it was enacted among other things that whenever the Governor in Council shall be satisfied that any native tribe, or section of a tribe, or any considerable number thereof, have since the 1st of January, 1863, been engaged in rebellion against Her Majesty's authority, it shall be lawful for the Governor in Council to declare that the district within which any land being the property or in possession of such tribe, or section, or considerable number thereof, shall be situate, shall be a district within the provisions of the said Act, and the boundaries of such district in like manner to define and vary as he shall think fit:

"And whereas the Governor in Council is satisfied that certain native tribes, or sections of tribes, having landed properties and possessions in the lands described in the Schedules hereunder written, have been engaged in rebellion against Her Majesty's authority:

"Now, therefore, I, Sir George Grey, the Governor as aforesaid, in exercise of the power vested in me by the said recited Act, do hereby, with the advice and consent of the Executive Council of the Colony, set apart as an eligible site for settlement for colonisation the lands described in the Schedule to this Proclamation, being lands described within the said proclaimed district of Middle Taranaki, and the Governor doth declare that the lands described in the said Schedule are required for the purposes of the said Act, and are subject to the provisions thereof, and doth reserve and take such land for such purposes as aforesaid.

"Given under my hand and seal, at the Government House, Auckland, and issued under the seal of the Colony of New Zealand, this 30th day of January, in the year of our Lord, 1865.

"G. GREY.

"GOD SAVE THE QUEEN."

[SCHEDULE.]

"MIDDLE TARANAKI.

"All that block of land at Taranaki bounded on the north and west by the sea, on the east by the Waitara River from its mouth to the

the Waitara to the crossing place of the Kairoa and Waimate Road, junction of the Manganui River, and by the Manganui River from thence on the south by the said road to its junction with the Wanganui and Taranaki coast road, and thence by a straight line from the said junction of roads to the sea at its nearest point; excepting all lands within the said boundaries held under Grant from the Crown."

Similar proclamations at the same date were issued respecting lands in Waitara South and Oakura, described in the following Schedules:—

WAITARA SOUTH.

All that block of land at Taranaki bounded on the north by the sea, on the east by the Waitara River, from its mouth to the junction of the Manganui River; on the south by a straight line from the junction of the Manganui and Waitara Rivers to Tarurutangi on the Waiongona River, and on the west by a straight line to the sea at Waitaha; excepting lands within the above described boundaries held under Grants from the Crown.

OAKURA.

Bounded on the north by the sea, on the east by the Omata Block from the sea to where the boundary of the Omata Block is cut by the native pa running between the Patua and Pouakai ranges, thence by a straight line running between the above mentioned ranges till it cuts the Haugatahua river, thence by the Hangatahua River to the sea, except the block of land known by the name of Tataraimaka.

On the 2nd of September the following districts were proclaimed:—

NGATIAWA.

Bounded on the north-west and north by the sea from the mouth of the River Waitara to the tunnel at Parininihi, and thence by a straight line in a direction due east (true bearing) for a distance of 20 miles; on the south-east by a straight line from the eastern extremity of the said northern boundary in a direction south 39 degrees west (true) till it intersects the straight line between the summit of Mount Egmont and Parikino on the Wanganui River; on the south by the said last named straight line from its intersection with the said south-eastern boundary to its intersection with the Kairoa and Waimate Road; on the west by the eastern boundary of the Middle District of Taranaki proclaimed under the New Zealand Settlements Act, 1863, from the point last named to the commencing point at the mouth of the River Waitara.

NGATIRUANUI.

On the north-east by a straight line bearing on the summit of Mount Egmont, commencing at the Kairoa and Waimate Road and drawn thence to Parikino on the River Wanganui; on the east by the said river to the sea; on the south-west by the sea from the mouth of the said River Wanganui to the Waimate stream; and on the west by the said Kairoa and Waimate Road from the said Waimate stream, which last or western boundary is also part of the eastern boundary of the said district of Middle Taranaki; excepting all lands held by or under the Crown prior to the date of this Proclamation.

NGATIAWA COAST.

Bounded on the west and north-west by a line drawn straight from the summit of Mount Egmont to the source of the River Waiongona, thence along the said River Waiongona to Tarurutangi, thence straight to the junction of the Rivers Manganui and Waitara, thence along the said Waitara to the sea, thence along the sea-coast to the tunnel at Parininihi; on the north by a straight line in a direction due east (true) from the said tunnel at Parininihi for a distance of 20 miles; on the south-east by a straight line drawn from the eastern extremity of the said northern boundary in a direction south 39 degrees west, till it intersects the straight line between the summit of Mount Egmont and Parikino on the Wanganui River; and on the south-west by the said straight line last named from its intersection with the said south-eastern boundary to the summit of Mount Egmont.

NGATIRUANUI COAST.

Bounded on the north by the River Hangatahua from its mouth to the southern angle of the Oakura district, and thence by a straight line passing between the Poukai and Patua (Kaitake) Ranges to the point where the Native path passing in the same direction intersects the south-western boundary of the Tapuae Block to the River Mangoraka, thence by the said River Mangoraka to its source, thence by a straight line to the summit of Mount Egmont, and thence by a straight line to Parikino on the River Wanganui; on the south-east by the said River Wanganui from Parikino to the sea, and on the south-west by the sea from the mouth of the said River Wanganui to the mouth of the said River Hangatahua; excepting all lands within the said boundaries held by or under the Crown prior to the date of this Proclamation.

The total area of land north of the Waingongoro River confiscated under orders in Council and dealt with under the New Zealand Settlements and Continuance Acts was 934,325 acres. Of this area, 47,800 acres were laid out as Military Settlements; viz., 45,681 acres as rural lands, 1,115 acres as suburban, and 1,004 in townships. The districts were Pukearuhe, Urenui, Tikorangi, Huirangi, Manganui, Mataitawa, Manutahi, Oakura, Koru, Ahuahua, and Okato. Of the total area confiscated, 35,000 acres were allotted to the Military Settlers, 6,622 acres were returned to the natives or reserved for their use, and the remainder was allotted for education and other reserves, or devoted to roads.

South of the Waingongoro River, an area of about 50,000 acres was laid out in military settlements, forming collectively the Patea district, the towns being Kakaramea, Ohawe, and Makoia. It was hoped at the time when these settlements were established that the men when released from military duty would settle down upon their allotments, and becoming permanent settlers in the Province would tend by their numbers to ensure peace and security; but from a variety of causes the Military Settlements scheme did not result in the immediate permanent increase in the population anticipated, and even before the expiration of the three years residence required to establish a title to the land allotted under their terms of service, a large proportion of the original military settlers had left the Province, settlers, and the sons of settlers, taking their place in the corps, and the reversion of their land as substitutes.

In 1866, when the prescribed three years of service had elapsed and the men became entitled to a grant of their allotments unfettered by any conditions, the great majority of the military settlers then remaining in the Province either sold or mortgaged their land and left, and by the end of 1867 probably not more than a tenth part of the men introduced under the Military Settlements regulations remained in the Province. Of the eleven towns laid out north of the Waingongoro, the majority had not a single house upon them, whilst the most populous could scarcely boast of a dozen. The bulk of the rural allotments had passed into the hands of settlers. One great cause of this general exodus was that when the Military Settlements scheme was adopted the great requirement of the colony was men, and the immediate exigency of this requirement was such that there was no time to select men who might be expected to utilize their land beneficially and become permanent settlers. But the chief cause of the departure of numbers of those who would have proved themselves useful Colonists, was the total inability of the Provincial Government after the settlements had been handed over to the Province either to provide work for these men, or to open communication between their allotments and the settled centres of the district. Isolated from the original settlement, and without any employers of labor among them, the men had no other alternative in most cases than to part with their land, more especially as the financial position of the Province was such that little could be done to aid them in opening up the roads and bridging the streams. .

So severely was this strain on the Provincial Treasury felt, even in the little that was accomplished in respect of opening up roads through confiscated lands, that although the military settlements were handed over fully surveyed and with a fair population located on them, without expense to the Province, yet the expense actually incurred, or estimated as being necessary for opening road communication between them and the original settlement, constituted the chief groundwork of all the applications from the Province to the General Government for financial aid. By degrees, however, these lands have been traversed by roads, and though the original Military Settlers no longer occupy them, they are rapidly being utilised, either for cultivations or pasture, and support a fair and increasing population. These remarks apply equally to the magnificent Patea district, now the most flourishing portion of the Province.

In addition to the military settlements, and in order to keep up the line of communication between them and New Plymouth, blocks were laid out at Waitara, including the town of Raleigh and suburban districts of Waitara East and West, at Opunake, and on the Patea River at Carlyle. At various times auction sales of town and suburban allotments in these localities were held, and over 20,000 acres of land sold in the Taranaki County District, realising over £10,000.

During the years from 1868 to 1871, great expectations were entertained of the phormium trade, and large works were erected at Opunake, the centre of a very extensive flax district, involving an expenditure of several thousand pounds by the projectors and undertakers of this industry. Had the results hoped for been realised, the district would have progressed rapidly, as the natives showed every disposition to throw open their lands to capitalists; but unfortunately the trade collapsed, and the site of the town of Opunake was for a long period all but deserted by Europeans. The only acquired rural land is an area of 735 acres, formerly allotted to Major C. Brown and Captain R. C. Hammerton for services in connection with Militia and Volunteers.

By a special arrangement with Military Settlers, the settlements of Hawera and Manutahi-Patea were formed, the Government granting 10 acres of land to each man who would consent to hold the positions in those localities. Flourishing towns are now springing up in those districts, the town of Carlyle having been established by Government, and that of Normanby and others in the Patea County by private speculation.

Under the several Acts bearing on the confiscated lands, powers were reserved to His Excellency the Governor to return portions of these lands to the natives, and to make reserves for native and other purposes within their boundaries. There has accordingly been returned to natives in this district, or reserved for them, an area of about 170,000 acres.

It was perceived at an early date that the most judicious course which could be adopted in dealing with the confiscated lands would be to promote their settlement and occupation as speedily as possible, and various schemes were propounded with a view to this end.

In the years 1865 and 1866, a lengthened correspondence was carried on between the Ministry and His Honor H. R. Richmond, the Superintendent of the Province, on the subject of the settlement of the confiscated lands, an offer being made by the Government that the Provincial authorities should take over and administer them as part of the territorial estate. Among the letters which passed is one from the Hon. Sir Julius Vogel to the Hon. E. Stafford, dated 14th September, 1865, forwarding a scheme for the speedy utilization and settlement of the districts acquired by confiscation, and which is farther interesting as containing the first germs of the

Immigration and Public Works Policy, since inaugurated under the administration of the writer of the letter. This communication, favorably reported on by the Superintendents of Auckland and Wellington, was, with the correspondence between the Ministry and the Superintendent, laid before the Provincial Council of Taranaki, when a resolution was carried to the effect that it was not expedient to recommend the adoption of the scheme proposed. In fact, such was the condition of the Provincial Revenue, and so avowed was the impotence at that time of the Province to utilize these lands, that nothing could be done to further their settlement; nor were the Provincial authorities in a more favorable situation financially even at a later date had not the General Government intervened.

The insuperable difficulties with which the Provincial Government had to contend were : firstly, the question of unmolested occupation being secured to purchasers. It was felt that purchasers of lands within the confiscated boundaries would require some farther and stronger guarantee than that of the Provincial Government of the acquiesence of the former native owners of the soil in its confiscation and subsequent sale, and that such guarantee could be given only by the lands being administered by the General Government of the Colony. Secondly, the financial position of the Province was such that even if the land had been handed over free from native encumbrances yet the preliminary cost of surveys—no inconsiderable item in forest lands—and of opening up communications by roads, would have been beyond the resources of the Provincial exchequer. Under these circumstances the bulk of the confiscated lands in the Taranaki district remained unutilized until in 1873 the Government adopted the system of obtaining the concurrence of all natives interested in any block of land subject to the confiscation proclamations in its alienation, paying a certain amount of compensation to dispossessed owners not implicated in the rebellion. Under this system land to a very considerable extent has been acquired in the district within the boundaries of the confiscation, the title to which is clear and uncontested.

The Moa, Waitara-Taramouku, Kopua, Pukemahoe, Onaero-Urenui-Taramoukou-Ruapekapeka, Waipuku, Waipuku-Patea, Manganui-Te Wera, Huiroa, Otoia, Ahuroa-Ratapiko-Manawawiri-Mangaotuku, Mangaehu, Kataroa No. 1, and Pukekino, in all about 253,000 acres, have been handed over to the Provincial authorities, and since the Abolition of Provincial Institutions to the Waste Lands Board, to be dealt with as Waste Lands of the Crown. Other lands have also been acquired but are not yet handed over.

The Waste Lands Board, constituted under the Taranaki Waste Lands Act, 1874, and recognised by the Land Act, 1877, the Commissioner of Crown Lands, Mr. Charles Douglas Whitcombe, being its chairman, and Messrs. William Morgan Crompton, Thomas Kelly, Arthur Standish, and William Neilson Syme its members, commenced proceedings in January, 1875, and its first land sale was held on the 20th of February in that year. Since that date other sales of rural, suburban, and town lands in the Moa and other acquired districts have been held, a special feature in which has been the sale of portions on terms of deferred payments.

On the 23rd of January, the town of Inglewood, in the Moa district, was established by the Provincial Government; and in December, 1877, the village of Waipuku, and the town of Stratford on Patea, by the Waste Lands Board.

Besides these transactions, arrangements were made with Colonel Robert Trimble, a gentleman who arrived from England in 1875, for the purpose of settling in Taranaki, for the sale to him of 2,000 acres of land, under the 66th Clause of the Taranaki Waste Lands Act, 1874, in which provision was made for special settlements. In 1876, a block of 2,000 acres was sold by the Government to Messrs. Jones and McMillan, and in 1877 Mr. A. Cracroft Fookes was permitted to take up 5,000 acres on the Mountain Road, under certain conditions, for the purpose of forming the Midhirst Special Settlement.

CHAPTER XXVI.

THE CONCLUSION OF THE WAR.

GENERAL CHUTE, on taking the command of the forces in New Zealand, determined on crushing the rebellion and avenging the murders which had been perpetrated on the West Coast. The return of the Volunteers and Native Contingent from the East Coast afforded him a favorable opportunity for prosecuting this design, and on Saturday, the 30th of December, 1865, he marched from Wanganui with the following force :—
Royal Artillery, commanded by Lieutenant Carre, 1 subaltern, 2 sergeants, and 30 gunners; H.M. 14th Regiment—1 captain, 1 subaltern, 4 sergeants and 101 rank and file; Native Contingent, under Major McDonnell, consisting of about 200 men of all arms; Transport Corps—45 drivers, 45 drays with two horses each. At Wereroa the force was joined by the Forest Rangers, under Major Von Tempsky, numbering 45 men.
On the 2nd of January, Dr. Featherstone, the Superintendent of Wellington, accompanied by several influential native chiefs joined the force, and on the following day the force was again strengthened by a detachment of the second battalion of the 14th Regiment, commanded by Lieutenant-Colonel Trevor, and consisting of 1 subaltern, 4 sergeants, 6 buglers, and 120 rank and file.
On the 4th of January, the force marched upon Okotuku, a strong position on the top of a forest clad hill, which was taken without much difficulty, but most of its rebel defenders escaped during the assault into the forest, where they were unsuccessfully pursued by Major Von Tempsky and the Forest Rangers.
On the 6th, the General with his men marched upon Putahi, a strong rebel position on the banks of the Whenuakura River, and at daybreak on the 7th the pa was assaulted and taken without much loss on the side of the assailants.
On the 9th, the General marched towards Otapawa. On the 11th, the force was joined by Lieutenant-Colonel Hassard, with 120 men of the 57th Regiment.
On the next day the united force marched to Ketemarae, and encamped at 4 p.m. within a mile of Otapawa, where it was joined by Lieutenant-Colonel Butler of the 57th. Here the house, called Taiporohenui, where the Land League was established, was taken and destroyed.
At 2 a.m. on the 18th of January, the following force marched for the attack upon Otapawa: —Royal Artillery—3 guns, with the necessary complement of gunners and drivers; 14th Regiment—200 men, under Lieutenant-Colonel Trevor; 57th Regiment—180 men, under Lieutenant-Colonel Butler; Forest Rangers—36 men, under Major Von Tempsky; Native Contingent—200 men, under Major

McDonnell. The pa was garrisoned by 300 rebels, who were mostly concealed in rifle pits, but it was taken in twenty minutes, and consigned to the flames. The enemy's loss was 50 killed, and a proportionate number wounded. The British casualties were severe, nine being killed, among whom was Lieutenant-Colonel Hassard, who fell while bravely leading his men to the attack, and 14 wounded, including Major McDonnell.

At 2 a.m. on the 15th, the force was again on the march, the Native Contingent being under the command of Ensign McDonnell, the brother of Major McDonnell, who was wounded at Otapawa, the advance on this occasion being made on Ketemarae. The native settlement of Ketemarae was one of the oldest and most venerated villages in New Zealand. It formed a converging point for several paths, leading to various parts of the island, was a halting place for travellers, and a centre for the dissemination of news. The pas in this neighborhood were found to be deserted and all were burned, but a body of rebels made an unsuccessful attempt to cut off a straggling party of the assailants.

THE MARCH THROUGH THE FOREST.

On the 17th of January, General Chute with his force commenced to march from Ketemarae through the forest on the east side of Mount Egmont to New Plymouth. We have already mentioned that in pre-colonial times the natives had a path leading from Pukerangiora, on the banks of the Waitara, to the shores of Cooke's Strait, and that the Brothers Nairn, with gangs of natives under instructions from Mr. Wicksteed, the New Zealand Company's Agent, cut a bridle path along this route, but at this time these forest paths, by the growth of vegetation and by disuse, had become nearly obliterated. At 4 a.m., the General marched from Ketemarae, with 240 men of all ranks, of whom 54 were Forest Rangers, and 68 members of the Native Contingent. The transport service consisted of 67 pack horses, with their drivers, and 24 saddle horses. General Chute advanced in front, accompanied by the following staff:—Colonel Carey, D.A.G.; Lieutenant-Colonel Gamble, D.Q.M.G.; Major Pitt, A.M.S.; Captain Leach, acting A.D.C.; Mr. Commissary Strickland; Surgeon Gibbs, and Dr. Featherstone, Superintendent of Wellington. Each man carried a water-proof sheet, a blanket, a great coat, and two days' supply of biscuits. The entrance into the forest was a broad dray track, which led through a succession of small plantations with several whares in them; and fences, whares, and everything combustible were set on fire as the force proceeded onward. During the day they crossed four gullies, two considerable streams, and made about $9\frac{1}{2}$ miles journey.

On the 18th they started at 5.30 a.m., the Forest Rangers forming the advanced guard, and the 14th the rear guard. The forest now became more dense and difficult of passage, and the supplejacks *Ripogonum scandens*, formed a net work which had to be cut away.

On approaching the Patea River, gullies became numerous and deep, and the underwood still more dense. The river was crossed at noon, and the force then halted till 3 p.m., in order to allow the baggage to come up. The men then marched three miles farther, having cut their way through thirteen miles of forest, crossed one river and thirteen gullies.

On Friday, the 19th of January, the force started at 7.30 a.m., the men having had time to take a good breakfast, and to give the horses a little food to prepare them for the difficulties of the day. The Forest Rangers again formed the advanced guard, leading the column, and cutting a passable road, working with a good will, bridging swamps and gullies, and cutting passages round the fallen monarchs of the forest. The best and most easily obtained material for road making was found to be the trunks of tree-ferns, which when laid side by side gave a firm footing to the horses over the swampy places. The force halted at 3 p.m. on the banks of the Maketawa River, a clear and rapid stream, conveniently shallow, and about seventy feet wide. The pack horses did not arrive at the camping place till 6 p.m. The force this day passed one of the worst gullies yet met with, and six rivers in a march of six miles. Provisions now began to run short, but the horses were in good condition, and being relieved of their burden of rations were loaded with the men's bundles.

On Saturday the 20th, the force again moved at 7.30, the weather being gloomy, and nothing but a leaden sky to be seen through the dense foliage over head. Anxious to see where they were, Ensign Churchward of the 14th, and several men of the force, climbed the trees, and discovered that the peak of Egmont bore S.W., proving that the force had pushed its way well round it. This evening the last of the rations were served out. The supply would have lasted longer had not the natives desired their full supply at starting, part of which they left behind them. Fifteen gullies and seven rivers were passed this day, and a journey made of eleven and a half miles. Two objects were now very desirable of attainment—to reach supplies and convey them to the troops. In order to reach these ends, Mr. Commissary Price bravely volunteered to start that night for Mataitawa in the Taranaki district, and Captain Leach and Ensign McDonnell, with ten of his ablest natives, also volunteered their services. This heroic little party started before the pack horses came up, and had little or no provisions for their journey, and no track over the gullies and precipices in the benighted forest. The rain fell in torrents, but they pushed on until Mr. Price became so exhausted, that he had to lie down under a tree. Covering him with a blanket, and giving him a wet biscuit, his comrades left him in his damp and dreary couch while they pushed onwards. They made but five miles during the night, but by 10 a.m. on the following day they had the satisfaction of reaching Mataitawa. Here with alacrity provisions were obtained and forced into the forest, but meanwhile 400 men had divided their last biscuit, and were doubtful as to the success of the forlorn hope which had pushed forward. Without tents or provisions, they had bivouacked in the forest during that wet and dismal night, yet not a murmur escaped from any, nor was there a sick man in the whole force.

On Sunday, the march was resumed, but the day was wet and gloomy, and the Forest Rangers were worn out with the pioneering work. Working parties of the 14th, under Colonel Carey, were now sent to the front. Fifteen gullies and four rivers were crossed this day, and at 3.30 p.m. the force halted, after performing a march of four miles. The General, who had exerted himself all day in bringing up up the rear, did not reach the camp till 9 p.m. This evening one of the horses was killed for a meat ration. By the prudent foresight of Mr. Strickland the men had received a half ration of rum in the morning, and still had a little biscuit left. They stowed themselves away under trees and brushwood as best they could, but during the night it rained so heavily that refreshing sleep was out of the question.

The morning of the 22nd broke gloomily over the force, and the fates seemed to have declared against them. Beneath was a quagmire, and above a constant shower of rain. The Native Contingent, driven by want of food through their own imprudence, ran through the forest on the previous day, and some of the Rangers with them, so that this morning not a brown skin was seen among the force in the foodless forest. The horses showing signs of fatigue a halt was ordered, and a day's rest taken. At night another horse was killed for rations, his heart being reserved for the General. That evening Captain Leach returned from Mataitawa, leading a party of the 43rd and 68th, under Lieutenant Palmer, laden with supplies of biscuits and groceries.

On the 23rd, being the seventh day of their journey in the forest, and the 3rd day of the rain, the troops had a comfortable breakfast, and started at 7 a.m. Before ten, a messenger met the advanced guard, announcing that two fat bullocks, biscuit, rum, and groceries were coming on, and were only a few miles a-head. When the column reached the camping ground at 3 p.m., the men were abundantly supplied with fresh meat, biscuit, and groceries. During their eight hours' march the troops had crossed twenty-one gullies and three rivers, and had made but six miles, wading deeply in mud.

On the 24th, the weather was still gloomy, and the land very soft and wet. Six gullies were crossed this day, and an advance made of four miles.

On the 25th, a march of five miles without a gully brought the force out of the forest. The sun shone warmly and brightly upon the men and refreshed them. At 10.30 a.m. they halted in the Mataitawa valley, enjoying the warmth of the sun, and drying their clothes and blankets. At noon the men fell in, and marched to the Waiwakaiho, where they encamped. The weather was fine, and arrangements were made by Colonel Carey with the Military Store

Department in New Plymouth for the supply of such comforts as the men required.

On the 27th, at 10 a.m., General Chute at the head of his force marched into New Plymouth on his return southward by the coast. Here a substantial dinner was set before the men, and beneath a triumphal arch erected over the Huatoki Bridge the General was met by the Superintendent of Taranaki, and the leading men of New Plymouth, and presented with the following address :—

"To Major-General Trevor Chute, Commanding Her Majesty's Forces in New Zealand.

"Sir :—I have been deputed by the inhabitants of this settlement to express to you their sense of the benefit you have conferred on them, and on the Colony, by the operations just now successfully concluded between Wanganui and Waitara. Without entering on any invidious questions, it is allowable for us to state the fact that the recent march through the bush inland of Mount Egmont is the first in which a large body of regular troops have been led for several days together through the difficult forests of New Zealand. Having from the beginning of the present troubles maintained that the war could not be ended, beyond the chance of re-kindling, until our forces should habitually penetrate the bush in pursuit of the enemy, it is peculiarly gratifying to us to see the happy issue of these first bold movements, and we are bound to acknowledge the practical sagacity which dictated and the courage which undertook and executed the operations. But we have not merely to admire the plan and conduct of the operations—we have to thank you warmly for the vigorous course you have adopted, as closely affecting our personal interests. At this particular moment the matter is of special importance to us. The war, which has languished on for six years, has taxed the treasure and the patience of the empire beyond endurance, without effecting its object—the establishment of law and order; and whilst the empire is weary, the colony seems to be on the eve of financial and political convulsions, mainly from the same cause. The extinction of the struggle this summer may yet arrest the threatened evils, or at least place the settlements of the North Island in a condition of strength and security, which will render constitutional changes less utterly destructive of prosperity and hope than they would be at present. The capture of Okotuku, Putahi, Otapawa, and Ketemarae, and the march in the rear of Mount Egmont will contribute greatly to this result. These operations have shown that against British forces, regular and irregular, New Zealand has no impregnable fortresses; they have shown that British courage, and British arms, can penetrate wherever man can hide; that there is no security for rebellion; and that the only course open to the hostile natives is frank submission to the just and equal law which the Empire and the Colony hold out for their acceptance.

"In the name of the settlers of Taranaki I beg to thank you for the wise and courageous course you have taken, and the officers and men under your command who have so gallantly and successfully carried out your plans.

"H. R. RICHMOND,
"Superintendent of Taranaki.
"New Plymouth, January 27th, 1866."

General Chute having courteously accepted the address and replied to it, the force moved on, and at 3 p.m. reached Oakura, where it encamped for the night.

On the 28th, the force resumed its march across Tataraimaka and Okato, and encamped at the Stony River.

On the 29th, the General was reinforced by 70 men of the 43rd, and by Captain Mace's Mounted Corps. At noon, Warea was reached, and Ensign McDonnell with his Native Contingent was ordered to scour the country, and, if possible, find the track leading to the Warea pa.

At 3 a.m. on the 1st of February, the General moved silently out of camp, with a force of 450 men of all ranks, to attack Waikoko, a strongly fortified position, situated about six miles inland. At daylight he met Captain Corbett's party at a place previously appointed. Emerging from the scrub and dense bush the force reached a large clearing, at a point about 500 yards distant from the pa. The 14th were on the right, the 43rd on the left, the Forest Rangers in the centre, all in skirmishing order, and the Native Contingent formed the reserve. The enemy silently watched the movements of the force until the General ordered the advance, when a heavy fire was opened from the pa, which was responded to by a British cheer, and a charge which soon drove the rebels from their position. The whares were soon in flames, and Waikoko was speedily a mass of ruins. Only four dead bodies were found. On the side of the British, one man of the 14th was shot dead, and a sergeant of Corbett's Rangers and two friendly natives wounded.

On the 2nd, the force reached Te Namu, where some prisoners were taken, and other natives took the oath of allegiance.

On the 6th, the force reached Patea, and on the 7th the campaign ended, after active service of five weeks and two days.

While General Chute was passing through the bush, Lieutenant-Colonel Butler of the 57th was operating with a flying column on the coast from the camp at the Waingongoro. On the 18th of January he moved out of camp with one field gun, 200 men of the 50th and 97th Regiments, and about 120 friendly natives, and proceeded in the direction of Oukuti, which he found destroyed. He then went to Tiwitiri Moana, where three bodies were discovered, one being that of Hohepa, a chief of considerable importance. This pa was destroyed, but the bulk of the defenders escaped as usual by the rear, and pursuit was impossible. Fifteen cart loads of potatoes were taken, and the cultivations destroyed. The troops returned to the Waingongoro camp the same evening.

On the 20th, Lieutenant-Colonel Butler marched out of camp at 10 a.m., with 20 of the Military Train, under Lieutenant Creagh, 80 men of the 50th, and 100 of the 57th, also about 120 of the Native Contingent, with the intention of attacking a strong position, called Ahipipi. He detatched the Native Contingent along the left bank of the Waingongoro River, with directions to cross it at the edge of the bush, and endeavor to get in the rear of Ahipipi in order to intercept the retreat of the rebels. He then advanced directly upon the position, and found it deserted, but the rebels fired upon his party as they were destroying the whares and wounded one man of the 57th severely. The Native Contingent then pursued the rebels into the bush, and in so doing came upon a large village. The pursuers receiving support from a party of the 57th, under Sir Robert Douglas, the village was attacked under a heavy fire, and was taken in about twenty minutes. A number of the enemy carried off a body with great care, which was supposed to be that of a great chief. A substantial and well-furnished European built house erected close to the flagstaff was destroyed in common with everything to be found, including cultivations. The destruction of this place was considered of importance, as it was newly built by the rebels, with unusual care, and was the head-quarters of the fanatics of the neighborhood. In this affair five rebels were killed, and one man of the Native Contingent wounded.

After these events, nothing of an important military character occurred in the Province for some time. The Imperial troops were gradually withdrawn until July, 1867, when the last detachments of the 50th were removed, and Taranaki was left without a single soldier of the Imperial Army. After an interval, two companies of the 18th were stationed at New Plymouth, but they were shortly afterwards sent to Adelaide. There was no proclamation of peace, nor any guarantee of safety given to the settlers, but many persons were compelled by necessity to return to their farms, while the rebels maintained a sullen truce.

Owing to the great depression of trade, consequent on the removal of the troops, efforts were made to obtain wealth by preparing the fibre of the phormium for the home market, by boring for petroleum at the Sugarloaves, and by attempts to manufacture the iron sand.

On the night of the 7th of January, 1867, the Waiwakaiho Bridge, which had been built of iron-wood in 1858, at a cost of £2,405, was swept away by a flood, and landed on a small island some ten chains distance down the stream.

On the 7th of November, 1867, an unfortunate affair occurred at Manutahi, near to Mataitawa. A young native, named Inia, who had stolen some clothes from a Military Settler, named Marshall, was apprehended and given into the charge of John Daniel Roby, also a Military Settler, until a policeman could be obtained from New Plymouth. Roby loaded his rifle, and took the prisoner into one of the rooms of the Manutahi Hotel, and fastened the door. After some time the report of the rifle was heard, also a scream and a crash. When the room was entered, Roby was found lying on the floor, mortally wounded, and it was seen that the Maori had escaped by leaping through the window. It was supposed that Inia had thought that Roby intended to shoot him, and that in his terror he seized the rifle while Roby was off his guard, and shot him with it. Inia escaped to Kaipakopako, but was given up to the police. He was tried and found guilty of manslaughter.

During 1867, the first portion of the township of Raleigh, at the mouth of the Waitara, was sold.

In January, 1868, the Government ordered the raising of the Armed Constabulary Corps, and Major Von Tempsky was sent to Patea to take command of the force raised in that district.

On the 16th, the Tasmanian Maid, a small iron steamer which had rendered important services at the Waitara during the war, was wrecked on the long reef off New Plymouth by an error of the steersman.

On the 4th of February, Governor Sir George Bowen landed in Wellington with his family, from the s.s. Kaikoura.

On the 15th, the Waiwakaiho Bridge was again opened for traffic, after being rebuilt and having iron cylinder piers, and two spans added at a cost of £1,500.

In February, Mr. H. R. Richmond was appointed Resident Magistrate of New Plymouth. Shortly after which Mr. Flight retired from the same office on a pension.

On the 19th of May, the Royal Hotel, which stood at the corner of Liardet and Devon-street, was burned, and a lad named Peter Hillam was consumed in the flames.

DISTURBANCE AT PATEA.

In May, complaints having been made by the settlers at Patea of the natives stealing their horses, and Captain McDonnell having had a favorite racer stolen, Mr. Booth, the Resident Magistrate, issued orders to Captain Page to take 100 men and demand the lost horses of the natives. The Maoris received Captain Page peaceably, and promised to restore the animals. Signs of impending mischief were, however, evident by the burning of the huts formerly used by the military at Warea and Waihi.

On the 10th of June, Sergeant Cahill and Privates Squire and Clarke were brutally murdered by the rebels while engaged in putting a log on a saw pit.

On the 12th, a trooper named Thomas Smith was shot while in the act of mounting his horse at Waihi, and was afterwards dreadfully mutilated with tomahawks.

Endeavors were at once made by the Government to collect a force from various quarters for the quelling of the rising rebellion. Major Von Tempsky, who had been ordered to Auckland, was sent for, and Colonel McDonnell, Captain Ross, Captain Page, Captain Newland,

and other officers were ordered to proceed to the disturbed district. Major Hunter, in the absence of Colonel McDonnell, was at this time in command at Waihi.

On the 29th, Captain Newland and his company embarked at New Plymouth in the Colonial steamer Sturt for Patea, and on the following morning the Mounted Corps, under Sergeant Bennett, proceeded thither overland.

THE ATTACK AT TURUTURUMOKAI.

The Turuturumokai Redoubt was situated about three miles south of Waihi, and was a place of some strength, being situated on a knoll, and surrounded by a ditch and breastwork. Here were stationed 25 men, under the command of Captain Ross, who in false security slept in a whare outside the redoubt.

At 4 a.m. on Sunday morning, the 12th of July, the sentry inside the redoubt saw a Maori creeping in the fern outside the ditch, and shortly afterwards the sentry outside perceived in the twilight the outlines of a human form, and challenged twice and fired. This was the signal for a yell, a rush, and a volley from the rebels, by which Lacy, the outside sentinel, received a wound in the shoulder. The redoubt was then assaulted by the rebels, and the awakening garrison, panic struck, leaping over the embankment, were cut down by the enemy outside. Captain Ross rushed from his whare to the gate of the redoubt, firing a rifle handed to him by Lacy, the wounded sentry, and emptying the chambers of his revolver in a hand to hand encounter with the foe. Falling in the gateway with a bullet through his head, he called out, "I am done for; men, you must do the best you can for yourselves." Four men held a corner of the redoubt, but the rest were either shot down, tomahawked or had escaped.

On hearing the firing at Waihi, Major Von Tempsky and his men at once mounted and started off in the direction of the redoubt. On approaching it they saw the natives actively engaged in the attack, but the rebels finding themselves about to be charged in the rear, quickly retired to the bush. Finding that he could not cut the rebels off, Major Von Tempsky rode to the redoubt, where a shocking sight awaited him. About three feet inside the gateway lay Captain Ross, frightfully tomahawked, and with his heart cut from his body, and not far from him, near the gate, were the remains of Gaynor. In one of the angles of the redoubt lay the bodies of Sergeant McFadden, Corporal John Blake, and Private Shield, Captain Ross' servant, weltering in their blood, and on the parapet on the outside was the body of Private Holden. Lemon, the canteen keeper, lay alongside a whare on the outside of the redoubt, with his heart torn out, and his body cut to pieces. The following is a list of the casualties incurred in this unfortunate affair:—Killed—Captain Ross, Sergeant McFadden, Corporal Blake, Constables Shields, Holden, Ross, A. Beamish, Swords, Gaynor, Lemon. Wounded—Constables Lacey, Beamish, Kershaw, Flanagan, Tuffin. Total, 10

18

killed, and 5 wounded.   Only 3 dead bodies of rebels were found.

On the 29th, at about 10 a.m., as the escort was returning from Waihi to Patea with the carters who had conveyed supplies to that outpost, it was fired upon by an ambuscade of 70 or 80 rebels. The escort consisted of eleven of Von Tempsky's men, and six mounted troopers. Two of Von Tempsky's men were wounded—one through the groin dangerously, and the other in the calf of the leg. As the attack took place close to Waihi, Von Tempsky and his men heard the firing and at once ran to the rescue. Getting between the rebels and the bush they gave them a volley, after which they were seen carrying away their dead, but the number killed was not ascertained.

During the month news arrived of the escape of 200 rebel prisoners, in the schooner Rifleman, from the Chatham Islands, and of their landing at Whareongonga, in Poverty Bay.

On the 10th of August, 43 Volunteers left New Plymouth for Patea in the Colonial steamer Sturt, under the command of Lieutenant Roddy.

CAPTURE OF TE NGUTU O TE MANU.

On the 21st of August, Colonel McDonnell left Waihi at 7 a.m., with a force of 230 men, in order to attack the stronghold of the rebels at Te Ngutu o Te Manu (the beak of the bird). Considerable delay took place at Waingongoro, there being a freshet in the river. After the force had proceeded some distance the rain commenced to fall, and continued to pour during the rest of the day. When the expedition arrived about two miles beyond Pungamahoe, breast works and rifle pits were seen flanking the road, and it was evident that an ambuscade had lately lain there, as fresh tracks of natives' feet were visible. When the force was within 500 yards of the enemy's position a strong palisading was seen, and Colonel McDonnell, Sergeant R. Blake, and a few men went forward to reconnoitre. The natives were heard to be singing, and apparently had not the slightest idea of the approach of the British. The Colonel then went back to the force and ordered an advance. On approaching the palisading the men found a back track along which they rushed into the pa with a terrific yell, the bugles at the same time sounding the charge. Volley after volley was poured into the village, and the natives after firing fled, leaving nine dead behind them. About fifteen or twenty pounds of powder, in pound canisters, was found and destroyed. Bags of bullets of all descriptions were also found, also two revolvers, a double barrelled gun, and a quantity of breech loading ammunition of native manufacture. The casualties on this occasion were :—

Wellington Rangers, Captain Page's Company—Killed: Private R. Wallace, Private W. A. Kerr. Wounded: Private Thompson, Corporal Lloyd, Bugler Middleton, Private Sedgewick. Captain Buck's Company—Killed: Private H. Garey. Wounded: Private J. Garey.

Armed Constabulary—Wounded: Private Collopy.

Major Von Tempsky's Company—Killed: Private McCoy. Wounded: Private Whiteside, Private Hope.
Major Hunter's Company—Wounded: Private Dyer, Major Hunter's servant.
The brothers Garey were shot in the retreat by the hovering rebels.
At this engagement the Rev. Father Rolland was present, and administered the consolations of religion to the dying under fire.

THE REPULSE AT RUARURU.

On the 7th of September, at 3 a.m., a force consisting of 250 Europeans and 100 Wanganui natives left Waihi for the purpose of attacking Ruaruru, the stronghold of the chief Titoko Waru. It was divided into three divisions, No. 1 being under the command of Major Von Tempsky, with Sub-Inspectors Cummings, Brown, and Roberts, Captain Palmer, Lieutenants Hastings and Hunter, Ensign Hirtzell, and about 140 men. No. 2 was commanded by Major Hunter, with Sub-Inspectors Newland and Goring, Captains Buck and O'Halloran, Lieutenant Rowan and 108 men. No. 3 was composed of Wanganui natives about 100 strong, and was under the command of Captain W. McDonnell, Kawana, Hunia, Kempi, and other chiefs; the whole force was commanded by Colonel McDonnell. Dr. Walker accompanied No. 1, and Acting-Assistant Surgeon Best, No. 2 division. After the force had crossed the Waingongoro and entered the bush, the main track to Te Ngutu o Te Manu was followed for some distance. The column then, under the guidance of the Kupapas, entered the bush on the right, and after a tedious march arrived in the rear of Ruaruru at 2 p.m. A few bark huts were seen and a tent. Here the natives killed a child by dashing out its brains, and took a little boy prisoner. The force then proceeded, and under heavy fire took up a position in a narrow valley, through which ran a stream of water. At this place the force remained about ten minutes exposed to a heavy fire from the pa in front, and from the bush on both sides. Trooper Hogan was here shot in the thigh, and Lieutenant Rowan through the face, the ball breaking both his jaws. It was now discovered that the enemy had sharpshooters posted in some large rata trees, which commanded the pa. Volley after volley was poured into these trees without effect. The men now began to drop fast, and the force got uneasy. Seeing this, Major Von Tempsky asked for permission to assault the pa with his division, and soon afterwards Major Hunter made a similar request. Colonel McDonnell, however, would not consent, fearing that the position was too strong for a successful attack, and that it was commanded by the natives posted in the trees. The wounded were then collected and placed under a strong escort of some 80 or a 100 men, which was commanded by Colonel McDonnell, with Major Hunter and Sub-Inspectors Newland and Cumming. Von Tempsky was now left with his force to cover the retreat, exposed to a heavy fire. He walked up and down in front of his men, endeavoring to persuade them to take cover, while they, partially disorganised, kept exposing themselves in parties of twenty or thirty. Von Tempsky then fell, but accounts differ as to the precise mode of his death. Immediately he fell Captain Buck ran forward to recover his body, and he too fell to rise no more. Lieutenant Hunter then ran forward, and his gallantry cost him his life. About the same time Captain Palmer fell mortally wounded. There were now no officers left with that portion of the force which was nearest to the enemy, the confusion of the men under fire increased, and they felt that they must escape as best they could. The repulse was complete, and the rebels closely pursued the retreating men. The dead, and wounded who could not walk, were left behind, and some of the wounded were dragged to the pa and burnt to death. The force under Colonel McDonnell kept well together, and by the aid of the Kupapas reached the camp at 10 p.m., with all the wounded it had started with, Von Tempsky's division having received the full brunt of the fury of the rebels.

The casualties on this occasion were :—

Killed—Major Von Tempsky, Captain Buck, Captain Palmer, Lieutenant Hastings, Lieutenant Hunter, Corporal Russell, Constable Elkin, Privates Finnessey, Hart, Gilgru, Israel Davis, E. G. Farram, Hughes, Lumsden, Grant, Deeks, and Wells.

Wounded—Lieutenant Rowan, Dr. Best, Constables Houston, O'Brien, O'Connor, Burke, Hogan, Walton, Fulton, Shannigan; Sergeant Towey; Privates McGeneskin, Harris, Caldwell, McManus, Walden, Griffiths, Locker, Quinsey, Melvin, Hamblyn, Holloway, Hyland, Flynn, Dire.

Missing—Darlington and Downs.

This terrible defeat acted so injuriously upon the force which had been hastily collected, that it became partially disorganised, and Von Tempsky's men having lost their leader took their blankets and left the district.

MAJOR VON TEMPSKY.

Gustavus Ferdinand Von Tempsky was the second son of Lieutenant-Colonel Von Tempsky of the Prussian service, and was educated at the Military College at Berlin, and eventually obtained his commission in the 3rd Regiment of Fusileers in 1844, but being of a roving disposition, with an intense abhorrence of routine and red tape, and also strongly imbued with a love of adventure, he made up his mind to give up his profession, and accordingly started with some of his countrymen for the Mosquito shore on the Eastern coast of Central America, intending to found a new colony. The British Government at that time had established a sort of protectorate there, and had appointed R. Walker, Esq., as Consul General and Diplomatic Agent, to represent British interests on that coast. The emigration scheme turned out a failure, but Von Tempsky was made Captain to form an irregular force of Mosquito Indians, who did good service against the Spaniards, and in leading and guiding the British officers and crews of H.M.S. Alarm, s.s. Vixen, and brig Daring, against the Spanish stockades of Castillo, Viojo, Sarapequi, and San Carlo, which were taken. Here the Consul General met with a fearful death, having slipped overboard from one of the boats, and been immediately devoured by alligators before assistance could be rendered. Von Tempsky having lost his most intimate friend in this horrible way, now seems to have become partially disgusted with his post, and gold being discovered in California about this time he essayed to try his fortune there.

After remaining some little time in California he started backward, and landing at Mazatlan, on the west coast of Mexico, in the Sierra Nevada and Rocky Mountains, he, with a friend, determined to pass through Central America, which he did till he arrived at Blewfields on the Mosquito shore. This journey forms the subject of an excellent work called "Mitla; or, Travels in Mexico and Central America," of which the gallant Major was the author. After staying at Blewfields for a short time he married the daughter of the Commandant of the Station, and then set sail for England with his wife and father-in-law.

Once again he left Europe, this time bound for Victoria, where Mrs. Von Tempsky had a married sister. At first he turned his attention to agricultural pursuits, but some time after the Government having planned an expedition to explore the interior, candidates to take command of the party were enquired for. Von Tempsky came forward for the appointment, but Burke was the successful man. A feeling of national pride that the interior should be explored by a Briton was probably the bar to Von Tempsky's success in this matter. He was, however, offered the sub-command, but refused it. About this time rumours of the discovery of gold at Coromandel, New Zealand, reached Victoria, and as great depression existed at that time in Australia, Von Tempsky at once sailed for New Zealand, and proceeded to Coromandel, where his knowledge as a practical miner aided the Government considerably in developing the resources of that gold field.

On the Waikato war breaking out in July, 1863, he offered his services to the Government, and was appointed an Ensign in the Forest Rangers in August, 1863. From this time to November of that year he was attached to the Flying Column, which was engaged in scouring the Henua Ranges, in whose fastnesses the rebels had congregated. He next was engaged at the Maukn, where the natives had entrenched themselves behind some logs in a bush clearing, and fired a volley at the Rangers at a distance of twenty yards, but fortunately missed them. After this, in company with Captain Thomas McDonnell, then a Sub-Inspector of the Defence Force, he stole at night to Paparata, where the rebels were assembled in great force, and hiding in the flax continued during the whole of the next day to observe the movements of the enemy. Reaching the Camp at Whangamarino the next night, he, with Sub-Inspector McDonnell, received the thanks of General Cameron for his gallantry, and for the information conveyed. This was one of the most hazardous services rendered during the war, there being at least 500 natives in the vicinity of the spot these officers visited. For this service both were promoted to the rank of captain.

Von Tempsky's next action took place on the 11th of February, 1864, at Mangapiko on the Waipa, where, in the quaint words of his despatch to the Lieutenant-General, he says:—"My men with promptitude surrounded the thicket, and entering the same revolver in hand *extracted*, in a short time, seven natives." For this duty he was mentioned by General Cameron in his despatches to the Governor.

On the 22nd and 23rd of February he was in action at Rangiawhia, which lasted two days. After this fight the return of the Forest Rangers was thus described by an eye-witness—"They were loaded with pigs, potatoes, spears, tomahawks, cooking utensils, and all kinds of Maori goods."

On the 2nd of April, 1864, he took part in the siege of Orakau, behaving with his usual courage, and for which he was promoted to the rank of Major. After this action Waikato was subdued, and Von Tempsky's sword rested till the breaking out of the war in 1865. When the Government determined to chastise the rebels at Wanganui, Von Tempsky's Company of Forest Rangers were asked to volunteer for service in that quarter. The officers and half the men acquiesced in the request. When at Wanganui they were asked to go with Major Brassy's expedition to Opotiki, for the purpose of chastising the murderers of the Rev. Carl Sylvius Volkner and others. This was in the absence of Von Tempsky, who was away at the time on leave. Von Tempsky proceeded to the East Coast, expecting to meet his men there, and in their absence joined Major Brassy's force as a volunteer. After this he returned to Wanganui with the object of inducing his men to volunteer for the East Coast. Having gained the consent of his men to proceed he marched with them to Wellington, where he received orders to put himself under the command of Lieutenant-Colonel Fraser. This so vexed Von Tempsky that he refused to proceed, and resigned his commission.

In November he recalled his resignation, and took command of a company of Forest Rangers, composed of men from the European and Maori Militia of Wanganui, under orders for service at Patea. He then went to Auckland, but on the renewal of the disturbance at Patea was sent to Waihi. He was present at the assault of Te Ngutu o Te Manu, and fell nobly doing his duty before Ruaruru. He was one of the bravest of men, and scarcely received from the Government the consideration which his high qualities entitled him to. His commission as Major in the First Regiment of Waikato Militia bears date 4th of April, 1864.

Shortly after the defeat at Ruaruru, Colonel McDonnell gave up the command, and was succeeded by Colonel Whitmore.

On the 30th of September, an escort while on its way from Manawapou to Patea, was fired on by an ambuscade at Manutahi, and one man was killed.

Early in October, a settler at Kakaramea, named McCullock, went out to look for his sheep and never returned.

On the 16th, Thomas Collins, of New Plymouth, was murdered and dreadfully mutilated, while crossing the Manawakawa River.

THE REPULSE AT OKUTUKU.

On November the 7th, Colonel Whitmore made an attack on Okutuku, with a mixed force of 266 Europeans and 80 Maoris, but was repulsed after a hard fight, which lasted from 8 a.m. to 1.30 p.m. The men behaved well and retired in good order, but were followed by the rebels to within 700 yards of the Wairoa Camp. Major Hunter fell at about 30 yards from the pa, while leading a storming party. He was struck in the thigh by a ball which severed the femoral artery, and bled to death. The casualties were :—

Killed—Major Hunter, Sergeant Kirwin, Constables Lee and Satler, Privates Path, Urquhart, and one not named. Wounded—Constables Eastwood, Dolan, Monk, Thompson, Wesley, Williams, Cooksley; Privates Cole, Kelly, Foot, McDowell, Vance, Keane, Mepa, Lindar, and five Wanganui natives. Missing—Constables Kennedy, R. Thompson, Poole; Privates Brown, Kenneally, Norman, Savage, Rogers, Nicholls, Devon, Negus, Kenally.

THE BROTHERS HUNTER.

The brothers Major William Hunter and Lieutenant Henry Hunter arrived in Auckland in the spring of 1861. They were both natives of the County of Antrim, Ireland, and were grandsons of Bishop Magee, the author of a standard work on the "Atonement," and nephews, by marriage, of the Rev. Hugh McNeil of Liverpool.

The elder brother, William, who was a student in Trinity College, Dublin, when the Crimean war broke out, led away by martial ardor abandoned the University, and obtained a commission in the Antrim Militia Rifles, and after undergoing the regular course of training at Hythe, under Colonel Pitt, became Adjutant of the Regiment, in which capacity he served for five years. At the close of the Crimean war, when the Militia were disbanded, Major Hunter, accompanied by his brother Henry, emigrated to Auckland. Coming out with letters of recommendation to several of the leading persons in Auckland, they without difficulty obtained situations under Government.

The elder brother was during the year, 1862, assistant clerk to the Auckland Provincial Council, in which capacity he became known to and appreciated by many public men. After this he went down to Wellington to attend the first session of the General Assembly that was held there, and was on board the s.s. White Swan when she was wrecked. Those who were on board the vessel perceived the sterling stuff of which he was made. In the midst of the danger he was perfectly cool and collected. So efficiently did he discharge the duties required of him during the session at Wellington that he was offered permanent employment as clerk assistant, by the Hon. Mr. Bartley, the Speaker of the Upper House; but the war breaking out in Waikato in 1863, he abandoned the Civil Service for service in the Colonial Forces, when the war was almost at the doors of the citizens of Auckland. Colonel Pitt was then engaged in raising the First Waikato Regiment, and William Hunter was at once gazetted Captain and Adjutant of that Regiment, which post he held till the regiment was disbanded in 1866. While he held that post it was admitted that although there were ten regiments of Her Majesty's regulars in the Colony that there was no more efficient officer, or more accomplished drill-master, than William Hunter in New Zealand.

His younger brother, Henry, after serving a brief period in the Post Office department in Hawke's Bay, also joined the 1st Waikato Regiment, and served throughout the Waikato war, and afterwards in the Wanganui and Taranaki campaigns. His genial manner endeared him to many, and none that knew him will ever forget the light-heartedness of one whose military career was like that of those who "march to death with military glee." Henry Hunter fell at Ngutu o Te Manu, leaving a wife and one child. William Hunter fell leading a forlorn hope on the Okotuku pa.

Titoko Waru, with his force of rebels, now approached towards Wanganui, burning houses, and creating great alarm, both in Wanganui and Wellington.

On the 21st of November, the news of the massacre in Poverty Bay by Te Kooti, and the escapees from the Chatham Islands, was published in New Plymouth.

On the 24th, a great fire occurred in Devon-street, New Plymouth, and £10,000 worth of property was destroyed.

On the 28th, the barque Collingwood arrived from Waitangi, Chatham Islands, with 2 Europeans, 1 Chinese, 69 native men, 45 native women, and 38 native children. These people were located by the Government on the north side of the Urenui River. They were the descendants of the Ngatimutunga, who fled from Rauparaha, the celebrated warrior chief of Kawhia, to the Chatham Islands from Wellington in the brig Rodney, in 1836. They returned to Taranaki on account of having sold their lands in the Chatham Islands to Europeans.

Early in December, the Superintendent of Taranaki received from Dr. Pollen, of Auckland, a copy of a telegram which had been forwarded to him by Mr. Searancke of Waikato, to the effect that the Ngatimaniapoto feeling angry at the refusal of the other Waikato tribes to sanction a general rising in that district, had uttered a threat that they would go to the White Cliffs, in the Taranaki district, on their own account. The Government Agent forwarded it so that the Provincial Government might be on its guard, but stated that as Rewi, the greatest chief of the Ngatimaniapotos, was against any aggressive movement, the likelihood of its being carried out was very improbable. The Superintendent caused the information to be conveyed to the settlers at the White Cliffs and Urenui, and Mr. Parris placed some trustworthy natives on the look out at the White Cliffs to guard against the possibility of a surprise, as it was deemed to be impossible for an armed party to march along the coast beyond the cliffs without detection during their journey. After the native scouts had been employed in this service for a short time they were dismissed, because no danger was apprehended by the Provincial Government.

THE MASSACRE AT THE WHITE CLIFFS.

On Saturday, the 13th day of February, 1869, excited by the success which had attended the arms of the rebels under Te Kooti and Titoko Waru, and encouraged by the fact that the whole of the Imperial and Colonial troops had again been withdrawn from the Taranaki Northern outpost, a *taua*, or war party of Ngatimaniapoto, the section of the great Waikato tribe residing at Mokau, approached Pukearuhe, the British redoubt at the White Cliffs.

Pukearuhe is situated about 36 miles from New Plymouth, and commands the approaches from the Mokau and Waikato country. To the south it affords a view of the country for at least two miles, but from the eastward it is commanded by a range of hills, distant from it about 500 yards. There is, however, a deep gully between these hills and the redoubt, which affords a protection from any sudden attack.

The *taua* approached in broad daylight, and found two Europeans at the blockhouse, whom they enticed away by telling them there were pigs on the beach for sale. Milne went first, and was tomahawked on the path leading to the beach. Seeing that Richards, the other man, did not follow, the party returned, urging him to come and look at the pigs. The unfortunate man descended the hill, and was killed near to where Milne fell. The *taua* then rushed up to the redoubt, and found that Lieutenant Gascoigne and his family were absent in their field of corn and potatoes. Lieutenant Gascoigne looking up saw the natives at the blockhouse, and at once proceeded towards them, carrying his youngest child ; Mrs. Gascoigne and the other children followed him. On arriving at a little stream at the base of the hill on which the blockhouse stood, Lieutenant Gascoigne gave the child to his wife, and went forward to meet the Maoris. Approaching them they shook hands with him and accompanied him to the door. Upon his raising his hand to open the door he was struck from behind and fell. Soon after Mrs. Gascoigne came with her children, and she and the little ones were killed. The murderers then tomahawked the house dog and the cat. About sunset Mr. Whitely was seen approaching on horseback, but he was not recognised until he descended the hill which led to an old pa.

After crossing the stream and ascending Pukearuhe he was ordered to return, but refusing to do so, he and his horse were shot. The blockhouse and huts were then burned.

This frightful atrocity was first discovered on the following Monday, by a young man named Macdonald, who immediately took the news to New Plymouth.

On the following day an armed party proceeded to the Cliffs in the s.s. Wellington, and recovered the bodies. The remains, gory, mutilated, and partially decomposed, were brought up to New Plymouth, and interred with military honors in the public cemetery where an obelisk of trachyte has been erected to their memory bearing the following names:—

> Rev. John Whiteley, aged 62 years.
> Lieutenant Bamber Gascoigne, aged 40 years.
> Annie Gascoigne, aged 27 years.
> Laura Gascoigne, aged 5 years.
> Cecil John Gascoigne, aged 3 years.
> Louisa Annie Gascoigne, aged 3 months.
> John Milne, aged 40 years.
> Edward Richards, aged 35 years.

Mr. W. N. Searancke, Resident Magistrate at Waikato, in a letter to Dr. Pollen, gave the following account of these murders:—

"The actual murderers at the White Cliffs were a half-caste lad, a son of a European, named Frank Philips, residing at Mokau Heads; Wetere, a son of the late Takerei, of Te Awakino, near Mokau; Herewini, a son of the late Peketai, formerly residing at the Waitara, subsequently of Mokau; and Te Tana of Mokau Heads. These four actually committed the murders. Mr. Whiteley was shot by Wetere. He was told to go back and refused. His horse was then shot. Mr. Whitely then sunk on his knees and commenced praying; while so doing he was shot at twice by Wetere with a revolver, and missed. Wetere then went up close, and shot the unfortunate gentleman dead."

THE REV. JOHN WHITELEY.

The Rev. John Whiteley was born of Christian parents at Kneesal, Nottinghamshire, England, on July the 20th, 1806. From childhood he was religiously disposed, and in his 20th year became a a decided, and, as he believed, an accepted Christian. At this period he became a member of an Independent Church, but shortly afterwards his connection with that body of Christians was severed by his removal to the vicinity of Newark, where he threw in his lot with the Wesleyans, and became a local preacher. In 1831, he was accepted as a candidate for missionary work. He was married on the 4th of September, 1832, at a small parish church in the Newark circuit, and proceeded with his wife to the old Mission House in Hatton Garden, London, where he received a very kind reception.

After receiving recognition as a Missionary Minister at Lambeth Chapel, he proceeded to Portsmouth, and there embarked with his wife, on the 5th of November, 1832, in the ship Caroline, Captain Treadwell, bound for Hokianga, New Zealand. Early in the following year the ship reached the coast of New Zealand, but the weather being rough Captain Treadwell declined to enter the Hokianga River, and took the vessel round the North Cape to the Bay of Islands, where the debarkation was safely effected. The Wesleyan station at that time was at Mangungu on the Hokianga, the original station at Wangaroa having been destroyed by the natives in 1827, and there was but one missionary there. Mr. Whiteley proceeded to his post overland, and found his solitary brother awaiting his arrival. Here he learned the Maori language, and qualified himself for the great work of his life. In 1837 he was visited by the Rev. N. Turner, the Wesleyan Pioneer Missionary of New Zealand, who in search of health had come to revisit the scenes of his early labors. On the 17th of November of that year, Messrs. Whiteley and Turner set out to visit Honruru and other places on the eastern coast, where a good work had begun among the natives. By 7 p.m. they reached the foot of Mount Taniwa, the camping ground of native travellers. Here they erected, in native fashion, a breakwind of the fronds of the Nikau palm, and after taking tea, and performing their devotions, they wrapped themselves in their blankets and slept soundly. By sunrise they were on the top of the mount, which is a remarkable cone, capping a high range of hills. Here, the beauty and grandeur of nature repaid their toil in climbing the peak. At an immense depth, just below them, were silvery streams lighting up the panorama of forests and vales spread out below them. On the east coast, skirted by a low thick fog, was the noble Wangoroa Bay, with its bold cliffs, and the island guardian of its ocean gate; and on the west, beaming its welcome to the rising sun, their own lovely Hokianga. Far reaching in the distance beyond their sight was the North Cape of our sea-girt home. They saw the coast line of cliffs, and sands, and craggs, laved by old ocean rolling in his majesty, and in spirit they heard the grand and harmonious anthem of the waves, east and west. Here they tarried for half-an-hour, and indulged in thoughts of New Zealand worthy of Christian Missionaries. Descending by the eastern side they travelled over hill and dale, crossing one serpentine steam nearly twenty times. They reached the first native village in the Honruru Valley an hour before noon. The people, thirty or forty in number, including children, were busy in their plantations and much surprised by their visit. Shaded by a copse in a sequestred dell, the whole tribe assembled for worship. A youth named Matthew, whom Mr. Turner had baptized at Mungungu twelve months before, had been their teacher; and it was richly assuring to find that hearts, hardened by threescore years of heathenism, had been subdued by the Spirit, under the teaching and prayers of the babe in Christ. Matthew received a few books, and was much encouraged for further labor. Having halted for two hours the Missionaries travelled on up the lonely valley, observing as they went traces of a large population in former days.

They next tarried at a village whose chief had lately been baptized by the name of Joseph Orton. Mr. Whiteley was remarkable as a pedestrian. Few Englishmen, even renowned explorers, could excel him; but his companion in travel was tired out, not having before walked so many miles in one day. Their wash from a calabash, and a cup of tea, were very refreshing. They then conversed till evening with the people. Mr. Turner preached to about seventy people on a traveller's theme, Philip and the Eunuch. Several native helpers had lately gone among this people, and had led many of them to God; and now they earnestly desired the appointment of a Missionary. It was in the very spot were Samuel Leigh had thought of beginning his labors, and was in some respects a most eligible and commanding position. But the people were now too few to have their wish gratified. A bed of fern in Joseph Orton's verandah afforded rest till daybreak.

After prayers, at five o'clock, they resumed their travels. The roads being muddy, and the rain falling heavily, they were four hours, instead of two, in reaching Kohumaru. As they approached the village they heard the bells ringing for worship. The people had not been aware of their coming, and gladly deferred worship till they had changed their clothing and refreshed themselves. Forty persons were present, in whose hearts desires for salvation had been begotten by the agency of native teachers. The Missionaries were storm stayed, and held another service in the evening. They sought the road at six the following morning, and by eleven arrived at Mr. Lever's, three miles from Wangaroa. That gentleman, who had been accustomed to sit under Mr. Turner's ministry in Hobart Town, received them with much pleasure. After refreshment he took Mr. Turner in his boat to visit his first New Zealand home. The journey of three hours was amidst the familiar scenes of former years; and a rush of memories of mercies, trials, dangers, and deliverences filled his mind. Wesley had suffered nothing by the lapse of time. Indeed, its native loveliness had been somewhat increased by the growth of scented groves of sweet-brier. But as the Missionary stood once more on ground hallowed by toil, by suffering, by prayer, and by a tender consecration, the silent air seemed weighted with melancholy. At his feet was all that remained of his own manual work—a few broken bricks. He looked to the right and left as if for those he had known; but there were no family groups circling round their fires, no children sporting in the bushes, and he felt the desolation. He sought the spot where his first child had lain. The soil was sunken and disturbed, and told of the despoilers' hands. The little one's sepulchre had been in his garden; his own hands, when younger, had trained that garden's trees. Though now all traces of any enclosure had disappeared, there were lovely flowers and fruits. He gathered some roses to carry home, for there were other sympathies with the silent spot—he plucked them as God's own emblems.

The valley had been harvested. Sin, war, and disease had been the weapons! Though for three hours he travelled the familiar walks, now covered with grass, he saw but a small remnant of the tribes. Of those whom he had known ten years before, only two old people remained.

Heavy rains detained them till noon next day. Their course homeward lay through the Otangaroa, which they found in high flood. The natives tested the stream-depth, here and there they found footing with their heads above water, they then conveyed the Missionaries across. Two Maoris took hold of Mr. Turner's arms, other two of his legs, and with the water supporting his weight as he lay upon it between the two couples of bearers, he was partially carried and partly floated over. Mr. Whiteley was conveyed over in the same way. They made slow progress through a country almost untravelled, and overgrown with bushes and fern, and at length lost their way and were benighted. With their clothing drenched, every tree and bush dripping, the ground deluged by the down pour of many hours, and without shelter, or the apparent means of procuring it, they were more than weary in their evening's discomfort. They set too, however, to make the best of it. All hands gathered bushes, and within an hour they had constructed a partial shelter. The natives got two dry pieces of wood from a hollow tree, and by rubbing them together obtained a fire. The Missionaries dried their clothes, reduced their discomfort as much as they could, and by the light of their camp fire at midnight read the holy word. They then in that dense wild forest rested beneath the Almighty's shade and rose unharmed. It took an hour to regain the overgrown path, a circumstance not unusual in New Zealand travel. Upon a hill top they passed one of the big guns of the ship Boyd. Years before some Hokianga natives had conceived the idea of securing it for their great pa, to be used as an arm of defence in time of war. They had dragged it over hill and dale, and through streams, until food and courage failing they had abandoned it, and it remained on this hill top, a witness of their folly. Travelling down the mountains the Missionaries crossed one stream sixty times. At four o'clock they reached their boat at Mangamuka, and by twilight reac'ed their homes, thankful for the travelling merc'es of six days.

A ter resid' ig for a few years at Ho'sianga, Mr. Whiteley removed to Kawhia, and there among the Waikato tribes spent the best of his days. Strong, active, abstemious, loving the country and people, he was not troubled with sickly longings for home, or sentimental languishings for refined society, but as a good soldier and servant of Jesus Christ he nimbly trod the narrow and devious paths, paddled his canoe up the rivers, or travelled on horseback long distances over the open wilderness, or along the wide reaches of the solitary sea-beach in search of the villages of the dusky race he had given his life to serve. Sitting in the rush-built hut upon a cushion of fern he would partake with the people of their homely supper, from the steaming oven, and after the meal would hold "karakia," or devotional service, singing with his flock the evening hymn in their own tongue, and to an air perfectly hideous to most European ears, but musical to him. Then after refreshing sleep, in the early hours, he would awake at the voice of the bird, proceed to some neighboring stream, shave, perform his ablutions, not forgetting his feet, return to the pa, hold karakia, breakfast, and depart to some other portion of his large diocese, there to repeat the proceedings of the previous day. Without forgetting that he was a civilised Briton, so identified did he become with his people, and so readily did he fall into their habits of thought and catch the idiom of their language, that he became one of the best Maori preachers, and obtained great influence over the native people. Shortly after the foundation of the New Plymouth Settlement, he was chiefly instrumental in inducing the Waikato tribes to manumit the Ngatiawa slaves they took at the siege of Pukerangiora. In 1844, he, at the special request of Governor Fitzroy, attempted to smooth the ill-feeling which arose between the freedmen and the pioneer settlers of Taranaki. In 1856, in consequence of the Puketapu feud, Mr. Whiteley was stationed at New Plymouth. Here he labored amidst all the scenes of alarm, misery, and blood-shedding, with which this province was afflicted for so many years, preaching both to friends and foes, now in the camp of the British, and now in the war pa of the Maori. There was no outpost too remote for the missionary to reach, and he has frequently entered a blockhouse on a Sunday wet to his loins by wading through swollen rivers. He labored for some years in the endeavor to impart instruction to the natives at the Grey Institution on the Mission Reserve at Ngamotu. He was instrumental in causing the erection of a native chapel on the Kawau Pa in New Plymouth, and when, during the war, the pa and chapel were purchased by the Government, it was chiefly by his exertions that another native chapel was built at the Henui. In 1859, he accompanied the present writer with Rev. J. Fletcher, Messrs. Webster, senior, Hulke, Burton, and Knight, with a party of natives on a long forest journey from Bell Block to Mount Egmont. At length the good old man finished the work which was given him to do. It was his custom to ride out to some remote post on Saturday, sleep there on Saturday night, rise and hold early Sabbath service, and then proceed homewards, preaching at all the villages on his way. In pursuance of this plan he left New Plymouth on Saturday, the 13th day of February, 1869, on horseback for Pukearuhe, "fern root hill," an out-post in the White Cliff district in the extreme north of Taranaki. He was not unconscious of danger, for he had written a warning letter to the Government concerning this very outpost. As the old missionary rode along, now on the margin of the high sea cliffs, with the spectacle of Ruapehu in front and Egmont on his right, both lifting their snowy crests from the bosom of the dark forests to the bright blue sky, and the dancing wavelets flashing the reflected sunlight in the watery abyss on his left, now cantering along the sandy beach amidst the iridescent bubbles of the sea foam, little did he think how black a crime was being perpetrated on the spot he was rapidly approaching. Pukearuhe had that day been stained with the blood of a young English mother of 27, and of her three babes, with the blood of three harmless men, and even with the blood of their domestic cat and dog. The Missionary crossed the stream at the foot of the hill and commenced to ascend the steep path, when from among a war party of 20 Ngatimaniapoto, headed by a chief, who had been baptized as a believer in a merciful Saviour, and by the name of Wesley, voices were heard exclaiming, "hokia! hokia!"—go back! go back? Then there was a discharge of arms, and the missionary's horse fell. Disengaging himself from the dying beast, the aged minister fell on his knees, and clasped his hands in the attitude of prayer. Arms were again discharged; five bullets pierced his body, and so he passed to his everlasting rest.

With the death of Mr. Whiteley, the war in Taranaki was ended. The Government were unable to punish the murderers, but to this day the blood-stained cliff of Pukearuhe has been held by a garrison of the Armed Constabulary of New Zealand.

CHAPTER XXVII.

PEACE.

AFTER nine years of turmoil and bloodshed, peace was restored to Taranaki, but the restoration came about in such a dubious manner that the joy which usually attends the cessation of hostilities was withheld from the long-suffering people of the district. By many, the massacre at the White Cliffs was looked upon as presaging another and still more terrible chapter of war. Many settlers fled from their farms to New Plymouth, and a few with their families left the Province with the intention of not returning until the rebellion should cease. There was also a temporary revival of military activity. A force was sent to the South to surround Titoko Waru, and another to the North to make reprisals on the Mokau murderers. Colonel Whitmore embarked some of the latter in the Colonial s.s. Sturt, and proceeded to the Mokau Heads. Finding the country very difficult for military operations, he merely fired a few shells on to the shore and returned. The refusal of the Maori King to aid Titoko Waru and the Maori rebels, together with the paucity of Colonial troops, and the poverty of the Colonial exchequer, induced the Government to cease military operations on the West Coast. Gradually, therefore, it became apparent that the war was at an end, and gradually a sense of security was restored to the settlement. The change from the intense excitement of war to the quiet of a small agricultural and pastoral settlement was very great. No longer the reveille was sounded at daybreak from Marsland Hill to arouse the garrison and the inhabitants of the besieged town, and to give the weary night pickets license to leave their posts for their home and their firesides; no longer the "alarm" called all men off duty to arms, and to face the foe; and no longer the mournful dead march wailed out its sorrowful strains over the remains of the fallen brave.

Owing to the drain made upon the Colony by the war, the peace was attended by great commercial and financial depression, and New Plymouth suffered most severely in this respect by the entire withdrawal from it of the Imperial troops and military establishments.

THE IRON SAND.

Along the shores of Taranaki exists a very considerable quantity of magnetic iron sand, which has been washed out of the tufa which surrounds the base of Mount Egmont by the rivers and carried to the sea beach. It appears to be a sublimate of iron and titanium, produced by volcanic agency, and converted into a black magnetic oxide while in a heated state by contact with heated steam. Its analysis is as follows:—

Magnetite	71.0
Titanite	8.0
Quartz and Olivine	21.0
	100.0

It produces in smelting from 50 to 61 per cent. of iron of the finest quality, the tensile strength of which has been discovered by experiment to be greater by 33 tons 5 cwt. to the square inch than that of the best English iron. The iron, when converted into steel, has been put to the most severe tests by many eminent steel and tool makers in Great Britain, and has been admitted by them to be unsurpassed by any in the world; its closeness of grain, brilliancy of polish, keenness of edge, elasticity and strength exciting general admiration, and leading to a unanimous statement that it must some day supersede all other brands of steel for the finer and more expensive branches of the cutlery and edge tool trade. In 1848, Mr. John Perry, carpenter, and an old settler of the Province, made an attempt to smelt this sand by erecting a small furnace on the banks of a small stream which flows into the Huatoki River on the Carrington Road. Mr. Perry was encouraged in this work by His Excellency Governor Grey, who promised him a lease of the sand if his experiments were successful. Mr. Perry found a great difficulty in the fineness of the sand, which made its way to the bottom of the furnace before the fire could operate upon it with sufficient power to smelt it. Some small quantities of iron were, however, produced by him, and forged into small articles by Mr. Wood, the blacksmith. After this, Mr. C. Sutton made some experiments in the same direction on the town cliff, near to Mount McCormick, but was unsuccessful.

In 1858, the Provincial Government of Taranaki granted a lease of the iron sand to Captain Morshead, a retired officer of the Hon. East India Company's Service, who went to England for the purpose of endeavoring to raise a company to work the ore. Captain Morshead, returning unsuccessful from his mission, in 1869 a firm from Wellington, trading under the name of Henochsburg and Co., erected a furnace on the South Road, just outside the boundaries of New Plymouth, and attempted to work the sand. Partial success attending these operations, the firm was expanded into a company, bearing the title of the Pioneer Steel Company. Failing to make the metal flow freely from the furnace, the company suspended operations, and deputed Mr. Chilman to the iron masters of England to represent to them the value of the ore, to obtain information as to the best method of reducing it, and to sell the works if possible and raise a new company. Mr. Chilman returned, having effected the sale of the lease and

19

interest of the company to Mr. Walduck, and with some valuable information.

Mr. Walduck failing to make use of the works, or to avail himself of the interest of the Pioneer Company, another Company was formed chiefly by the exertions of Mr. E. M. Smith, who had discovered a method of preventing the choking of furnaces by the iron sand by forming it with clay into compound bricks before subjecting it to the fire. This Company bore the name of the New Zealand Titanic Steel and Iron Company (Limited). Its proposed capital was £50,000, in 5,000 shares of £10 each, with power to increase to £100,000. Of this capital £20,000 was called up and expended in works at the Henui, including a blast charcoal furnace on the best American plan, and a powerful engine and apparatus for producing a hot blast. After the works had been completed, and everything was in readiness for commencing operations, the Company shut up the place and refused to charge the furnace. At the earnest solicitation of the shareholders residing in Taranaki, and on their guaranteeing to protect the Company from loss or damage, permission was given for experimental operations to be conducted. The first of these was an experimental reduction of ore which was chiefly hæmatite from the Parapara mine at Nelson. The next experiment was that conducted under the supervision of Messrs. E. M. Smith and D. Atkinson, by which iron sand alone was reduced. On Saturday the 23rd of September, 1876, the furnace was tapped, and 3 tons 15 cwt. of metal in pigs was produced, which has since been tested in England, and reported to be iron of the best possible quality. After these experiments the furnace was blown out and the works have since remained in a quiescent state.

PROVINCIAL GOVERNMENT.

On the 15th October, 1859, Mr. F. A. Carrington succeeded Mr. H. R. Richmond in the Superintendency of the Province, and was re-elected to that office on 22nd November, 1873. At the end of 1876, Provincial institutions were abolished by the "Abolition of Provinces Act, 1875."

THE LAND FUND.

By the "Financial Arrangements Act, 1877," the compact of 1856, under which certain sums were paid to the Northern Provinces in order that the Southern Provinces might enjoy their own land funds, was broken up, the Act providing that the land fund of the colony should become general revenue, except 20 per cent. which is to be paid back to the Counties for local purposes, and except in the case of the Provincial District of Taranaki, which is to receive one-fourth of the land fund of the district for the purpose of assisting to construct a harbor at New Plymouth. From the time the compact of 1856 had been ratified by the "Public Debt Apportionment Act, 1868," to the Abolition of the Provinces, Taranaki received the sum

HISTORY OF TARANAKI. 291

of £2,200 per annum as interest on the £32,000 which had been allotted to it by the Act of 1868, and by this sum the Provincial Government was almost entirely supported, the Province having no land fund owing to the refusal of the Maoris to part with their waste lands to the Government.

LOCAL GOVERNMENT.

With the exception of the formation of new districts as colonisation has extended, the Road Districts have remained unchanged since 1858. For several years the town of New Plymouth was treated simply as a road district, and its roads were repaired by rates raised under the provisions of the Roads and Bridges Ordinance, and expended under the supervision of Commissioners. But in 1863 special provisions were made for the improvement of the town by the constitution of a Town Board by an Ordinance of the Provincial Council. This Ordinance, with some amendments, remained in force till the 11th of August, 1876, when, by the exertions of Mr. W. H. Scott and other members of the Town Board, New Plymouth was proclaimed a Municipality by His Excellency the Governor. On the 22nd of September, 1876, the following gentlemen were elected members of the New Plymouth Borough Council—J. Ellis, R. Chilman, W. H. Scott, A. Laird, D. Callaghan, T. E. Hamerton, A. Standish, J. M. Vivian, and Walter Read, and Mr. L. H. Cholwill was chosen town clerk. On the 11th of October following Arthur Standish was elected the first Mayor of the Borough. The towns of Carlyle, Raleigh, Hawera, and Inglewood have Town Boards, established under the provisions of the Town Boards of Taranaki Ordinances of 1872 and 1875.

In 1876 the town of New Plymouth was raised, and a stone bridge erected over the Huatoki River. This improvement, which was in many respects desirable, was necessitated by the construction of the railway in the town. Since the establishment of the Municipality, extensive improvements have been made in the Borough. Bridges have been built, streets formed and metalled, and other important works effected. In February, 1878, the assent of the burgesses was given to the raising of a loan of £25,000, on the security of the endowments of the Borough— some of which, through the exertions of the Mayor, had been then recently obtained- for the construction of water works, gas works, and the general improvement of the streets of the Borough.

On the abolition of the Provinces, Taranaki was divided into the Counties of Taranaki and Patea. Taranaki County is entirely within the limits of the Taranaki Province, but Patea County is partly within the Wellington provincial district. Taranaki County is bounded towards the north by the eastern boundary of Kawhia County, which is formed by the centre of the Mokau River from its mouth to its most northerly source, and by a right line thence to the Rangitoto Mountain ; towards the east by a right line to the source of the Ongaruhe River, and thence by the centres of the Ongaruhe, the Ngahuinga (or Tahua), and Wanganui Rivers to the junction with the Tangarakau River; thence towards the south by a right line to the eastern corner of the Mangaotuku Block, thence by the southern boundary of that block to its south-west corner, thence by a right line to the eastern corner of the Ahuroa Block, by the eastern boundary of the last mentioned block to the Patea River, thence by the centre of the Patea River to its source in Mount Egmont, by a right line thence by the source of the Taungatara River, and by the centre of the last mentioned river to its mouth; and towards the west and north-west by the ocean to the mouth of the Mokau River, the commencing point.

Patea County is bounded towards the north by the southern boundary of the County of Taranaki hereinbefore defined, from the mouth of the Taungatara River to the summit of the western water-shed of the Wanganui River, near the eastern corner of the Mangaotuku Block: thence towards the east by lines from hill to hill along the said summit of the said water-shed by Mataimoana, Taumatarata, Taurangapiopio, to Paparangiora, thence along a ridge separating the watersheds of the Waitotara River and Kai-iwi Stream to Tutukaikatoa; thence by a ridge and the summit of the Rangitatau Range to the nearest corner of the Auroa Native Reserve, thence by the northern boundary of the Waitotara Block to the Waitotara River, and thence by the centre of that river to the ocean; and towards the south-west by the ocean to the mouth of the Taungatara River, the commencing point.

The County of Taranaki is divided into three Ridings, namely:—Moa Riding, Omata Riding, and Waitara Riding. The first representatives of these Ridings were—Moa Riding: R. Trimble, T. Kelly, W. Courtney; Omata Riding—H. Brown, H. D. Vavasour, W. Berridge; Waitara Riding—F. L. Webster, B. C. Lawrence and J. Rattenbury. Colonel Robert Trimble was elected the first chairman, Mr. J. B. Lawson county clerk and treasurer, and Mr. T. K. Skinner the first permanent engineer, Mr. G. F. Robinson having been at the first establishment of the County Council partially and temporarily employed in that capacity. The "Counties Act, 1876," being of an indefinite and permissive character, time will be required for the full development of the county system. At present the County Council of Taranaki has taken over the management of the main roads and the principal bridges, but in all probability the various Road Boards will be merged into it, and the whole of the roads and bridges outside of the municipalities and beyond the jurisdiction of the Town Boards will be subject to its administration.

IMMIGRATION AND PUBLIC WORKS.

To raise the Colony from the depression under which it labored by the drain on its resources consequent on the Native Rebellion, Sir Julius Vogel projected a scheme for promoting immigration and public works. This scheme was embodied and given effect to by the "Immigration and Public Works Act," and "Loan Act, 1870." By the authority of these Acts large sums of money were borrowed in the London market and applied to the purposes of bringing immigrants to the Colony and of constructing railroads and other public works. Various sums from these funds were at times voted by the House of Representatives for Public Works in Taranaki, but only a portion of them were expended in the province. In 1874, the sum of £20,000 was voted for opening up the track leading from Mataitawa to the shores of Cook Strait, near Hawera. The duty of administering this money fell on Major Atkinson, who gave His Honor F. A. Carrington, Esq., the Superintendent of Taranaki, and Mr. Kelly, the Provincial Secretary, *carte blanche* to expend it, the result of which was the opening up of the Mountain Road from Sentry Hill and the Junction Road, and from the Meeting of the Waters to Inglewood and onwards towards the Patea River. In the Session of 1877, a further sum of £10,000 was voted for the completion of this road.

On the 21st of August, 1873, the first sod of the New Plymouth and Waitara Railway was cut at New Plymouth amidst great rejoicings by Mrs. Henderson, daughter of F. A. Carrington, Esq. This line was opened on the 14th of October, 1875, after which a branch was extended along the Mountain Road, and was opened for traffic to Inglewood on the 29th of August, 1877. The first portion of this line was constructed by Brogden and Co., Railway Engineers and Contractors, of England, under the superintendence of Mr. Henderson. The line was surveyed by Mr. C. W. Hursthouse, who is at present the Resident Engineer of the line, and is engaged in extending it towards Patea. In June, 1874, Mr. W. M. Burton was appointed Immigration Agent to the Province by the Provincial Council, and shortly afterwards proceeded with Mrs. Burton to England, *viâ* San Francisco, where he was engaged for three years lecturing in the agricultural districts of the East of England, and in superintending the embarkation of emigrants for Taranaki.

NEW PLYMOUTH HARBOR.

In 1866, Messrs. Balfour and Doyne were employed by the Provincial Government to survey the New Plymouth roadstead for a harbor site. This work was executed by these gentlemen, and plans of harbors at the Sugarloaves and opposite to the town projected by them at a cost of £2,000. In 1866, the Provincial Council passed the Harbor Trust Ordinance, which set apart Mount Eliot, some land at the seaward end of Brougham Street, and at the mouth of the Huatoki River for harbor purposes. In 1875, the Provincial Council passed the New Plymouth Harbor Board Ordinance, constituting a Harbor Board consisting of nine members, six of whom were to be elected by the members of the Provincial Council, and three to be appointed by the Governor in Council, vesting the harbor reserves and one fourth of the land fund of the Province in the Board, and empowering it to raise a loan for harbor purposes of £350,000. In 1877, an Act of the General

Assembly was passed limiting the borrowing powers of the Board to £200,000, and simplifying the mode of raising the loan. The first members of the Board were:—elected by the Council—Majors Atkinson and Brown, Messrs. Syme, F. A. Carrington, A. Standish; appointed by the Governor in Council—Messrs. T. Kelly, H. Weston, and G. Curtis. Mr. Carrington was chosen chairman and treasurer, and Mr. J. B. Lawson, secretary. In 1876, a new plan for a harbor at the Sugarloaves was projected by Messrs. Carruthers and Blackett, connected with which was a scheme of a central prison at the harbor works. At the time we write, Messrs. Carruthers and Blackett's harbor design is under the consideration of the Governor in Council, while the central prison scheme has apparently fallen through.

THE ELECTRIC TELEGRAPH.

On the 10th of June, 1871, the electric telegraph was open from New Plymouth to Opunake. On the 15th of April, 1872, communication was opened with Wellington, partly by telegraph, and partly by mounted messengers, who rode to and from Opunake and Hawera, between which places the natives would not suffer the telegraph line to be erected. On the 29th of June, 1876, direct telegraphic communication was obtained with Wellington by the Mountain Road; and in February, 1878, Waitara was placed in connection with the telegraph system.

JUDICATURE.

For many years Captain King, R.N., officiated as Resident Magistrate of the district, but when, by reason of his age, he was compelled to seek retirement, he was succeeded on the bench by Mr. Flight, who in his turn succumbed to age, and was succeeded by Mr. H. R. Richmond, who filled concurrently the offices of Superintendent and Resident Magistrate. Mr. Richmond having fulfilled his term of office as Superintendent, and failing to obtain re-election, this arrangement fell through, and Mr. Harry Eyre Kenny, a barrister of considerable promise, who had for some time efficiently filled the office of Registrar of the Supreme Court and Clerk of the Resident Magistrate's Court, was appointed Resident Magistrate, and has since in conjunction with that office been appointed District Judge. In the early days, Mr. Donald Maclean, afterwards Sir Donald, held the office of Inspector of Police. He was succeeded by Mr. H. Halse, who was succeeded by Sergeant Dunn, who was succeeded by Sergeant Duffin. At the commencement of 1878 the Civil Police and Armed Constabulary were amalgamated, and Mr. Sub-Inspector Kenny was appointed to command the division performing civil police duty in New Plymouth.

THE LITERARY INSTITUTE.

At the foundation of the Settlement, the New Plymouth Company sent out a copy of the "Encyclopædia Brittanica," as the nucleus of a public library for New Plymouth; this has been religiously preserved, and around it from time to time have clustered other works, until the library has assumed large proportions. The Taranaki Institute consists of a general library, and a library of reference, containing a total of 3,000 volumes, also a free reading room, well supplied with periodical literature and newspapers.

EDUCATION.

In the early days of the settlement the education of the young was sadly neglected. No provision was made for general instruction by the Plymouth or New Zealand Company, or by the Government of the Colony; the district was also too sparsely populated, and the people were generally too poor for private teachers to hope for support in the pursuance of their avocations. Mrs. and the Misses King rendered important service in the instruction of the female children of the more wealthy classes, and Messrs. Murch, Sharland, Batkin, and Beardsworth at different periods gave instruction to the boys of New Plymouth. Many of the poorer children were taught to read in the various Sunday Schools of the town, and Mesdames Homeyer and Parker kept preparatory schools. Many children, however, grew up without instruction. During the war the children who were sent as refugees to Nelson received instruction in schools specially opened for them by the Government, and also in the Nelson Public Schools. When the families returned from Nelson the Wesleyans established a school, which was conducted by Mr. and Mrs. Schofield, and afterwards by Mr. and Mrs. Collis.

In 1857, the Provincial Council passed the Education Commission Ordinance, which authorised the Superintendent to appoint a Commission to enquire into, and consider what system of Education should be adopted for the Province. In 1868 the Council passed an Ordinance for making provision for the establishment and maintenance of schools in the Province. The result of this legislation was that a few schools were established, but the funds at the disposal of the Provincial Government were so small, that the system of instruction inaugurated by it was very imperfect. In 1874, His Honor the Superintendent held meetings in the various districts surrounding New Plymouth, for the purpose of testing public opinion respecting a projected provincial measure for placing public education on a sound basis by the levying of a household rate of £1 per annum for its support. Notwithstanding very great opposition to the scheme, the Council passed an Educational Ordinance dividing the Province into two Districts, constituting Boards and levying a household rate. The members of the Boards were elected by the people, the first members of the New Plymouth District being:— A. Standish, H. A. Atkinson, B. Wells, H. R. Richmond, C. W. Hursthouse, H. Govett, and Mr. W. N. Syme. B. Wells was chosen chairman, W. Northcroft secretary and treasurer, and W. M. Crompton inspector. The funds of the Boards consisted of the household rate, the rents of lands set apart for education purposes, and grants from the Provincial Government. By the exertions of the Boards a very great improvement was effected in the educational system of the districts. The teachers were encouraged by the increase of their very small salaries, the blockhouses scattered about the country were utilised as school houses, and many new school buildings were erected and schools established in various parts of the Province. In 1877, a Colonial Act of a provisional character came into operation, by which all the public schools of the Colony were brought under the control of the General Government, and in 1878, by the Act of the session of 1877, public education became free, secular and compulsory, and was provided for out of the general revenue of the country in connection with educational endowments.

THE HOSPITAL.

Dr. Peter Wilson for many years performed the duties of Colonial Surgeon in New Plymouth, his patients being chiefly Maoris. Since the war the hospital has been chiefly a local institution, and is now supported by the Borough and County Councils. Dr. T. E. Rawson has for many years filled the office of Provincial Hospital Surgeon, and Mr. and Mrs. Hill that of Steward and Matron.

THE BOTANIC GARDEN.

In 1875, by an arrangement between the Provincial Government, the Board of Education and the Board of Public Trustees, which was ratified by the Taranaki Botanic Garden Act, a large piece of broken land at the south of the town of New Plymouth, and abutting on the Carrington Road, was set apart for a botanic garden and recreation ground. The Board of Trustees consists of T. King (Chairman), R. Bayley (Hon. Secretary), R. C. Hughes, J. Gilmour, H. Ford, J. T. Davis and T. Colson.

ACCLIMATISATION SOCIETY.

During the war pheasants were introduced from Nelson. On the 27th of January, 1871, skylarks were introduced from Nelson by Mr. H. R. Richmond. Since then sparrows have been introduced from Auckland by Mr. A. Colson, and greenfinches from Nelson by Mr. Harley. The society has introduced the Indian mainah from Nelson, and partridges, blackbirds, thrushes, and goldfinches from England, by the aid of Mr. Burton, the Immigration Agent. The society is supported by fees paid for licenses to shoot game and by donations. Mr. C. D. Whitcombe is the Secretary.

Fresh victories of peace are being gained year by year; fresh fields are gained from the leafy and wooded wilderness; roads, railways and telegraphs are being extended, explorers are out in the interior searching for metals and minerals, and for lines of communication with other districts; local government promises to operate beneficially, attempts are being made to provide the district with a haven for ships, and the towns with the comforts and luxuries of civilised life. The pioneers who came to the wilderness in the full vigor of manhood are now aged, but they can look backward on the heroic struggle they have endured in their endeavor to plant an empire under southern skies, and look forward to the fruit of their labors which their children will possess as an inheritance.

CHAPTER XXVIII.

THE TARANAKI PIONEERS.

MR. F. A. CARRINGTON.

FREDERIC ALONZO CARRINGTON was born at Chelmsford, Essex, England, in the year 1807, and is the son of Captain William Carrington, afterwards barrack-master at Douglas, Isle of Man, whose father and grandfather were Senior Prebendaries and Chancellors of the Diocese of Exeter and cadets of the family of Carrington of Sponton, in Yorkshire. Mr. Carrington was specially instructed by the distinguished military engineer, surveyor and draughtsman, Robert Dawson, the father of Colonel Dawson, R.E., C.B., for the duties of the Ordnance Survey Department. He was appointed to office by His Grace the Duke of Wellington, Master General, and the Hon. Board of Ordnance in January, 1826. He surveyed tracts of country in Gloucester, Worcester, Hereford, Monmouth, and Glamorgan shires; triangulated, surveyed, and minutely delineated a continuous piece of country from Brecknockshire, through Glamorganshire, to the Bristol Channel. He revised blocks of original survey work in various parts of England, and—consequent on the Reform Bill of 1832—to a large extent determined on the ground and described for the Commissioners the Parliamentary boundaries of Boroughs in the districts from Bristol to Manchester. He compiled and reduced for engraving many of the original surveys, and minutely delineated in the field large tracts of country in different parts of England; he also, in the map office in the Tower of London, made the finished drawings of the Hills from Hertford to Halifax in Yorkshire for publication, embracing more than a thousand square miles of country.

In 1839, Captain Smith, of the Royal Artillery, who had then recently been appointed Chief Surveyor to the New Zealand Company, called at the Surveyor General's Office in the Tower of London for the purpose of consulting Mr. Carrington and his brother concerning certain duties devolving on him in his new capacity. In the course of his enquiries Captain Smith spoke in such glowing terms of New Zealand as to induce the young surveyor to desire to proceed thither, and shortly afterwards, by the advice of Sir Hussey Vivian, the Master General of the Ordnance, and by the offer of great inducements, he arranged to accept the appointment of Chief Surveyor to the Plymouth Company of New Zealand. It was arranged that his duties should be to select and found the settlement, and to purchase land for the Company, and that in addition to a salary of £350 |per annum he should be supplied with rations for himself and family, and should receive the sum of 4d. per acre for all lands surveyed by himself and staff, and 1 per cent. on the price of all lands sold. Mr. Carrington sailed from London in the ship London, and arrived in Wellington in December, 1840. Colonel Wakefield having kindly placed at his disposal the barque Brougham, Mr. Carrington explored various parts of the coast, and under many difficulties selected, surveyed, delineated, and laid out the settlement of New Plymouth. Owing to the native difficulties which beset the settlement, and the differences of the New Zealand Company with the English Government, Mr. Carrington's services were dispensed with in 1843, and in 1844 he arrived in England. On the 6th of June, 1844, Mr. Carrington gave evidence before the Select Committee appointed by the House of Commons to inquire into the state of the Colony of New Zealand, and into the proceedings of the New Zealand Company. Mr. Carrington took to England a large and valuable collection of specimens and curiosities, consisting of bird skins, insects, Maori mats, models of canoes, war clubs, spears, native knives, nets, fish hooks and lines, musical instruments, carvings, coal, limestone, and marble, iron sand, and specimens of indigenous timber. These articles were exhibited at a *soiree* at Sir Roderick Murchison's house in Belgrave Square, London. The Prince Consort called to see the exhibition, and expressed himself much pleased with it. The marble was specially admired, and was pronounced to be superior to that of Carrara. The specimen was said to have been procured somewhere between the Waipa and the Mokau.

Mr. Carrington received the following testimonial from the Court of Directors of the New Zealand Company :—

"New Zealand House, 4th May, 1849.

"Sir :—Having laid before the Court of Directors of the New Zealand Company your letter of the 2nd instant, I am instructed to inform you that the Directors have much pleasure in stating that you were employed as Chief Surveyor of the Plymouth Company of New Zealand and the New Zealand Company for the Settlement of New Plymouth, from June, 1840, to March, 1844; that the sole cause of your leaving the service of the latter Company was the suspension of its colonising operations occasioned by differences (since adjusted) with the Home Government ; and that the zeal and ability which marked your performance of the several duties with which you were successively entrusted in exploring the country, selecting a site for settlement, designing and laying out the allotments and roads, and in delineating the features of the ground, were at all times such as to call forth the perfect approbation of the Court.—I have, &c.

"T. C. HARINGTON,

"F. A. Carrington, Esq."

From 1844 Mr. Carrington was occupied in delineating and modelling country, superintending and directing the surveying, and getting up Parliamentary plans and models for Parliamentary Committees on projected railways, waterworks, and harbors in England and Scotland.

So much did Mr. Carrington excel in the art of modelling country, that he received on one occasion at Buckingham Palace the approbation of the late Prince Consort for his works, and Sir Robert Peel and Dr. Buckland paid visits to his studio.

The *Times* of September the 5th, 1849, thus notices his model plan of the Midland Counties:—

"Mr. F. A. Carrington, of 10, Henrietta Street, Covent Garden, has just executed a model plan of the Midland Counties, which as a work of art is extremely interesting, and well deserves to attract public attention and patronage. Upon this plan are delineated with the greatest accuracy the varying surfaces of that great district which stretches from Lincoln westwards to Congleton in Cheshire, from Congleton northwards by Manchester to Burnley, thence eastward by Bradford and Leeds to South Cave on the Humber, and from the Humber south to Lincoln. Within this parallelogram are marked out the sites of 46 cities and towns, innumerable villages, parks, woods, roads, railroads, and canals; the great natural watersheds of the country, and the sources and windings of the Trent, the Mersey, the Derwent, the Don, and other rivers and streams are also traced. The mountain ranges, the extent of plain, and the physical peculiarities of the country are all definitely defined, and a bird's-eye view of the whole is obtained so complete, satisfactory and simple as to distance entirely every other form of topographical illustration.

"In a military point of view such works as this are of incalculable importance, but in these days of agitation for peace it is doubtful whether, were such the only uses to which his labors could be turned, Mr. Carrington's ingenuity would meet the reward which it deserves. His system of surface delineation and plan modelling, however, has far higher merits. It is, perhaps, the best means that has yet been devised for regulating the lines of drainage, as by it the lowest levels of any given district can be determined at once, and thus the nearest approach be made to that natural law which guides the course of rivers, and renders them the great means for carrying off superfluous water to the sea. The present system of sections and contour lines gives but a partial knowledge of the character of the ground, inasmuch as the undulation can only be shown where the traverse is made with the level. To contour ground for practical purposes is also very expensive, and to do so in towns with strict accuracy is impracticable from the obstructions offered by the buildings. Moreover it is impossible on a contour map to discover the direction in which the lowest level of a district runs, and valuable and indispensable as sections are, they fail to supply that comprehensive and detailed whole which is so desirable in designing and carrying out any great work.

"We understand that Mr. Carrington many months ago offered to complete a model plan of the Metropolis and its environs, from Greenwich to Chiswick, for the sum of £4,500. He offered if ten or twelve copies were taken to do the work at 4d. per acre; and there can be but little doubt that such a model plan would have been most useful in introducing a proper system of drainage into the Metropolis. By its aid every Commissioner could see at a glance what ought to be done, and the new works might have been set agoing without all the delay and expense which have arisen in connexion with the Ordnance Survey. The Commissioners of Sewers rejected Mr. Carrington's offer, and thus an interesting branch of art suffers.

"Mr. Carrington was fifteen years in the Ordnance Survey Department. He was also employed by the New Zealand Company in selecting and surveying some of their settlements, and the large experience which he has had in that particular department of art to which he has devoted himself, makes it a matter of public interest that he should meet with encouragement to persevere. His model plan of the Midland Counties has been visited and admired by many of the most distinguished and scientific men of the country."

At the great Exhibition of 1851, Mr. Carrington was awarded the prize medal for models of country.

From 1851 to 1856 he was employed in making three special journeys to California and other parts of America, and one to Paris and Belgium, for the purpose of reporting on speculative business connected with the London Stock Exchange, and respecting projected railways and contract works in Paris, and for the purpose of valuing an estate in Belgium.

In January, 1857, Mr. Carrington again left England with his family for New Zealand, with the view of erecting iron works, and bringing into commerce iron from the iron sands of Taranaki, making a survey for a harbor, occupying his own land, and managing the property of others as an agent. The native rebellion breaking out shortly after his arrival, he offered his services to the Government, and was appointed engineer for the purpose of making roads in Taranaki. In September, 1869, he was elected Superintendent of the Province, which office he continued to hold till the abolition of provincial institutions in 1876. For many years he has represented the Grey and Bell district in the House of Representatives, and he is a member of the Harbor Board.

For many years he strove to obtain compensation for lands selected by him on the banks of the Waitara in the early days of the settlement, for Messrs. Sartoris and Downe, but which were first seized by the natives, and afterwards by the Government as a site for the town of Raleigh, and in the Session of 1877 he obtained his long sought object.

Sir Roderick Murchison has given the following testimony of Mr. Carrington's ability :—

"He possesses a remarkable faculty in delineating the true physical features of any tract, and I have no hesitation in saying that if I wished to be satisfied in my own mind of the real relations in detail of any piece of country, I should feel entire confidence in his faithful report upon it. His geometrical measurements may be most entirely relied on."

Mr. Carrington also holds testimonials as to his professional ability from General Pasley, R.E., Major-General T. Colby, R.E., Colonel Mudge, R.E., Sir John Rennie, C.E., F.R.S., and from Sir. H. T. De la Beche, the geologist.

CAPTAIN HENRY KING, R.N.

The half-masted ensign on the flagstaff at Mount Eliot on the afternoon of June the 6th, 1874, announced to the people of New Plymouth that a chief had fallen, and the intelligence soon spread abroad that Captain King was dead. The deceased officer had long passed the usual bounds of human life, being at the time of his death in his ninety-second year. He was the last survivor of those who took part in the battle of St. Vincent, and after fighting his country's battles he came out to Taranaki to do battle with the wilderness, a hale man of fifty-eight, an age at which most men seek repose. After his arrival he lived a second life of thirty-three years in the Colony, taking his full share in the arduous work, excitement and perils of a pioneer. At last his vital force showed signs of exhaustion, and on May the 30th, just a week before he expired, he was seized with paralysis of the throat. On the following Tuesday he revived, was cheerful, and even jocose; this revival however, proved to be but the last flicker of the flame of life, for he speedily relapsed into a comatose state, which ended in death.

Captain Henry King was born at Torquay, Devonshire, England, on the 7th of April, 1783. He entered the Royal Navy as midshipman on board the Namur, Captain Sir James Whitshead, on the 27th of November, 1795, being at that time but twelve years and eight months old. He was present at the battle of St. Vincent, which took place on the 14th of February, 1797, the Namur forming a part of the fleet under the command of Admiral Sir John Jervois, afterwards Lord St. Vincent. Mr. King served five years in the Namur, distinguishing himself by many acts of daring in connection with cutting-out expeditions, and left his ship with the rank of third lieutenant. He next joined the Canopus, Captain Sir G. Campbell. There, at the recommendation of his captain, he was promoted to a second lieutenancy. His next ship was the Ambuscade; after serving in her for some time, he was appointed to the Unité, a vessel which afterwards lay for many years as a convict hospital hulk off Woolwich Arsenal. He was invalided from this ship, having his leg broken in three places by the topsail tie falling upon him. On his recovery he was appointed first lieutenant of the Sea Horse, Captain, afterwards Sir Alexander Gordon, and served in her in the Potomac and at the taking of Alexandria in the American war of 1812-14. A number of merchantmen at Alexandria, laden with corn, cotton, and tobacco, requiring a convoy, the Sea Horse was ordered to perform that service, and successfully conducted the fleet through the midst of the enemy; for this service Mr. King obtained his promotion to the rank of commander, Sir Alexander Gordon, in his official letter to Vice-Admiral Cochrane giving an account of his operations in the Potomac, dated from H.M.S. Sea Horse, Chesapeake Bay, September the 19th, 1814, thus speaks of his first lieutenant :—

"So universally good was the conduct of all the officers, seamen, and marines of the detachment, that I cannot particularise with justice to the rest, but I owe to the long tried experience I have had of Mr. Henry King, first lieutenant of the Sea Horse, to point out to you that such was his eagerness to take the part to which his abilities would have directed him on this occasion, that he even came out of his sickbed to command at his quarters, while the ship was passing the batteries. The first two guns pointed by Lieutenant King disabled each a gun of the enemy."

Peace being shortly after this proclaimed, Captain King retired from active service. In March, 1852, he was gazetted post captain on the retired list.

On his retirement from the service Captain King went to reside in his native Devonshire, where he soon became actively engaged as a barge master on the Bude and Holsworthy Canal, conveying a shelly sand from the sea-coast to the interior, where it is extensively used as a manure. On the establishment of the Plymouth Company for colonising New Zealand, he was appointed Chief Commissioner of the Company, and came out to the Colony in the Amelia Thompson, arriving in New Plymouth on September the 3rd, 1841. Immediately on his arrival he was appointed Police Magistrate, his appointment being published by Governor Hobson's command in the Wellington Gazette of September, 1841. In consequence of the amalgamation of the Plymouth and New Zealand Companies, he was shortly after his arrival superseded in his commissionership by Captain Liardet, R.N. In connection with his brother-in-law, Mr. George Cutfield, formerly a naval architect in Plymouth Dockyard, Captain King settled on the suburban section now known as Brooklands. Shortly after his arrival he took a voyage to Sydney, and returned with a cargo of cattle for the settlement in the barque Jupiter. After this he never again left the settlement. At an early period he was appointed Resident Magistrate, in connection with which office he acted as Government factotum for many years. In those days crime among the European settlers was so infrequent that he had to commit but one person for trial during ten years that he exercised judicial functions. The conduct of the natives, however, demanded of him the utmost amount of discretion. The handful of peaceful country farmers who at that time formed almost the entire European population of the settlement, neglected by the Home Government, poor, and defenceless, were at the mercy of a band of insolent unmanumitted slaves and returned refugees of the Maori race, and the threats and war-dances of these people were successfully met by the brave but judicious old Captain with the only possible effective weapon—diplomacy.

In 1852, Captain King retired from active life, receiving a piece of plate from the settlers as a token of their grateful recognition of his services. In March, 1860, the breaking out of the Maori rebellion necessitated his retreat from the pleasant villa at Brooklands within the lines of New Plymouth. On the 8th of February, 1861, his only child, Captain William Cutfield King, of the Taranaki Volunteers, a young man of great promise, was killed by a party of rebels in ambush, within sight of a garrison of British troops on Marsland Hill.

If the gallant deeds of this brave Naval officer are lost sight of in England in the midst of the galaxy of glorious achievements effected by his contemporary heroes, his peaceful, but no less honorable and useful services in the foundation of the Province of Taranaki will be honorably remembered in the Colony for ever.

MR. CHARLES BROWN, SENR.

Mr. Charles Brown was born in 1786, and was in early life a Russia merchant, but failing in business through the substitution of fringe whalebone for bristles, and the anticipation by Britain of a war with Russia, he devoted the remainder of his days to literature and art, and to the society of literary men. He was intimate with Charles Wentworth Dilke, John Hamilton Reynolds, Thomas Hood, Leigh Hunt, Walter Savage Landor, Lord Byron, and had brotherly affection for Keats. Mr. Brown was of Scotch extraction, the family tradition being that his father left Long Island with a Bible as his sole property, and proceeded to London, where, by wisdom, prudence, and industry he attained affluence and a good position in society.

In 1809, when Mr. Brown was 23 years of age, he composed a Comic Opera, which was performed at Drury Lane Theatre, and for which he received a silver ticket, admitting him for life to the theatre. The following is one of the songs of the opera:—

THOU ART ALL TO ME, LOVE.

[Sung by Mr. Braham in the Comic Opera of "Narensky; or, the Road to Yaroslaft," at the Theatre Royal, Drury Lane. The Poetry by Charles Brown, Esq. The Music by Mr. Braham, London. Printed by Goulding, D'Almane, Trotter and Co., 20, Soho Square, and to be had at Westmoreland Street, Dublin.]

> The Summer gale that gently blows,
> Joys not to meet the balmy rose
>   As I delight in thee, love.
> The rosebud opening to the view,
> Loves not to bathe in morning dew,
>   As I delight in thee, love.
> Oh! thou art all to me, love,
>   All my heart holds dearly,
> Never loved a village swain
>   So truly, so sincerely.

The bee exults not in the sweets,
Enriching every flower she meets,
As I delight in thee, love.
The lark rejoices not to rise
At early morn in cloudless skies,
As I delight in thee, love.
Oh! thou art all to me, love,
All my heart holds dearly,
Never loved a village swain,
So truly, so sincerely.

In June, 1818, Brown and Keats started on a walking tour among the English lakes, and the Highlands and Islands of Scotland. During this tour Keats, who had an hereditary tendency to consumption, caught a severe cold among the swamps of the Island of Mull, from which he never thoroughly recovered. The summer of 1819 was spent by the two friends in company at Shanklin, in the Isle of Wight. There they amused themselves by sketching the beautiful scenery of the Island, and by conjointly writing the tragedy of "Otho the Great," Mr. Brown supplying the fable, character, and dramatic conduct, Keats the diction and verse. The two composers sat opposite at a table, and as Mr. Brown sketched out the incidents of each scene Keats translated them into rich and ready language. In August the friends removed to Winchester, where they shortly afterwards parted for a time, Keats remaining at Winchester and Brown going to London. A gloomy letter of Keats took Mr. Brown back to Winchester in September, and the two friends shortly afterwards proceeded to London. After reaching town, Keats ruptured a blood vessel in his lungs, and Mr. Brown was unremitting in his attention to him. During the winter Mr. Brown occupied himself with drawing. In February, 1820, Keats in a letter to Rice says, "Brown has left the inventive and taken to the imitative art. He is doing his forte, which is copying Hogarth's heads." On the 7th of May the two friends parted never to meet again; Mr. Brown determined on a short tour in Scotland, Keats being too weak to accompany him remained behind. After Mr. Brown had gone, Keats fancied that a trip to Italy would do him good. Mr. Severn, the artist and composer, agreed to accompany him to Rome, and the two set out on their journey, before Mr. Brown's return from Scotland. As soon as Mr. Brown heard of the increasing illness of Keats he lost no time in embarking at Dundee—this was in September, 1820, and he arrived in London only one day too late. Unknown to each other the vessels containing these two anxious friends lay a whole night side by side at Gravesend, and by an additional irony of fate, when Keats' ship was driven back into Portsmouth by stress of weather, Mr. Brown was staying in the neighborhood, within ten miles, when Keats landed and spent a day on shore. Nothing was left to Mr. Brown but to make his preparations for following Keats as speedily as possible, and remaining with him in Italy, if it turned out that a southern climate was necessary for the preservation of his life. On the 23rd of February, 1821, Keats died at Rome, having received the almost womanly care of Severn, and before his friend Brown could reach him.

. A letter from Mrs. Dilke, to her father-in-law, in 1820, has the following :—

"There has been a wager between Dilke and Mr. Charles Brown. It was made on Christmas Day. The conversation turned on fairy tales—Brown's forte—Dilke not liking them. Brown said he was sure he could beat Dilke, and to let him try they betted a beefsteak supper, and an allotted time was given. They having been read by the persons fixed on—Keats, Reynolds, Rice and Taylor—the wager was decided in favour of Dilke. Next Saturday night the supper is to be given; beef steaks and punch—the food of the Cockney school."

Shortly after the death of Keats Mr. Brown retired to Italy, and took up his abode at Florence. On the 12th of November, 1822, he wrote to Mr. Dilke, "When Lord Byron talked to me of the Vision of Judgment I interrupted him, for a Blackwoodish idea came across my mind, with "I hope you have not attacked Southey at his fire side," when he expressed quite an abhorrence of such an attack, and declared he had not. There never was a poor creature in rags a greater radical than Byron. My qualms were satisfied much in the same reasonable way as they were executed, and my satisfaction will appear to you just as unreasonable. I was angry with him not for expressing an opinion on Keats' poetry, but for joining in the ridicule against him. He did so in a note forwarded to Murray, but soon afterwards, when he learnt Keats' situation and saw more of his works, for he had only read his first volume of poems and flew out at the passage about Boileau, he ordered the note to be erased, and this, foolish soul that I am, quite satisfied me together with his eulogium on Hyperion, for he is no great admirer of the others."

. In 1826, Mr. Dilke, with his son, visited Rome, and went with Mr. Brown to see Keats' tomb, which had been erected by Severn, then a rising artist, without permitting Brown to pay part of the expense of it. Mr. Brown was brought to tears, and young Dilke also cried. During his sojourn in Italy, Mr. Brown employed his time in writing for some of the London magazines, and translating. He was intimately acquainted with, and intensely enjoyed what has been called the frailer charms of Southern song. He hardly ever passed a day without translating some portion of that school of Italian poetry, and he has left behind him a complete and admirable version of the first five cantos of Bajardo's "Orlando Innamorato." He also to some extent followed art. The present writer has seen a series of heads, copied from Hogarth's "Rake's Progress," which was drawn at Florence in 1831, and so beautifully executed that he can fully appreciate the statement made by Keats while the two friends were living together at the Isle of Wight, that if Brown had taken a little of his advice he would have been the first palette of the day.

In 1833, Mr. Monckton Milnes met Mr. Brown at the villa of Landor, the poet, in the beautiful hill-side of Fiesole, and a friendship from that moment sprang up between the two which never ceased till Mr. Brown's death.

In the year 1837, Mr. Brown returned to England, and took up his residence at Laira Green, near to Plymouth. Here he edited the Plymouth Journal, and gave lectures on Shakespeare at the Plymouth Institution. These lectures he published in a collective form in 1838, under the title of "Shakespeare's Autobiographical Poems." The work bears mark of considerable ingenuity and research, and is an attempt to deduce Shakespeare's character and biography from his works. About this time he was busy editing Shakespeare's Poems. The chief task, however, which he set himself, was the publication of the "Remains of his friend Keats," few of which had escaped his affectionate care. The preliminary arrangements for giving them to the world were actually in progress when the accident of attending a meeting on the subject of the formation of a Plymouth Company for colonising a portion of New Zealand altered his plans and determined him to transfer his fortunes and the closing years of his life to this country. Before he left England he confided to Mr. Monckton Milnes' care all his collections of Keats' writings, accompanied with a biographical notice.

Mr. Brown was so eager to engage in colonial life that he despatched his only son to New Plymouth by the Amelia Thompson, which sailed from Plymouth Sound on March the 25th, 1841, and followed himself in the Oriental, which left Plymouth on the 22nd of June of that year, and arrived at New Plymouth on the 19th of November. The stern utilitarianism of pioneer colonial life such as existed in New Plymouth in those days must have been a great, and we should think distasteful contrast, to the life Mr. Brown had led in London and Florence, among the *elite* of literature and art. It was, we believe, with the hope of benefiting his son that he took this step. After seven months' residence in the colony, he suddenly expired in a fit of apoplexy, in June 1842. Mr. Brown was buried on the brow of Marsland Hill, in New Plymouth, facing the sea. A large slab of stone was placed over his grave, but when the hill was escarped and fortified during the war this rude memorial was covered with earth, and only a few old settlers can now point out exactly his resting place.

MR. RICHARD CHILMAN.

Mr. Richard Chilman was born in London, on the 6th of May, 1816, where his father was in business. He received an excellent commercial education, and became a skilful penman and arithmetician. When a youth of sixteen he embarked for America, and after travelling through Canada, and visiting New York, New Orleans, and other places in the States, he returned to London. In 1840, in his twenty-fifth year, and having recently married, he embarked with his wife at Plymouth, in the Plymouth Company's pioneer vessel the William Bryan, and arrived at New Plymouth on the 30th of March, 1841. On the passage, Mr. Chilman received from Mr. Cutfield, who had charge of the expedition, an appointment as clerk, which he held under the successive agents of the Plymouth and New Zealand Companies until the New Zealand Company ceased its operations. He then commenced farming at the little farm on the east side of the Henui River, near to the Beach. From thence he removed to a suburban section on the south side of the Devon Road, and nearer to the Waiwakaiho. In 1849 he removed to Mangorei, where he cultivated a farm in the forest, and planted an orchard. A representative constitution having been granted to New Zealand, Mr. Chilman, in September, 1853, was appointed Provincial Treasurer, which office he held till March, 1861, when he received the appointment of Collector of Customs at the Port of New Plymouth. He was also appointed Provincial Auditor, Receiver of Land Revenue, and Acting-Paymaster of the Province of Taranaki. Mr. Chilman was an energetic settler, and took a deep interest in the progress of Taranaki. He was Chairman of the Petroleum Company, the Opunake Flax Company, and the Pioneer Steel Company. He was one of the founders of the Taranaki Institute, and held the office of Treasurer for many years. He was a Justice of the Peace, a Trustee of the New Plymouth Savings' Bank, a Trustee of the New Plymouth Building Society, Chairman of the New Plymouth Harbor Board, and Warden of St. Mary's Church. Having obtained leave of absence of the Government, he, on May the 6th, 1871, left the Colony, and proceeded viâ San Francisco to England, for the purpose of inducing English capitalists to work the iron sand. He took great interest in the running of the sand at the Henui works in 1876. Latterly Mr. Chilman's attention was chiefly directed towards the obtaining of a harbor for New Plymouth, and with this end in view he labored asssiduously. Feeling his powers decline, he in 1876 obtained his superannuation, after which his constitution rapidly broke up, and he expired at his residence, Fern Dell, New Plymouth, on the 12th of March, 1877, in the 61st year of his age.

HISTORY OF TARANAKI. 309

SHIPS WHICH VISITED THE COAST OF TARANAKI IN EARLY TIMES.

	YEAR.
Yacht Heemskirk } Captain Tasman, December	1574
Fly-boat Sea-hen }	
Barque Endeavor, Captain Cook, January	1770
Ship Mascarin, Captain Marion du Fresne, February	1772
Barque William Stoveld, Captain Davidson, anchored off the Waitara and traded with the natives, who came out of the river in large canoes	1823
Bombay, whaler, anchored off Ngamotu, and landed Heberley and others	1828
Schooner Currency Lass, of Sydney, traded at Ngamotu February	1832
Ship Tory, Captain Chaffers, landed Dr. Dieffenbach at Ngamotu, November 28	1839
Brig Guide	1840
Barque Brougham, February 11	1841
Barque William Bryan, March 30	1841
Barque Amelia Thompson, September 3	1841
Schooner Regina, October 3	1841
Ship Oriental, November 18	1841
Barque Timandra, February 24	1842
Barque Jupiter	1842
Barque Blenheim, November 7	1842
Barque Essex, January 23	1843
Barque Thomas Sparks, May 29	1843
Barque William Stoveld, October 26	1843
Barque Himalaya, December 23	1343
Barque Theresa, March 19	1844
Barque Bella Marina, May 27	1844
Government Brig Victoria, June 31	1844
Barque Raymond, August 29	1844
H.M.S. Hazard, August	1844
Barque Slaines Castle	1845
—— Paul Jones, April	1845
—— Marianne, June	1846
Barque Madras, September	1846
Barque Ralph Bernal, October	1846
Barque Elom, January	1847
H.M.S. Inflexible, February 26	1847
Barque Cornwall, August 18	1849
Barque Poictiers	1849
—— Berkshire	1850

	YEAR.
——— Kelso ...	1850
——— Mariner	1850
——— Eden, October ...	1850
——— Phœbe Dunbar	1850
H.M.S. Acheron	1850
——— Victory, May 1	1851
——— Lord William Bentinck, January 6	1852
——— William Hyde, March	1852
Barque Cresswell, July	1852
Barque Gwalior, August	1852
Ship Joseph Fletcher, October	1852
——— St. Michael, December	1852
H.M.S. Faintome, December ...	1852
——— Tasmania, April	1853
Barque Cashmere, July	1853
——— Simlah, August	1853
——— Sir Edward Paget	1853
Barque Cresswell, August	1853
Ship Joseph Fletcher, September	1853
Ship John Taylor, November ...	1853
Barque Hamilla Mitchell, February	1854
Barque Lady Clarke, April	1854
Barque Eclipse, June ...	1854
Barque Cashmere, August	1854
Ship Joseph Fletcher, October	1854
Barque Monarch, October	1854
Ship Josephine Willis, January	1855
H.M.S. Pandora, March	1855
Barque Cresswell, June	1855
Barque Rock City, July	1855
Barque Duke of Portland, August	1855
Ship Egmont, November	1855
Barque Cashmere, November ...	1855
Barque Ashmore, March	1856
Barque Chatham, May ...	1856
Barque Inchinnan, July	1856
Barque Gipsy, October ·	1856
Barque Euphemeus, March	1857
Barque Cashmere, April	1857
Barque Kenilworth, July	1857
Barque Melbourne, August	1857
Ship Dinapore, October	1857
Barque William Watson, December ...	1857
Brig Duchess of Leinster, January	1859

SHIPS WHICH VISITED THE COAST OF TARANAKI IN EARLY TIMES.

	YEAR.
Yacht Heemskirk ⎱ Captain Tasman, December	1574
Fly-boat Sea-hen ⎰	
Barque Endeavor, Captain Cook, January	1770
Ship Mascarin, Captain Marion du Fresne, February ...	1772
Barque William Stoveld, Captain Davidson, anchored off the Waitara and traded with the natives, who came out of the river in large canoes	1823
Bombay, whaler, anchored off Ngamotu, and landed Heberley and others	1828
Schooner Currency Lass, of Sydney, traded at Ngamotu February	1832
Ship Tory, Captain Chaffers, landed Dr. Dieffenbach at Ngamotu, November 28	1839
Brig Guide	1840
Barque Brougham, February 11	1841
Barque William Bryan, March 30	1841
Barque Amelia Thompson, September 3	1841
Schooner Regina, October 3	1841
Ship Oriental, November 18	1841
Barque Timandra, February 24	1842
Barque Jupiter	1842
Barque Blenheim, November 7	1842
Barque Essex, January 23	1843
Barque Thomas Sparks, May 29	1843
Barque William Stoveld, October 26	1843
Barque Himalaya, December 23	1343
Barque Theresa, March 19	1844
Barque Bella Marina, May 27	1844
Government Brig Victoria, June 31	1844
Barque Raymond, August 29	1844
H.M.S. Hazard, August	1844
Barque Slaines Castle	1845
——— Paul Jones, April	1845
——— Marianne, June	1846
Barque Madras, September	1846
Barque Ralph Bernal, October	1846
Barque Elora, January	1847
H.M.S. Inflexible, February 26	1847
Barque Cornwall, August 18	1849
Barque Poictiers	1849
——— Berkshire	1850

	YEAR.
——— Kelso ...	1850
——— Mariner	1850
——— Eden, October ...	1850
——— Phœbe Dunbar	1850
H.M.S. Acheron	1850
——— Victory, May 1	1851
——— Lord William Bentinck, January 6	1852
——— William Hyde, March	1852
Barque Cresswell, July	1852
Barque Gwalior, August	1852
Ship Joseph Fletcher, October	1852
——— St. Michael, December	1852
H.M.S. Faintome, December ...	1852
——— Tasmania, April	1853
Barque Cashmere, July	1853
——— Simlah, August	1853
——— Sir Edward Paget	1853
Barque Cresswell, August	1853
Ship Joseph Fletcher, September	1853
Ship John Taylor, November ...	1853
Barque Hamilla Mitchell, February	1854
Barque Lady Clarke, April	1854
Barque Eclipse, June ...	1854
Barque Cashmere, August	1854
Ship Joseph Fletcher, October	1854
Barque Monarch, October	1854
Ship Josephine Willis, January	1855
H.M.S. Pandora, March	1855
Barque Cresswell, June	1855
Barque Rock City, July	1855
Barque Duke of Portland, August	1855
Ship Egmont, November	1855
Barque Cashmere, November ...	1855
Barque Ashmore, March	1856
Barque Chatham, May ...	1856
Barque Inchinnan, July	1856
Barque Gipsy, October ·	1856
Barque Euphemeus, March	1857
Barque Cashmere, April	1857
Barque Kenilworth, July	1857
Barque Melbourne, August	1857
Ship Dinapore, October	1857
Barque William Watson, December	1857
Brig Duchess of Leinster, January	1859

BIBLIOGRAPHY.

Chapman's Centenary Memorial of Captain Cook's Description of New Zealand.
Appendices to the Journals of the New Zealand House of Representatives.
Report of the Select Committee of the House of Commons appointed to inquire into the State of the Colony of New Zealand, and into the proceedings of the New Zealand Company, 1844.
Life, Letters, and Literary Remains of John Keats, edited by Monckton Milnes, Lord Houghton.
Polack's Residence in New Zealand, from 1831 to 1837.
Travels in New Zealand, by Dr. Ernst Dieffenbach.
The Transactions of the New Zealand Institute.
Chips from a German Workshop, by Max Muller.
The New Zealand Journal, 1841, 1842, 1843.
Journal of Colonel William Wakefield.
Journal of Mr. E. J. Wakefield.
Reports of the Directors of the New Zealand Company.
The New Zealand Statutes.
The Story of New Zealand, by Dr. Thompson.
Papers of a Critic, by C. Dilke.
New Zealand Parliamentary Debates.
Men of the Time.
Life of the Rev. N. Turner, Wesleyan Missionary.
Grayling's History of the Taranaki War.
The Campaign on the West Coast.
The *Taranaki Herald*.
The *Taranaki News*.

Printed at the TARANAKI NEWS Office, New Plymouth.

www.ingramcontent.com/pod-product-compliance
Lightning Source LLC
Chambersburg PA
CBHW022017240426
43667CB00042B/907